MW00912580

FINDING NOTHING

"SMALL ELECTRICAL STORM IN ELEMENT COUNTY."

Gary Lee-Nova, *A Small Electrical Storm in Element County* (1973; recto).
Used with permission. Collection of the Morris and Helen Belkin Art Gallery.

FINDING NOTHING, Being a Treatise on
Absence, Neglect, How the Avant-Garde Learned
to See Vancouver (or Found Reason to Try),
Writing on the Edge/Margin/Line, Feminist
Birth Stories (or the Birth of Feminist Stories),
the VanGardes 1959–1975, a Type of Collage,
Concrete, Art in Unceded Territory, Indigenous
Cultures, Foreign Incursions, Surrealist Revolts,
& other sundry and otherwise subjects.

Gregory Betts

UNIVERSITY OF TORONTO PRESS
Toronto Buffalo London

© University of Toronto Press 2021
Toronto Buffalo London
utorontopress.com
Printed in the U.S.A.

ISBN 978-1-4875-0531-8 (cloth)
ISBN 978-1-4875-3198-0 (EPUB)
ISBN 978-1-4875-3197-3 (PDF)

Library and Archives Canada Cataloguing in Publication

Title: Finding nothing : being a treatise on absence, neglect, how the avant-garde learned
    to see Vancouver (or found reason to try), writing on the edge/margin/line, feminist birth
    stories (or the birth of feminist stories), the VanGardes 1959–1975, a type of collage,
    concrete, art in unceded territory, Indigenous cultures, foreign incursions, surrealist
    revolts, & other sundry and otherwise subjects / Gregory Betts.
Other titles: Finding nothing : the VanGardes, 1959–1975 | VanGardes 1959–1975
Names: Betts, Gregory, 1975– author.
Description: Includes bibliographical references and index.
Identifiers: Canadiana (print) 20210174005 | Canadiana (ebook) 20210175486 |
    ISBN 9781487505318 (hardcover) | ISBN 9781487531973 (PDF) |
    ISBN 9781487531980 (EPUB)
Subjects: CSH: Experimental poetry, Canadian (English) – British Columbia – Vancouver –
    History and criticism. | CSH: Canadian poetry (English) – 20th century – History and
    criticism. | LCSH: Avant-garde (Aesthetics) – British Columbia – Vancouver – History –
    20th century. | LCSH: Arts – British Columbia – Vancouver – Experimental methods. |
    LCSH: Vancouver (B.C.) – Intellectual life – 20th century.
Classification: LCC PS8159.7.V3 B48 2021 | DDC C811/.5409110971133 – dc23

This research was supported by the Social Sciences and Humanities Research Council of
Canada.

University of Toronto Press acknowledges the financial assistance to its publishing program of
the Canada Council for the Arts and the Ontario Arts Council, an agency of the Government
of Ontario.

 Canada Council   Conseil des Arts
for the Arts   du Canada

 ONTARIO ARTS COUNCIL
CONSEIL DES ARTS DE L'ONTARIO
an Ontario government agency
un organisme du gouvernement de l'Ontario

Funded by the   Financé par le
Government   gouvernement | **Canadä**
of Canada   du Canada

Contents

Illustrations

Acknowledgments

Books (on poetry) must be made by all. I was born in Vancouver in the moment after the period documented by this book – coincidentally, into a house on W 37th Street, directly across from Warren Tallman's famous abode. Consequently, from that remove, I join with all of the scholars attending to the trace of a transformative and rich era of cultural activity, thinking about what we can do with what Bowering calls unabashedly the "Vancouver renaissance." In my efforts to address a period not my own, I have been the grateful recipient of an enormous amount of help in this book by many people, who very generously gave me their time, insight, energy, and direction. What I realized rather quickly is that this topic is a subject of deep and very personal interest to many people. Those who shared their interest and, by doing so, made this book possible, include Joan Haggerty, Stan Persky, bill bissett, Jean Baird, Robert Hogg, Michael Turner, Warren Dean Fulton, Judith Copithorne, Catherine Parayre, jwcurry, Ellie Nichol, Tony Power, Gregg Simpson, Ray Ellenwood, Aaron Vidaver, derek beaulieu, Daphne Marlatt, Gladys Maria Hindmarch, Stephen Collis, Donato Mancini, Pierre Coupey, Jason Camlot, Darren Wershler, Yves Laroque, George Bowering, Carol Reid, Carole Itter, Laura Moss, Brian Dedora, Dean Irvine, Colin Browne, Robert McTavish, Karis Shearer, Gary Lee-Nova, Scott Watson, Anna Tidlund, David Kloepfer, Ian Wallace, Janet Marie Rogers, Karen Tallman, and Felicity Taylor. I thank you all for the conversation, insight, and guidance. I would also like to thank Jan Milligan, the interlibrary loan guru at Brock University Library, without whose diligence I would not have been able to access a fraction of the weird, strange, and wonderful texts documented in this book. Thanks to Mark Thompson and Siobhan McMenemy from the University of Toronto Press. A Social Sciences and Humanities Research Council Standard Research Grant, as well as various forms of internal funding from Brock University, assisted in the research for this book. I would like to thank my research assistants, Julia Polyck-O'Neill, Mathieu Aubin, and Eric Schmaltz, who are all now publishing important work on the Vancouver avant-garde. On a more personal note, I am so deeply enamoured with Lisa Betts, my partner in all of this, who held it all together as I scuttled around from archive to archive, sometimes crossing literal and metaphorical oceans to do so. I raise a glass of sake to you all.

Portions of this manuscript were presented at Exile's Return: An Editing Modernism in Canada Colloquium (Sorbonne, Paris), the Modern Language Association annual conference (Boston), Approaching the Poetry Series conference (Concordia, Montreal), and Discourse & Dynamics: Canadian Women as Public Intellectuals (Mount Allison, Sackville), and in invited public lectures at the University of Birmingham, the University of Nottingham, Roehampton University, the Université Sorbonne Nouvelle, and the University of Innsbruck. All of these events facilitated essential discussions and conversations that pushed the book forward into its form here and now.

Introduction: Finding Nothing

the HEAD, by way of the EAR, to the SYLLABLE

Charles Olson, "Projective Verse" (19)

The story of the literary avant-garde in Vancouver is the story of the ear leading the unwilling eye into the future.

Peter Culley, "Because I Am Always Talking" (191)

The sixties were an historical moment that fomented a revolution in education, racial divisions, anxieties about national security, consumerism, Aboriginal mobilization, anti-Americanism, the search for national identity, clashes between capital and labour, innovations in public policy, and debates surrounding the family, health, and the environment. It was an era deeply shaped by the Cold War, and by the unprecedented, albeit unequally distributed, prosperity, an uncommonly youthful population, a shift to post-industrialism, and a new cultural politics.

Lara Campbell, Dominique Clément, and Gregory S. Kealey,
Debating Dissent: Canada and the Sixties (6)

If you don't look, you will see nothing. But what if you do look – and still see nothing? Neuropsychologists have shown that the closer something is to what we already know, the better we remember it. In fact, we see what we already know clearer, and tend to fear new things and recognize them poorly.[1] Attention, it turns out, is a closed loop. For evolutionary purposes, the brain developed a preferential bias for what we already know, which probably served our ancestors quite well. It is an imperfect solution to survival in the present, however, as it equally works to limit our ability to hear

---

1 Robert Zajonc (1968) proposed a "mere exposure effect" after his experiments in human cognition uncovered a strong linear relationship between exposure and positive attitudes. Zebrowitz and Zhang (2012) confirmed his experiment and discovered the means by which racist grouping and attitudes can be diminished by repeated exposure. Herzmann et al. (2011) found a significant impact of exposure on memory.

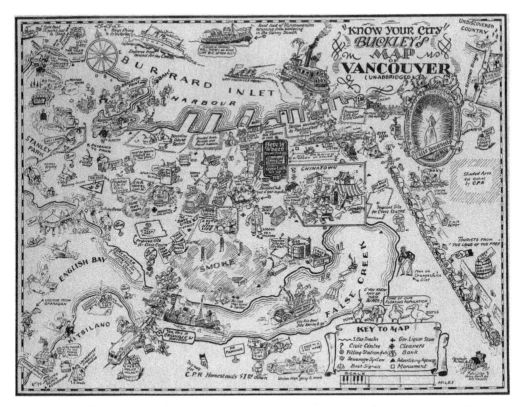

Figure I.1 Buckley's *Know Your City* map of Vancouver, 1930. Source: City of Vancouver Archives, AM1594-: MAP 318.

new things, register new voices, and learn from cultural exchange. Daphne Marlatt's breakthrough book of prose-poetry *Rings* (1971) uses the trope of the ring, the ring of men's speech, the closed ring of borders, to articulate her desire to break exclusive loops, to break the rings that erase her, and re-imagine the importance of the gaps. (Her poetic novel *Ana Historic* [1988], in contrast, is set in the space outside of that erasure, outside of exclusionary history, as it were.) While it likely provides little to no comfort to those who are not heard to know that biological structures contribute to their erasure, it does increase the magnitude of the problem and also suggests more precise methods for change. To contest such mendacious erasures, a strategy toward their correction begins by rejecting the established categories of knowledge, redefining them in conscious manner, and repeating them until they are etched into the human psyche. Gertrude Stein's point that "there is no such thing as repetition" ("Portraits" 166) finds its full resonance here, as each iteration does in fact change the depth at which our memories of the world are inscribed into our brain's matrix. The more we are exposed to an idea, the more it becomes something we already know. This is how new ideas enter into the closed loop of memory.

This book, titled *Finding Nothing*, takes up the problem of the closed loop of memory and looks at how in one place new ideas and new models of modernist art production broke through and changed the way people remember art and literature in that place. By attending to transnational cultural flows, and what happens to local cultures when foreign ideas swamp and dislodge them, this book documents a consistent and recurring pattern of transnational aesthetics flowing into Vancouver and erasing or disrupting what came before – hence, one sense of "finding nothing" is the disavowal of the value of pre-existing cultures in the city. In the context of such a discussion, it is important to acknowledge the appropriation of Indigenous land by settlers who "found nothing" of value in Indigenous models of land-use and culture and merely took the land without treaty. The land was never ceded (hence, decolonial activists and scholars have found nothing legally transferring the land to England or, by extension, Canada). The litany of voices not heard at the outset of Vancouver's settlement, of people and peoples erased, is starting to gain recognition today, in what might be called this current period of cultural unsettlement. Vancouver was mapped by the British (1792), settled as Gastown (1867), and registered as Granville (1870) for a short time, before being renamed and incorporated as Vancouver (6 April 1886), in honour of the British explorer Captain George Vancouver (1757–98). Vancouver is, in fact, an Anglicization of the Dutch name Van Coevorden, denoting somebody *from* the city of *Coevorden* in the Netherlands, the town Vancouver's ancestors had left for England. The name of this Canadian city, then, is tied to multiple geographic displacements, while displacing others in its usurpation of title. The area now covered by the sprawling metropolis had a variety of other pre-colonial names in the traditions of the Skwxwú7mesh Úxwumixw (Squamish), xʷməθkʷəy̓əm (Musqueam), and səl̓ilwətaʔɬ təməxʷ (Tsleil-Waututh) nations, whose overlapping territories had been claimed without treaty or negotiation by the European settlers.

When Alexander Mackenzie arrived at the Pacific Ocean, riding in a canoe borrowed from the Nuxalk nation, he met the vista of the ocean and mountains just six weeks after Vancouver had passed on his second voyage. He painted his name onto a rock overlooking what would become the city, with the message "Alex Mackenzie / From Canada by land / 22nd July 1793." It was as if the arms of Empire were closing in from sea and land. The land he surveyed was unfathomably lush. In the ensuing decades, however, sawmills were set up in Burrard Inlet, leading to an aggressive clear-cut logging tradition that opened ever more space for a future that was rising from an increasingly decimated land. Vancouver quickly grew from a port to a village to a city with Mackenzie registered as one of the heroes that pulled it into being from absence (see Figure I.2). Meanwhile, Indigenous use and access to the land continued to decrease. Pushed out of the city officially (though *insistently* still present in the city), the vast territories of the səl̓ilwətaʔɬ təməxʷ First Nation have been reduced to a small reservation, Burrard Inlet #3, on the outskirts of town. Similarly, the 6,732 square kilometres of Skwxwú7mesh Úxwumixw traditional territories stands in stark contrast to the 28 square kilometres now maintained by the Nation, including the small village of

Figure I.2 Sir Alexander Mackenzie Elementary School, photographed on 17 July 1930 by W.J. Moore. Source: City of Vancouver Archives, Sch P1 36.

Ustlawn in North Vancouver. The xʷməθkʷəy̓əm, meanwhile, whose traditional territory encompasses all of the Greater Vancouver Area, live on a small reserve within the city itself. "Here," as Marian Kargbo writes, they are "living in a community where there are no industries, and yet outside [their] immediate surroundings is a very large and sophisticated community to which [they do] not belong" (15). The non-standard English orthographies of these Nations' names will become familiar only with constant, repetitious reminders of their belonging in the linguistic geography of Vancouver. I use them here deliberately, to aid in the process of that gradual recognition.

Their land had been seized through the doctrine of *terra nullius*, a colonialist mode of negating Indigenous title by determining ownership entirely in reference to European standards, traditions, and institutions.[2] If the land had not been cultivated to European models of agriculture, it was considered fair game for appropriation. This approach to the land is anathema to Indigenous practices and cultural models, where interaction with and mutual recognition of the land shapes essential identity. Living with and learning from the land are incommensurate with the requisite to use and exploit it or lose it. Thus, Syilx (Okanagan) author Jeannette Armstrong

---

2 Though the Proclamation of 1763 might seem to contradict the application of *terra nullius* to British Columbia, in connecting the appropriation of Indigenous land to the doctrine I am following the precedent of scholars like Chelsea Vowel (2016), Vasiliki Douglas (2013), and, especially, John Borrows in his article "The Durability of Terra Nullius: Tsilhqot'in Nation v. British Columbia" (2015). Furthermore, the Assembly of First Nations points out that the doctrine was accepted by the Canadian Supreme Court as a legitimate means to "extinguish Indigenous rights" across Canada (see Assemby of First Nations, *Dismantling the Doctrine of Discovery*). Stuart Banner, in his 2007 book *Possessing the Pacific*, writes, "British Columbia was the only part of Canada that the British treated as terra nullius" (195).

writes, "the land constantly speaks. It is constantly communicating. Not to learn its language is to die" ("Land Speaking" 146). The consequences of detachment from the land are echoed in the fear of detachment from community (and, in Armstrong's article, from Indigenous languages). Lee Maracle explains the social implications of erasure to the Stó:lō people: "the concept of zero means nothing. It is represented by a circle devoid of all life. This has no meaning for the living or the dead, but it is useful in teaching young children to interact in a positive social fashion. A child learns that if she doesn't obey the laws of the people, she will suffer great nothing-ness in her interaction with women and men" ("Oratory" 63). Here, we start to see the consequences of finding nothing – a resounding horror, staring into the face of death itself, the great and final erasure.

The settlement of Vancouver and its renaming can be thought of as the first of a series of silencings – attempts at reducing the presence of previous inhabitants and delicate ecosystems to nothing. Settlers were taught by governments and religious leaders to not hear Indigenous voices, to disregard the delicate balance that had been achieved between humans and lush nature. Instead, man (defined, in this case, as the thinnest band of citizenship: white, male, European, and wealthy) had been granted dominion over the land and its riches. Thus did the global spread of Euro-pean colonialism arrive in the Pacific Northwest. This is an important stage in the advancement of the Anthropocene, the name commonly given to our current era, being the Earth's sixth mass dying, this time caused by an explosion of human popu-lations and dominance of the planet. The naturalist Edward O. Wilson has proposed another name for the period: the Eremocine, the age of loneliness, when humans find themselves increasingly isolated as species disappear into extinction (see *Half-Life: Our Planet's Fight for Life*). The Eremocine might also be useful in this particular context to refer to the linguistic loneliness of the English language that was forced upon local populations in a blatant attempt to erase all other linguistic communi-ties in the greater Vancouver area and reduce them to nothing. From June 2018, however, with land claims cases still roiling through the courts, Indigenous place names have begun reappearing throughout the city on official signs (see "Vancouver Gives"). Indigenous languages and place names – including more established ones like Haida Gwaii and the Salish Sea – will only re-naturalize with repetition and regular use. Through such efforts, the idea of Vancouver as a polyphonic, decolo-nized space might take hold, just as with concerted, collective effort we may yet hold the ultimate devastation of the Anthropocene at bay. These require shifts in the very categories that structure our thinking. We either change how we think and see, or the things we set about erasing a century and a half ago will disappear, with devastating consequences. The future of the city (with much broader implications by extension) depends upon the outcome of such questions.

Finding nothing of value in the sustainable intersection of human and nature, the settlers that built Vancouver on the unceded land sought value in the commodities they could recognize. The place has been, in the 130 years since its naming (or the 152 since its first settlement by Europeans, and the over two centuries since contact), a site of violent, relentless erasure. The Indigenous communities were pushed further and further away, eventually scooped up into the residential school system that was created explicitly to erase the cultural difference completely. Residential schools opened in nearby Chilliwack (1860) and Victoria (1863), and then in the city itself (1899) with the overt mandate of erasing Indigenous culture and assimilating all of the errant nations across the new country. The forests were massacred and the wildlife sacrificed in the relentless pursuit of capital. The life-preserving topsoil was ripped back inelegantly in the ongoing quest for minerals and precious stones (especially coal, silver, gold, later copper, zinc, and lead). British Columbia confederated with Canada (1871) and swiftly received the promised railway (1885) from Canada, by land, less than a century after Mackenzie's arrival. Upon its completion, the Canadian government passed the Chinese Immigration Act (also 1885) to prevent the fifteen thousand Chinese workers who helped build the railway from bringing their families here, and to encourage them to return to China. A generation later, abused and battered workers of all racial backgrounds in the province were scooped up when capitalism seemed to stall in the 1920s and 1930s. They were ported by trains on these very rail lines to concentration camps (called "relief camps") to labour hard for bare subsistence (Howard and Skikavich n. pag.). A powerful account of the street battles and workers' resistance during this period is contained in Irene Baird's *Waste Heritage* (1939); Wayson Choy's *The Jade Peony: A Novel* (1995), meanwhile, represents the same period but without overlooking (erasing) the Chinese Canadian experience. The model of the work camps would be redeployed in 1942, when Japanese Canadians were arrested, and their homes and goods confiscated, their rights erased to nothing, while they were placed in internment camps. They were free to leave these camps, but having no possessions and displaced in hostile territory, they were effectively trapped in the ghost towns of aborted gold rushes. They became what Giorgio Agamben has called the "homo sacer" (see *Homo Sacer*), figures of derision pushed outside the boundaries of civil protections. They were not allowed to return to the coast until 1949, years after the end of the war, which had been a convenient pretence for the overt State racism. These erasures scraped back the history of that once-lush land, erasing even the traces of its having been scraped, to make room for the emerging City of Vancouver.

When the subjects of this book arrived in the city, in the wake of such epochal violence, they, too, found nothing. They came in a remarkable wave of arrivals that began in the 1930s and accelerated heavily in the 1950s, but still they could not see what they did not know to look for. The colonial process had been so effective that there was barely a trace of that displaced *something* that had been there before. And, of course, as we know about vision and perception, what might have been seen was essentially invisible to preconditioned eyes. What is striking about the generation

Figure I.3 Distribution of food by Rev. Andrew Roddan of First United Church to unemployed at City dump. Photo taken September 1931. Source: City of Vancouver Archives, AM54-S4-: Re N4.4.

that began assembling in the city in the 1950s, however, is that their writing shifted its subject position out of the colonial mentality just enough to begin to stop the erasing. In order to locate themselves, they began listening. They took themselves and their city as their subjects and found a very different story than what they had arrived believing. Fred Ribkoff notes that Daphne Marlatt wrote in order to become "at home in her body" (232). What she discovered inside, however, and documents throughout *Rings* and her subsequent works, is the entanglement of the self in the socio-political world. In order for the body to be at home, place and language must also be reconciled – what she describes as "the whole field of consciousness" in *What Matters* (74).

Marlatt and her cohort began creating new categories of knowledge to make sense of the city they were excavating or salvaging (a metaphoric shift of profound significance from the modernist discourse of "mining" or "discovering" or "inventing"). In remarkably short order, they consciously retrained their perception to become open to

Figure I.4 Cover of Daphne Marlatt's *What Matters: Writing 1968–1970* (1980). Used with permission of the author.

the shocking confluence of voices, sounds, and linguistic textures of Vancouver. Being colonials, by habit and tradition, it is no surprise that many of them learned from foreigners from the big metropolitan centres elsewhere. The American poet Charles Olson became a hero to many, in part for his instruction to delve even further into the complexity of place: "'Man is estranged from that with which he is most familiar.' – Heraclitus [...] History is the new localism, a polis to replace the one which was lost in various stages all over the world from 490 BC on, until anyone of us knows places where it is disappearing now" (*Special View* 25). The Vancouver writers who followed his instruction became, through this historical consciousness, the first generation to start to reverse the overlapping erasures, the enforced nothings, of Vancouver.

Except that they weren't. This oft-repeated story, too, of the singular achievement of the 1960s generation performs its own kind of erasure. Generations of writers had come

Figure I.5 Charles Olson in Vancouver in 1963. Photo by Karen Tallman. Used with permission.

before the writers of the 1960s, had started the listening process, the documenting, the tough recoil of the blanket of nothingness that colonial eyes cast over a landscape (smothering the people who live there). Acclaimed writers like Dorothy Livesay, Earle Birney, Malcolm Lowry, E. Pauline Johnson, Phyllis Webb, Rae Verrill, Ethel Wilson, Annie Charlotte Dalton, and many others struggled against the weight of the blanketing silence that lay between the Eurocentric literary traditions and the actual land they lived upon. Those previous generations had built the institutions – including the University of British Columbia (UBC) creative writing program – that attracted the next to come to the city and that fostered the 1960s foment, as will be discussed throughout this book. A new kind of realism was required, one that rushed full-bodied and whole-throated into the present. It was an awkward but completely essential transformational moment, setting up the ongoing decolonial processes that Vancouver still wrestles with today. This book looks at the process by which a generation, working from many local and international precedents and foundations, came to see through that devastating erasure and start, hesitatingly, errantly (in today's less forgiving parlance, still *problematically*), to hear the whole field. Certainly, this book will revisit many of the familiar narratives of Vancouver's 1960s literary and cultural explosion, but, by approaching these stories from a transcolonial vantage, it will also make space for many of the voices lost in the habitual telling of the story of Vancouver's ongoing emergence – finding them in the nothing – and documenting how the transition from colonization to the present moment's attempts at reversing systematic erasure came to be.

Finding Nothing addresses a scattershot array of sixteen years of experimental writing in Vancouver that reinvented the culture of the city, and that has helped Canadians at large to re-imagine writing here and to bear witness to our internalization of colonial violence. Vancouver is a key site of the transformations that swept English Canada at this time. Indeed, one of the origins of the surge in experimental arts can be traced to a meeting in 1958 in Vancouver,[3] where Marshall McLuhan spoke to a group of broadcasters at the University of British Columbia in the library (the very library that would become a centre for experimental art under the tutelage of Alvin Balkind). It was in that meeting that he first uttered the phrase that helped to inaugurate a new era – "THE MEDIUM IS THE MESSAGE." Shortly after, Vancouver poets and artists began thinking about the medium of their art with a shocking new clarity. They began experimenting aggressively with the boundaries between the arts and established an intermedia zone for art creation whose effects are being felt to the present day. This zone developed into an artists' association called, appropriately, the Intermedia Society (1967–72). As Alvin Balkind writes of the McLuhan-inspired coalition, they "made one of the first contributions anywhere in the world – and certainly in Canada – to a particular kind of collaborative avant-garde. The element of collaboration was rooted in a strong, functional democracy that demanded a loose-limbed, flexible, less-structured, co-operative approach to artistic endeavour" ("On Ferment" n. pag.). By 1965, the fervour had spread to the point that UBC's annual Festival of the Contemporary Arts was themed "The Medium Is the Message" in tribute to his influence.

Even McLuhan wasn't the first, though, to recognize the changes underfoot. Paul Tiessen has already noted how ideas about culture and technology that McLuhan would later popularize were already circulating throughout the English-speaking world, including in Vancouver in the 1940s through the writings of novelist Malcolm Lowry and film doyen Gerald Noxon ("From Literary Modernism" n. pag.). Lowry and Noxon argued that, as Canada took its place in the global village, it was the physical bodies of regular Canadians that would most profoundly feel the impact of that shift, largely as a result of the mass media. Vancouver was already awash, Tiessen adds, in "a conversation, really a critical idiom, which in its content and tone broadly anticipated elements of Marshall

---

3 While this date is routinely invoked, no scholar has been able to track down the actual event at which he made this comment. McLuhan's grandson Andrew McLuhan discovered an undated handwritten note by Marshall that reads "used the phrase in June (?) 1958 at Radio broadcasters conference in Vancouver. Was reassuring them that TV could not end radio" (McLuhan 2020). In 1975, however, McLuhan began a lecture at Georgia State University by listing the date as 1957. McLuhan, however, did not speak in Vancouver in 1957. He was, however, invited to "The Radio Seminar" from 5 to 9 May 1958, a joint event organized by the University of British Columbia and the British Columbia Association of Broadcasters. McLuhan's talk was titled "Revolution in Communication."

McLuhan's post-World War II work."[4] Vancouver was not unique in this regard. The conversation Tiessen documents was also happening throughout the Western world. The city, however, was uniquely positioned to respond to this kind of thinking and to take up the implications in art, especially because of the impact of figures like Noxon, Lowry, and later Sheila Watson, who was closely associated with McLuhan. The modernist legacies of the city, such as those of Lowry, Noxon, Watson, and others discussed in the chapters that follow, established the conditions for the avant-garde flowering that followed between 1959 and 1975. Conveniently, there was a lack of any countervailing set of conservative art institutions or entrenched aesthetics to stem the tide (in fact, the art institutions aided and abetted the spirit of experimentation that emerged).

1 When American Literature Moved to Vancouver

In the ongoing advance of science, contemporary quantum physics has happed upon an old Buddhist riddle – that there is no such thing as nothing.[5] Instead, there is only the absence of patterns (or tools) that allow us to see the fullness of nothing (or measure its composition, in the case of physics). Seeing something as nothing is to admit a blindness about what is actually there. For instance, the most celebrated moment in the period in question reveals how the particular focus of this book alters a familiar narrative – finding something where nothing had been presumed.

Finding Nothing's narrative of transnational cultural flow, and what happens to a local culture when something new and disruptive arrives, begins in the summer of 1963 when a large group of American avant-garde writers descended upon the city of Vancouver to share their poems and insights with a younger generation of aspiring mostly Canadian writers. It was an exciting moment for a diverse coterie of literary-minded students in the city: authors they had been reading and studying were now suddenly in their midst. Of course, the Americans were in town for the now widely acclaimed Vancouver Poetry Conference (VPC), an event that had evolved from a university course conducted by University of British Columbia English professor Warren Tallman called, plainly enough, "English 410: Poetry Writing and Criticism" into, by the professor's own estimation, a "Götterdämmerung poetry klatsch" ("A Brief" 117) of cutting-edge literature. Leading American poets Robert Creeley, Allen Ginsberg, and Charles Olson were hired to teach the course with Tallman that year. The class ran from 24 July through to 16 August and featured lectures,

---

4 See also Miguel Mota and Paul Tiessen's critical introduction to *The Cinema of Malcolm Lowry* (1990), in which they document his medium-consciousness and his transcultural reading of popular media.
5 See Ethan Siegal's 2016 article "What Is the Physics of Nothing?" for a useful overview of the field, including an array of ways of thinking about nothing as absence, as the pure context for things (*chora* in philosophy), as cosmic vacuum, and so on.

Figure I.6 The
American poets in
Vancouver, 1963.
Allen Ginsberg, Robert
Duncan, Donald Allen,
and Charles Allen in
the Kerrisdale home of
Warren Tallman. Photo
by Karen Tallman. Used
with permission.

readings, workshops, and discussion by Olson, Creeley, and Ginsberg, as well as
three other American poets of note, Robert Duncan, Denise Levertov, and Philip
Whalen. One lone Canadian, Margaret Avison, presented her work at the event. She
was, in fact, the only author not affiliated with either the Black Mountain College or
the Berkeley Renaissance.[6] She was, however, recognized as somewhat simpatico (if
not completely compatible)[7] with the others. Indeed, after hearing Avison read from
her book manuscript at the conference, Levertov, acting as an advisory poetry editor
for W.W. Norton, would request and publish Avison's collection *The Dumbfounding*

6 "Black Mountain" specifically refers to a college in Black Mountain, North Carolina, that closed in 1956,
   but also more generally refers to a school of poetry that emerged from associated faculty in the 1950s. The
   Berkeley Renaissance circle, in the words of scholar Terry Ludwar, "centred on Blaser-Duncan-Spicer, [and]
   had as a source of group identification men as the beloved" (27). Olson, Creeley, and Duncan were faculty at
   Black Mountain College; Levertov fell under the influence of the group after becoming an American citizen
   in 1955. Ginsberg and Whalen were not directly associated with the Berkeley Renaissance, but as iconic
   Beat poets are often included in the more broadly imagined San Francisco Renaissance. This corresponds to
   the grouping in Donald Allen's iconic *New American Poetry 1945–1960*, in which Olson, Creeley, Duncan,
   and Levertov are grouped as Black Mountain Poets and Spicer, Blaser, Ginsberg, and Whalen are grouped as
   San Francisco Renaissance poets. Avison's work is not included in the anthology. Blaser, who would become
   Canadian after moving to Vancouver, was not invited to attend the VPC.
7 Avison writes, "I was aware of being separate, Canadian, more formally dressed, and often in awe. The great
   gain from such discomfort was the fact that Denise Levertov and, oddly, Charles Olson, perceived this. They

Figure I.7 Portrait of Margaret Avison (1963). Photo by Karen Tallman. Used with permission.

Margaret Avison (1918–2007) was a Toronto-based poet with a reputation for producing exquisite, multilayered lyric poetry that explores complex moral and religious themes. In 1963, she was primarily acclaimed for *Winter Sun* (1960), a collection of poems written in Chicago in 1956. Her second collection, *The Dumb-founding* (1966), was published by W.W. Norton and edited by Denise Levertov following a conversation they had in Vancouver in 1963. Over her career, Avison won two Governor General's Literary Awards and the 2003 Griffin Poetry Prize.

(Sarah 62). Tallman, an American expat, was more diffident about her inclusion, however, and sneeringly dismissed her participation "as a concession to national whatever pride" in a letter to Robert Creeley (Letter 8). The material conditions of the event, it being a university-course-based class, precluded the participation of the older modernist writers in the city, including established Vancouver writers, like Earle Birney and Dorothy Livesay, who were not invited to participate, as well

---

often manoeuvred me back into the circle of talk, inconspicuously" (*I Am Here* 145). It wasn't just social and personality differences, though: "Only eight months earlier, my stance had been theirs [...] Believing in Jesus now unfixed all my prior values" (146). Despite being well received, and welcomed into the conversation, she had to leave the conference prematurely and abruptly when she learned of her father's sudden death (147).

as contemporary poets who were not students, like Frank Davey and Phyllis Webb. Canada and Canadian literature, including Vancouver and British Columbian literature, were left out and firmly set aside (effectively erased) in the moment of the event's arrival.

As Vancouver's young literati received them, one of those visiting Americans broke off from the organized activities to pay tribute to a cutting-edge Canadian not on the program. It was Allen Ginsberg who left for an afternoon visit with Stella Gysin, mother of Brion Gysin, the Canadian expatriate then living in Paris. Ginsberg had been associated with Gysin in New York City, in Tangier, Morocco, but especially in Paris at the Beat Hotel on the rue Git-le-Coeur – where Gysin was busy inventing various new literary forms, including permutation poems, digital poems, performance art poetry, and most famously the cut-up technique that the likes of William Burroughs, Kathy Acker, David Bowie, and many others would go on to explore in a flurry of groundbreaking novels, poems, and songs. Gysin developed the technique from his friend Tristan Tzara, with whom he was acquainted through their mutual involvement in André Breton's Surrealist movement in the 1930s. Gysin was the only Canadian member of the group prior to the Second World War (though he, like Tzara, was expelled for aesthetic violations). In Gysin's post-Surrealist experiments with cut-up, collage, gridwork, and multimodal performances, he was leading the international avant-garde on new aesthetic adventures. He returned to Canada, to Toronto and Vancouver, during the Second World War to study the Japanese language and its calligraphic writing system with the Canadian army. He was stationed at the University of British Columbia campus, where the poetry conference took place less than two decades later. He had intended to become a spy, but the war ended before he had the chance to finish his training in Vancouver and deploy into the field. With the new skills he learned in Vancouver, though, Gysin moved to New York City and got connected with the action painters and eventually the Beat authors, who admired his calligraphic fusion of asemic text, improvisation, and mysticism. Thus, for almost half a century, Gysin worked at the centre of the international avant-garde. As William Burroughs, Gysin's collaborator and closest friend, said of his art, "I see in his painting the psychic landscape of my own work. He is doing in painting what I try to do in writing [...] What [Francis] Bacon hopes to do Gysin has done repeatedly" (qtd. in Geiger 125). Gysin was moved by the human kindness of Ginsberg's private tribute in Vancouver (Geiger 21–22), but Ginsberg's visit disrupts the familiar story of what happened in Vancouver in 1963 and what it means for the avant-garde history of the city and the country. The 1963 poetry conference has been variously declared the germinal moment of Canadian avant-garde poetics and hailed as "one of those serendipitous historical moments when the marginal momentarily occupied the centre" (Butling et al. 144), an event marked by "legendary" anecdotes of the great Americans in outmoded Canada (145). Tallman, the conference organizer, was given the highest praise for his efforts with the

Figure I.8 Allen Ginsberg dances with Karen Tallman in the Tallman house in Kerrisdale. Photo by Warren Tallman. Used with permission.

conference and beyond by Creeley: "It's as if Warren brought not only the US and Canada together in such interests, but that he really brought western Canada's poetry into the international world it now helps to define and keep possible" ("Warren Tallman Elegy"; see Appendix A). The VPC was an important progenitor of and model for subsequent legendary literary events, including the Foster Poetry Conference in Montreal later that year and the Berkeley Poetry Conference in 1965, in which Jack Spicer made his final public appearance. On its own, though, Vancouver was a gelling moment for the New American Poetry group, as it was the first time the aesthetics of the group had been presented as a coherent phenomenon in an international context. The conference, as Lewis Ellingham and Kevin Killian claim, "brought all these notable spirits together for the first time" (267).

It was all quite *something*.

Yet, despite the importance of the event to Canadian avant-gardism, it was only in Ginsberg's off-program private visit, never previously acknowledged in any of the scholarship on the event, that earlier or concurrent avant-gardisms in Canada were admitted and acknowledged. Indeed, while the writing of diverse generations of Anglo-American authors was interrogated for value and relevance, no discussion or even renunciation was afforded to Canada's avant-gardes – such as the Automatists, the Canadian Vorticists, and the Cosmic Canadians, whom I have discussed in other contexts, and all of whom had significant connections to Vancouver in the early 1960s[8] – let alone other individual and more local initiatives or authors. As Avison reflected, "the whole project was to introduce 'these new voices' from south of the border [...] O you Americans!" (Avison, Letter n. pag.). It changes the narrative significantly to realize that those same American authors had Canadian peers – with Vancouver connections – that were never acknowledged in the conference. Ginsberg's tribute thus serves as a useful reminder of the limitation of the mythology of the conference as a sudden flowering in a desolate climate. Indeed, the story of the VPC is often used as something of an origin story for modernism and avant-gardism in Vancouver, despite the already existent legacies of both in the city. That story, as others have remarked, rehashes the depressingly colonial narrative of culture moving from the imperial centre to the unenlightened margins. The locals are praised, not for what they contribute to the growth of culture, but for how well they mimic the source of imperial culture. This book is called *Finding Nothing* in part in reference to this sense of the erasure of local culture as represented in the VPC. In founding *Tish* editor, and future poet laureate of Canada, George Bowering's own words, "I hadn't thought about Canadian poetry. I didn't even think about thinking about Canadian poetry" (Bayard and David 81). As the communication theorists Gregory Bateson and Jurgen Ruesch note, all new knowledge and insight involves the erasure of old knowledge and insight (see *Communication: The Social Matrix of Psychiatry* passim). In this case, the neglect of Canada's and Vancouver's literary history in the VPC and, perhaps more problematically, in the narrativization of the VPC, displaced the true story of modernism north of the border and has perpetuated the habit of erasure and silencings that has characterized Vancouver culture from its outset.

Accordingly, many of the histories of the VPC rely upon the strategic erasure of literary activity in Vancouver and, more generally, in Canada, as well as the significance of cultures from other marginalized groups outside of the thin band of poetic production. It was, indeed, at one point in the history of Canadian literature, for a significant cohort, exciting to imagine and depict modernist culture arriving into the country as a kind of liberating epiphany that broke the doldrums of an illiterate or provincial folk. But just as the land itself was not empty when the first European settler-colonialists arrived, and just as Indigenous cultures were not without value

---

8 While they are discussed in more detail in the subsequent chapters, it is worth acknowledging here that Jack Shadbolt, a prominent artist associated with the Canadian Vorticists, and Lawren Harris, the most prominent Cosmic Canadian, were living in Vancouver at the time and actively making experimental art. Shadbolt, in fact, was a founding member of the Intermedia Society, which will be discussed throughout this book. Of course, they were primarily painters and not recognized as immediately relevant to the concerns of the poets gathered at the VPC, who do not appear to have discussed any visual artists. Pierre Coupey, famous for founding and editing the *Capilano Review*, brought to Vancouver his significant connections with the Montreal Automatists when he came in 1964. By the 1960s, the Automatists had already gained national and international attention and were renowned figures in Canadian arts and letters. Automatist signatory Françoise Sullivan performed in Vancouver at the Festival of Contemporary Arts (1967).

Figure I.9 Brion Gysin in Paris, 1959. Photograph by Ian Sommerville. © the Brion Gysin Estate and the William S. Burroughs Trust, used by permission of the Wylie Agency LLC.

Brion Gysin (1916–86) was one of the stalwart figures of the international avant-garde in the twentieth century. He was born in the Canadian military hospital on the grounds of Cliveden, Taplow, England, and raised in Edmonton, Alberta. After secondary school, he arrived in Paris as a teenager and became Canada's first member of André Breton's Surrealist movement. He introduced the cut-up method, which he developed from his friend Tristan Tzara, to writers like William S. Burroughs and Kathy Acker. Gysin developed a unique gestural, asemic painting style that developed from his training with the Canadian army, in the Second World War, to become a spy.

though they were treated as such, it is no longer sufficient to imagine the Vancouver, let alone Canadian, cultural landscape through such a hierarchical and colonial lens. In fact, Ginsberg's private visit attests to a secret network of internationalized avant-garde production that was already flowing across the border (indeed, flowing both ways) and throughout Canada well before the conference. Acknowledging and accounting for the avant-garde in Canada requires a more flexible model of modernism that reads cultural production with more attention to the border, and to how globalization facilitates the flow of culture across borders. The transnational movement of culture as constant coordinates of cultural life in the city long predates 1963. And indeed, the story of Vancouver's avant-gardes, of their turn away from colonial silencing, needs a more sophisticated narrative that is aware of the confluence of global cultures and local cultures already manifest and interacting in the city well before this particular group of Americans arrived. Vancouver, in other words, had already modernized, and the VPC was not the onset but a galvanizing moment of self-realization of this cultural shift, this turn toward a whole-field consciousness. Furthermore, the tools the Vancouver authors took from the American poets were specifically oriented toward perceiving the locus as a site of confluence of material and mythological forces acting upon the individual. The New American poetics, as I discuss in more detail below, sought to overcome the alienation of author from place and page by situating them in the full dynamism of this confluence: "one loves only form, / and form only comes / into existence when / the thing is born // born of yourself" (Olson, "I, Maximus" 7). Modernist poets and novelists in Vancouver, however, had already begun the work of mapping out this kind of perception of space, place, and history of the city, long before the Americans came to town.

2 Vancouver, via a Brief Digression on Modernism

The story of Vancouver's transformation in the 1960s requires some sense of the literary movement known as "modernism," of what it was and how it came to Canada. Canadian and American modernist literature begins in Paris, where artists from around the world congregated en masse in the early twentieth century to address, contest, and attempt to direct all of the changes that had been precipitated by the arrival of modernity and industrialization. The city's black-metal Eiffel Tower, the world's largest structure when it was finished in 1889, served as a central symbol for the arrival of a new era. It helped that established nineteenth-century authors, such as Guy de Maupassant, contested the "giddy, ridiculous tower" for heralding the onset of a "ghastly dream" (qtd. in Harvie 95). Today, we call that ghastly dream modernism itself, and many of its distinctly urban, disjunctive, and geometrical features are anticipated in the tower. It was in that context, in 1897, that French Symbolist poet Stéphane Mallarmé published a rather jangly, fragmented poem called "Un coup de dés" with a decidedly enigmatic title that would come to have an enormous impact on Vancouver's avant-garde: the full title translates as "A throw of the dice will never abolish chance." The poem overlays the story of a shipwreck with gambling imagery so as to highlight an existential randomness within human culture: thus, it concludes, "All Thought expresses a Throw of the Dice" (165). The text moves back and forth across the page with a new kind of typographical freedom, opening up the page as a spatial/visual realm. Everything is changing, it announces; nothing is permanent: like a dream "all reality is dissolved" (163). After Mallarmé, the poem was free to explore the full extent of space on the page.

While all periods introduce a certain amount of chance and change into the world, a dramatic acceleration of widespread transformation characterizes the historical period we call modernity. Literature in North America was not immune to these forces, as the writers' relationship to the page and to the idea of writing altered in the period. American poet E.E. Cummings, for instance, took up Mallarmé's

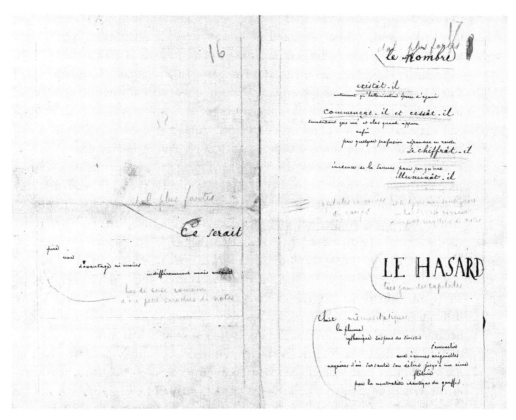

Figure I.10 Page detail of the maquette of Stéphane Mallarmé's *Un coup de dés jamais n'abolira le hazard* (A throw of the dice will never abolish chance), as delivered to typesetters in 1897.

experiments with the placement of words on the page and began organizing his writing to maximize visual effect. American-British poet and critic T.S. Eliot explored the crisis suggested by Mallarmé's notion that culture is ultimately superficial and inherently random. Eliot wrestled with Mallarmé's provocative proposition that language could create its own reality.

Culture at the time seemed unstable and was still drifting from the shock of a number of radical nineteenth-century ideas in religion, economics, politics, and popular art that undermined many of the ideological pillars of Victorian society. The theory of evolution, for example, implied by extension that the Bible was not literally true, a heretical position before Charles Darwin's *Origin of Species*, published in 1859. This shift created the very troubling question of what was true, if not the word of God? Karl Marx's economic theories, which were first published in 1842, also introduced the disruptive idea of class mobility and the notion that workers should have the right to own their own labour. The United States, following its period of reconstruction after the Civil War, was still adjusting to its emancipation from slavery. Women were actively and aggressively advocating for their right to vote. Communist revolutions inspired by Marx in Paris (1871), Russia (1917), Germany (1918), Bavaria (1919), and Hungary (1919) marked the emergence of a new kind of political struggle. Society was in upheaval and would soon descend into global wars not unrelated to the arrival of modernity. All of these struggles and vagaries would have an impact on North American modernist literature and create an atmosphere charged with the spirit of revolution and change.

At the same time as all of the above, technological advancements, including the emergence of a mass media, swiftly altered and upset the traditional hierarchy of the arts. A wave of futurist artists emerged who championed the progress of technology and celebrated the enormous scale of cities like Paris and New York. As the American expatriate novelist Henry Miller exclaimed: "Such a huge Paris! It would take a lifetime to explore it again" (171). Walter Benjamin set about, but never finished, a new kind of lifetime collage text in response, jotting down notes and quotes about the marvels of Paris in his *Passagenwerk* (commonly known in English as *The Arcades Project*). The central question for artists of the period became their relationship to such novelty: to either pursue it with utopian abandon, or else fight it and try to preserve an inherited culture. Those who went to Paris and other European centres went to discover new possibilities. These modernist writers positioned themselves as participants in or even progenitors of the radical transformations underfoot. Thus, American poet Ezra Pound offered up a famous motto for writers to "make it new" (*Make*) – a plea for writers to enhance the intensity of the changes underfoot. Indeed, the embrace of an emerging or possible culture rather than a stalwart defence of the old is one of the characteristics of modernist literature.

Harkening back to the harsh metallic symbolism of the Eiffel Tower, a group of artists and writers associated with Pound and Eliot even began identifying themselves as a "Cult of Ugliness" (Pound, "Serious" 45). Their writing was filled with violent and jarring imagery and marked by complex stylistic features such as collage, bricolage, and fragmentation. "Civilization's going to pieces," wrote F. Scott Fitzgerald in 1925 at the beginning of *The Great Gatsby* (14). Despite the pervasive bleakness, however, there is still an inherent optimism beneath the despair, as the violence and existential alienation depicted in these modernist works perform a kind of cleansing, cyclical ritual. Gatsby, for instance, by the end of the novel, still believes in "the orgiastic future that year by year recedes before us [...] tomorrow we will run faster, stretch out our arms farther" (141). T.S. Eliot's devastating long poem *The Waste Land*, from 1922, concludes with revivifying (even if dangerous) waters returning to a desiccated landscape. That same year, Canadian painter Lawren Harris published a small book of free verse poems called *Contrasts* that juxtaposes ephemeral urban decay with eternal

Figure I.11 Guillaume Apollinaire's *Calligrammes; poèmes de la paix et da la guerre, 1913–1916* (1918). Source: Private collection of the author.

spiritual integrity. Though the book was largely overlooked, its publication was a clear indication that international modernist culture had arrived and found purchase in Canada. Harris brought that spirit to Vancouver when he moved there in 1940, and became an important guide in advancing modernist art and literature in the city.

"City Heat"
Lawren Harris, *Contrasts: A Book of Verse* (1922)

The streets are hot under the sun,
Surging with animal heat,
Sucked to the surface
Through pores, through angers, through feverishness
By the sun.

The heat jiggles along every street,
Reverberates from the scorching pavement,
Hot brick walls, stone walls and side walks –
Runs everywhere
With licking-hot, laughing tongues
Driven by the sun.

The breezes are dead,
Only the slow undulating coarse stench
From hot meals, dead meats,
Stinking steam, sour milk
And sour sweat
Moves –
Soughing swamp breathings
In the pestilential city.

Babies in the heat,
The sick in the heat,
Pain in the heat,
Noises running the waves of heat,
Metal-hot, nasal noises,
Cryings, bawlings, clangings
And wearied voices
Ringing in the head
Like the close-singing remoteness
Of delirium.

From out the city
Oozes forth
A sticky, cloying, stinking thickness,
Sucked to the surface
By the sun.

The transformations introduced within modernity were emphatically extreme. Consider, as one example, the impact of developments in electricity: at the end of the nineteenth century, for the first time ever, city streets were suddenly awash in electric light, opening up the night. A swath of inventions, from radio to cinema, quickly followed, and the Eiffel Tower itself was used for radio transmissions. The electric elevator, invented in 1880, allowed buildings to grow taller, and the skyscraper was born, lit up and down like an enormous torch held up as if in defiance against the stars. Apollinaire's 1912 poem "Les Fenêtres" (published in *Calligrammes* in 1918) considers the transformation of the urban landscape with the increased height: "Towers / Towers are the streets / Well / Wells are the squares / Wells / Hollow tree sheltering vagabond mulattoes" (29). The future of modernity is transcultural and, anticipating Eliot, hollow. The poem, as Timothy Mathews argues, establishes a clear resistance to the "adoration of the modern" (31). Strikingly, in this posthumously published poem, Apollinaire connects the spread of modernist landscapes from Paris all the way to Vancouver:

> to the north
> Where raccoon hunters
> Scrape the fur skins
> Glittering diamond
> Vancouver
> Where the train white with snow and lights flashing though the dark runs away from winter
> Oh Paris
>
> (29)

To be clear, Apollinaire never visited the city, but uses it in the poem as the marker of how far modernity's transformations had reached. In 1890, electric subways were first commissioned and a network of rapid-transit tunnels was swiftly burrowed beneath all of the major, bustling cities. Daily life – especially in the cities – was utterly transformed, suddenly electrified from below ground to above the clouds. Earle Birney wrote his iconic poem "Vancouver Lights" (1941) about the "troubling delight" of seeing his city suddenly awash in electric light: "we are a spark beleaguered / by darkness" (72). Modernism is, accordingly, intimately connected to such monumental and distinctly urban transformations. Birney's poem highlights the presence of those forces of change in Vancouver, and the complicated ambivalence with which such changes were often received.

Literature had to change. As Canada's avant-garde novelist and painter Bertram Brooker argued, "books like those of Henry James, George Meredith and Joseph Conrad simply cannot be written by a man who has just breakfasted with an electric toaster at his elbow and whose morning meditation in the garden has been disturbed by ukulele-music trickling out of the sky" (197). Brooker's prose, especially his 1936 novel *Think of the Earth*, catalogues the impact of the new electrified environment. By mid-century, Marshall McLuhan had developed a complex and widely influential philosophy about the impact of electricity, citing it as the most important technological development in Western civilization since the printing press. A new kind of human consciousness had begun to emerge in the "electric age," he argued (*Understanding Media* 1). The question was, how should books be written now?

For many North American writers, Canada and the United States did not prove to be productive environments in which to address such a question. Both places, but for different reasons, felt too resistant to modernity's changes, too caught up in unsophisticated nationalisms or traditionalisms, to permit the kind of literary experimentation that was needed to effectively grapple with the radical changes underfoot. Brooker protested such conditions directly: "We have welcomed new architectural forms like the grain elevator and the skyscraper. But in the arts where form is divorced from mechanics – notably in literature and painting – we permit ourselves to be greatly disturbed by ingenuity, originality, and the invention of new contrivances, new moods, new modes" (198). The conditions that Brooker describes contributed to a mass exodus of a generation of many of North America's most prominent authors to Europe. Ezra Pound moved to London in 1909, and then to Paris in 1921; T.S. Eliot moved to Paris in 1910, and then to London in 1914. H.D. moved to London permanently in 1911. After the First World War, another group – including Ernest Hemingway, Gertrude Stein, F. Scott Fitzgerald, John Dos Passos, and Canadian writers Morley Callaghan, John Glassco, and Brion Gysin – relocated to Paris. It was in Paris, after all, that America's best precedent for modernism, Edgar Allan Poe, was first recognized as an important author.[9] The group of exiled authors who left in the twentieth century became known by a famous quote by Stein, who declared: "You are all a lost generation." Hemingway used the line as an epigraph to his 1926 novel *The Sun Also Rises*, which depicts the expatriate literary community in Paris fretting about their existential rootlessness. "Cheer up," his protagonist says: "All countries look just like the moving pictures" (18).

Laura Doyle and Laura Winkiel's response to this globalized sense of modernism is useful to account for the transnational nature of Vancouver's cultural character. Their work seeks to break down nationally dependent frames of reference for the interpretation and study of modernism and relocate cultural flows on a global scale. From this vantage, modernism appears as a dynamic global phenomenon moving through diverse landscapes, meeting in places like Paris or Vancouver and interacting with complex and multidirectional precedents and locally situated politics. This *geomodernism* includes investigating "how canonical white Anglo modernism is itself determined by contact-zone clashes and reversals and how it, too, is haunted by ghosts – the repressed ghosts of an African modernity,

---

9 Charles Baudelaire's essay "Edgar Allan Poe: sa vie et ses ouvrages," first published in April 1852, was the first major consideration of Poe's work (Sova 295), despite which fact Baudelaire's 1848 translation of Poe was actually the fourth translation of Poe into French.

an Atlantic modernity, a subaltern modernity. That is, we begin to see all kinds of modernisms as they make themselves and are made from the *outside in*" (3; emphasis in original). It is a reversal of horizons, then, that allows us to rethink modernism in broader terms, beyond the well-established discourse of modernism as a one-way flow of influence, as a series of productive tensions between the global and the local, the technological and the traditional. In this study, that reversal will include acknowledging the First Nations inhabitants in relation to the avant-gardism that emerges from this place. Through the reversal of colonial habits of erasure, we can start to think about how the work of this intermediary generation of authors participated in a transcolonial network, responsive to the overlapping histories of colonization in Canada, including in their resistance to British and American cultural models, to central Canadian dominance of the industry, and, in the more recent decolonial turn, to the ongoing Canadian replication of that colonial heritage.

Such a model becomes especially useful in engaging with the inherited modernist trope of exile, wherein many modernist authors confronted within themselves the deeply personal and cultural (and hegemonic) implications of locus – where the idea of place is rendered sharply political by including the history and condition of global colonialism in the constitution of locality and personal identity. Acknowledging dynamism and movement, along with the violent regimes of colonial power, as a foundational constituent of modernism is especially useful in situating the work of Brion Gysin, who was at one time considered "the hippest man in the world" (Davis, *Old* 197), and who left Canada and crossed the Atlantic in search of the repressed ghosts and subaltern voices of Africa. In many respects, he sought to make *himself* a "contact-zone clash" of international modernisms and displaced peoples, self-consciously opened and remade from the outside in. He was a site of transcolonization, and he sought to attend to that clash. What made Gysin "hip" was precisely his ability to straddle and smoothly navigate multiple geographies (North America, Europe, Asia, and Africa), genres (painting, literature, sculpture, and music), and cultures (avant-garde, academic, military, union, etc.). And just as Doyle advocates, Gysin searched beyond the boundaries of Western notions of enlightenment for antidotes to the crises of modernity. Indeed, Doyle's resistance to what she terms "liberty plots" ("Liberty" 52), or the recurring pull of spiritual emancipation within modernist narratology, accords with Gysin's own interest in undoing his inherited cultural models rather than making them anew. "Finding nothing" in this sense is a literary trope of confronting the juggernaut of transcolonialisms, undoing cultural imperialism, seeking knowledge beyond the self, and encountering the void. The French philosopher and affiliate of Surrealism Georges Bataille once wrote, "To be conscious of not being everything, as one is of being mortal, is nothing. But if we are without a narcotic, an unbreathable void reveals itself" (xxxii).

In the aftermath of the Second World War, a period that scholars increasingly discuss as "late modernism,"[10] optimism fuelled by the triumph over fascist Nazi Germany combined with a deep suspicion of the Western culture that had produced that horror. Writers and artists sought out alternatives, whether looking back to the avant-garde movements from before the war, such as Surrealism and Dadaism, or else in pursuit of new liberated states of consciousness. In Quebec in the late 1940s, the Automatist group developed from the Surrealists a pursuit of liberation through irrationalism and spontaneous art. The New York School of Poets and the Beats in the 1950s and 1960s developed a stream-of-consciousness vernacular style to depict the possibility of liberation in the context of a cloistered, violent society. Jack Kerouac's 1957 novel *On the Road* epitomizes the new possibilities of freedom in America (and prompted bill bissett, as a teenager living in Halifax, to hit the road the next year). Frank O'Hara's poetry from the same period captures the urgency to communicate directly in Cold War paranoiac America. In Canada, a group including novelist Sheila Watson, poet and playwright Wilfred Watson, visual artist and designer Harley Parker, and novelist John Reid, among others, collected around McLuhan to follow up on both Wyndham Lewis's ideas of the media's impact on society and McLuhan's theories of the electric age. Thus, Sheila Watson's 1959 novel *The Double Hook* imagines a village in British Columbia without media that descends swiftly into violence (see Figure I.12). It is a paradox (hence her title) that modernism has not been able to solve: namely, that increased "civilization" is accompanied by increased violence. Indigenous communities across Canada would likely see no contradiction in such a position. Strikingly, as Sarah Walbohm (among many other critics) has noted, in order for Watson to establish her sense of modernist crisis, she erases all markers of Indigenous culture (save the mythological figure Coyote) from her representation of British Columbia (80). All her characters are left with is a series of fragments of past cultures with which to try to resuscitate the wasted landscape surrounding them. In a world on the precipice of a third world war, this time charged with the possibility of nuclear apocalypse, the urgency of modernism's longing for a lost stability seemed ever more pressing, ever more desperate, as this possibility receded ever further into the future.[11]

---

10 See, for instance, Tyrus Miller's *Late Modernism: Politics, Fiction, and the Arts Between the Wars* (1999), Anne Fitzpatrick's *Late Modernism* (2006), Robert Genter's *Late Modernism: Art, Culture, and Politics in Cold War America* (2011), and Charles Daniel Blanton's *Epic Negation: The Dialectical Poetics of Late Modernism* (2015).

11 I argue in my MA thesis, "Severed from Roots: Settling Culture in Sheila Watson's Novels," that the strategic erasure of historical details in *The Double Hook* produces a distortion that finds its possible resolution only in her other novel, *Deep Hollow Creek*, which interrogates the Indigenous–settler relationship more forcefully.

This compelling and imaginative first novel introduces an original talent to the Canadian literary scene. Sheila Watson writes with extreme economy and directness about the complexities of human nature and human destiny. A sharply experimental approach to the novelist craft has resulted in an unusual pattern of composition that will immediately strike the eye. No less striking are the stark reality of the images evoked and the austere beauty of the prose.

THE DOUBLE HOOK

SHEILA
WATSON

the Double Hook

Figure I.12 Original hardcover dust jacket of Sheila Watson's 1959 novel *The Double Hook*. Cover designed by Frank Newfeld. Used with permission.

Watson was not the first modernist, or even avant-gardist, active on the West Coast. The arrival of modernist literary culture in Vancouver can be traced back to at least 1935, when Dorothy Livesay moved to the city. She came with almost a decade's worth of experience of organizing and editing the political little magazine *Masses* and producing radical avant-garde literature in support of communist revolution in Canada. She also spent 1931–2 at the Sorbonne in Paris completing a thesis on the influence of Symbolist poets like Baudelaire, Mallarmé, and Apollinaire on English modernists like Pound, Eliot, Auden, and Spender (Percival 120). As Dean Irvine writes, Livesay "bridges the histories of modernist and leftist magazine cultures in a way that no other figure [...] does; she is the one individual who persistently traverses modernist and leftist cultural formations" (27). After arriving in Vancouver, she published her iconic revolutionary poem "Day and Night" in the first issue of *Canadian Poetry Magazine*, edited by E.J. Pratt, and proceeded to help establish the magazine *New Frontier* as a new leftist literary cultural forum (Irvine 58–65).

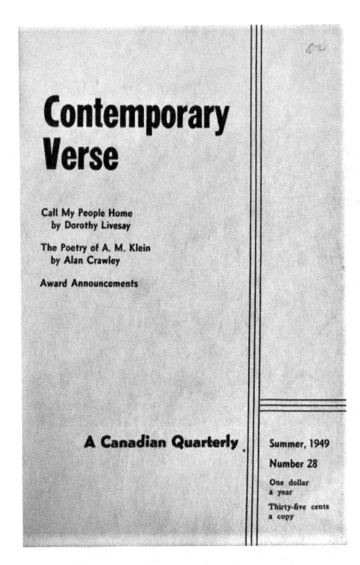

Contemporary Verse

Call My People Home
by Dorothy Livesay

The Poetry of A. M. Klein
by Alan Crawley

Award Announcements

A Canadian Quarterly

Summer, 1949

Number 28

One dollar
a year

Thirty-five cents
a copy

Figure I.13 Cover of
Contemporary Verse 38
(Summer 1949).

This institutional skill-set and activist mentality proved crucial in establishing another new British Columbian literary magazine called *Contemporary Verse* in 1941, which she co-founded with Alan Crawley, Doris Ferne, Anne Marriott, and Floris McLaren. While it was "not an avant-garde magazine" (Irvine 79), *Contemporary Verse* quickly became an important forum for modernist writing in the country, especially by female authors. It was also the first identifiably modernist magazine in Vancouver, and one of the first in Canada. Crawley, Livesay, and McLaren[12] were also

---

12 Crawley and Livesay were members of the Vancouver Poetry Society, but it is unclear whether McLaren, who lived in Victoria, was actually a member. Grant Hurley notes that she presented a public lecture on poetry to the group on 28 January 1939 (59).

all members of the nascent Vancouver Poetry Society, which published a magazine of its own called *Full Tide*, though it was less committed to the new modernist forms. When Birney took over the editorship of the *Canadian Poetry Magazine* in September 1946 (after getting hired as a professor at the University of British Columbia), he pulled its eclectic aesthetics firmly into the modernist camp. Vancouver, suddenly, had two prominent modernist magazines, a more conservative third publication, and a firmly established little-magazine culture.

Livesay capitalized upon the opportunity with two significant publications. An entire issue of *Contemporary Verse* was given to publishing her radio play "Call My People Home," a text that contested the ongoing internment of Japanese Canadians long after the war had ended. The text speaks out against the silence of Vancouver's colonialist erasures. She also published "Vancouver" in *Contemporary Verse*, a poem that offers a psycho-geographic romp through the masculine violence of the city. By the time *Contemporary Verse* folded in 1953, two other little magazines had come and gone – the *Western Free-Lance* (one issue in 1942, edited by Geoffrey Asche) and *pm* (three issues from 1951 to 1952, edited by Yvonne Agazarian). Rather than imagining themselves as conduits of national or international modernist culture, both of these short-run magazines focused almost exclusively on the Vancouver scene. That there was a scene, by 1953, was undeniable. No magazine, or author, had yet sought to take a firm stand in the flow of modern culture, but many worked hard to connect the city to national and international aesthetic initiatives.

"Vancouver"
Dorothy Livesay, *Contemporary Verse* 31 (Spring 1950), 15–16

The city is male, they said: a champion
Caught in a stance; a warrior dreaming.
Indolent he sprawls, arms flung around a mountain
Feet among the Fraser's fishes, head in evergreen.
The city is a sleeper no one dares to waken
Though time is ripe and innocence untaken. [...]

The city is male, they said: smelling the sweat
Squeezed as a log boom's launched
Into False Creek; as a stevedore unloads
The sick-sweet copra; hoists high
The outgoing wheat, matey and muscular. [...]

The city is male, I said: a hunter haunted
Sniffing the north: on the cool mountain's snow
Seeing a shadow; through the forest floor
Hearing a footfall or an echo go.

Then, with gun cocked – he's taken for a gangster –
Nabbed by his own police, stabbed in the back.
Now bleeding in the dens of Chinatown
Is stuff in closests, left until the stench
Wrenches the roof off, and explodes the bomb.

O body lying shattered, limbs of man
Tossed in a doorway for the maggot sun:
City unburied, shall I approach you now
Open and undeterred?
What, if your arms say nothing and your mouth
Cries out unheard
Can you awaken yet, out of this sleep
And proclaim the Word?

Modernist prose had taken root in the city as well. Though Northrop Frye found it not quite modern enough for contemporary readers (655), other critics claimed that Ethel Wilson's novella *Hetty Dorval* (1947) is marked by themes "typical to both popular modern and high modern writing" (Willmott 103). Still, its modernism is ambivalent enough that Desmond Pacey could even describe it as "old-fashioned" for its narrative voice (61). Her third work, *Swamp Angel* (1954), in contrast, achieved a rare symbolic intensity and was widely praised by critics as an important accomplishment for Canadian modernist fiction.

While the Canadian authors were modernizing, international modernists began arriving, too. The British anarchist scholar George Woodcock (who had been born in Canada) moved to Vancouver in 1949 and brought with him all of his social connections to literati such as George Orwell, Stephen Spender, and W.H. Auden, among other notables. Shortly after arriving in the country, Woodcock organized a reading by British poet Dylan Thomas at the University of British Columbia in 1950,[13] and

---

13 For a full account of Thomas's reading on 6 April 1950, see Floris McLaren's "Dylan Thomas in Vancouver," *Contemporary Verse* 31 (Spring 1950): 26–7.

a second reading downtown at which Malcolm Lowry attended and played host to the great poet. One of Woodcock's colleagues was tasked with collecting Thomas in the morning, and discovered that he, Lowry, Birney, and two unnamed women had spent the entire night drinking and carousing (Bowker, *Pursued by Furies* n. pag.). By morning, only Lowry and Thomas were still going strong (Salloum, "John" 76). It was not long after moments like these, as I detail in chapter 5, that the British Surrealists also began arriving in the city. As Birney mused of this period: "I was beginning to feel no longer marooned" (*Spreading Time* 139). Thomas's portrait of the emerging city, in contrast, was less enthusiastic:

> Today is Good Friday. I am writing this in a hotel bedroom in Vancouver, British Columbia, Canada, where yesterday I gave two readings, one in the university, one in the ballroom of the Vancouver Hotel, and made one broadcast. Vancouver is on the sea, and gigantic mountains doom [sic] above it. Behind the mountains lie other mountains, lies an unknown place, 30,000 miles of mountainous wilderness, the lost land of Columbia where cougars live and black bears. But the city of Vancouver is a quite handsome hellhole. It is, of course, being Canadian, more British than Cheltenham. I spoke last night – or read, I never lecture, how could I? – in front of two huge union jacks. The pubs – they are called beer-parlours – serve only beer, are not allowed to have whiskey or wine or any spirits at all – and are open only for a few hours a day. There are, in this monstrous hotel, two bars, one for Men, one for Women. They do not mix. Today, Good Friday, nothing is open nor will be open all day long. Everybody is pious and patriotic, apart from a few people in the university & my old friend Malcolm Lwry [sic] – do you remember Under the Volcano – who lives in a hut in the mountains & who came down to see me last night. Do you remember his wife Margery? (103)

Wilson's *Swamp Angel* appeared the same year that Malcolm Lowry left his seaside shack in Dollarton, near Vancouver, where he lived from 1939 to 1954. His father, who maintained power of attorney over him on account of his alcoholism, had sent Lowry to Canada with the hope that the isolation would settle him down. Lowry bought a series of small "squatter" shacks on the shores of the Burrard Inlet (quite near the səlilwətaɬ reservation), and led a quiet life writing, swimming, and rowing. The Canadian editor of *Experiment* magazine, and Lowry's old Cambridge chum, Gerald Noxon visited him there multiple times and described him as being "out of touch with people [...] He had been working more or less in the dark" (qtd. in Salloum, *Malcolm* 25). Most of the writing and revising of Lowry's second novel, *Under the Volcano* (1947), happened in Dollarton, though a fire prompted a quick exit to Ontario, where Lowry finished his modernist "masterpiece" (Grace 9) in Niagara-on-the-Lake. The novel cemented Lowry's reputation as one of the giants of late modernist prose: as Patrick McCarthy writes, "If Joyce is one of the avatars of

Figure I.14 Malcolm Lowry in Dollarton (1937–54). Photographer unknown.

high modernism, Lowry speaks for the next generation" (1). As if in anticipation of that link, Noxon had published Lowry's fiction alongside James Joyce's then work in progress (which would become *Finnegans Wake*) in *Experiment* magazine.

While Lowry is rarely regarded as a Canadian author to any critic outside Canada, he lived here for a decade and a half and made some important friendships in Vancouver, especially with Birney, who published him in *Canadian Poetry Magazine* and in a special issue of the British magazine *Outposts* dedicated to Canadian writing. Recognizing Lowry's status and ability as an author, Birney facilitated publication in other Canadian modernist magazines as well, including *Contemporary Verse* and *Here & Now*, and over thirty other magazines throughout the English-speaking world (Salloum, *Malcolm* 67–69). Birney also edited a selection of these Canadian poems for Lawrence Ferlinghetti's City Lights Books, published in 1962. At the very least, these connections demonstrate Birney's commitment to imagining a local modernist writing. On the other hand, Lowry's Canadian connections are undeniably significant – starting with the fact that more than half of his 479 extant poems were written in

British Columbia (Ackerley 112). The impact of the presence of a great author was widely felt. Curt Lang and Al Purdy were regular vistors to the Lowry home in Dollarton, where they would read each other's poetry and drink themselves to unconsciousness. From those visits, Lowry wrote Ralph Gustafson in 1957 to recommend that he include Purdy's poetry in *The Penguin Book of Canadian Verse* (Salloum, *Malcolm* 103), which he did. Dylan Thomas and A.J.M. Smith also visited him there, as did the mystical Rosicrucian poet Charles Stansfeld Jones. Though Paul Tiessen describes Lowry's early life in Dollarton as "Thoreau-like" and isolated (Introduction 1988 2) and notes that in "Canada he was cut off from direct regular communion with literary people" (Introduction 2015 xxii), Lowry circulated and socialized with the Canadian modernists in the city and region, few in number as they were.

3 Finding Nothing (or, the Avant-Garde Flowering That Was the 1960s)

In 1952, Birney wrote a comedic radio play called *The Damnation of Vancouver* that mused about the necessary destruction of Vancouver (by H-bomb or flooding), arguing that it had already replicated the failures and shortcomings of the modern world and it might be too late to generate some truly novel cultural alternative. When one of the characters admits that "only in your absence can I think to speak" (69), however, Birney is acknowledging what would become a major theme of Vancouver avant-garde writing between 1959 and 1975, including his own: namely, the undoing of knowledge, discovering the importance of silence, disturbing the impossibility of presence, and tracking language's ideological complicity. I have taken to thinking of this cultural shift by settlers in the city as a great unsettlement. Indeed, with a dawning awareness of ecological devastation, and of Canadian complicity in imperialist violence, there developed a general suspicion of the civilization the settler population had foisted upon the continent. During the period in question, Toronto poet Dennis Lee fell into a profound but depressing silence upon confronting the globalized situatedness of his words. Brion Gysin, in contrast, revelled in shattering the fraught prism of language: "Rub out the word," he gleefully instructed his readers (see Figure I.15). From a similar sense of breaking language to create ideological openings, Vancouver poet and editor bill bissett exclaimed, "[W]e are chasmsounds" (Untitled 1965). Though there is a sense of alienation in these chasms or limits of communication, avant-garde artists began embracing the linguistic basis of alienation as a source of inspiration and aesthetics. It was through destruction that a shift in consciousness began and Vancouver's unique cultural alternative emerged. Instead of celebrating a will-to-power, or a hunger to make things new, this avant-garde began investigating the potential of selflessness and of undoing some of the harmful legacies of modernity and colonialism. It was the political, mystical, aesthetic, and social potential of these chasmsounds that the first wave of Vancouver's

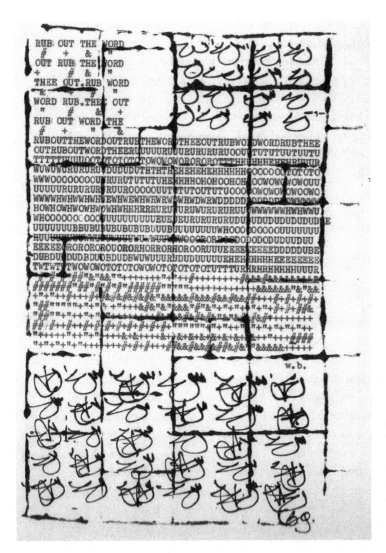

avant-garde set out to map. They sought to remake their entire socio-political land-scape through their discovery of nothingness, in all its complexity, and by opening themselves up to what-may-be, some new kind of open community, on the other side of the wreckage.

How different, then, to confront the city from a slightly different perspective, out-side of the displacing, colonialist gaze that recognized nothing of value happening there, and to consider the complex cultural interaction and competition that was, in fact, already at play in the early 1960s. The city was not empty, nor was it culturally barren even in avant-garde production. Despite the current and oft-repeated narra-tivization, there was avant-garde revolutionary literature in the city. Consider visual artist and sometimes poet Ian Wallace's sense of the city mid-century: Vancouver "attracted a bohemian and hippie culture which has had widespread influence throughout the globe. There were many specific regional artistic influences, including the local history of modernist art from Emily Carr to Jack Shadbolt, Gordon Smith, BC Binning and Iain Baxter of N.E. Thing" (qtd. in Janssen 138). Wallace was a pivotal figure in the intermedia experimentation that erupted in the city in the 1960s and became even more prominent in the decades that followed through his infusion of conceptual painting into photography. Hardly cut off from the world, in the late 1950s and early 1960s, Wallace "was inspired by [his] exposure to the best avant-garde art of the time" (139). Wallace describes his art of the period as "zero-degree representation," borrowing the term from Roland Barthes in reference to an increasingly reductive, minimalist approach to art. He was working toward "an erasure of the image in painting." He connects this pursuit of "radical 'emptiness'" to the modernist crisis of representation and a general climate of socio-political revolt. The possibility of art crushing its cultural inheritance from within, without abandoning the broken husk to nihilistic collapse, was for Vancouver's downtown arts community deeply inspiring. It offered "refuge for the roving spirit of alienated subjectivities. This is the nexus of avant-garde practice and the logos of western rationalism" (140). In 1974, Wallace delivered a lecture at the Art Gallery of Victoria on blank pages, empty spaces – themes he would develop in his two enormous *Attack on Literature* panels that sought to extend the visual impact of French Symbolist poet Stéphane Mallarmé's "Un coup de dés." The work, which included collaged images from European avant-garde cinema, was a response to poetry using a montage of film stills. The idea of nothing, it turns out, was also a way into avant-garde practice.

For many artists living between 1959 and 1975, Vancouver offered a dynamic milieu of globalized ideas, technologies, and ideolects that moved through the city and interacted with the complex and multidirectional precedents and situated politics already active there. It was, in many respects, a contact zone of cultures, aesthetics, and politics, many of which were marked by a spirit of contestation, including sometimes violent clashes with authorities, and a more general spirit of uncovering, including experiences of profound ecstasy and insight. Its proper context begins in the 1940s and 1950s, when painters in the city such as Bruno Bobak, Molly Bobak, Lawren Harris, Don Jarvis, Toni Onley, Jack Shadbolt, Ian Wallace, and Takao Tanabe developed the modernist legacy and practice of Emily Carr: "this cultural vanguard," as Vancouver Art Gallery curator Daina Augaitis writes, "was anything but dry and dull [... They] advocated for an improved society that would counter the catastrophic effects of World War II" (19). Likewise, writers such as Lowry, Birney, Livesay, and Phyllis Webb not only experimented and advanced modernist forms and practices, but they too created institutions that empowered generations of future writers to work from their innovations. These artists and authors laid the foundations for the next generation by creating the institutions that would house and foster this future work, including the new art department at the University of British Columbia, the

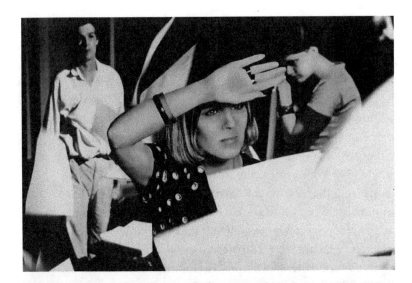

Figures I.16, I.17
Detail of Ian
Wallace's *An
Attack on Literature*
(1975). Used with
permission. See
Figure 7.3 for a full
reproduction.

new creative writing program at UBC, the expansion of the Vancouver School of Art
(VSA), literary and scholarly magazines, and the creation of the interdisciplinary
Festival of the Contemporary Arts (FoCA), which actively opened up the advances
in visual art to the literary and film communities in the city. Coupled with the founding of Simon Fraser University (SFU) in 1965, the hirings alone associated with these
institutions brought or helped keep a significant population of key avant-garde artists in the city – for instance, Roy Kiyooka worked at the VSA from 1960 to 1965,
Warren Tallman at UBC from 1956 to 1986, and Robin Blaser at SFU from 1966 to
1986 (not to forget Robert Creeley at UBC in 1963–4).

THE MEDIUM IS THE MESSAGE

This presentation, which is to be held in the Armouries, University of B.C., on
3rd and 5th Feb. during the Festival of the Contemporary Arts, is of especial
interest since it was born largely as a result of a combination of ideas inspired by events at the four previous Festivals.   Chief among these inspirations
has been the dance group of Ann Halprin, which appeared here in 1961; the pro-
gramme put on by the musician John Cage together with the Merce Cunningham
Dancers in 1962; the presentation of the San Francisco Tape Music Centre in
1963; and, last year, the work of Gerd Stern with its emphasis on "collaged"
combinations of poetry, painting, photography and sound.   Also last year, the
presence of Marshall McLuhan, whose brilliant philosophy of contemporary communication media is helping us toward a new understanding of the cogent role these
media play in shaping twentieth century life.

The presentation in the Armouries (we have been calling it "The Armouries Show
of 1965") was also certainly influenced by "happenings" which have been staged
by artists in New York, San Francisco, Paris and elsewhere in recent years.
These have characteristiclly involved a great deal of audience participation -
not in the sense of a sing-along, but in the sense of spontaneous, unselfconscious activity which, in its simplest aspect, results from the audience
having to walk among the events which are occurring around them.   Thus the
contact with the presentation is different from the typical auditorium experience where the audience is static, and also from the typical gallery experience where the presentation remains fixed.   But since the audience is "on
stage", its very presence makes it an integral part of the show, and part of
the who.e complex of events.   McLuhan has said of our age "...a re-focussing
of aims and images to permit ever more audience involvement and participation
has been inevitable".

In the arrangement planned for the "Armouries Show", the audience will influence
the course of action by its presence and will also have the opportunity to
manipulate the media, consciously and spontaneously, by choosing paths of movement, casting shadows, picking up reflections, making sounds, and so on.

Various media will be involved: painting, sculpture, architecture, photography,
projection, physical movement, words, electronic tapes - all in various combinations, and expressed in a variety of unusual techniques.

(cont.)

The Festival of the Contemporary Arts 1965 (cont.)
THE MEDIUM IS THE MESSAGE

What message, what idea will all these attempt to convey?   No other than the
message of the media themselves.   McLuhan says that, in the past, "the message,
it seemed, was 'content', as people used to ask what a painting was about.   Yet
they never thought to ask what a melody was about, nor what a house or a dress
was about.   In such matters, people retained some sense of the whole pattern
of form and function as a unity .....Specialized segments have shifted to total
field, and we can now say 'the medium is the message.'"

The Medium is the Message has been prepared by:

> Helen Goodwin, Physical Education
> Iain Baxter, Fine Arts
> David Orcutt, Extension
> Cortland Hultberg, Music
> Abraham Rogatnick, Architecture
> Takao Tanabe, Vancouver School of Art
> Alvin Balkind, Fine Arts
> Sam Perry, film-maker
> Roy Kiyooka, Vancouver School of Art
> Helen Sonthoff, English

and with the assistance and co-operation of students in various faculties at
the University and at the Vancouver School of Art.

Figure I.18 Press release for the Festival of the Contemporary Arts 1965, subtitled
"The Medium Is the Message." Source: Private collection of the author.

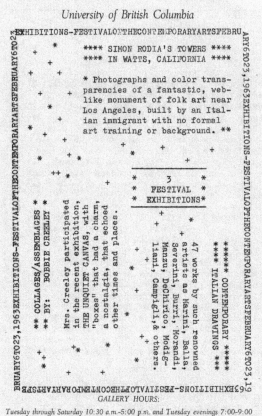

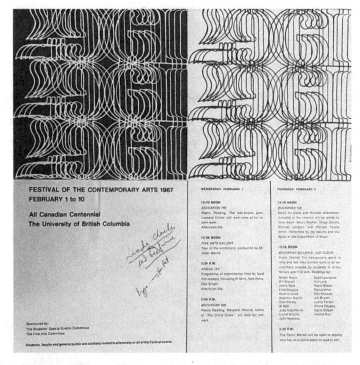

Figures I.19, I.20, I.21 Brochures for the Festival of the Contemporary Arts 1965, 1968, and 1961. Source: Private collection of the author.

With this institutional infrastructure in place, the period that followed was marked by a series of pivotal events, any one of which could serve as a representative of the dynamic forces at play in the city during this period. The FoCA at UBC became an annual extravaganza and ran from 1961 to 1971. The success of the first festival, which featured Marshall McLuhan and Robert Duncan, among others, created a template for large-scale experimental arts events in the city. Intended initially to help promote the new Arts Department at UBC, it became an enabler of cross-disciplinary interaction that featured many of the most prominent thinkers and artists of the time investigating contemporary media and communication. Beyond McLuhan and Duncan, other artists and thinkers featured at the festival included John Cage, Robert Creeley, Jack Spicer, Jackson Maclow, Michael McLure, Margaret Mead, Walter Gropius, Sir Herbert Read, Margaret Atwood, Françoise Sullivan, and more. The avant-garde films of Andy Warhol, Jean-Luc Godard, Bruce Conner, Sam Perry, and the Kucher brothers were all screened, alongside experimental dance, music, and theatrical performances. The festival directly inspired three other large-scale events, all with significant or exclusive literary content, including the VPC (1963), the Trips Festival (1966), and the Concrete Poetry Festival (1969). Surrounding these landmark events was a buzz of constant activity including that distinctly 1960s confluence of poetry readings, performance art, jazz, rock music, public lectures, demonstrations, riots, happenings, protests, and be-ins. The venues for literary publication expanded rapidly in the city, with a steady stream of new publishers and magazines regularly appearing and often also quickly disappearing. Literature was leaving the page, leaving the classroom, for the streets and open air. Revolutionary discourse peppered the rhetoric of the activity as various political causes helped to focalize the urgency of what needed to be changed. As Diane di Prima wrote in *Blewointment*: "None of us knows the answers, think about / these things. / The day will come when we have to know / the answers" ("Revolutionary Letters #9" n. pag.).[14] In Vancouver, the emergence during this period of a number of dynamic, experimental art movements coincided with the rapid expansion of supporting art and academic infrastructure. In terms of the cultural geography, the terrain was bounded on one side by UBC, with its experimental visual arts scene and nascent literary community, and on the other by SFU, with its newly established creative writing program. Fourth Avenue, in between (close to UBC, downtown, and nearby English Bay), served as the epicentre of Vancouver's alternative culture, including playing host to the *Georgia Straight*, the alternative newspaper that grew out of the hippie and poetry communities. From Kitsilano through the downtown, artists and writers gathered in a rich melange of

---

14 Di Prima was an American author, though she did try to immigrate to Canada with her partner, which was "still the golden freedom land for us" (Letter to Bill Bissett n. pag.). Unfortunately, they found the immigration process "too hard" and abandoned the move.

public and private art galleries, bookstores, cafés, clubs, and collective spaces, including the New Design Gallery, the Cellar, and the Vancouver Art Gallery, which each played an important role in fostering the intermedia movement in the city. From this locus, I want to read Vancouver's avant-garde work not as singular to Vancouver, but as part of a network of global movements, local politics, and (Canadian) art history. I want to track the period between colonial silence (and the reproduction of colonial silences) and decolonial resistance. I want to study, more precisely than has been done before, how the blinding barriers of literary canons, literary traditions, and colonial centres began to fall. Something erupted in the early 1960s in Vancouver, a drive to rupture all categories of knowledge, to create new patterns, new possibilities of seeing, to let the whole field in. Rather than a comprehensive literary history or a first-hand account (which I don't have), then, this approach might be thought of as a "microhistory" with a transnational frame, to twist a phrase used by Heather Murray in her study of book history in Canada. She describes microhistories as "rooted in the attempt to incorporate peripheral or marginal events, figures, and communities into the historical picture" (406). The microhistory seeks to "understand an historically situated mentality" marked by anomalies and networks of communities (408). To borrow the words of Daphne Marlatt, writing in Vancouver in 1970, "not writing a history of the city. want to let the city speak *thru* the poems, its things, its persons. not trying for breadth, scope (cover the *whole* city – can't) but depth (uncover), cut thru different time strata at once" (*What Matters* 154; emphases in original). In Vancouver, a series of interrelated, anamolous avant-gardes emerged from the confluence of politics and art, each with a different orientation to the moment. I read these avant-gardes, the VanGardes, together with the intermedia art scene, the local Dadaists, nouveau Surrealists, combative Marxists, feminists, and Red Power activists, as part of the globalized phenomenon I have identified as "geomodernism." They uncovered new approaches to art making by borrowing freely from international art movements and applying them loosely to the local scene unfolding in their midst. Finding Paris, or London, or New York, or San Francisco, or nothing, in Vancouver.

Vancouver Presses and Magazines

Though it is often depicted as a marginal and quiet community, Vancouver was rife with small and mid-sized presses and literary magazines during the period in question. The following is intended to be taken not as an exhaustive list or a complete editorial history of each publishing venture (especially those that carry on after 1975), but rather as a sketch of the abundance of publishing activity happening in the city at the time.

Presses and Book Publishers

Robert Reid (Later Robert Reid and Takao Tanabe; 1946–62; eds. Robert Reid and Takao Tanabe. Imprint: Pica Press)

Klanak (1958–74; eds. Alice McConnell and William McConnell)

Nevermore Press (1960–64; ed. Geoge Kuthan)

Alcuin Society (1965–present; ed. Geoff Spencer)

Very Stone House (1965–8; eds. Pat Lane, Seymour Mayne, bill bissett, and Jim Brown; imprint: Talonbooks)

Tishbooks (1962–4; ed. Frank Davey)

Returning Press (1966; ed. Judith Copithorne)

Flye Press (1966–70; ed. David UU)

Blew Ointment Press (1967–83; ed. bill bissett)

Daylight Press (1967–72; ed. Lionel Kearns)

Periwinkle (1963–5; ed. Takao Tanabe)

Morris Printing (1967–76; ed. Charles Morris)

Sono Nis Press (1968–present; ed. J. Michael Yates)

Talonbooks (1967–present; eds. David Robinson, Jim Brown, Janie McElwyne, et al.)

The Wolfe Press (1969; eds. Helen Wolfe Sontoff and Jane Rule)

Pendejo Press (1969; ed. John Mills)

Hairy Eagle Press (ed. Stephen Scobie)

Intermedia Press (1969–81; eds. Ed Varney and Henry Rappaport)

Beaver Kosmos Folios (1969–73; ed. George Bowering)

William Hoffer (1969–84; ed. William Hoffer)

Blackfish Press (1970–82; eds. Allan Safarik and Brian Brett)

Vancouver Community Press (1970–4; eds. Dennis Wheeler, Stan Persky, and Scott Watson)

The Poem Company (1970–present; eds. Ed Varney, Henry Rappaport, and J. MacDonald)

Air Press (1970–3; ed. Bertrand Lachance)

J.J. Douglas (1971–present; eds. Jim Douglas and Scott McIntyre; later renamed Douglas & McIntyre)

Pacific Trans-Power Publications (1971; ed. Henry Rappaport)

HESHE&ITWORKS (1971–92; eds. Gerry Gilbert and Carole Itter)

Pulp Press (1971–83; eds. Steve Osborne, Tom Osborne, Jon Furberg, D.M. Fraser, and Greg Enright)

Kanchenhunga Press (1972–8; eds. Miki Sheffield and Robert Bringhurst)

Air Press (1973–7; eds. Bertrand Lachance and Arthur Richardson)

Press Gang Publishers (1974–2002; eds. Joanne Arnott, Shani Mootoo,
   Sheila Baxter, et al.; collective members: Persimmon Blackbridge,
   Chrystos, Ivan Coyote, Lynnette D'anna, Elana Dykewomon, Kar-
   lene Faith, Sky Lee, Lee Maracle, Daphne Marlatt, Nancy Richler,
   Betsy Warland, and Rita Wong)

New Star Books (Formerly Vancouver Community Press; 1974–present;
   eds. Lanning Beckman, Stan Perksy, and Gladsy Maria Hindmarch)

Cobblestone Press (1975–91; ed. Gerald Giampa)

*A special addendum to acknowledge Tim Lander, the street poet who
self-published countless chapbooks and sold them himself during the
1960s.*

Literary Magazines

Contemporary Verse (1946–52; ed. Alan Crawley)

Thunderbird (1946–9; ed. John Green, Alan Dawe, and John Wardroper)

P.M. (1951–2; ed. Yvonne Agazarian)

Raven (1955–62; eds. Michael Ames, Douglas Howie, Desmond
   FitzGerald, Edward Aho, and David Bromige)

Prism (1959–present; eds. Jan de Bruyn, Earle Birney, Jack Zilber, Michael Bullock, et al.; later renamed to Prism International)

Tish (1961–6; eds. Frank Davey et al.)

Motion (1962; eds. Robert Hogg and David Cull)

Blewointment (1963–84; ed. bill bissett)

Limbo (1963–7; ed. Murray Morton)

Imago (1964–71; ed. George Bowering)

Talon Magazine (1964–8; eds. Dave Robinson, Jim Brown, and Janie
   McElwyne)

The Open Letter (1966–2014; ed. Frank Davey; later renamed to Open
   Letter)

Expression (1966–70; ed. Michael Bullock)

Up the Tube with One I (Open) (1966–77; eds. Chuck Carlson and
  Patrick Lane)
The West Coast Review (1966–90; eds. Frederick Candelaria and Har-
  vey deRoo)
Iron (1967–78; ed. Brian Fawcett)
Georgia Straight (1967–present; eds. Dan McLeod, Pierre Coupey,
  et al.)
Pacific Nation (1967–69; ed. Robin Blaser)
Western Gate (1968; eds. Al Birnie and Pierre Coupey)
Beaver Cosmos Folio (1968–71; ed. George Bowering)
radiofreerainforest (1968–70; ed. Gerry Gilbert)
Amphora (1968–present; ed. Wil Hudson)
Contemporary Literature in Translation (1968–78; ed. Andreas
  Schroeder)
Ballsout: A Magazine of Unpleasant Verse and Impolite Prose (1969–
  72; ed. Bertram Maird)
Georgia Straight Writing Supplement (1969–70; eds. Stan Persky and
  Dennis Wheeler)
Free Media Bulletin (1969; eds. Jeff Wall, Ian Wallace, and Duane
  Lunden)
The Indian Voice (1969–84; eds. Mrs. "Kitty" Bell, Chief John L.
  George, and Donna Doss)
Blackfish (1970–8; eds. Brian Brett and Alan Safarick)
Rage (1970; eds. unknown)
New Leaf: An Independent Newspaper for an Independent Canada
  (1970–2; eds. unknown)
Air (1971–3; ed. Bertrand Lachance)
The Canadian Fiction Magazine (1971–present; eds. R.W. Stedingh
  and Geoff Hancock)
Circular Causation (1969–70; eds. Scott Lawrance and George
  Heyman)
Event (1971–present; eds. David Evanier, Leona Gom, et al.)
Empty Belly (1972–8; ed. Charles Tidler)
Georgia Grape (1972; ed. Stan Persky)
Lodgistiks (1972–6; eds. Gregg Simpson and David UU)

The Capilano Review (1972–present; ed. Pierre Coupey, asst. ed.
   Gladys Hindmarch)
The British Columbia Monthly (1972; eds. Bob Amussen and Gerry
   Gilbert)
Iron II (1975–6; ed. Brett Enemark)
Room of One's Own (1975–present; ed. the Growing Room Collective;
   later renamed Room)
NMFG (1976–9; ed. Brian Fawcett)
Periodics (1977–81; eds. Daphne Marlatt and Paul de Barros)
Scarabeus Magazine (1978; ed. Martin Guderna)
Melmoth/The Vancouver Surrealist Newsletter (1981–4; eds. Michael
   Bullock and Martin Guderna)
Raven (1979–82; eds. Scott Lawrence and Jorj Heyman)
See/Hear Productions (1968–71; ed. Jim Brown)

4 The Problem of Nothing: A Short Interlude on the Theory of the Avant-Garde

What is the avant-garde? Who is the avant-garde in Vancouver? In an article on the *Jacket2* magazine website, Vancouver poet and professor Stephen Collis asks plaintively, "[D]oes the term 'avant-garde' do any productive, liberatory work anymore?" ("The Call" n. pag.). It is a common concern among contemporary experimental writers, scholars, and literary-minded activists. It cycles back to the familiar refrain that postmodernism highlights the avant-garde's ineffectiveness against the systems it seeks to dismantle. Masculinist and militaristic in origin, the avant-garde now is often said to perform indistinguishably from the boom and bust cycles of capitalism itself. Is it just another recurrence of the colonial pattern of violent erasures and displacements? More recently, American critics like Cathy Park Hong, Sueyeun Juliette Lee, and Craig Santos Perez (among many, many commentators) have questioned the cultural exclusivity of the avant-garde as a bastion for especially white and male practitioners to maintain racial and gender privilege, arguing that as a mode of literary production it remains entrenched in and supportive of oppressive networks of power. The debate is particular to the United States, however, where the lines between avant and identity-based poetics are especially strict. Lee's critique of contemporary American avant-garde poetry smartly shifts the discussion away from the limitations of that particular brand by acknowledging a broader field in which to imagine avant-gardism:

> I recognize that my framing of this dilemma in terms of "caring" and seeming to have a "personal stake" may seem ridiculous for those interested in the avant-garde. I argue, however, that the avant-garde has always *immensely* cared, and has always *immensely* had a personal stake in what it produces. To erase these considerations from the debate is to efface the true promise of the avant-garde – to license us full access to ourselves.
>
> (n. pag.; emphases in original)

Not only does Lee's attention to affect and the avant-garde provide a useful and functional answer to Collis's question, but she also helps to articulate a central premise of *Finding Nothing*: the avant-garde is always, by name and definition, the productive, liberatory dynamic at work in literature. Revolutionary work presumes the possibility of a better or ideal social contract, but that begins by re-imagining interpersonal relations and daily life. If the radical affect disappears, so does the avant-garde. Similarly, Daphne Marlatt once defined "radical" literature as that which alters and expands the sense of what constitutes a "normal part of community life" (Milne 249). The writing remains radical until its proposition has become normalized (or the forces of cultural conservatism dismantle the garde). In this way, the natural entropy of a particular garde can be measured by the extent to which its strategies for challenging oppressive networks of power have been advanced or displaced by other strategies. When a movement is no longer useful in fulfilling its own socio-political ambitions (and the ambitions of the avant-garde are always entwined with socio-politics), it has the choice of either institutionalizing and protecting its deficiencies by becoming a living archive or just decommissioning. In either case, its status as avant-garde shifts from contemporary disruption to yet another delimited case in literary history.

This shift in definition highlights a central confusion in the study and deployment of the term "avant-garde" over the past 150 years, for what was once avant-garde is not always avant-garde except as an archival descriptor. It has become common for critics to speak of a historical avant-garde that differentiates the specific avant-garde nodes of activity from modernism in general. It is to recognize a diverse set of nineteenth- and twentieth-century writers that organized proto-military art collectives in the name of a specific set of aesthetic or socio-political criteria and distinguish these advocates from their contemporaries, the modernist writers who were not necessarily so aligned or so future-oriented. The Vorticists, Dada (later the Dadaists), the Surrealists, concrete poets, the Situationists, and Fluxus, among many other groups (these are the ones with direct relevance to the current discussion on Vancouver experimental writing), all established aesthetic collectives for the sake of advocating a new world order or else a new world consciousness. Their respective manifestos are the codification of that advocacy, just as their essays function as programs for extending their movement. As old gardes fail, however, the moniker "avant-garde" shifts from being a description of their commitment to revolution and social activism to an achievement that, once conferred, becomes an indisputable, bestowed-upon status. Recognizing these failures and backing away wholesale from the discourse of socio-political revolution that informs avant-gardism, the term "post-avant" is a more appropriate description of the experimental but post-revolutionary aesthetics of many contemporary experimental writers. Even so, the avant-garde remains a functional description of the place where liberatory impulses are encoded into literature and yet also the codicil of its own demise. In other words, the concept has been around long enough that it now has a history – a history of movements that are paradoxically no longer avant-garde in the present. Is it necessary to clarify that exhausted gardes might yet serve avant purposes in new contexts and periods?

The criticisms of avant-gardisms' complicity are not without merit. For well over two centuries now, since the advent of modernity itself, change, disruption, and even revolution have been built into the very fabric of capitalist life. Modernism and the avant-garde subset are both, in many respects, reactions within and against the conditions of perpetual disruption that stem from the conditions of modernity (including its advancement of transnational colonialism). Bruno Latour understands the term more particularly in relation to chronology and historical change: "Modernity comes in as many versions as there are thinkers or journalists, yet all its definitions point, in one way or another, to the passage of time. The adjective 'modern' designates a new regime, an acceleration, a rupture, a revolution in time" (10). If modernity conditions the revolution, recognized as a dynamic, multifaceted agent of change (or the self-consciousness of change, as Susan Stanford Friedman characterizes it [*Planetary* 10]), then we can situate modernism and avant-gardism both in terms of how they differently respond to the changes wrought by its arrival. For whereas the modernist responds to the revolution occasioned by the sweep of modernity,[15] whether that response takes the form of lament in elegizing modernity's

---

15 For modernist critics like Stanford Friedman, modernity unleashed an incredible wave of technological change, including changes that fundamentally undermined the quotidian beliefs of Western citizens. She offers a model of treating modernism as a response to modernity, the rapid socio-political and technological changes of the late nineteenth century: "Modernism, for many, became a reflection of and engagement with a wide spectrum of historical changes, including intensified and alienating urbanization; the cataclysms of world war and technological progress run amok; the rise and fall of European empires; changing gender, class, and race relations; and technological inventions that radically changed the nature of everyday life, work, mobility, and communication" (*Planetary* 51).

These she calls "domains of change"; hence "modernism is a force of change effecting change as much as it intersects other domains of change. Thus, I am suggesting that we treat modernism as the domain of creative expressivity *within* modernity's dynamic of rapid change, a domain that interacts with other arenas of rupture such as technology, trade, migration, state function, societal institutions, and so forth" (52; emphasis in original). This reverses the hierarchy and privileged role of the creators of discourse, those who seem to transcend the ideological bubble of their context.

dominion over globalized cultures or retreating into intellectual elitisms or otherwise, the avant-gardist self-consciously attempts to harness and direct that revolutionary condition in specific directions. In André Breton's words, "[p]oetry would hold no interest for me whatsoever if I didn't expect it to suggest to me and some of my friends a specific solution to the problems of our lives" ("Reply to a Survey" 83). It is important to bear in mind that, as Joe Bray, Alison Gibbons, and Brian McHale write in the recent *Routledge Companion to Experimental Literature*, "aesthetic avant-gardism continues to be allied with political radicalism in a number of twentieth- and twenty-first century artistic and literary movements" (1).

In recognizing that the historical avant-garde began as a subset of modernist writing, we can start to recognize how contemporary avant-gardes respond to the conditions of modernity as well as to the legacies of modernist and avant-garde writing. Thus, when we start to think about how these concepts relate to a specific locale like Vancouver from 1959 to 1975, we can see how the generations of artistic responses to modernity from all around the world became available to contemporary authors, who could extend the experiments that preceded them or combine them in strange, anachronistic fashion. For instance, to help celebrate Michael Morris's 1969 exhibition of concrete poetry, a movement that emerged in the 1950s, Sherry Baker organized an evening called "Cabaret Voltaire" with re-enactments of sound poetry from 1916 (see Figure I.22). If Latour's sense of modernism is distinct in time, late modernism in Vancouver was characteristically out of time. bill bissett breezily positions James Joyce, William Shakespeare, and Aristotle on the side of "language fascists" and American imperialists in his 1971 book *RUSH: what fuckan theory*, whereas Gertrude Stein, Led Zeppelin, Louis Riel, and bpNichol were all said to be on the side of the "language revolushun" and forging a path forward. Time was unhinged, and history collapsed into a collage of simultaneity. In this way, the idea of a "microhistory" is useful here for connecting a very small community to the broader "ambiguities of the symbolic world, the plurality of possible interpretations of it, and the struggle which takes place over symbolic as much as over material resources" within historical aesthetic communities (Giovanni Levi qtd. in H. Murray 409).

Peter Burke cautions that microhistories, in delving deeply into the ideology of a specific community, tend to obscure their own ideological premises and methods (see 9–12). I have tried to address this problem of being too embedded in a subject by treating the local as the manifestation of global cultural flows, and connecting Vancouver's avant-garde moment with the broader experience of transcolonialism in the city. This accords well with Heather Murray's understanding of the work of microhistory, in recognizing the use of "micro in the sense of being situated at a particular point or conjuncture, and as located within larger webs or networks" (411). In accordance with the kind of study that considers subsets of groupings within a particular locus, Murray advocates thinking about communities over nations and even cities as "the primary point of influence or identification" (413). What is particularly

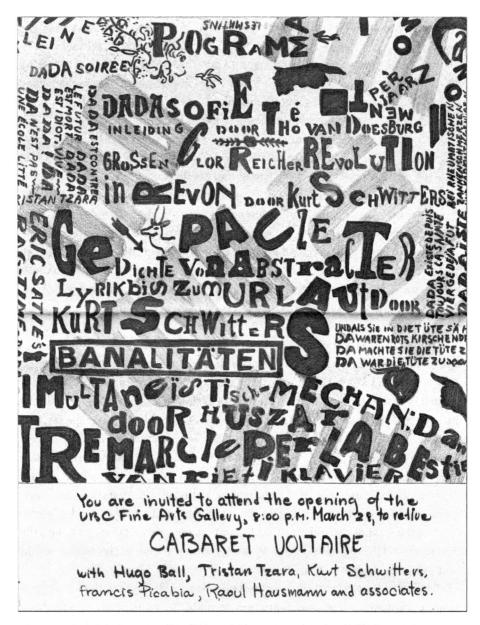

Figure I.22 Poster promoting the "Cabaret Voltaire" evening of sound poetry and avant-garde performances that was organized by Sherry Baker at the University of British Columbia. Collection of the Morris and Helen Belkin Art Gallery. Used with permission of the author.

striking about the avant-garde is its self-conscious, group-conscious relation to possible futures – those that are envisioned and publicly advocated and articulated. This raises the possibility of using microhistories to map out microfuturisms and the competing visions advocated by different avant-garde collectives even within the same city. It also opens up the possibility for reading a particular moment, the Van-Gardes 1959–75, as negotiating broader historical processes, in particular the shift from colonial silence to decolonial resistance.

Beyond the historical frame, the ongoing relevance of the avant-garde, and an underlying assumption of this book, stems from the paradox of avant-gardism as a performative function of literature. There is a history of literary contestation that makes sense of and facilitates the ongoing participation of literature in anti-oppression struggles. This history is also a burden, however, especially inasmuch as it has become a hermetic tradition that defines the category of the avant-garde based on its own precedent, and even more problematically because the conventions of avant-garde tradition (a phrase that is pointedly oxymoronical) inevitably run counter to the ambitions of the present gardes. For instance, when avant-gardists reject identity politics – or what, in Canada, might be better understood as transgressions in radicalized subjectivities – or deny the radical tremor within decolonization, they are highlighting their own belatedness, inscribing their names on the crypt walls of literary history. When writers, however, use their writing in the service of a revolution of the quotidian, of aesthetics, of ideology, they are assuming a place at the front lines of culture and manifesting the spirit of the avant-garde.

In the context of this book, there are three very distinct phases or types of avant-gardism under consideration. The first section monitors the arrival of a foreign garde into Canada and measures the impact of its domestication and hybridization into Vancouver. This is a key phase in the transition from a colonized space into a more liberated consciousness. Place (or locus) was a central feature of *Tish* poetics, inspired in part by their regional anxieties and early sense of marginalization from Eastern Canada. As *Tish* founding editor Frank Davey commented in a famous interview with all of the first-era *Tish* editors: "very important for *Tish* was the sense that most of us had of being marginalized [...] Marginalized in terms by being Canadian in North America; marginalized by being west coast and British Columbian in the Canadian context" (Niechoda and Hunter 93). They didn't go far enough in their resitance to colonial patterns to recognize their own replication of colonial or marginalizing tendencies, of course, but they started to transform literary subject positions in encouraging ways. As Canada began to emerge from its colonial history (Canadians still used a British passport in 1946, after all, and the Union Jack is still an official flag of Canada to this day, alongside the Maple Leaf) and the warp of a colonial mentality, it became a radical transgression in subjectivity to place value on the land without reference to the colonial centre. The regional dispute that figures so largely in so many studies of *Tish*, the short-lived battle between Eastern and Western Canada, evaporated in the more pressing push of writing place, of pulling Canada and its smaller locales out of a neglected, colonial, and conservative literary past into a successful, post-colonial, and experimental literary present. These geographic politics surrounding

Tish, amid other late modernist concerns, had a significant influence on the nature of their variation of avant-garde aesthetics. Their aesthetic response to geography, their *geopoetics*, adapted the New American poetic ideal of using language to unveil the unique energy of a particular place (even as the *Tish* poets resisted the nationalist discourse that also flowed in abundance during the period, and, of course, neglected the politics of gendered and racialized bodies in their shared locus). But the fact that they wrote from the unique milieu of Vancouver distinguished them (whenever they wrote successfully) from the writing of any other place. Thus, while the *Tish* poets embraced a foreign aesthetic, the geopoetic orientation of that poetics demanded that they respond to their locality and question in verse the relationship between place and language. Bowering explains the writing process of this poetic: "Olson told us to dig exhaustively into our local concerns. We began to do so, and the geography, history, and economics of Vancouver became the grid of our poetry" ("Alphabiography" 309). This opening up of literary potential through a shift in colonial consciousness marks the *Tish* collective as an avant-garde network, even though a source of their inspiration was admittedly derivative of an older garde from the United States and their sense of socio-political change was diffuse. As Robert Bringhurst writes, "[t]hey wanted to be *read*. And they weren't content to be read and nodded at politely; they wanted to be castigated or praised. They wanted poetry to have a place in life, to be something somebody cared about, as people cared about baseball scores and politics and dinner" (25; emphasis in original). It wasn't that provincial isolation had been overcome, or its colonial heritage reversed, but there was now a place for local art. It was an opening, the beginning of *something*.

Working from *Tish* and the VPC, chapter 2, on the second editorial period of the magazine, and the subsequent sections of this book explore the rise of a different intermediated consciousness that displaced or, more generously, extended the New American poetics. Importantly, it was not derivative of any earlier garde, but aligned with the front lines of culture around the world. In chapter 3, on the emergence of Blew Ointment Press, I explain the shift through the rise of an intense interest in the work of Marshall McLuhan on the impact of media and especially electrically modelled interdisciplinarity. From a linear, individualist orientation with a clear sense of universal harmony there arose a mosaical, collectivist orientation with a sense of the world and universe as being in radical flux. The artists in question combined McLuhan's "vision of multidisciplinary projects that acknowledged popular culture and advancements in technology" (K. Wallace 31) with the rise of collage-based art procedures to create an explosion of idealistic intermedia experimentation. Whereas the *Tish* group was interested in documenting their personal, individual experience of and engagement with place – the permeated *self* – the avant-garde intermedia community sought to integrate the people of Vancouver into both their art and the art-making process – the permeated *polis*, the whole field. The Intermedia Nights at the Vancouver Art Gallery, for instance, embodied the fusions this garde sought to enable: "As an experimental program it achieved its purpose, making a tangible and living experience out of some of the new art forms being developed in the sixties [...] these new art forms are designed to get onlookers involved and to take part in the experience [...] Divisions between audience and performer and exhibit largely disappeared" (N. Wilson n. pag.). McLuhan theorized in *The Gutenberg Galaxy* that the mechanical detachment of the capitalist citizen was directly connected to the linear arrangement of type in a line of text. As this new garde in Vancouver increasingly explored the visual impact of text and language, the linear arrangement of text on the page largely disappeared. Instead, as documented in chapters 3 and 4 on the emerging interdisciplinary community that emerged, freed by the legacy of Mallarmé, they created complex experiments in linguistic collage, in concrete and visual poetry. There was a presumption in this avant community that their radical openness in form and community could provoke widespread socio-political change. In other words, the intermedia experimentation and the related smashing of the line between art and society pushed art to the front lines of a broad socio-political battle of the collective imagination of Vancouver. In such an experimental and politicized context, it is not surprising that Surrealism found firm purchase in the city. Chapter 5 looks specifically at the eruption of form in Vancouver's Surrealist work and connects that profound psychological uncovering with the recognition of Indigenous art and culture. The Parisian Surrealists were the first avant-garde group to study the art work and colonial circumstance of the Indigenous Nations in British Columbia. Vancouver, consequently, became a preferred centre for especially British Surrealists during the Second World War, creating a network of radical and disruptive work for over half a century. It is striking that contemporary Indigenous artists in British Columbia, in the midst of the resurgence, took influence from Surrealist art that was itself inspired in part by Indigenous artists in British Columbia.

While the first five chapters of the book explore aesthetic avant-gardes, chapters 6 and 7 register the resurgence of a radical avant-gardism in Vancouver. While acknowledging the abundance of Marxist writing in the city, the final chapters specifically address the rise of feminist consciousness. There emerged a new genre of writing that channelled the material consciousness of the intermedia community into direct attention to the politics of the human (gendered) body. It is in this section that we can register the contemporary insistence on transgressions in radicalized subjectivities as avant-garde, and return to the far-reaching work of Daphne Marlatt, Gladys Maria Hindmarch, Helen Potrebenko, Joan Haggerty, Gwen Hauser, Audrey Thomas, Phyllis Webb, and others as progenitors of new directions in writing as in consciousness. They deliberately staged the female body as a site of public discourse, thereby opening up discourse to the subjective experience of female citizens. This helps to bridge the colonial era and the radically decolonizing work that emerged from the 1980s and continues on to the present. This final section opens up a critique of dominance of a particular model of white masculinist rebellion as the template of avant-gardism,

Figure I.23 Promotional photo of bill bissett and the Mandan Ghetto, including Roger Tentrey (poet, musician), Martina Clinton (poet, painter), Harley McConnell (drums), Terry Beauchamp (guitar), Gregg Simpson (poet, painter, drummer), and Ken Patterson (harmonica). Source: University of British Columbia Rare Books and Special Collections, Intermedia Society Fonds, A4 B3 2–8 1518/255.

without abandoning the idea of avant-gardism as the unique combination of art and revolutionary politics. Such a critique is bolstered by contemporary modernist studies that are increasingly and insistently moving beyond American and European measures, moving beyond the normative experience of heterosexual masculinity, by which all other forms of modernism are judged and to which all others must be compared. Instead, as Stanford Friedman argues, scholars of twentieth-century literature

must look across the planet, through deep time, and vertically within each location to identify sites of the slash – "modernity/modernism" – and then focus our attention on the nature of the particular modernity in question, explore the shapes and forms of creative expressivities engaging that modernity, and ask what cultural and political work those aesthetic practices perform as an important domain within it.

("Periodizing" 487–8)

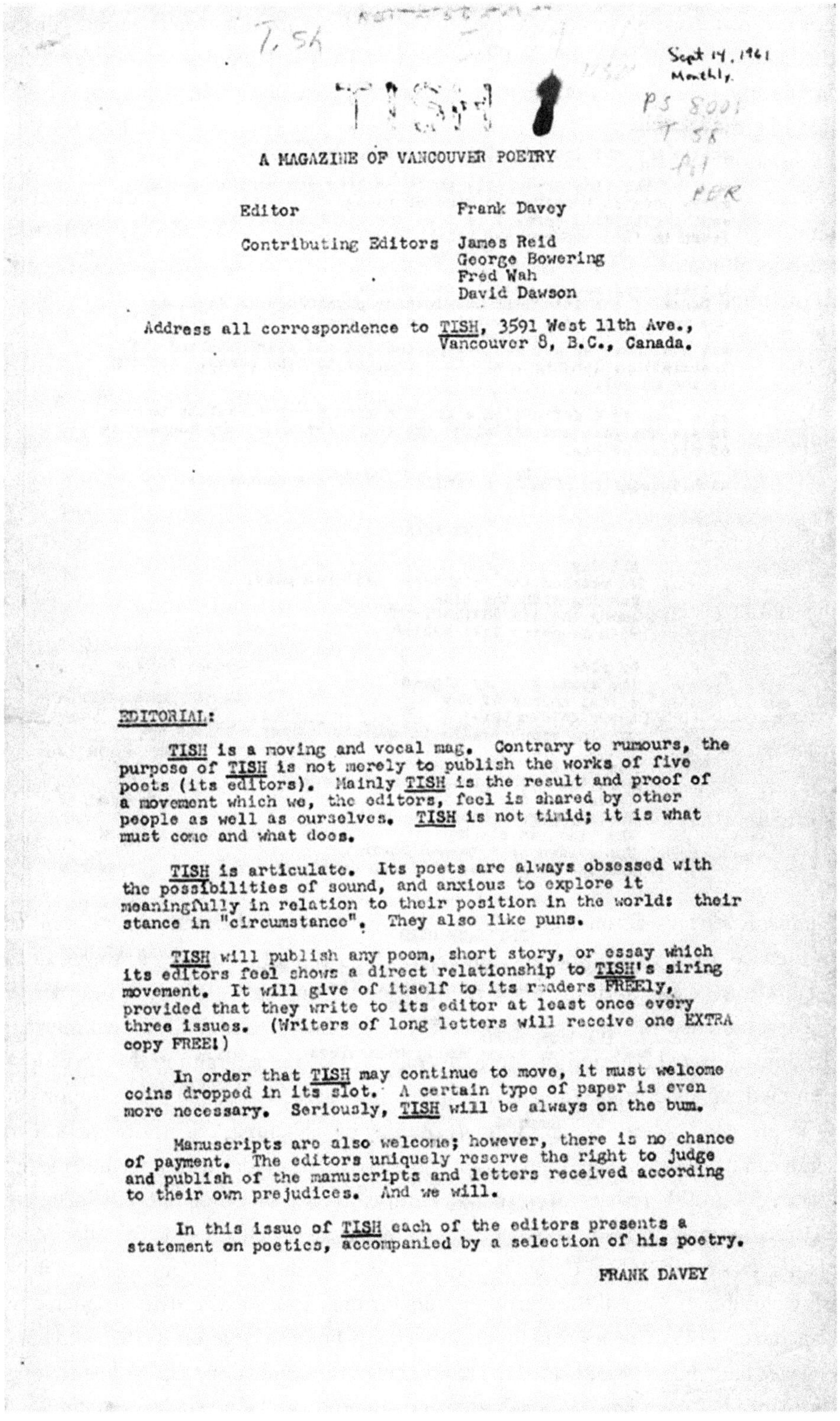

Sept 14, 1961
Monthly.

TISH

A MAGAZINE OF VANCOUVER POETRY

Editor: Frank Davey

Contributing Editors: James Reid, George Bowering, Fred Wah, David Dawson

Address all correspondence to <u>TISH</u>, 3591 West 11th Ave., Vancouver 8, B.C., Canada.

EDITORIAL:

<u>TISH</u> is a moving and vocal mag. Contrary to rumours, the purpose of <u>TISH</u> is not merely to publish the works of five poets (its editors). Mainly <u>TISH</u> is the result and proof of a movement which we, the editors, feel is shared by other people as well as ourselves. <u>TISH</u> is not timid; it is what must come and what does.

<u>TISH</u> is articulate. Its poets are always obsessed with the possibilities of sound, and anxious to explore it meaningfully in relation to their position in the world: their stance in "circumstance". They also like puns.

<u>TISH</u> will publish any poem, short story, or essay which its editors feel shows a direct relationship to <u>TISH</u>'s siring movement. It will give of itself to its readers FREEly, provided that they write to its editor at least once every three issues. (Writers of long letters will receive one EXTRA copy FREE!)

In order that <u>TISH</u> may continue to move, it must welcome coins dropped in its slot. A certain type of paper is even more necessary. Seriously, <u>TISH</u> will be always on the bum.

Manuscripts are also welcome; however, there is no chance of payment. The editors uniquely reserve the right to judge and publish of the manuscripts and letters received according to their own prejudices. And we will.

In this issue of <u>TISH</u> each of the editors presents a statement on poetics, accompanied by a selection of his poetry.

FRANK DAVEY

Figure I.24 Cover of the first issue of *Tish* (14 September 1961). Source: Private collection of the author.

For the most part, I set aside the question of modernism, and even late modernism, throughout this study to delve into the nature of the particular *micro*-avant-gardism in question. The rise of radical avant-gardism in Vancouver, which, in fact, continued to grow and become even more of a palpable force in the period after the one in question, signals a remarkable consciousness of the globalized forces at play in the city. It is here, then, in the context of reading the material body into a material landscape, that my discussion of Vancouver avant-garde literature from 1959 to 1975 finds its ultimate focus. For as these authors politicize and globalize their experience of their bodies, their insistence upon taking possession and control of their subjective experience registers as a radically transgressive act. As the transcolonial body rushes forth from its veiled silence, a space opens for the rush to sound of negated things – communities, orientations, races, and nations. There is no such thing as nothing, and never was.

5 The VanGardes

the HEART, by way of the BREATH, to the LINE

Charles Olson, "Projective Verse" (19)

Print teaches habits of privacy and self-reliance and initiative. It provides a massive visual panorama of the resources of the mother tongue which preliterate peoples know only by ear. [...] In the past thirty years all of our traditional disciplines in the arts and sciences have moved from the pattern of lineal cause to configuration.

Marshall McLuhan, "Electronic Revolution: Revolutionary Effects of New Media" (3, 4)

Finding Nothing is devoted to exploring the interfusion of the literary communities in the city. To recognize the interlinked spaces of shared aesthetics, however, does require some effort at distinguishing and disentangling each from each in order to make some sense of what is at stake in their commixture, and in their own internal dynamism over the period of approximately sixteen years. Framing this investigation by designated years, and starting that frame in 1959 when so much important work preceded it, bears the unfortunate but inevitable hallmark of arbitrariness. The same can be said of all attempts to mark the arrival of modernism into the city, for instance – and there have been many attempts to date that moment. For instance, Warren Tallman, in his widely circulated and frequently cited essay "Wonder Merchants," describes Robert Creeley's February 1962 reading at the University of British Columbia as "one of the starting points for the exceptional activity in poetry in Vancouver" (175). Creeley read for over two hours before a large, captivated, and fully engaged audience. He concluded the reading with the confession that "it's been a long time since I've experienced such energy and attention, and I'm very, very grateful."

Given the intensity of the audience he encountered, it is strange to consider this moment a point of origin: the interest in literary arts, including the performance of poetry, was already advanced to the point of sophistication with, as Tallman notes, "a fineness of attention to the poems" (176). Tallman admits that most in the audience of hundreds of students were unfamiliar with Creeley's work (which, at the time, was mostly confined to small press, avant-garde publications), but were attuned to advanced techniques in experimental poetry. Where, then, did the interest in poetry come from? It was already mature by 1962, and it didn't come syllogistically and anachronistically from Creeley's reading. *Tish*, of course, had already been publishing for a year by that point, the Festival of the Contemporary Arts was into its second year, and *Prism* was three years old. Creeley's peer Robert Duncan had, in fact, already visited, lectured, and read twice in the city by that time. *Prism* had been already active at UBC since the end of the 1950s, a publication that poet Robert Bringhurst has described as "its best, most adventurous periodical" (23). Bringhurst also acknowledges the first modernist little magazine in Vancouver, *P.M.* (edited by Yvonne Agazarian), which lasted from 1951 to 1952. Beyond these specific markers, a fuller, proper contextualization of the literary interest and acumen of those students would have to acknowledge other UBC English professors than Tallman as well, such as Roy Daniells, who was deeply versed in modernist poetics (Djwa 9) and had taught future avant-garde authors such as Sheila Watson and Margaret Avison and introduced them to the field, or Earle Birney, one of Canada's most acclaimed mid-century poets. Marshall McLuhan's student Leon Surette (who did a PhD with McLuhan on Ezra Pound) also began teaching avant-garde poetry at UBC in 1962, as did the poet Marya Fiamengo. Widely acclaimed lesbian novelist Jane Rule began teaching at UBC in 1956 (though her classic novel *Desert of the Heart* was not published until 1964). The wider context of Vancouver also merits further attention. Consider that when African American poet Langston Hughes came to UBC to give a lecture in 1958, he did a remarkable performance with accompaniment on the Vancouver program *The 7 O'Clock Show* on CBC. At the CBC studio, he might have encountered Eleanor Collins, the first Black woman to star in her own TV show. *The Eleanor Show* first aired in 1955, the same year that the Cellar cooperative jazz club opened downtown and began broadcasting live jazz performances weekly from a variety of guest musicians, dancers, and artists. The point of taking note of these activities being that things were opening up in Vancouver and evidence of that shift abounds throughout the 1950s and 1960s.

Indeed, the points of origin for avant-garde literary production in Vancouver 1959–75 proliferate and could, without any grave misrepresentation, be traced back to the origins of poetry itself (I do spend some time meditating on Aristotle's poetics in subsequent chapters). Despite this fact, and limiting the frame of discussion to the microhistory of a key dynamic at play in a local context, all of the productive aesthetic tensions that I map out in this book have roots in key events that took place in Vancouver in 1959. In that year: Robert Duncan came to Vancouver for the first time to perform his poetry and lecture on the New American open verse poetics; Marshall McLuhan also came back to the city to lecture on the end of linear cultures and the revolutionary onset of a new electrically infused collage or mosaic modality; the American Beat poet Kenneth Patchen began his groundbreaking intermedial collaboration with Vancouver musician Al Neil; American-born Canadian novelist Audrey Thomas moved to the city; and, perhaps most significantly for our purposes, bill bissett moved to Vancouver. Jamie Reid, one of the founding editors of *Tish*, recalls meeting bissett that year: "The first time I actually spoke to bill bissett was in 1959, when I was finishing grade thirteen at King Edward High School [... bissett was the] embodiment of the truly hip, a real Ginsberg, a real Kerouac, right [t]here in Vancouver" ("The Pome Wuz" 15). Reid elaborates on the centrality, originality, and difference of bissett's approach to art and lifestyle:

> bill was the product of the original Vancouver bohemia, the one that was rooted in downtown Robson Street, the real early bohemia, not the American-media-created bohemia, the so-called "counter-culture" of Fourth Avenue that emerged after the middle 1960s, though bill was raging at the centre of that later movement, too. (16)

McLuhan, in 1959, argued that in the emerging world of the artist of the electronic age "we see the disappearance of the old oppositions between art and nature, business and culture, school and society" ("Electronic Revolution" 5). In Vancouver, dating from 1959, bissett was both consciously and organically seeking to overcome the barriers between art and lifestyle. That same year, George Woodcock, at the behest of the head of the Department of English at the University of British Columbia, launched *Canadian Literature*, "the first review devoted only to the study of Canadian writers and writing. It will – we have added – throw a concentrated light on a field that has never been illuminated systematically by any previous periodical" (Editorial 3). The second issue that same year featured an extended, important study of Margaret Avison's poetry by Milton Wilson. We have, then, in one year the confluence of the internationally significant representatives of two primary aesthetic orientations in Vancouver during the period in question, open verse and collage, the onset of Vancouver's involvement in brash and exciting intermedial experimentation, the arrival of Canada's pre-eminent forum for the conscious study and elucidation of its literature, and the meeting of a founding editor of *Tish* and the founding editor of *Blewointment*. Nineteen fifty-nine was also the year that Roy Kiyooka – who would become a significant figure in Vancouver's Surrealist renaissance – moved to Vancouver from Regina and that Frank Davey met future *Tish* editors Robert Hogg and George Bowering (he had met Gladys Hindmarch and Judith Copithorne in September 1958), as well as first meeting Lionel Kearns, Carol Bolt (née Johnson), and Warren Tallman (Davey, *When* 79–93). Organic links flowed through the campus, drawing the literary community together. Hindmarch read a story by George Bowering in *The Raven*, and in the cafeteria told her professor (Tallman) how much she enjoyed it. He pointed across the room and said, "You should tell him himself. That's George over there." She did approach him and introduced herself. The two, with Lionel Kearns, began hanging out in 1959 and going for daytime drives to the Spanish Banks, Stanley Park, and the Endowment Lands (Hindmarch, email interview with author). That fall, they joined the Writers Work-shop, a collective that included Davey and Judith Copithorne, among others. Nineteen fifty-nine was the year that Toni Onley staged the exhibition of abstract collage work at the Vancouver Art Gallery that established his reputation (*Breathless Days* 4). It was the year that BC author Sheila Watson published her avant-garde novel *The Double Hook*, catapulting female authors from the West Coast to the forefront of experimental Cana-dian writing. Beginnings are arbitrary, but this year presents an exemplary microcosm of the energy, optimism, and innocence of the decade and a half to come. It was also the year that all of the *Tish* poets began reading Ginsberg and the Beats.

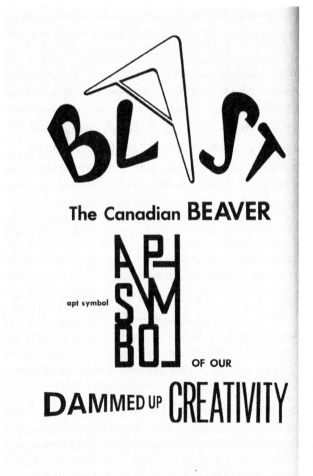

Figure I.25 Pages from Marshall McLuhan's *Counterblast* (1954/1969). Typography by Harley Parker. Source: Private collection of the author. Used with permission of the Estate of Marshall McLuhan.

If 1959 is the somewhat arbitrary beginning of this period, 1975 represents a useful if also somewhat unnatural demarcation point. The terms and possibilities of avant activity had, by that point, changed considerably. The initial rush of activity in the 1960s was followed by a significant rise in materialist consciousness that helped to politicize many of the assumptions of contemporary art practice, avant or otherwise. It was no longer enough to want to try something new; consciousness awakenings and resistance to the juggernauts of transnational capitalism and Empire, Western and white supremacy, and patriarchy and heteronormativity disturbed the utopian innocence of the 1960s. Alas, stung by the combination of residential schools and the Sixties Scoop, the Indigenous community was still decades away from the start of its cultural renaissance, but new literary venues and initiatives emerged, including a Vancouver-based Indigenous newspaper in response to an increasing materialist consciousness that was deeply critical of colonialist tendencies by Canada and its dominating neighbour. The *Indian Voice* was founded by the Indian Homemakers Association of British Columbia, a non-profit collective of Indigenous women, and began publishing its newsletter in October 1969. Featuring a range of anti-colonial position papers, community news, and political poetry, the newsletter grew into a newspaper and established a province-wide network of Indigenous spaces representing 140 bands in shared resistance to the Trudeau government's White Paper (that proposed ending the special legal relationship between Indigenous people and the Canadian state), settler claims on unceded land, and general reservation conditions. The poetry in the newspaper (ranging between three and seven poems per issue) is strident, populist, and determined to directly articulate the dire circumstances of Indigenous quality of life at the time. As Patricia Barkaskas argues, women were central to the role of the *Indian Voice*, using the forum as "an important intervention into the dominant Native nationalist discourse about gender and claims to Indigenous identity" (3). The centrality of female leaders in the Indigenous-led efforts toward decolonization continued in the era that followed and extends unbroken into the present. The newspaper, meanwhile, successfully published over 100 issues until 1984 when it disbanded. Contemporary Indigenous avant-garde artists like Marie Clements and Janet Marie Rogers have responded to the *Indian Voice* and the Indian Homemakers Association of British Columbia in their work. Rogers notes how, against the wash of colonization, the *Indian Voice* helped to establish "unification/through common discrimination," even though too many government agents and even Indigenous leaders were "walking in opposite directions / (not) listening to the women / even the little Home-Makers / scared'em" ("MOQW/MOQW?ESPEYE?WIXT" 130–1).

Publishing houses and magazines appeared in the late 1970s and throughout the 1980s, such as Press Gang Publishers for feminist and anti-capitalist work in 1974 and *Room of One's One: A Feminist Journal of Literature and Criticism* in 1975 for feminist writing. Within the period in question, the shift toward overtly political content can be registered in *Blewointment*'s increasingly politicized orientation and increasingly leftist revolutionary character. Indeed, the period after the one explored in *Finding Nothing* is dominated by the politically charged, contestatory writing that stems from this shift – culminating in the enormous Women & Words conference in 1983, which featured over a thousand feminist authors, academics, and activists, and all the subsequent changes wrought by decades of activisim: Japanese redress, the closure of the residential school program, recognition of Indigenous title, the acknowledgment and apology for the Komagata Maru incident, the establishment of a national enquiry into the epidemic of MMIW (missing and murdered Indigenous women), and so on. The avant-gardes have many active fronts.

The 1959–75 frame has specific relevance for politically oriented radically avant verse in the city. In 1959, Milton Acorn, Roy Lowther, Pat Lowther, and other writers in the city founded the Poets for Peace reading group, which orchestrated reading series and political-literary discussion groups. The group published an important anthology of nineteen British Columbian poets in 1960 to protest the testing of nuclear weapons in the province. The story of that group ended in tragedy, however, when Roy Lowther murdered his wife in 1975, an act that sent shock waves throughout Vancouver and, indeed, Canadian arts communities. As Christine Wertheim notes, Roy killed his wife, the exquisite poet Pat Lowther, because of professional jealousy and maniacal (patriarchal) possessiveness, but also because her writing had moved too far from his radical leftism by experimenting with intermedial collage and radical lyricism. Her tragic murder helps to establish the boundary for this study, the point of disillusionment at which the idealism inherent in the avant-garde pursuit of new literary forms and social realities dissolved into (temporary) meaninglessness, the most troubling manifestation of finding nothing.

The literary groupings that follow, primarily but not exclusively the *Tish* poets, the downtown scene (who were also the Kitsilano scene), the intermedia community, the West Coast Surrealists, and the feminists, are related to one another, infused and overlapping socially and aesthetically. Any bifurcation is exaggerated, but there is yet an important difference between open verse and collage, especially as practised in Vancouver, that invites deeper investigation as a productive fissure in a burgeoning scene. In the simplest terms, the difference can be explained through the importance of the voice, the line, and the sound of the language in open verse, which stands in contrast to the materiality of the letters, the full-page space, and the visual impact of language in collage. In McLuhan's terms, this is the difference of a poetry shaped by the dominance of the ear versus the eye. This simplification will be elaborated in the chapters that follow, but for now it is enough to note that the difference led to discrete venues for the exploration of each mode: for instance, in a greatly truncated list, *Tish*, *Talon*, the *Georgia Straight Writing Supplement*, *Motion*, *Imago*, and *Blackfish* focused on publishing, exploring, and promoting open-field poetics; meanwhile, publications like *Blewointment*, *Circular Causation*, *radiofreerainforest*, and the *Capilano Review* and art world institutions like the Intermedia Society, the

THE CAPILANO REVIEW

Figure I.26 Cover of the *Capilano Review*, Fall 1975/Spring 1976 double issue. Source: Private collection of the author. Used with permission.

Mandan Ghetto Gallery, the Sound Gallery, the Western Front, and the annual Festival of the Contemporary Arts were all committed to promulgating multidisciplinary collage. As the *Capilano Review* editor Pierre Coupey notes: "I thought of every issue as a collage. How each piece would speak forward and speak back to each other. They had to interweave. It had to be alive that way. It couldn't be discrete things. It had to be an organism" (Interview 2019).

By 1975, given the intense openness of the collage mindset, it seems inevitable that any and all of the divisions of the early 1960s dissolved into irrelevance. In 1974, Warren Tallman had already declared the datedness of the sixties aesthetics by noting that it "was clear that by 1968 the American story of Modernist writing had been pretty much told through in Vancouver. Most of the Vancouver poets were by this time out from under the American influence into a Modernism of their own devising" (*Godawful* 184). Jason Wiens, for his part, argues that – when you actually look at the writing coming out of the so-called New American branch in Vancouver – the influence of the New American authors has been greatly "exaggerated" ("I May Be Trying to Tell What I Renounce" 84). Regardless, as the New American influence waned, and it clearly did, the borders between the aesthetic communities increasingly blurred. Witness the surfeit of riches in the Fall 1975/Spring 1976 double issue of the *Capilano Review*, which contains representative samplings from of all the Vancouver gardes tracked in this book (not identified or divided as such in the magazine, of course): from the *Tish*/New American scene, there is work by George Bowering, Lewis Ellingham, Jack Spicer, Robin Blaser, and Robert Duncan; from the *Blewointment*/downtown scene there is work by Maxine Gadd, bpNichol, and Gerry Gilbert; from the intermedia/visual arts community there is work by Cathie Falk and Claude Breeze, and an extended profile of both Iain Baxter and the Western Front; from the Surrealist group there is work by Gary Lee-Nova (plus selections from the Toronto Surrealists A. Frank and Theresa Moritz); and from the feminist community there is work by Carole Itter, Audrey Thomas, Daphne Marlatt, and Gladys Hindmarch (who conducted an interview with bpNichol and Pierre Coupey for the issue). There is a contribution from John Bentley Mays, the Toronto artist who collaborated with William Burroughs (who, around that time, endorsed the Western Front's mayoral candidate, Mr. Peanut), Victor Coleman, and bpNichol on a three-hour radio play called "Audiothon." The issue functions as a remarkable anticipatory companion, perhaps even summary, of the work that happens in this book.

In a compelling moment of retrospection in this issue, at the end of a long interview with Nichol by former *Tish* editors Daphne Marlatt and Gladys Hindmarch, the discussion turns to the problem of literary influence especially for young writers. Tellingly, when Nichol was asked about the trap of such formative influences, he answered by describing how he managed to avoid becoming a parodic derivative of New American aesthetics before he left Vancouver in 1964:

> BPNICHOL: The whole superstar system, for instance, is a consumption of the artist: you pays your money and you gets your meal, like at concerts or restaurants really. It's to break with that whole consumption thing and say that language does not have to be a consumptive process. Let's use it both ways.
>
> GLADYS HINDMARCH: Listen, I just thought of a question I wanted to ask about that. At the point that you're fairly young, you tend to slip into what aesthetic is around you, or to be found out through accident, usually through some sort of thing that there's some friend or some writing that leads to one other thing. But like, how bound are people in some sense by that aesthetic that they come up into or slip into? Like for me, it's been very hard to break out of in some sense, the whole Black Mountain [...] Like, okay, by admiring their aesthetic, their person, I made them heroes in a way that wasn't necessary. And I think every young writer is going to do that, in some sense. And so it's many other accumulations and layers that you're dealing with.

BP: I'll tell you the way I handled it is I hid out. [...] I hid out and Dave Phillips and I were each other's audiences, and we believed all sorts of things. And this left us free to roam and ramble. [...] I was very afraid of being overwhelmed by somebody who had a much more clearly articulated aesthetic, and that it would be very easy to slip into. This is what enraged me with the later issues of *El Corno Emplumado*: you had all these guys using Creeley's breathline that were not Creeley, and as a result, their language lacked an energy charge; it was just sheer boredom. And it was total misunderstanding of everything the man was about. I'm sure he must have interpreted it as an insult. And I say, how else could you see it? [...] And it's all those sorts of forms that not only dishonour the writer, they're a consuming of the writer again.

(Nichol Interview with Gladys Hindmarch et al., 344–5)

Figure I.27 "Kissing" portrait of bpNichol. Photographer unknown. Source: The Estate of bpNichol. Used with permission of the Estate of bpNichol.

Though based in Toronto, Nichol was an active poet in the *Blewointment* fold. He published thirty poems, comics, and visual poems in eight different

issues of the magazine (3.1, 9, 10, 11, 13, 14, and 16), and co-published dozens of books with bissett. He also commissioned bissett to write a book of
literary theory, which became the Canadian postmodern classic *RUSH: what
fuckan theory; a study uv language* (1972). His exploration of sound and
visual poetry was directly inspired by bissett, and his publishing venture a
self-conscious attempt to do in Toronto what bissett was doing in Vancouver. In a letter to David UU in the early 1960s, Nichol clarified the divide he
recognized in Vancouver poetics explicitly: "Tish & Blew Ointment present
the split view [...] Vancouver & Kenneth Patchen become major influences i
only recently have fully incorporated" ("from bp to David fr *Spanish Fleye*"
23). bissett and David UU were co-editors in Nichol's grOnk venture when it
was launched in 1967.

Figure I.28 School portrait of
Gladys Maria Hindmarch. Used
with permission.

In Vancouver in the early 1960s, Nichol wasn't looking for a master to follow, and consciously avoided the master-discourses that dominated aesthetics at UBC. His resistance catapulted him into new terrain, indeed into the avant-garde: "there is a way in which I know that the concrete and the sound poetry allowed me to move untrammelled" (345). It required leaving Vancouver, though, to claim the necessary mental space and begin building up a new community, a new garde in Toronto that could avoid becoming a parody of the centre. (In contrast, Scott Watson notes that Michael Morris, who also left Vancouver but returned in 1966, avoided such devotional slavishness by ironizing the parodic centre–margin relationship and turning that problem into the focus of his work ["Mirrors" 69] – especially evident in his iconic painting *The Problem of Nothing* [1966; see cover], which includes a speech bubble echoing the aesthetic styles that surround/subsume it.)

Despite the overlap in the communities, the aesthetic boundaries between these forums were pronounced especially during the early part of the period in question; open-field verse appeared in all of the collage forums (naturally, *everything* appeared in them), but visually oriented works were strictly kept out of the open-field forums. There is one noteworthy exception to the exclusion of visual work from the *Tish*/New American/open verse scene: bill bissett published just one short poem in *Tish* (noteably, a slight lyric about the phallus). He was also invited to design the cover for the penultimate fifth issue of *Tish*'s short-lived offshoot prose magazine *Motion* in October 1962. Meanwhile, after his time with *Tish*, while living in Victoria, Davey launched *The Open Letter* (later just *Open Letter*), which began as *Tish* did with a series of editorials alongside representative examples of poetry. This journal would become the pre-eminent forum for discussions of avant-garde aesthetics in the country and played a major role in galvanizing and advancing the field as a field in the latter half of the twentieth century. In the second issue, though, Davey begins by noting, "McFadden and Nichol send visual poems – which mode I still find irrelevant to what I know as poetry. For me poetry is of language, and language is still of sound with rhythm in stress and pitch" ("Dear Fred" 3). That boundary remained noticeably unblurred until the 1970s, when Nichol became a special editor of *Open Letter*. So, while the venues and the literary ambitions were, in many respects, aesthetically discrete, most of the people involved in them were common citizens in a rather small artistic community. They interacted, debated, and experimented with many modes and mediums, irrespective of the borders between each. George Bowering dabbled in concrete poetry (see Figure I.26). Lionel Kearns produced some of the country's most compelling and important examples of visual poetry. His iconic poem "The Birth of God" (see Figure I.29) highlights the interrelation between presence and absence, something and nothing. Many avant-gardists lived in small, often crammed communes and raised children together. The lines of aesthetic and social entanglement overlapped

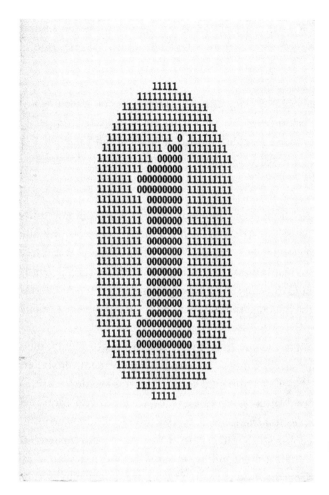

Figure I.29 Lionel Kearns's *The Birth of God* (1965; Trigram Press, 1968).

and webbed the city – but Nichol's sense of the "split view" yet helps to elucidate the transitions and divergences in the overlapping communities. It is our (impossible) task to engage with the too-tidy divisions between the gardes, and their equally too-messy interfusions.

This book, while mapping out the particular contours and contradictions of the city's avant-gardisms, and the international currents they intersected and interacted with, will also consider why Vancouver erupted in experimental activity during the period in question. It has been said by many scholars and observers that Vancouver was notably ripe for the interfusion of art disciplines precisely because it lacked an entrenched history and notoriety in any specific aesthetic direction (this is the positive reversal of the "finding nothing" trope; there was nothing in their way, nothing to stop them). The institutions were not barriers to this activity. As the Vancouver artist Marina Roy writes, "avant-garde artists often found support from the cultural establishment (the Canada Council, the Vancouver Art Gallery)" (62). Furthermore, as Peter Culley writes,

> the systemic structures of class and ideology that maintain the illusion of writing's autonomy did not have to be laboriously broken down, having been erected haphazardly in the first place. As the sixties proceeded, the decentralization and fluidity that resulted from this made it hard to tell where the literary culture ended and others began. (193)

The scenes in question appeared at precisely the moment when the dominant institutions of the city were first being constructed, such that artists were not initially imbued with a sense of ostracization from the networks of aesthetic power. They were involved in creating those institutions. Institutional alienation would eventually and inevitably come, as would the *salon des refusées* and the alternative, contestatory institutions determined to challenge the conduct and habits of the city's public and commercial art institutions.

The Intermedia Society, one of the country's first artist-run centres, embodied in many respects the optimism and openness of the mid-decade Vancouver sixties. Caroline Bayard argues that it was instrumental in the "progressive de-centring" of Canadian art discourse from an entrenched focus on Toronto and Montreal (116). Intermedia, she argues, "established the particular interaction between life- and art-style which was to become so characteristic of Vancouver and turned out to be an essential part of the environment bill bissett and the Western Canadian avant-garde emerged from." Intermedia was invited to program an annual week-long festival at the Vancouver Art Gallery (VAG) beginning in 1968. As the *Province* reported, the optimism for the possibilities of getting the public involved in art and art-making ran high: "There will come a time when society, in an ethos which has made human labour obsolete, will need to create its own music and poetry – its art forms which will be different from historical art forms, but which will nevertheless offer perhaps more satisfaction" (N. Wilson n. pag.). The gallery developed a unique "Special Events program" specifically to facilitate the combination of music, video, film, lectures, dance, literature, and performance by local artists. They and Intermedia were partners in the creation of an arts culture in Vancouver. *Everything* was on the table.

But let me be careful not to present too saccharine or sanguine a portrait of the period. There were faults and fissures and battle lines that ran throughout the city. *Tish* pissed off a lot of downtown artists, and marginalized women and BIPOC authors. Even Jamie Reid, *Tish* editor, turned against his own writing from the early 1960s: "I conscientiously went through my old [*Tish*] work and read it aloud to myself at home, and when I read it aloud to myself at home I found that it nauseated me to

Figure I.30 Intermedia logo designed by Gary Lee-Nova (c. 1970). Source: University of British Columbia Rare Books and Special Collections, Intermedia Society Fonds, A4 B3 2–8 1518/414. Used with permission.

my stomach. It would be impossible to read it with any kind of fervour" ("Reading" n. pag.). Instead, starting from 1968, he began advocating for an anti-imperialist revolutionary literature – a radical avant-garde – to serve the working class in Canada. Lee Maracle's autobiographical *Bobbi Lee, Indian Rebel*, written in 1975 and published in 1980, depicts her experience in Vancouver in the 1960s and 1970s. She includes a disturbing (*problematic*) scene at SFU where an irate, radicalized former *Tish* editor, in fact Jamie Reid, chastises her protagonist for advocating for Native rights, as this was taken to be an affront to his proletarian internationalism (135). Meanwhile, George Woodcock described McLuhan as "the actual destroyer of our civilization, a glorying in what he had done in transforming language into incoherence. I thought this is the ultimate act of barbarism" (Interview n. pag.).[16] Roy Kiyooka, in contrast, published a letter to Sheila Watson in *Transcanada Letters* about her doctoral supervisor McLuhan, complaining of his *conservatism*: "will the real M.M. get his nose out of the stacks and stop writing abt the death of literacy?" (Letter 110). The conflict between artistic and activist communities was becoming a subject in and of itself.

Interdisciplinarity as a concept even eventually came under direct attack. In 1975, the head of the Canada Council Visual Arts and Film section, Luke Rombout, became the director of the Vancouver Art Gallery and issued what Andrew Witt describes as "the most regressive statements concerning the gallery's earlier experimental projects" (n. pag.). Rombout explained why and how he began his tenure at the gallery by eviscerating its interdisciplinary orientation and cancelling the Special Events programming:

> The Gallery gained its reputation during those years substantially for the Special Events program, not so much for what was done in the visual arts [... E]ven though they attracted a very particular and very loyal audience [...] people who were interested in the development of the visual arts, including collectors, had turned their backs on the Gallery [...] The first change I made was to virtually cancel the Special Events program. I was determined to bring the Gallery back to being involved in the visual arts.[17]

The dismantling of the city's interdisciplinary infrastructure and partnerships (alongside the increased siloing of national funding structures) and the professionalizing of the city's public, private, and even artist-run gallery spaces all contributed to a dramatic shift in the way art was made in Vancouver from the mid-1970s on. The experimental poets, for one, were no longer freely welcomed into the production and exhibition of new visual art. Collaborations continued (and continue) to happen, but the institutional support of those crossovers diminished. By the time Rombout had arrived at the VAG, Intermedia was three years gone, and already replaced by the more substantial, more professional, but less accessible Western Front. As Keith Wallace notes,

> the Western Front assumed its own peculiar form of institutionalization. As only invited artists could exhibit, perform, produce a video or stay as part of the artist-in-residence program, this policy created a perceived exclusivity during the 1970s, one that alienated a considerable segment of the local art community and basically ignored the public.
>
> (36)[18]

---

16 The occasion of this was comment was a visit in 1959 by George Woodcock and his wife to a seminar held by McLuhan in his famous coach house at the University of Toronto.

17 Witt quotes this passage from Keith Wallace's essay "A Particular History" (36), though it originally comes from an essay Rombout wrote for *Vancouver: Art and Aritsts 1931–1983* called "Personal Perspectives."

18 In the 1970s, the Western Front was a critical literary forum in the city, indeed the country. Guided by bpNichol's principal collaborator, Steve McCaffery, the Western Front launched an ambitious series

Jamie Reid, telephone interview, 26 January 2014

I left Vancouver in 1969. I was working with the Communist Party of Canada [Marxist-Leninist]. [Jack] Spicer, you see, was a Trotskyite, but broke with it. There were divisions all over the place. Spicer said, "You can't write anything, can't do anything without politics. You can't even go to bed with someone without politics." He wrote a whole series of poems about living in California, seeing produce from the orchards being destroyed because they couldn't be marketed. He watched fruits burned, he wanted to kill the people responsible. There is an allegorical politics at work in all of his writing, even in his book on the Holy Grail. All the figures in that book are in a political conspiracy of one kind or another.

In '66, I helped organize the first be-in [in Vancouver] with Country Joe and the Fish. It was the same community as the Trips Festival, and I was sympathetic to the hippie crowd. I regarded myself as more hipster than hippie, but I was involved in starting an organization to legalize marijuana. I realized, though, that marijuana could not be a central issue. It wasn't going to change anything, one way or another. But I remember in '65 or '66 [Timothy] Leary and Ram Dass arrived with LSD. That led right to the Grateful Dead and Big Brother. By '68, I had converted to Communism, but that too was disillusioning [...]

As a [Marxist-Leninist] Communist, I don't believe in anarchism. There needs to be an authority to regulate society. We need some form of regulative apparatus that depends upon a knowledge of how the things we are regulating actually work.

As the 1970s wore on, alienation and disillusionment became increasingly common hallmarks of Vancouver's artistic discourse. A spirit of contestation entered into the city, fostered by the rise of police harassment and violent riots that darkened the mood and shattered what remained of any naïve optimism. The belief that

---

of experimental events. As Peter Culley writes, "Of all the writers who have visited the Western Front, McCaffery is the one who has made the fullest and most consistent use of all its social and technical permutations [...] The institutional encouragement of such extremes of literary practice was a mantle that throughout much of the 70s and early 80s the Western Front carried alone" (96).

"collaboration and new electronic media would signal the dawn of a new utopian consciousness" (Roy 59) faltered, and in its place came world-weariness and battle-hardness. Meanwhile, the possibilities for real political change felt at a more personal level also began to come into focus. The 1970 report of the Royal Commission on the Status of Women in Canada, for instance, provided a set of practical targets (167 in total) to improve material conditions for Canadian women, especially in the realms of employment equity, maternity, harassment, discrimination, and marriage. The report tracked the rise of the Women's Liberation Movement, and the fact that Canada had signed the Universal Declaration of Human Rights in 1948, recognizing in principle the full and unequivocal equality of men and women. Noting the discrepancy between the ideals of the Universal Declaration and the lived experience of women in the country, the report begins optimistically: "The stage has been set for a new society equally enjoyed and maintained by both sexes" (xi). Women's collectives coalesced and fought to achieve the optimistic and specific possibilities envisioned by the report. From this resurgence in the women's movement, a new wave of women-centred arts collectives emerged in Vancouver, including the Women's Alive Group (a television production company), ISIS (a media distribution centre), Reelfeelings (in film production and radio), and Women in Focus (in television and film production and advocacy), alongside a tight network of women's meeting groups that included many female authors. These groups were formed "with a unified feminist voice in mind" (Roy 63), but they presaged the activist groups that followed that explored discrimination beyond that against women, including race, sexual orientation, and class and trans identities.

In other words, if modernism began as a response to new phenomena, it became by mid-century a splintered admixture of variegated local, national, and international cultural responses to rapid change, including responses to the various layers of modernist cultures themselves. It was disorienting, and the boundaries of meaningful identity came under enormous pressures. Brion Gysin realized the transnational geopolitical context of his art and chose to renounce his Canadian identity and align himself with unadorned internationalism: he declared himself "the man from nowhere" ("Cut Me Up" 43). His transformation muddied the waters surrounding his identity enough that in 2010, when Vancouver's UBC Fine Arts Gallery – a short distance from where he had been stationed with the Canadian army in the Second World War – launched a retrospective exhibition that included his works, they described him in their catalogue copy as "American" (*Breathless Days* 13). While Gysin's national effacement can be read in the context of modernist ambitions for universal culture and/or disaffection from the same, the claim of being "from nowhere" also implies Canada's lack of cultural cachet as a centre for modernist or avant-garde literary production. It was a pointed critique of unhip Canadian colonial society.

Vancouver during the early 1960s was particularly prone to this sense of detachment and marginalization from the thresholds of power and culture. For instance,

Tallman describes Canadian writers in Vancouver pre-*Tish* as "working in isolation: There was no coherent scene whatsoever"[19] (Niechoda and Hunter 85). Pierre
Coupey, who would go on to play an instrumental role in creating an intellectual
community in Vancouver, characterizes the city in the early 1960s in similarly stark
and unflattering terms: "Vancouver seemed a small slice of hell, raw, rough, impov-
erished, frontier, unsophisticated, and narrowly Anglo" (Interview n. pag.). Modernism, particularly the Anglo-American modernism that New Modernist Studies
seeks to decentre, promised access to the thresholds of cultural power. Rather than
cobble together the fragments of a discontinuous and nascent – even subaltern –
modernism of their own, many of the Vancouver writers in the early 1960s glommed
on to the rhetoric and aesthetics of high Anglo-American modernism as a means of
integrating the city into the international circuit, of making it sophisticated, cultural,
indeed real, even if imitative.

The fact of Vancouver's close proximity to culture seems to have taken some of the
early 1960s writers by surprise. Consequently, and in retrospect, Davey confessed
to the "embarrassing [...] frivolity [...] pedantry [...] snobbery [... and] glibness"
(Introduction 9) of early *Tish* editorials. bpNichol agreed, adding that in rereading
Davey's early creative work "one clearly encounters a young writer, cocky, obsessed
with issues of craft (& still interesting on that level), but without a full grasp of the
implications of the philosophy he was moving towards" ("Introduction" 246).[20] It
is almost as if they were caught off guard at having been read or at least at having
their words taken seriously, surprised to have discovered themselves within a rich, if
dispersed, network of Canadian and international experimental writers who cared
deeply about the implications of aesthetic choices; as if they too felt themselves to be
"men from nowhere" right up until the point that they realized they were not alone,
that they were already somewhere.[21] Like Gysin, the *Tish* authors (in an appropriately unsigned editorial) rejected the nation as an appropriate context in which to
read their writing: "Canada does not exist except as a political arrangement for the
convenience of individuals accidentally happening to live within its arbitrary area"
(*Tish No. 1–19* 155).

However, Gysin's emergence from out of the accident of Canada led him to a more
existential problem of the arbitrariness not just of specific national borders but also
of human culture *in toto*. In contrast, the *Tish* authors merely preferred to locate

---

19 In this interview, conducted in October 1985, Gerry Gilbert responds with a rebuttal: "Warren? There
    was a coherent kind of downtown scene of artists and writers, an inner-city group that had gone on and
    grown up and out of the traditional Vancouver scene" (85).
20 Nichol's comments appear in the introduction to Davey's *Selected Works*, where he elected to omit
    everything prior to 1970. The work that followed is "vastly superior," he explained (247).
21 Gender issues and *Tish*, whose editors debated naming the magazine *Cock*, are addressed in more detail
    below, but particularly in chapters 1 and 2.

their experience in a more particular, regional and civic context; they were never really authors or artists from nowhere (a profound rejection of culture as spiritual and intellectual foundation, a radical misanthropy); they were always, especially in the writing at the beginning of their careers, from the West Coast. Thus, the *Tish* counterpoint to Gysin's iconic dilemma "I am that am I?" might be Bowering's over-confident boast: "I know / where I am" ("Tuesday Night" 136). Or, as Robert Duncan writes in his review of the first year of *Tish*, and his welcome to "the novices of Vancouver," highlighting David Dawson's "Tentative Coastlines" serial poem in particular: "The shores are shores of Vancouver, of an actual place that is also a spiritual beachhead [...] it is a reality of the City the poets live in" ("For the Novices" 253, 255). "An actual place," "a reality": Vancouver, via its novitiates, had been recognized by American modernism and secured a presence; hence it was no longer nothing. Though this kind of thinking suggests a colonial authority extending into a marginal outpost, as Friedman points out, it can also be understood as a reflection of the dynamic negotiation of the culture of competing modernisms (see "Planetary" 51).

The Vancouver avant-garde literary community covered by this study of the period between 1959 and 1975 began as the writers there shucked the sense (however mistaken it might have been) of the city as an inevitably marginal, desolate space. They discovered their close proximity to international modernism and discovered that the tools of international modernism and avant-gardism were also available to them to use for their own purposes. It seems strange, in retrospect, that they appear to have been remarkably unaware of the advances of modernist writing made by previous generations in the city – of the rich legacy of writers such as Livesay, Birney, and Lowry, especially. Regardless, this study tracks the growth predicted in Duncan's "spiritual beachhead" and the optimistic, indeed occasionally utopian, output that followed this prediction. While Margaret Atwood could still detect the "isolation of Vancouver and its consequent cultishness" in publications as late as 1971 (82), the growth and emergence of the city as a literary centre of avant-garde activity can be quantified in the emergence of a remarkable spectrum of experimental magazines, alongside the creation of a number of small literary presses open, if not welcoming, to avant-garde production. It can be discovered in quieter moments, like Daphne Marlatt's private desire "to be present, to a place i could take on as home (with the response-abilities that implies)" (*What Matters* 8). It can be discovered in the grander moments of spatial possession, like Ed Varney's epiphany on the Lions Gate Bridge: "I can feel anything I want. / I want to fly. / The clouds are like fire" ("On Lions Gate Bridge" 5). Unlike the rather concentrated and halting efforts of prior Canadian avant-gardes, the Vancouver of 1959 to 1975 represents an extremely prolific period of activity. Hundreds of books were published, hundreds of magazines were issued (not to mention the appearance of Vancouver's writers in countless magazines across the country, the United States, and beyond). The city could boast of there being multiple bookstores available to experimental writing and a range of

Figure I.31 Ian Sommerville and Brion Gysin, Paris, 1962. Photographer unknown. © the Brion Gysin Estate and the William S. Burroughs Trust. Used by permission of the Wylie Agency LLC.

reading series that served different aspects of a vibrant community. Denizens of the city could boast of the vibrant literary activity and, very soon in the period under consideration, did begin boasting of its literary accomplishments.

They became not nothing.

Coda: Gysin's Vancouver

In his visits to the city, and in the time he lived there, Gysin never interacted with the artists in Vancouver. His influence arrived circuitously through transnational flows of culture into the city, energizing an aesthetic atmosphere that facilitated intermedia, post-language experimentation. Pierre Coupey, for instance, after publishing one of the first visual poems in Canada, received a significant grant from the Conseil des arts et des lettres du Québec in 1964 to advance his concrete poetry. He went to Paris and used the money to enrol in art school at the avant-garde Académie Julian, where Henri Matisse, Hans Arp, Fernand Léger, and Robert Rauschenberg had all trained. As befits Paris, he went for a stroll in the 6th arrondissement

(Saint-Germain-des-Prés) searching for *something* and happed upon a small gallery broadcasting a strange voice into the street. The voice was chanting ungrammatical variations such as "Junk is no good baby, baby junk is good, good baby is junk." It was Gysin, of course, and Coupey was struck dumb. A man in the doorway saw his interest and ushered him in to the gallery, where the walls were blanketed by an international exhibition of concrete poetry. The man in the doorway was Henri Chopin, the French pioneer of visual and sound poetry, who would become the official "War Editor" of the *Georgia Straight*, which Coupey helped found in 1967. When Chopin learned Coupey came from Canada, he immediately asked, "So you are aware of Marshall McLuhan?" Coupey bought a copy of *Understanding Media* that afternoon. Coupey befriended Chopin, who gave him a small archive of sound recordings and books, which Coupey took with him to Vancouver a few months later. He had intended to do a one-year master's degree with Earle Birney at UBC, though Birney had temporarily relocated to Toronto by the time Coupey arrived. Still, Coupey stayed with the program and even presented his amassed sound poetry recordings and visual poetry at the 1966 Festival of the Contemporary Arts at UBC. Robert Duncan and Ian Wallace were both in the audience that day. Wallace already owned books by Gysin and William Burroughs, having come back from City Lights Books in San Francisco after a weeklong road trip with Tom Burrows in 1965. Reading and hearing Coupey's presentations of Gysin's work, alongside the other material that Coupey presented, was a watershed moment for Wallace, who experimented with visual poetry and collage for the next five years, before founding the unofficially named Vancouver School of Photoconceptualism with Jeff Wall. Duncan, meanwhile, was inspired to rush off and record an album of sound poetry (Coupey, Letter to Henri Chopin n. pag.) that has, alas, been lost to history. Wall, meanwhile, developed this interest in Burroughs into his widely acclaimed *Landscape Manual* (1969), which freely borrows its style and methodology from Burroughs's *APO-33* (1965) and its theories of language and art from McLuhan: as he writes, "[T]he shape of the language determines the shape of our reactions to interactions with the physical" (10). The medium is the message. In the short-lived *Free Media Bulletin*, Wall writes about *APO-33* and Burroughs's cut-up novel *Nova Express* (1964) in his essay "Meaningness" as an ideal model for achieving an anti-harmonic "irreconcilable dualism" (n. pag) that allows things to exist together paratactically without relation or logic or hierarchy. Burroughs, of course, credits Gysin with pioneering the method.

Similarly, Judith Copithorne fell under Gysin's influence by chance and happenstance. After being encouraged by bissett to attend a poetry reading by Kenneth Patchen, who was performing in Vancouver with Al Neil's band ("A Personal" 55), she was, as they used to say, turned on and tuned in. She dropped out of UBC and committed to becoming a full-time artist – a poet. Shortly thereafter, she made her own pilgrimage to San Francisco and to Lawrence Ferlinghetti's City Light Books,

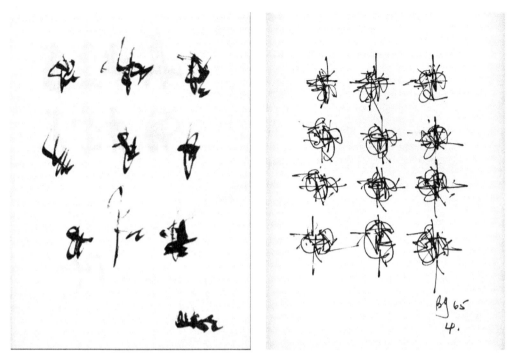

Figures I.32, I.33 On the left, an untitled page from Judith Copithorne's book *Rain* (1969), published by bpNichol's Ganglia Press in Toronto. On the right, Brion Gysin's "4" (1965). Copyright © the Brion Gysin Estate and the William S. Burroughs Trust, used by permission of the Wylie Agency LLC.

where she encountered visual-textual crossover work by Henri Michaux and Gysin (Barwin n. pag.). Though unaware of Gysin's Canadian roots and more limited connections to Vancouver, she credits that encounter with giving her "a lot of clues" about the possibilities of visual poetry. Whether consciously or not, Copithorne explored very similar asemic calligraphy as Gysin's for a period during the late 1960s.

The story of Ginsberg's visit to Gysin's mother, Stella, meanwhile, did eventually become something of a local legend among a small coterie of artists in the city. Her life in Vancouver had led to Brion visiting regularly throughout the 1950s and 1960s, and again upon her death in January 1966. Years later, the Western Front chose to acknowledge and indeed beatify her by posthumously dubbing her a "local saint." She was a remarkable woman, having nursed Brion back to health in New York City in 1947, surrounded by the action painters and his community there, and later having visited her son in his residence at the famous Beat Hotel in 1962, where she met the Beat writers, shortly after Gysin launched the Dream Machine at the Louvre's Museé des Arts Decoratifs (Geiger 174–5). But it was only after Ginsberg's visit in 1963 that her connection to the international avant-garde was acknowledged at home in Canada. As Gysin wrote in 1986 in tribute to Ginsberg's generosity: "His visit made her into the lady with a salon for Pacific poets who has been posthumously beatified by the local avant garde movement known as the Western Front. Thus do poets dispense their beatitude" ("An Encomium" 125).

Coupey visited Gysin a few times in Paris in the 1980s, when Gysin's health was deteriorating. Michael Morris spoke to him on the phone several times in the same period (Michael Morris Interview). The stigma of being from "nowhere" had shifted; nowhere was now sending out emissaries that he received attesting to *not nothing*, as if evidence of *something*. When I spoke to Morris, in his Vancouver studio apartment, about these links, he jumped up, walked me down the hall, and, to my surprise, knocked on his neighbour's door. There lived Bryan Mulvihill in an apartment decorated with paintings by bill bissett and Brion Gysin. Mulvihill, it turns out, was close friends with Gysin, who taught him calligraphy and cut-up methods. Thus does culture flow across borders, seep into communities, and appear as if by a throw of the dice.

1–19 Thoughts on *TISH*, 1961–1969 (A Document of Response)

1

"Tish" is an anagram of "shit." The Vancouver student editors who launched the little poetry magazine *Tish* in September 1961 took the name from a lecture by Robert Duncan delivered in the home of their UBC professor Warren Tallman. Duncan's meditations on the socio-spiritual significance of shit connected to the Vancouver poets' "sense that too many of modern Canadian poems were synthetic, impersonally fashioned objects [...] After a few tentative and facetious suggestions we adopted the phonetic inversion suggested by Duncan himself" (Davey, Introduction 8–9). Despite being a famously combative group of young rebellious men, the UBC students backed away from the more overtly confrontational stance and opted for an empty signifier, a neologism with a veiled insider's joke. Of all the anagrams of those four letters that they could have chosen – shit, shti, siht, sith, sthi, stih, hsti, hsit, hits, hist, htis, htsi, isht, isth, ihst, ihts, itsh, iths, tsih, tshi, this, thsi, tihs, tish – there are only three that are not neologisms. All three words in those combinations of letters – hits, this, and shit – have become Canadian magazines since *Tish*.

There have been a number of anagrams in Canadian literature following *Tish*, but very few before or with such deliberative intention. Still, the anagram has become an increasingly important form in Canadian literature since 1961: bpNichol's poem "Not What the Siren Sang but What the Frag Meant" (1967), for instance, uses the device as a means of generating new word combinations that create enciphered networks of significance within the words of his poem, which is a tactic similar in spirit to *Tish*'s attempt to uncover new options for poetry in Canada. Hence, in Nichol's poem "autumn" becomes "umantu," which divides into "um tu," which is rearranged as "mu ut" and expanded to become "munaut," which reveals "monotony," and so on. The poem, which jokes about what "tall men" cannot "tell men" (perhaps a veiled rebuttal of UBC professor Tallman), uses the anagram to parody the habits of conventional and linear language use and seeks new, mystical methods of recovering linguistic integrity and mystery. Nichol's poem is poignantly dedicated to Margaret Avison, whom he had befriended after leaving Vancouver in 1964 (Davey, *aka* 51). Steve McCaffery, Margaret Atwood, Christian Bök, and admittedly myself are just

Figure 1.1 Robert Duncan and Robert Creeley in Warren Tallman's home on W 37th Street, Vancouver, 1963. Photo by Karen Tallman. Used with permission.

some of the authors to have made concerted efforts exploring the technique of writing through anagrams in the years since *Tish*. Avison returned Nichol's gesture with a chapbook called *Sliverick*, comprised of neologistic words ("Norgul," "Porntottie," "Gnishgiddle," etc.) built of rearranged sounds of a crowd cheering.[1]

The anagram is a potent device for rendering language as material while still accepting its semantic resonances. It is thus a means of breaking language away from its spoken function by isolating visual properties of words and letters via their written arrangement on the page, and in doing so discovering new occultic possibilities and connections revealed by the rearrangement of the letters in page space. After his personal discovery of Dada and the Russian Zaum experiments of language fragments ("from bp to David" 23), Nichol experimented aggressively with the full possibilities of moving letters around in page space, interacting with language as material,

---

1 Following a similar vein, Seymour Mayne also explored this kind of concrete ideopoem, including the anagram, in his late 1960s books such as *Manimals*. He creates, for instance, strange creatures by the movement of letters. The poem from which the book gains its name begins with the stanza: "manimani / anianian / mamamama / animanim / malmalma." He lets the game proceed in the following poem, "Enigmanimal," which crescendoes with a forty-two-letter Germanesque creature. He describes such neologisms as "chants" in the colophon. Avison and Nicholesque paragrams also appear in *Mutatations*: "realigious / imbible [...] priestigious" (n. pag.).

and found a place for himself, and Canadian literature, within the burgeoning international concrete poetry movement.

Anagrams came to the fore of the emerging postmodern culture in 1964 after the discovery of Ferdinand de Saussure's notebooks of 1906, wherein the famous linguist drafted extended meditations on the function of anagrams in Vedic poetry (Shepheard 33). Post-structuralist theorists such as Jacques Derrida, Jacques Lacan, and Julia Kristeva, who would all come to have influence on Canadian writers, including those associated with *Tish*, developed Saussure's observations into a more comprehensive theory of language. As Kristeva writes:

> We accept the principles set out by Ferdinand de Saussure in his "Anagrams," namely:
> 1. Poetic language adds a second, contrived, dimension to the original word
> 2. There is a correspondence between elements, in both metre and rime
> 3. Binary poetic laws transgress the rules of grammar.
>
> (174)

This contrived dimension of language use, ripe for satiric inversion as with *Tish*, provokes a rupture in the semiotic order that post-structuralists theorized had revolutionary, liberating potential. Thus, while the nascent back-to-the-earth hippie scene was contesting the inherent hegemony of Western culture right down to orthography and grammar, leading French intellectuals were staging similarly provocative questions of the rules that structure language and culture. Nichol and bissett, among many others, fused such disruptive energies in their language revolution. McCaffery addresses the connection between the emergence of post-structuralist continental philosophy (especially Lacan's use of the "double structure" of reference and representation [McCaffery, "The Martyrology" 58], which influenced Kristeva's theory above) and Nichol's use of the anagram and pun in his 1986 essay "The Martyrology as Paragram," a link initiated in Davey's groundbreaking, postmodern essay "Surviving the Paraphrase" (9).

The *Tish* authors were interested in the relationship between language and voice, the aurality of language, and in writing from, to borrow a phrase from Charles Olson, "the union of the mind and the ear," because the "breath allows *all* the speech-force of language back in (speech is the 'solid' of verse, is the secret of a poem's energy)" (Olson, "Projective" 18, 20; emphasis in original). While Pound, Ernest Fenollosa, Saussure, and Nichol focused on the link between the visual dimension of language and the spoken word, the *Tish* authors held that the optical materiality of language was a mark of hollowed, empty speech. Davey, editor of the first series of *Tish*, would explain his disinterest in visual poetry in other contexts,[2] but meanwhile the

---

2 As Davey notes, "Indeed, visual poems were outside of the oral and linguistically based poetries of Tish 1 to 19, as well as outside my own practice" (*When* 232).

magazine never published any examples of the genre despite its thriving in Vancouver at the time. Thus, the name *Tish* embeds a satirical poetics into the entire project: having stripped language of the vitality of speech via the visually oriented anagram, "*Tish*" doubles the satire by anagrammatizing effluvia.

2

The first and only instance of the word "shit" in *Tish* 1–19 occurs in a letter to the editors by Mike Matthews in the fourth issue: "Title is good – too bad it couldn't have been just plain 'shit' but at least this way you get in a parody of *Prism*, and that's long needed doing" (*Tish*[3] 72).

3

Tish was the first magazine in Canada to take its name from an anagram. It is not the only Canadian magazine named by a neologism, nor is it the first as such. A decade earlier, Ezra Pound had inadvertently provided the name to the Montreal-based magazine *CIV/n* (1953–4), edited by Aileen Collins, in a letter to Louis Dudek (Irvine 244). While this is technically an abbreviation, in the same manner that *Tish* is technically an anagram, both have become neologisms in their development of a particular style of modernist literature associated with their name. The idea of the neologism stems from eighteenth-century France, where, beyond just designating newly coined words, it was used more specifically to denote the need for a new word arising because of some particularly innovative practice in literature. Both literary communities surrounding *Tish* and *CIV/n* were deeply connected to the emerging Black Mountain and San Francisco Renaissance schools of poetry, and both little magazines published many of the New American poets associated with those schools. As neologisms for an emerging modernist literary community in Canada, separated by geography, they share a siring influence.

After *CIV/n*, in 1957, Dudek founded the literary magazine *Delta* to complement his publishing work with Contact Press. In October 1962, *Delta* featured a special profile of Vancouver poets, including *Tish* authors Davey, Reid, Kearns, Bowering, David Bromige, Matthews, and Patrick Lane, with the help of Frank Davey. This was not the first Eastern publication to print *Tish* work, but it does present a poignant moment of reconciliation between Eastern and Western Canadian literary movements – unified by a shared

---

3 All page references to poems, editorials, and letters in the first nineteen issues are from *Tish No. 1–19*, edited by Frank Davey.

interest in New American poetics. Meanwhile, Davey, in his lead editorial for the issue, notes that the Vancouver literary scene had divided into "three distinct and purposeful groups of young poets" ("The Present Scene" 1). Though "these groups are all so different," he tries to unify them all in opposition to "the academic cleverness of [Earle] Birney" (2). Davey was unaware of the depth of Birney's interest in and commitment to visual poetic forms. In his book on Birney, Davey dismissed his various forays into visual work as the dabblings of a "linguistically oriented poet for whom concrete techniques are auxillary [*sic*]" (*Earle Birney* 63). Birney, however, published some of Canada's earliest visual poems and a landmark manifesto called "Poets and Painters" in 1957 that called for the fusion of the two arts and the "spontaneous working together of independent artists and their poetic contemporaries" (150). *Delta*, the next year, published what has been widely considered to be the first visual poem in Canada – Pierre Coupey's "The Alphabet of Blood" (Winter 1964). As previously mentoned, Coupey moved to Vancouver in 1965 hoping to work on a master's degree with Birney, who had, alas, already moved on.

4

Tish has been praised as a foundational literary magazine of Canadian modernism, but it is not immediately obvious why it has accrued this stature and influence. The magazine's impact cannot be explained by its primacy, for it was not the first modernist magazine in Canada (there are many examples dating up to half a century earlier[4]), nor was it even the first literary magazine on the UBC campus. *Raven* was an active literary magazine at UBC in the 1950s, followed, more pertinently, by *Prism* in 1959, which was founded under the tutelage of British Surrealist Michael Bullock as an extension of the UBC creative writing program. The second issue of that magazine featured work by Lionel Kearns, who would become the most frequent contributor to *Tish* not on the masthead.[5] Kearns's work first appears in the second issue of *Tish* (the first contribution by a non-editor), where his short biography describes him as a "lover of Mexico and Prism magazine" (44). *Tish* was not even the first, second, or third literary magazine in Canada devoted to exploring local engagement with New American poetics. Why was it so important?

One answer appears in the words of critic and poet Andrew Klobucar, who suggests that "Tish helped organize the Vancouver writing scene as a new site of

---

4 See Dean Irvine's "Immigrants, Exiles, and Expatriates" in *The Oxford Handbook of Modernisms*, which locates the emergence of Canadian modernist publication in the fin-de-siècle generation at the end of the nineteenth century (873–4).

5 Kearns was, in fact, invited to become an editor, but declined "because I couldn't agree with the ideas that all my funny friends had about writing and poetry" (qtd. in Niechoda and Hunter 92). The *Tish* collective would eventually publish his *Songs of Circumstance* under their imprint TISHBooks, which published only three books in total (though more had been planned).

literary production, and the group quickly established itself as the West Coast locus of 'avant-garde' writing [...] Its writers wrote not only to express isolation, but to end it" (14). Despite this generative role in the local cultural economy, Brian Fawcett offers a more circumspect and less generous assessment: for him, *Tish* represents

> a minor movement in Canadian poetry indebted to the New American Poetry movement in the U.S. [...] It's been a vehicle for lucrative academic careers for Davey and to a lesser extent for several of the others involved in the movement; and it has been an industrial resource pit that several generations of CanLit academics [...] have made careers out of mining. (n. pag.)

While the magazine had a (however major or minor) regional and even national role in the formation of national and avant-garde literatures, its most demonstrable impact was in helping to launch the careers of a set of influential Canadian writers and to help get those authors connected to literary communities in Eastern Canada and the United States. This is not an uncommon fact for most little magazines, yet the success of the *Tish* stable of authors has been remarkable: of the editors, George Bowering became the country's founding Poet Laureate and a two-time winner of the Governor General's Award (1969 and 1980), Fred Wah became the country's fifth Poet Laureate after winning the Governor General's Award (1985), and Frank Davey became the Carl F. Klinck Chair of Canadian Literature at the University of Western Ontario (1990). Combined, these three alone have published over 150 books of poetry, fiction, nonfiction, and literary criticism, alongside more than a thousand publications in magazines across the continent and beyond. Other influential contributing editors to the magazine include Daphne Marlatt (a member of the Order of Canada) and Dan McLeod (founder of the *Georgia Straight* alternative newspaper).

In the wider context of North American poetics, *Tish* has been acknowledged as the mouthpiece of the local literary community that gave rise to the Vancouver Poetry Conference in 1963, which was indeed an important turning point in the dissemination and promotion of both Black Mountain and San Francisco Renaissance poetics, especially as aligned, outside of the United States. As Alan Golding notes, the conference was the first gathering of these American authors after their grouping in Don Allen's *The New American Poetry* anthology of 1959 (195).

5

There are, in fact, at least two different and distinct manifestations of *Tish*, poignantly if coincidentally divided by the VPC. A more accurate description of the division is to note that it falls between the first nineteen issues and the subsequent twenty-five issues, which were edited by a different editorial board. Frank Davey is listed as editor for the first nineteen issues with "Contributing Editors" James Reid, George Bowering, Fred Wah, and David Dawson. Bowering is absent from the masthead in *Tish* 12, but restored in 13.

The next editorial period was much more unstable and difficult to map coherently. Dawson is listed as the editor for issues 20–24, with an editorial board made up of Peter Auxier, Dave Cull, Dan McLeod, Daphne Buckle (later Marlatt), and Gladys Hindmarch. The editorial board was in heavy flux for the next two years: Peter Auxier disappears from the masthead in *Tish* 24 (May 1964) only to reappear in *Tish* 26 (October 1964); Buckle is replaced by Bob Hogg in *Tish* 25 (June 1964); Cull exits with *Tish* 26 (October 1964), and Hogg leaves by *Tish* 27 (November 1964). McLeod became sole editor in *Tish* 25, but in *Tish* 28 (1965), the remaining group of four – Dawson, Auxier, McLeod, and Hindmarch – are all listed for the first time as editors of equal standing. After Hindmarch departed in *Tish* 30 (June 1965), and Dawson in *Tish* 31 (November 1965), only Auxier and McLeod remained. The two continued to edit the magazine alone until *Tish* 41 (February 1968), when the editorial board was reshuffled again to include Brad Robinson, Colin Stuart, and McLeod. Stan Persky edited issues 42 (1968), 43 (1968), 44 (February 1969), and 45 (April 1969).

Stan Persky, email interview, 27 September 2017

Behind all the names and dates, there is a tangle of interpersonal relationships. [Robin] Blaser and I arrived in Vancouver in spring 1966 from San Francisco (we lived together from about 1963 to sometime in 1968), and Rick Byrne was a student at UBC (from Montreal) with whom I was having a long affair. (Apologies for cluttering this up with used condoms full of wisdom, tubes of lubricant, and other detritus of affection.) I should mention that I was also a student at UBC during this period, and a campus activist.

[With *Tish* 44] I was the editor, and it was the first (and only) issue to carry the address of 2249 York Ave., which was a Kitsilano A-frame house a block up from the beach where several of us lived in the "York Street Commune." I had "inherited" the Tish mimeograph from Dan McLeod or Brad Robinson and it was installed in the basement of this house. The house became the base for Vancouver Community Press which later turned into New Star Books in the early 1970s, and continues to exist. The book series was, I think, inspired by a Warren Tallman admonition to me to pay attention to the local writers, and the series included George Bowering's Autobiology and my The Day, as well as chapbooks by a dozen or so poets. In between the last issue of Tish and the press there was The Georgia Straight Writing Supplement, a newspaper literary magazine of poetry and prose edited by Dennis Wheeler and me and which periodically appeared within regular issues of the Georgia Straight. It was graphically designed by Brian DeBeck, who also did a lot of the physical work on Tish and the press (he and I lived together in the commune for about 5 years, and he eventually married Karen Tallman – this could probably all be turned into a TV mini-series). So the end of Tish was "caused" by a political idea that poetry (and literary writing generally) ought to seek a broader, popular audience, rather than continuing the little magazine tradition. All of this of course connected to the political currents of the period and the question, What is writing for (in practical terms)? (We knew the unproblematic answer in literary terms)

However, what would be *Tish* 44 (February 1969) includes a prank announcement of a new editorial period, an imaginary third series that began, covertly, three issues earlier in February 1968. The further details provided in the editorial attempt to only confuse the question of who was in charge and where were they going:

Now as you noticed, Tish 44 is called Tish D. While this may not mean much to the average Joe, it will (hopefully) send bibliographers, librarians, rare butterfly collectors, litter-rare-y experts, etc, climbing up the ivy covered walls. See, the reason why is because big numbers for little magazines are stupid. So we hadda make a decision. One choice would be just to call it Volume 4, Number 4, ten issues to a volume. But that wouldn't be accurate. The first series of Tish was 1–19, managed by Frank Davey. Now if the second batch 20–40 was really a volume, then we would call 41 volume 3 and renumber correspondingly. (The serial cataloguer in Moosejaw just died of cardiac arrest.) But 20–40 was a wandering in the desert period. However, it looks like 41 begins a new series of Tish. So we could call it by alphabet. But then again we don't want to be committed to go all the way to z, because ya can't tell in

Figure 1.2 Page detail from *Tish*, in search of money. Source: Private collection of the author.

advance how long a series is gonna go. Tune in next tishue, same time, same station, blah blah blah.

Also, it's now proper to reveal that since issue 41, Tish has been under the general editorship of Karen Tallman.

D (as in, guess what that you smoke, drop or shoot up) is a Tish-takes-a-trip issue, held together by the fact that all the writers are involved in communes, free schools, experimental programs, hippie-rural-reconstruction and the like. (Reading it again, more seriously, it's an issue of folk-writing). (Persky n. pag.; emphasis added)

In private correspondence, Persky confirmed that it was merely a "joke" that teenager Karen Tallman had become the editor. Persky noted that the rather condescending joke stemmed from the fact that the issue was composed largely of writing by her friends from the free school. As another example of literary hijinks in the issue, Persky attributes his own poem "Five Variations on the Earth" to Jack Spicer. The self-deprecating notes in Persky's editorial – the "wandering in the desert" quip and fear of big numbers for a diminutive publication – provide a remarkable contrast to the overconfident editorials in the first series.

6

The most important issue of *Tish* is the very first issue, published in September 1961, which begins with the self-declaration: "TISH is a moving and vocal mag" (Davey, "Editorial" 13). It is the fact of the magazine's existence and its aesthetical difference – which includes exploration of proprioceptive lyricism ("moving") and speech-based metrics ("vocal") – from the established norms of Canadian literary publication that mark the arrival of a unique literary community in Vancouver, as in Canada. These aspects of the magazine's legacy are firmly established in the first issue. The first issue is primarily oriented toward self-definition and self-actualization and for this reason includes six editorials, one by each of the contributing editors and two by Davey. In these editorials, they outline the magazine's emergence from a specific "siring movement" (13) that I have already referred to in this chapter as the New American poetics. Poets and artists referred to by name in the issue include Marc Chagall (15), Paul Goodman, Robert Browning, William Wordsworth, Charles Olson, Gerry Mulligan, Stan Getz (17–19), Olson (again), and Allen Ginsberg (19–21). The last page entices readers with the promise of an essay on Philip Whalen by Reid in the next issue. This issue concludes with a euphemistic pun elaborating on the anagram root of their name: "TISH is a fine kettle of fecis" (30).

7

Tish 1 includes twenty poems by members of the editorial board. Every subsequent issue would include contributions from at least three of the five editors and often more than that. Though they would quickly open up the magazine to outside contributors, the five editors largely drove the content of the first nineteen issues.[6]

8

Tish 1–19 itself can be divided into at least two groupings, delineated by the shift in their motto from "A Magazine of Vancouver Poetry" to "A Poetry Newsletter." *Tish* 4, the first with the altered masthead, begins the introduction of the new position in a rather confused and contradictory manner. On the one hand, the poems by two Montreal poets are accompanied by a statement of the magazine's intentional exclusivity, aesthetic singularity, and rejection of eclecticism: "TISH guest pages are intended merely to show what the editors liked best of the material received. We often reject good poems; we publish only poems such as these which we believe reflect a purpose and technique somewhat similar to our own" (75). Despite that singular focus, an editorial note in the same issue attempts to universalize the *Tish* collective: "Tish is designed primarily as a poetry newsletter, to the intention of keeping poets & other interested people informed on what is happening in Vancouver – its

6 Overall, despite their connections to broader Canadian and North American literary communities, the other poets (forty contributors in total) published were heavily concentrated in the UBC community, including David Cull, who published in twelve issues and who would become a contributing editor in issue 20, Lionel Kearns, with twenty-four poems and one essay published in eleven different issues, Dan McLeod, published in four issues, Robert Frances Grady, three issues, R.S. Lane, three issues, David Bromige (a previous editor of *Raven* magazine), three issues, and Warren Tallman, two issues.

writing, its tastes. We are looking for the latest work of poets anywhere" (88). David Dawson's editorial in *Tish* 5 explains the policy shift in more detail:

> TISH is now a poetry newsletter, an organ designed to tell its readers WHAT'S GOING ON in Vancouver. That is, we seek to define the scene as completely as possible. We have discarded the format of a magazine of poetry because we find it too narrow (or too broad) a framework for what we have in mind.
>
> After four issues we now know what we want to do. [...] We print poems which conform to our taste, poems which move somewhat in the same direction as our own. This is true, not only of poems submitted by the readers, but of the poems submitted by the various co-editors as well. The desired result is a selection of poetry which indicates our poetic stance, which defines our scene. (91)

Notably, the ever-increasing differences between Vancouver-at-large and the more localized literary clique within UBC are elided. Despite this shift in policy toward more openness and greater representation of Vancouver's literary community, *Tish* 5 includes work by the co-editors, two poems by Lionel Kearns, and only one "guest" poem by influential New American and Black Mountain poet Larry Eigner. The move to definition of the Vancouver scene includes a significant effort at erasure of efforts beyond their cohort.

Tish 6 introduces a further change in editorial mandate: "The readers have finally convinced us that poeticizing ad ad etc. was not getting us anywhere, and that poetry was infinitely more valuable. This month we have poetry" (111). Subsequently, the number of editorials sharply declined, while the number of contributors outside of their inner circle rose significantly for the remainder of *Tish*'s run, even across editorial periods. Ironically, considering the shift away from editorializing, the core assignment given to participants at the VPC in 1963 was the production of *Tish*-style editorials on their own work: as the ad in *Tish* informs, "On the basis of these meetings students will write a critique explaining and justifying their own verse practice" (396). Gladys Maria Hindmarch's journal was published in 2020 as part of her collected writings, *Wanting Everything* (edited by Karis Shearer and Deanna Fong). Instead of polemic, though, her writing turns to chance and diffidence to think through the significance and impact of her experience: "Thinking about what I have written I realize how very little I was there at all" ("The Vancouver" 201).

9

The second most important issue of *Tish* is the twenty-first issue. In this issue, the little magazine finally fulfils the mandate of a poetry newsletter better than any of the preceding issues by directly reporting on the Vancouver Poetry Conference

University of British Columbia, Summer 1963 Poetry Offerings

INFORMATION

From July 24 to August 16, 1963 the university will offer (1) English 410, a credit course in poetry writing, (2) an Extension Department non-credit course in contemporary poetry, and (3) a series of four Friday Readings -- as follows:

1. English 410 (credit course), $66. Limited to 45 students, the course will be conducted by Robert Creeley, Allen Ginsberg, and Charles Olson with Margaret Avison, Robert Duncan and Denise Levertov contributing. It will consist of morning lecture sessions and afternoon workshop sessions. The morning sessions will consist of lectures, panels and discussions by the poets on the basis of which students will write a critique demonstrating their understanding of modern verse writing. For the afternoon workshop sessions the students will divide into groups of 15 and meet with the poets to discuss the problems and possibilities of their own verse practice. The poets will rotate among the groups so that, for instance, one group of students will meet with Mr. Creeley the first week, with Mr. Ginsberg the second and with Mr. Olson the third; etc. On the basis of these meetings the students will write a critique explaining and justifying their own verse practice. Students registered for this course will be expected to attend the non-credit evening sessions.*

1a. English 410, Auditors, $33. A limited number of auditors, who may attend the morning lecture sessions but not the afternoon workshop sessions, will be accepted. If such is your desire, please indicate on the accompanying application.

2. Extension Department, non-credit course, $12 ($6 for credit course students). The course will consist of 11 Monday, Wednesday, Friday evening meetings from Wednesday July 24 through Friday August 16, 1963. Margaret Avison, Robert Creeley, Robert Duncan, Allen Ginsberg, Denise Levertov and Charles Olson will contribute readings and panel discussions designed to improve understanding of contemporary poetry. No pre-requisites, no assignments. For information contact Department of University Extension, U.B.C., Vancouver, B. C.

3. Friday Readings, $5. On successive Fridays, July 26, August 2, August 9 and August 16, Robert Duncan, Allen Ginsberg, Denise Levertov and Charles Olson will read their poetry. These readings are part of the non-credit course but others may attend them as a separate series. Tickets available from Department of University Extension or from Vancouver bookstores, approximately June 1st.

*NB Because enrollment for the credit course is limited to 45 students, permission to enroll is necessary. Those interested should consult the accompanying application and forward the appropriate information to Robert Creeley, English Department, University of British Columbia, Vancouver, B. C. at once: first come, first serve. Notices of acceptance will be forwarded as soon as possible.

Figure 1.3 Original informational press release for English 410, which has come to be known as the Vancouver Poetry Conference. Source: Simon Fraser Special Collections and Rare Books, Warren Tallman Fonds, MsC 26.

and documenting "WHAT'S GOING ON in Vancouver" (Dawson Editorial 1). The VPC, which was not really a conference but has stabilized in the popular and scholarly consciousness under that title, ran from 24 July to 16 August 1963 and was advertised in *Tish* 18 under the oblique title "Poetry Offerings" (396). It was to be "(1) English 410, a crdit [*sic*] course in poetry writing / (2) an Extension Department non-credit course in contemporary poetry / (3) a series of four Friday Readings." It was, less circumspectly, a galvanizing moment in North American poetics that grew out of the same community of interest in Vancouver that had led to the creation of *Tish* in the first place. In many respects, it was the culmination of the aesthetic questions that the *Tish* editors had been exploring since their initiation into modernist writing. The Vancouver "novitiates" were now suddenly given the opportunity to sit in attendance with the writers who had inspired them. In many respects, it is appropriate that the first editorial period ended just prior to the VPC with this significant moment of arrival into the midst of contemporary poetics.

The first independent issue by the new editorial board, *Tish* 20, is a transitional document. It is rather overwhelmed by the retrospective voices of the old editors George Bowering, Frank Davey, Fred Wah, and David Dawson as they seek to make sense of their former magazine and its accomplishments. By this point in 1963, the ambitions of the original editors had shifted significantly: their short-lived experiments with book publishing under the TISHBooks banner had failed and been shuttered, as had their extension into experimental prose through the partner magazine *Motion* (whose sixth and final issue was released in December 1962). As evidenced by the editorials in *Tish* 20, there was a decided lack of interest in the future of the magazine. Davey concludes with notable ambivalence, "[T]he magazine may continue to be Vancouver's most popular literary magazine for many more issues" (Editorial 10). Between these familiar editorials, however, there is a surprising dearth of the old garde's poetic voices. Instead, the poetry is supplied exclusively by five of the six new editors (only Hindmarch did not contribute any creative work) and one short poem by *Tish* friend and eventual editor Bob Hogg. While *Tish* 20 is a transitional issue, looking backwards for the purpose of memorialization, it also performs some of the same self-definition and self-actualization gestures as the very first issue of *Tish*. Only one of the poems in the issue, however, introduces anything resembling an aesthetic break from the previous editorial mandate. Hogg's poem on the last page of the issue announces a "strange communion" that seems to undo the relevance of the fundamental categories that orient New American poetics – especially the notion of the I and the individual as the central conduit for energy transfer in the poem (14). Poignantly, his poem was published above an announcement noting that the VPC was "happening / here now" (14) and that the next issue would attempt to respond to the event.

Tish 21 manages to look back at the just-finished conference from an entirely new aesthetic perspective. The break is significant and is poignantly announced by a lead editorial by Dawson on the cover:

OLSON/CREELEY/LEVERTOV/DUNCAN/GINSBERG/WHALEN/AVISON

a document of response: but how to give the texture of those 3 wks, of the poets & poems, of that (to me) "event" in the larger sense of the word? to record, point by point, what was said is a massive task, & one which might not be useful here & now. impressions then, of what was said. some facts. poems of that 3 wk period. "poetic gossip." extensions of the event. further events.

the only possible form: a type of <u>collage</u>.

so, from the journals kept by various people during the conference, bits & pieces. whatever we found of interest, or amusing, or revealing. flashes of insight. moments of anger, frustration. all more or less "cut-up," in some mad order – to give (perhaps more accurately than in any other way) the texture of the conference: a document of response. (1)

The editorial establishes a new paradigm for literary production beyond New American poetics. The shift from a proprioceptive (a situated-body-in-the-landscape consciousness)[7] to a collage modality signals a shift from the dominance of the ear to the eye, from an active role in the creation of a locus through a singular consciousness to the more passive representation of the multiple consciousness and multiple loci coexisting in the world. As Daphne Marlatt notes: "We didn't know how to capture it all. There was so much, so many people involved. We had to open things up" (Interview 12 December 2019).

Beyond a handful of conventional lyric poems, a collagic compilation of thoughts and observations from the journals and notes of the contributing editors dominates the issue. These commentaries range from quotes and phrases by the featured poets to reflections on the shared attributes of their aesthetic and even to the attire they wear: "Philip Whalen, a clean-looking blonde haired man. His blue shirt is unbuttoned Belafonte style. He wears a tweed jacket, and white running shoes" (4).[8] "Duncan is smartly attired in an orange shirt, orange socks, and

---

7 The focus of this book is not on Olson's poetics per se, nor on the New American moment, but on how they were received and taken up by the Vancouver authors. For a more details study of Olson directly, see Robert Von Hallberg's *Charles Olson: The Scholar's Art* (1978), Alan Golding's *Go Contrary, Go Sing: Charles Olson's Early Poetry and Poetics* (1980), Judith Halden-Sullivan's *The Topology of Being: The Poetics of Charles Olson* (1991), and Paul Christensen's *Charles Olson: Call Him Ishmael* (2014) for more.

8 The editorial that spans the issue has no clear author or any clear title. I have listed this text as published by the editor David Dawson under the generic heading "Editorial."

Figure 1.4 Allen Ginsberg at the VPC at University of British Columbia, 1963. Photo by Karen Tallman. Used with permission.

white canvas shoes." "Allen Ginsberg, wearing a dark, crumpled shirt unbuttoned so that the white undershirt is showing. The shoes he wears are worn away at the toes" (5). "Charles Olson in appearance is somewhat reminiscent of pictures of Papa Hemingway. He is immensely tall. His beard is grey, he wears workmen's khaki pants, a shirt, and carries and embroidered bag" (6). The overall effect of the collaged journal is to convey the intimate discourse and style of the New American poets among themselves and the intense interest in their presentation by the *Tish* editors. These poets were famous, beloved writers; consequently, the editors' interests went beyond the instructions on how to write to include observations on poetic comportment, on how to present oneself as a poet and as a creative person in the contemporary world. In her journal on the conference, Gladys Maria Hindmarch openly muses, "I wonder who I would most like to live like, to have as a model" ("The Vancouver" 204). In considering the suitability of each of the writers (Levertov was too "prissy"; Creeley "very nervous"), she makes clear to distinguish their writing from their bearing. Marlatt describes Ginsberg sitting with the students in the gardens and counselling them on general life concerns between classroom sessions (*The Line*). This focus on presentation and presence, of course, connects to the poetics under consideration: "Robert – the only place where you have any care and attention is where you <u>are</u>. There must be a 'criterion of completeness,' ie, how much awareness have we in preparation to meet our concerns? Why write poetry but to find the second where you are?" (6). It is unclear why not, but still notable that the attire of Avison and Levertov, the two featured female poets, is not reported on.[9] Hardly a sign of a conscious challenge to gender norms and expectations, the omission is rather more evidence of the general neglect the two female poets have received in critical responses to the conference.

By the seventh page of the journal collage there is a shift in tone as the entries begin to highlight differences between the featured poets as well as the importance of other aesthetics (such as the cut-up and collage) that have not been addressed in the conference:

> The best way to find out what <u>words</u> are saying, is to cut them up, rearrange them as Burroughs did with Time [magazine] – instead of, say, "short, fat hairy Harry Bridges," say, "short, fat, hair American Foreign policy" and all bias comes through beautifully. Burroughs also used two transistor radios with different news programs, one in each ear, and colors flashing, and even with his own writing to discover particular habits until now he can do it in his mind, without cutting it up. (8)

This passage signals not only Burroughs's novelty, but also the sublimation and extension of his aesthetic breakthrough into a new line of literary production. In other words, the editors were attempting to follow Burroughs's aesthetic approach, with its radical distrust of language, while reporting on an event that celebrated a very different school of writing and approach to language. Brion Gysin, the Canadian source of Burroughs's experiments with the cut-ups, is not mentioned at all.

10

This chapter, this assemblage of observations, takes its form and title from *Tish* 21: the first manifestation of the new beginning, the new line, promised by the conference.

11

Tish 1–19 editors who attended the VPC: Fred Wah, George Bowering, David Dawson, and Jamie Reid.

---

9 New York avant-garde poet Carol Bergé, however, did report on the women's clothing in her book on the VPC: "Denise is a white Peter Pan collar; Margaret Avison is a comfortable wollen sweater of indefinable age or color" (*Vancouver Report* 5).

Figure 1.5 Charles Olson, Vancouver, 1963. Photo by Karen Tallman. Used with permission.

Frank Davey, the only editor to not participate in the event, later tended to dismiss its overall significance. As he sniffed retrospectively in his memoirs of that summer:

> Me, I feel as if much of what I've done in Vancouver is completed, and much more needs to be worked through. I'm looking past the summer toward quiet moments for writing. [... The Vancouver Poetry Conference] also feels like part of the past rather than the future. [...] There are rumours that the writing workshop is less rich than people expect. (*When* 178–9)

He was less concerned about engaging with and/or reminiscing on the past, less distracted by the future, in his *Tish* 20 editorial, in his introductory essay to the book he edited on *Tish* 1–19, in his recent memoir, *When Tish Happens*, and in his frequent public talks on poetry in the period.

Tish 20–44 editors who attended the VPC: Peter Auxier, David Cull, David Dawson, Gladys Maria Hindmarch, Dan McLeod, Daphne Marlatt (née Buckle), Robert Hogg, and Karen Tallman.

Daphne Marlatt took a great deal of influence and direction from the event: "Everyone who was at that conference, at that summer school, had a personal stake in it. [...] It was exciting" (*The Line*). Robert Hogg usefully notes that it was not just important for the young Vancouver authors: "It was an avant-garde moment for the poets involved as well" (*The Line*). Olson himself, according to Robert Creeley's biographers, claimed that his four-hour reading on the last day of the conference was the best reading he had ever delivered (Faas and Trombacco 293). He was found in seclusion afterwards, emotionally drained with tears running down his face.

Lionel Kearns, the most frequent contributor to *Tish*, observes: "The conference was going pretty well twenty-four hours a day for some people, if not all people who attended. It was unlike anything that had happened before. So, it was a beginning" (*The Line*).

Tish editors who attended the VPC reunion on 14 August 2009 at the University of British Columbia: George Bowering, Fred Wah, Jamie Reid, Daphne Marlatt, Gladys Maria Hindmarch, and Robert Hogg.

12

What is collage? Art historians tend to date the birth of collage to 1912, when Pablo Picasso glued a small oilcloth to a still-life painting to create a work that he eventually called *Still Life with Chair Caning* (Hopkins 5). There are precedents for the act that stretch back to Mary Delaney (1700–88), the happy widow who found herself freed from an unhappy marriage, and who at age seventy-two took to paper and scissors to create astounding botanical images of flowers. She called them her "flower mosaicks" (Peacock 4). Church art, too, has various examples of incorporating three-dimensional objects into chapel frescos, but none of those precedents prepared audiences for the jarring juxtaposition of objects in Picasso's work. It marked the beginning of a new mode of aesthetic enquiry that challenged the separation of organic and mechanical production of art. The oilcloth includes the reproduction of a photograph of a chair caning, and thus fundamentally disturbs the notion of the integrity of the work of art: Picasso's painting is infected with another unacknowledged artist's work, indeed, the mechanical *reproduction* of another's work. Hopkins argues that collage was "a complex new hybrid in which the philosophical core of modernism received its most literal expression[, art as] an assemblage of fragments and various points of view" (5). The letters "JOU" jut out from Picasso's canvas, taken from "JOURNAL" (the document of quotidian experience) but parsed to highlight a new disruptive playfulness of art games ("jouer" means "to play," but "jou" is also Old French for "ego"). Emanating from the visual arts, in this way collage functions as a means of alienating the artist from their own work by privileging multiple consciousnesses rather than an individual consciousness, and approaching language as an external material, or tool, rather than as the organic expression of an individual's soul. As Elza Adamowicz observes, "[t]he raw material of collage is already cooked" (31).

Collage shares the production of a work's meaning between the artist, the audience/reader, and the previous producers of the material collaged. In doing so, it

Figure 1.6 Pablo Picasso, *Still Life with Chair Caning* (1912).

violates the core principles of intention, expression, and ownership of a work of art. The possibility of a unified, harmonious work of art surrenders to a network of evocations, associations, and polyvocalisms emanating from the work. Many of the old orders falter in its wake.

The cut-up is a literary extension of the collage technique. Experiments with collage led Tristan Tzara to invent the cut-up technique, which he originally termed "un poème dadaïste" as an extension of the Dadaist preference of "juxtaposition over sequential development" (Adamowicz 48). The reference to the cut-up method in Dawson's editorial above, however, refers specifically to the experimental prose work of Burroughs. Dawson mentions *Time*, a cut-up of *Time* magazine published in 1965 (where and how the editors saw this text before its broad circulation remains unclear). In the 1960s, Burroughs published three novels composed through the cut-up method: *The Soft Machine* (1961), *The Ticket That Exploded* (1962), and *Nova Express* (1964). As previously noted, he developed the technique from Brion Gysin, the Canadian avant-gardist mentioned in the introduction who had lived in Vancouver, who learned the technique from Tzara himself in Paris in the 1920s. Gysin was the only Canadian member of Breton's Surrealist group before the Second World War. He is not mentioned in the editorial collage of *Tish* 21, nor was he mentioned in the three-week proceedings of the VPC, even though Allen Ginsberg left the conference to visit Gysin's mother and pay his respects (Geiger 21).

13

The New American conception of the open form was infused with the spirit of collage, though marked by a poignant rejection of the value of unnatural (i.e., machinic) production as a critique or exposure of the fraudulence of the integrity of the work of art. Instead, they worked to re-establish a discourse of natural, unified, and holistic production within the realm of artifice. For Duncan, who among the New American poets invested the most in the idea of collage, the charge of poetic language develops from a notion of the ensemble toward an electric, mythical collectivism: "My sense of the total poem is that it is a community where every word is a worker. And none of them get to be idle" (Faas, "An Interview" 4). Peter Michelson critiques the politics of Duncan's notion of the ensemble and his use of a stabilizing cosmology within his poetry. For Michelson, Duncan's notion of multiplicity hinges upon Hegelian dialectics, and serves cosmic unity, rather than upon any attuned sense of alienation, multiplicity, or the historical, materialist dimension of myth and religion (25). The material, historical contingencies "cannot affect the cosmic order because 'IT' is an idea not subject to material influence" (32). Collage, in contrast, is a materialist, alienating method. The cut at the heart of the method that rips something from its material context and transforms it into an altered thing, a disjunctive presence in uncontrollable juxtaposition to other dislocated things, is at core predicated on alienation, fragmentation, and the dissolve of master narratives that might unify art and culture (or that, finally, motivate the troublesome workers who resist contributing to the production of meaning). Duncan's "grand collage" conception of poetry, then, presents an oxymoron in its attempt to re-establish cosmic unity by means of an essentially disruptive, aleatoric method. Similarly, it betrays an internal contradiction between form and content. Ironically, Olson's essay "Projective Verse," which maps out the new laws of open verse, was built out of "an assemblage of fragments" from his letters to Creeley that he collaged together (Molesworth 60). Olson's dicta on harmony and unification (such as "PAST IS PRESENT AT THE MOMENT OF WRITING") contradict, as Molesworth admits, "the radicality, the utter disruption" of collage (63).

To be clear, it is not ironic or contradictory but rather a testament to the close proximity of collage and New American poetics that Duncan's lifelong lover and

Figures 1.7, 1.8 1953 flyer for the King Ubu Gallery in San Francisco, featuring a portrait of Jess Collins and Robert Duncan by Elmer Bischoff.

partner was the visual artist Jess Collins, who specialized in the production of large-scale collages. Collins's work explored harsh and dissonant juxtapositions from wildly disparate cultural contexts. While the themes were similar to Duncan's with regard to a contemporary spiritual crisis, and the imagery was decidedly mythopoeic, and the two even collaborated on work together, Collins's collages worked in satiric and absurdist modes, whereas Duncan's poetry (as Michelson argues) was fundamentally idealistic. It is thus poignant that Collins, with Duncan's support, opened up the King Ubu Gallery in San Francisco in 1952 as a tribute to the 'pataphysical satirist Alfred Jarry. The gallery collapsed, however, and was quickly renamed the 6 Gallery, after the number of individuals involved, when Jack Spicer took control in 1954. Robert Rauschenberg, a master assemblist and collagist, was a student at Black Mountain College in 1948, 1951, and 1952 but did not make any collage works while there (Molesworth 60).

14

The first word out of the mouth of Jarry's most famous character, King Ubu, is "Shit" (Act 1, Scene 1 n. pag.).

Figure 1.9 Program for the opening performance of *Ubu roi* by Alfred Jarry on 10 December 1896 in Paris at the Théâtre de l'Œuvre.

15

The first words of Canadian 'pataphysics, being the local extrapolation of Jarry's project spearheaded by Steve McCaffery and bpNichol, were published in *Open Letter* – the journal founded and edited by Frank Davey after his departure from *Tish*.[10] The journal was unique in Canada for developing the *Tish* editorials into more protracted and diverse essays that went beyond poets explaining and justifying their own verse practice but stopped short of the academic peer-review model.

10 In 2003, McCaffery became the David Gray Chair of Poetry and Letters at the State University of New York at Buffalo, where Charles Olson and Robert Creeley both taught, and where Fred Wah went after leaving Vancouver and *Tish* for graduate school. McCaffery's post is in the Poetics Program, a program founded by Creeley in 1991. Davey devoted two issues of his journal *Open Letter* to essays on McCaffery's work, issue 6.9 (Fall 1987) and 14.7 (Fall 2011). McCaffery, in turn, edited issue 15.2 (Spring 2013), a special issue on Charles Olson. *Tish* editors Fred Wah and George Bowering also had special issues on their work. None of the women involved in *Tish* have been so honoured in the journal, which ceased publication in 2013.

Thus, while McCaffery and Nichol's work evinces an approach to language that is anathema to the *Tish* poetics, the creation of a space in which these two avant-garde poets were allowed to cultivate their practice and hone their "reservoirs of reported readings" (McCaffery, Introduction 12) is a reflection of the legacy of *Tish*.

16

The first discussion of collage in *Tish* appears in issue 17, with New York Fluxus poet Carol Bergé's short piece called "collage" – an ekphrastic response to Picasso's *Still Life with Chair Caning* (358). The piece, not written as a collage, creates a coherent consciousness that unifies the discrete images in the collage into a narrative of personal discovery. The meanings of the disjunctive images in Picasso's original are focalized through symbolic interpretation: "paris guanajuanto paris Firenze / shapes of eyes and hands // and now a simple closet / of myself knowing / white candle for belief / red candle for the past" (358). This endeavour, unlike the collage that inspired it, connects well to Frank Davey's prescription for good poetry in his essay "One Man Looks at 'Projective Verse,'" which he defines as "the personal song of a man interacting with the universe around and inside him" (103). In contrast, in collage the poet commits the sin of "sprawl," that is to say of "committing the unnatural [...] in a form 'outside himself' – an artificial self-created foreign both to nature and to himself as part of nature" (101, 102). Bergé would gain notoriety for publishing in 1964 the only book-length study of the Vancouver Poetry Conference, in fact an extended condemnation of the unnatural "asskissing of the 'foreign' Black Mountain school in Canada" (*Vancouver Report* 3). Her complaints range from the colonialism of Vancouver writers (including the obscenity of the naming of things in British Columbia after George Washington) to aesthetics, critiquing the organizers and speakers for "missing Canada [... T]he Vancouver Seminar was not, in that sense, seminal. I don't think anything bright, sharp or new came through" (16). The book was published in New York City by the less-constrained literary journal *Fuck You: A Magazine of the Arts*. Later, she became the sole editor of the avant-garde publication *Center*, which sought to foreground interdisciplinary, self-disruptive experiments with language.

In contrast, language, for Davey, as revealed in these early editorials, is a binding agent between an individual soul and the world they inhabit. At the time, he shared this belief with the other *Tish* poets: with George Bowering, for instance, when he writes, "I am the light & the way, / I, that I, that – / inner light [...] My nature / to correspond, to / project / to project the image" (18); with Fred Wah when he writes, "The smoothness / of her thighs is / one thing. // The memory / of a cedar bough's / softness is / the same thing. // These two things / in one I could / be master of. // And am." (24); and with Lionel Kearns when he writes, "In any authentic count-down / the word must remain / servant to the mouth" (46–47).

The faith in language's ability to project voice, to fashion environments, as well as to bridge the underlying unity of the universe into poetry falters over the course of *Tish*. The work of Sam Perry (whom Bergé praised as "incredible, multi-colored, multifaceted" [*Vancouver* 10]) provides a particularly useful demonstration of this transition. In *Tish* 10, he published an important essay called "Maximus of Gloucester from Dogtown: Charles Olson's Personal Locus." I describe this essay as important because it maps out the central *Tish* aesthetic in terms of historical contributions to literature, in the movement from Europe to North America as well as in the progression from Thoreau, Melville, and Whitman to Olson. Perry proposes that this movement amounted to writing ever closer to the American place. Olson's accomplishment especially with *Maximus*, then, is mapped out in terms of historical literary affect:

> Maximus measured the myth and from it I conclude that the soul, dependent, burns, and recognizing its dependence strikes out or hides from the certainty of death. Merry is a demi-god, his ritual with the bull is an American myth perceived by Olson measured by Olson as significant as any myths of distant times. Olson caught the big fish and made it stick with measurement. (209)

The language of measurement pervades Perry's assessment of Olson's contribution, as his essay highlights the means by which language achieves an inscrutable equivalence with the poet's place. Olson's achievement with *Maximus* in measuring out the material and mythic substructures of Gloucester enabled a similar endeavour in other American locales by successive writers:

> Olson's locus limited him to a certain part of the beach and to events that occurred there. He only travelled a measured distance from the peg. He couldn't move across American space to measure what happens in the big city, and the big city is a source of energy, the unique element of this society. His successors using his method with a Whitmanesque locus – the surface of their own skin – have charted the action of the big city. Creeley and Ginsberg and Kerouac are men travelling American space taking modern measure from their own space-time locus/wherever they are.
>
> (209; capitalizations corrected for consistency)

The city is messy, overwhelmed by multiplicity. Olson's writing is unified in form and content through the trope of its measure/measurement of locus. *Tish* became, naturally, an extension of this measuring endeavour, now extended to the particular locus of Vancouver with its rather nebulous, intersecting networks of national, colonial, and post-colonial mythologies (there is no mention of the violence embedded in surveying over Indigenous land, of course). Perry's essay was published as a stand-alone *Tish* book in 1963 as part of the brief TISHBooks venture. Tallman sent a copy to Olson and wrote to Creeley wondering about Olson's reaction to it. His response to it remains uncertain, but Gladys Maria Hindmarch depicts an intriguing exchange between Olson and Perry at the Vancouver Poetry Conference: "On Monday [August 5th, Olson] got at Sam for using words without defining in himself what he means. Sam spoke of moving on a ladder of steps out into the non-ordered to him chaos world. Olson insisted that it all had order, nature's order" ("The Vancouver" 201). It is striking that Hindmarch, in wrestling with how to record the VPC in her own journal, follows a tip from Ginsberg and Duncan and embraces chance, happenstance, and coincidence as methodology (201).

Olson's appeal to language functioning with a natural order underpins a review by Bowering of a book by Jack Spicer in *Tish* 16. Bowering begins the review on a defensive note: "I am the kind of reader who has always had trouble with any kind of surrealism, bringing suspicion, impatience, violated sense of order to the tumbling mixture of images" (324). He acknowledges Spicer's centrality to poetry in the San Francisco Renaissance community and tries to but cannot appreciate the confusion of images peppered throughout Spicer's *The Heads of the Town Up to the Aether* (1962). Bowering's review evidences a note of surprise and resistance at the emergence of a poetics that is ultimately mistrustful of language's expressive capabilities from a leader within his own community. As a caveat to that mistrust, as Stephen Collis documents, Bowering was still deeply influenced by Spicer's contributions to the serial poem form: he quotes Bowering admitting that "if I wanted my work to lean toward someone's it would be Spicer's" (qtd. in Collis "Of the Dissolved" 4). Even before this engagement with Spicer (that Collis dates from Spicer's Vancouver lectures in 1965), there are precedents in *Tish* before Bowering's review that imply and explore the limitations of language: in *Tish* 11, for instance, Lionel Kearns accuses Davey of seeming "rather naïve" for resisting form as artifice (223); in *Tish* 13, Red Lane's "Margins" presents a linguistic children's game around the inadequacy of language to provide essential answers to even basic questions (262); in *Tish* 15, Jamie Reid writes, "In face of the silence / which is in the world, / the one response, / the one possible response, / is silence" (307).

Perry did not publish again in the first editorial period of *Tish*, but his work in the second period includes a striking poem – indeed, perhaps the most experimental poem in the entire run of the magazine – that highlights and explores a fractured relationship between the poet and their language. His poem "Osseous Roots" in *Tish* 28, from January 1965, presents a series of permutations of a set of graphic images:

the two lips of one eye   pressed together
        squeezed /pursed as lips sphincter
are closed the lips pressed together are "closed"
                            clitoris

The two lips of one eye, pressed together
                    as mouth or sphincter or clitoris
~~to~~ defend, ~~to~~ stop penetration
stop ~~entering~~ inputing ingesting   deny entrance,
                    the two lips of my right eye
The two lips of one eye, pressed together as lips of mouth
sphincter clitoris defend passage block the putting into
(to ~~put between the lips~~ insert between the lips
defence the entrance   the entering
defend passage   defend insertions
          prevent insertions of certain
                         FLUIDS sperm flesh
           external
prevent ~~passage~~   passing   ~~liquids~~ fluids
               restrict narrow tighten to prevent passage
                    defend against the inputting
incoming or the outgoing
The two lips of one eye, pressed together
                    as lips of mouth sphincter
The two lips of one eye, pressed together as lips
                    of mouth or anus, defend
passage hinder input
               (9; deletions as in original; spacing approximate)

I quote this poem at length (it does carry on in similar manner for another twenty lines) to demonstrate its fractured language that works against the poem's expression. Expression is not a projection but a problem in this poem. The speaking voice turns the focus away from the depicted coitus to its inability to cross the bridge of communication. Some words are even written under erasure, a technique that would become popular a few decades later via post-structuralist theory to signal the inadequacy of expression.[11] Burroughs used this kind of foregrounded editing in his "bulletin" *APO-33*, poignantly published by Fuck You Press in 1965 (after *Tish* 28), which includes entire passages struck-through. Subsequent editions, most notably by Beach Books in 1968, did not correct these cancellation marks, but further stylized them. Perry's entire text, meanwhile, cycles through permutations of the same set of phrases and

---

11 In derek beaulieu's transcription of this issue, he removes the "cancellation marks and the offending text [...] in order to preserve the poet [*sic*] intended pacing and use of the page as compositional field" (11). His insinuation is that the technique is evidence of editorial process, not disjunctive form. I note that the poem repeats itself, corrects itself, and disrupts itself, even without the deletions.

images that depict blockage of internal communication and connection. The language remains exterior to the act; the coitus interrupted. In method, it echoes the work that Gysin was doing in his permutation texts from the same period, such as his instruction to "[r]ub out the word" and his question "I am that am I?"

Also, in *Tish* 28 is a collage poem written by Peter Auxier and Dan McLeod titled "Calling the Guide" (12) that depicts language in a crisis of instability. Jamie Reid protested in a letter in the next issue, by noting "that collage poem has a weirdly didactic feel to it, tho I can make little sense of the poem as a whole" (2).[12]

17

Despite the atypical appearance of collagic experimentation in *Tish* 28, *Tish* 22 clearly steps back from the radical, new avant-gardism introduced in *Tish* 21. This aesthetic retrenchment takes many forms, including an abundance of lyrical New American poems by Daphne Buckle, George Bowering, Peter Auxier, and David Cull, Dan McLeod's meditations on the "law" that governs consciousness and "the grace we / are called to" (2), a positive review of Beat novelist Kerouac, "the most interesting romantic novelist of the postwar time" ("Kerouac's Brother" 5) by Bowering, and a mostly negative review of *Blewointment*'s first issue by Gladys Maria Hindmarch. While Hindmarch is intrigued by the mosaical eclecticism of Vancouver's newest experimental magazine, she ultimately rejects the lack of control it presages: "part of me wants things more finished, more there" ("Review" 12). She articulates her dissatisfaction with recourse to a foundational principle of early *Tish* aesthetics: "I take it that all poems are meant to be heard, that poem on page is a transctiption [*sic*] of what sounds will be like music in air[,] auditory form." McLeod's poem also resists space as a principal coordinate of poetry, in preference for the unifying force of "the One that moves beneath" the words enabling consciousness (2).

Collage, however, and the cut-up method both privilege the visual objectivity of language over both the auditory sense and what McLuhan might extrapolate as the coherency of individual consciousness. In doing so, such works disrupt the unity McLeod appeals to and the polish/coherence Hindmarch prefers. In *Blewointment* editor bill bissett's words from the same period,

> the sentence paragraph is jail to the gggggggg gu ga free speech [...] each time different so also th spelling but that not just like sound but picture how it looks [...] ths aint no capitalist / pome ium tirud uv finding / th ownr [...] appreciate th diffrencus th voice cummin thru yu. (*pass th food* n. pag.)

---

12 In 1996, Reid actually produced a visual collage of his own – a collage of poets, Elvis Presley, and Babe Ruth dedicated to none other than George Bowering to accompany his book *Mad Boys*.

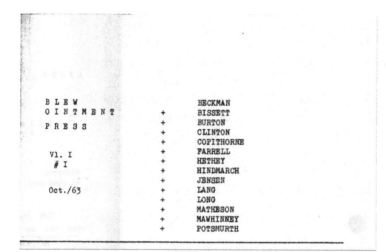

Figure 1.10 Table of contents from Blew Ointment Press magazine's premier issue in October 1963. Source: Private collection of the author. Used with permission.

The deliberate messiness of bissett's work as poet and editor, as with Burroughs and Gysin, undoes the illusions of individual control, undoes any underlying sense of harmony in the universe. bissett in the passage above connects the desire for control and universalism directly to a nefarious, predatory capitalism. In other works, such as *RUSH: what fuckan theory* or the "IBM" issue of *Blewointment* magazine (subtitled a "Saga uv th release uv human spirit from computer funkshuns"), bissett makes the link between single-consciousness lyric poetry, capitalism, and war overtly. *Tish* would not return to such radical, experimental ground for many years.

Like *Tish*, bissett's *Blewointment* was a magazine that responded to an outgrowth of aesthetic interest and activity in Vancouver in the early 1960s. It was launched in the fall of 1963[13] (having been first announced and advertised in *Tish* 21, adding to the importance of that issue) as in part a reaction against the aesthetic singularity that bissett and his network of downtown poets, painters, and musicians had witnessed in *Tish* and the VPC. In the first editorial of his new magazine, bissett ignores writing about the conference and instead articulates the mandate of the magazine in

---

13 Not surprisingly, there is some confusion about when the *Blewointment* venture actually began. The first issue is clearly dated October 1963, as in the image above, but the Vancouver Art Gallery claims the first issue was published in September 1962. When I first asked bissett, he said he remembered it (with pronounced uncertainty) starting in the fall of 1962. When I asked Copithorne, she said that she remembered receiving a first or early copy at the Vancouver Poetry Conference in the summer of 1963. The first corroborating textual responses to the magazine, including in *Tish*, as mentioned above, however, are all from the fall of 1963 or later. Given Copithorne's memory, and the fact that it was announced in *Tish* 21, it is possible bissett circulated a draft or preview of the issue to come at the VPC. bissett later wrote me and said: "n yes 1963 not 1962 as i oftn thot was th yeer uv th first blewointment publikaysyun yr book sounds sew xciting" (4 November 2019).

the form of a review of a National Film Board of Canada (NFB) film of Vancouver's downtown arts community:

> In a gestalt of montage wgich dug in / further and further into us you reveald the ques-
> tions / of all our lives / what can we know / what is eternal, outside us / what can we
> do / artists & poets, outside the abstracion / termed society which may or may not have
> an existential / value, are forced into these questions and/or activities / what can we
> do [...] you have made a visual / p o e m, which i think must be the artistic solution, / to
> show, to give, to make it be there [...] Your premiss was to show / these levels in action,
> to know eternity, and action / in the gestalt coherence of our control / and levels where
> we have no control. ("About" 103–5; spelling as in original)

The magazine became a global pioneer in the exploration of visual poetry and the collage aesthetic, sometimes going so far as to publish entire issues without clear indication of which author had written which poem. It was an attack on the possibility of control, of dominating language, of the discourse of mastery and control that shaped North American politics, poetics, and consciousness. While the open-field approach shares a similar resistance to cognitive closures of vari-ous sorts, it was precisely this intentional lack of control and lack of coherence that that had caused Hindmarch concern in her review, Bowering's resistance to Spicer's "surrealism," Davey's antipathy to disjunctive composition methods, and Reid's apprehension about not making "sense" of the elements in collagic work, as noted above.

18

Shit takes a central role in the narrative of the Blew Ointment Press, the maga-zine's publishing operation, which ran into public trouble after bissett published his poem "A Warm Place to Shit" in his 1971 book *Drifting into War*. The poem repeats the phrase thirty-nine times without any capitalization or spaces between the words: in other words, it sits a mess on the page. Buried in a decidedly innocu-ous small-press poetry publication by the low-profile publishing house Talonbooks, the book received little attention upon its release, despite containing provocative lines against "canadian complicity in vietnam," concrete poems depicting fellatio, and quips attacking apolitical Americanized poets: "yankee dog lovr a cours yu may think that art shud nevr deal with anything real or imagind that its supposd to be bullshit courz that then cud be yr problem but dont wondr why when th life bcums death eh nucklear baby" (n. pag.). Collaging in comic books, doctored pho-tographs, disintegrating photocopies, and other visual sources, the book is one of the high-water marks of literary collage in Canada and was predictably generally ignored.[14]

"A warm place to shit," however, became a notorious phrase when it appeared in a *Rolling Stone* article in October 1976 that quoted American secretary of agriculture Earl Butz making a racist joke on an airplane in the company of entertainer Pat Boone and other politicians; the punchline of the joke was "and third, a warm place to shit" (Dean 38). Butz was compelled to resign his cabinet post as a result of the widely publicized gaffe. Consequently, bissett's use of the phrase half a decade earlier was revived as a subject of controversy, and Vancouver's Progressive Conservative representatives dutifully raised the matter in the federal parliament. They objected to bissett having received federal funding from the Canada Council in spite of such obscene content. During the fallout and negative publicity, bissett received death threats, and the hallway to his lawyer's office was targeted with a Molotov cocktail. Though the literary community (led by Warren Tallman) rallied to bissett's defence, significant damage was done by the political interference over the next few years. Tim Carlson sums up the fallout tersely: "blewointment press took a 42 per cent cut in Canada Council funding in 1982. bissett sold it a year later" (47). Shitty. *Blewointment* magazine and press moved to Toronto with the sale. (To end with a more uplifting note, in 2019, the experimental noise band TZT serenaded bissett at his 80th birthday party with a musicalized version of "A Warm Place to Shit.")

19

The shift in styles, modes, and poetics – however hesitant – between the first and second editorial periods of *Tish*, poignantly divided by the VPC, marks the gradual introduction of a changing relationship to language. A space was opening up between the poets and their sense of their own connection to language that was enabling them to see language as material, as object, and eventually as ideological cultural product. In the post-*Tish* era, Daphne Marlatt would come to theorize this new relationship to language through the discourse of feminism and post-structuralism: "The Beginning: language, a living body we enter at birth, sustains and contains us. it does not replace the bodies around us [...] we know language structures our world and in a crucial sense we cannot see what we cannot verbalize" ("Musing" 223, 224). Rather than a universal unity found through language, for Marlatt it became the gaps in language that exposed the possibility of liberation and the forces obscuring it: "so many terms for dominance in English are tied up with male experiencing, masculine

---

14 George Bowering also wrote a generally ignored poem about shit called "It's There You Can't Deny It" in 1972 contrasting New York City's production of fecal matter with the Queen of England's.

hierarchies and differences (exclusion), patriarchal holdings with their legalities. where are the poems that celebrate the soft letting-go the flow of menstrual blood is as it leaves her body?" (225). Davey, in looking back on the discourse of the *Tish* editorials, admits the extremely gendered language of the period (*When* 195), but dismisses any particular institutional sexism within the *Tish*/New American milieu beyond the established habits of the period (197). Of course, that misses the point, and perhaps does so deliberately, which is precisely the fact that the language of the *Tish* poets contributed to the ongoing denigration of women as subjects within their own communities. The erasure of women as speaking subjects is constant in the editorials, such as in *Tish* 8, where Davey exclaims that "poets do not write as patriots, but as **men**" (155; emphasis in original), just as the reduction of women's role in society is constant in the many depictions of women in the poetry, such as in Davey's poem portrait of "all girls who / will make some man a good bookcase" (20), or of a lover: "And you / my sweet / live / as young womanhood has / and should / with body / flawless / all parts running smoothly / waiting / for use" (34). While an opening in aesthetic form, such writing continues the habitual erasure of women's voices and perspectives (let alone other marginalized subject positions).

In 2007, the American poets Juliana Spahr and Stephanie Young published an article about the erasure of women from literary cultures. In the study, called "Numbers Trouble," they took up a question asked by Jennifer Ashton about the presence and representation of women in literary journals by conducting an extensive survey of literary anthologies and journals in America (91). After they found that female representation in anthologies had barely changed from the 1960s through to the 1990s, hovering consistently around 22 per cent of contributors (94), they began expanding the object of their study to include books published and reviewed (96), literary awards (97), and literary faculty positions with and without tenure (98). They conclude the article with a call for "a feminism that begins with an editorial commitment to equitable representation of different genders, races, and classes but that doesn't end there" (100). The essay did not end there, but rather provoked a conversation that led to the creation of the non-profit feminist organization VIDA: Women in Literary Arts, which now orchestrates a massive annual "count" of gender representation across the American literary arts. The initiative spread north of the border in 2012, when Vancouver poet Gillian Jerome founded CWILA: Canadian Women in the Literary Arts to orchestrate a Canadian "count," publish feminist essays and analysis, and advocate on behalf of women writers in Canada. The work done by VIDA and CWILA has documented systemic bias in the literary industry. They continue to work to shatter what Lori Saint-Martin calls the paradox of innocence: "No publication will admit to a bias in favour of male authors, and yet the figures generally show that it exists. Nobody is doing it – and yet it's widespread. Nobody means for it to happen – and yet it happens all the time" (n. pag.). They also document when things change by looking at the math and seeing measurable difference. In the spirit of this work, then, and in the interest of starting to document the representation of gender in the mid-century Vancouver literary community, I want to use this approach to numbers to highlight the shift from the first editorial period to the second, a shift that might be characterized as the move from finding nothing to finding something.

Tish 1–19

0 female editors: 5 male editors – 0%
18 poems by women: 269 poems by men – 6%
1 review of work by women: 13 reviews of work by men – 7%
0 reviews written by women: 14 reviews written by men – 0%
0 essays/editorials written by women: 30 essays/editorials written by men – 0%
3 letters to the editor by women: 16 letters to the editor by men – 16%
1 short story by women: 0 short stories by men – 100%

Tish 20–44

3 female editors: 8 male editors – 27%
50 poems by women: 247 poems by men – 17%
2 reviews of work by women: 10 reviews of work by men – 17%
1 review written by women: 11 reviews written by men – 8%
1 essays/editorials written by women: 11 essays/editorials written by men – 8%
1 letters to the editor by women: 7 letters to the editor by men – 14%
5 short stories by women: 5 short stories by men – 50%

To be sure, the second editorial period of *Tish* marks a turn away from the patriarchal confidence in language and in the rigid gendered roles for men and women from the first editorial period. It does not achieve equal representation, but the active participation and valuation of women in the second series are pronounced. With the exception of the short story category, where they represent the only short story published in the first nineteen issues, women's participation and representation rise dramatically in the second editorial period. Looking more carefully at how the gender imbalance worked in the first editorial phase, it is striking to note that the exclusionary frame extends even to the privileged New American authors: of the seven invited poet-presenters at the VPC, *Tish* published original work by only Olson, Creeley, Duncan, and Ginsberg. Whalen did not publish any works himself but is the subject of an extended essay by Jamie Reid in *Tish* 2. They also published extended samplings of Jack Spicer and Larry Eigner. The poetry of the two invited female poets at the conference, however, Denise Levertov and Margaret Avison, as well as Hilda Morley, a poet at the Black Mountain College, was entirely excluded from the magazine. There are two small exceptions in the second editorial period, not relating to Avison but to Levertov's work, that are worth pointing out. First, in *Tish* 22, the first issue after the Vancouver Poetry Conference, Carol Bergé dedicates a poem to Levertov: "lady, / my hat's off to you" ("Reading the Poem" 6). Second, George Bowering offers a glowing review of Levertov's book *O Taste and See* in *Tish* 30:

> *O Taste and See*, accumulating poems from 1962 to 1964, is invested with a new strength. In these poems Miss Levertov continues to engage the sense perceptors, and now involves as well, the whole body, the heat of sex now, the whole body entering the act of the poem [...] highly recommended. (6)

Bowering's review appears in the same issue as the very first and only editorial in all of *Tish* written by a woman. Poignantly, Marlatt's editorial meditates on the earnest need to write through linguistic blockages where permission to write has been denied, and the importance of reconsidering form and method in encountering and writing from those forbidden spaces:

> A CARE, as in what you do with your boundaries (the dream) and surface (meeting-place), say of the poem, where the hand and its order to be a grace. Cared for / Or imagine the hell, as Lionel Kearns said, the "blockage between gut and / pennib," where permission is possible (and in fact given(?)). Perhaps not, and some attention to the process required. ("On Care" 2)

TWO

The Birth of Blew

Robert Duncan: "How can you be other than where you are?"
Robert Creeley: "The only I of the cosmos you know is yourself."
Exchange during the Vancouver Poetry Conference, 1963.

1 Harmony: Aristotle, Olson, and Vancouver 1959–1963

In this chapter on *Blewointment* magazine and press I want to situate the radical breach of its poetics and publishing style in the context of the influx of Black Mountain and San Francisco Renaissance poetics into Canada, as discussed in the previous chapter. Though Donald Allen's 1960 anthology *The New American Poetry* drew together disparate communities from across the United States, to expedite things somewhat, and as a reflection of how it was received in Canada, in this chapter I will continue to override the internal divisions and differences and refer to all of the groups in Allen's book as New American poets. This has the unfortunate consequence of separating the work from the particular context in which it was created, especially problematic in the case of Black Mountain College, which was a brilliant nexus of intermedia experimentation and avant-garde community-building. The distinctive networks of the Bay Area also have important conduits up and down the coast that, as discussed in subsequent chapters, played an important role in forming new aesthetic avant-garde communities. Really, though, my topic in this and the last chapter is the Vancouver scene and how they reacted to the arrival of this New American writing in their midst. To identify the fine point of aesthetic philosophy and periodization that divides the two scenes in Vancouver, *Tish* from *Blewointment*, perhaps improbably I'm going to turn to the poetics of the classical Greek philosopher Aristotle, whose *Poetics* (335 BC) were a mainstay of literary education and discussion even among those who disagreed with it. Aristotle's writing, in many respects, established the norm against which modern and avant-garde writers functionally distinguished themselves.

There are three key ideas from Aristotle that make him especially useful to this discussion. He is, of course, writing in dialogue with his teacher Plato's rejection

Figure 2.1 Back cover of the first issue of *Blewointment* magazine (October 1963). Source: Private collection of the author. Used with permission.

of poetry in *The Republic* (c. 380 BC) for its habitual misrepresentation of God, the Gods, and the good: "let us have no more lies of that sort. Neither must we have mothers under the influence of the poets scaring their children with a bad version of these myths [...] the lying poet has no place in our idea of God" (236). Aristotle in *The Poetics*, however, seeks to treat poetry unto itself by looking in upon its forms and methods, and by so doing articulate the ways in which literature participates in the ethical universe. The first of the three concepts that are particularly relevant to Vancouver is his notion that alongside language and music, one of the three constituent parts of poetry is harmony – which he defines in "On the Soul" as "a blend or composition of contraries" (650). Harmony is the means by which the pure internal soul meets and interacts with the impure external universe without losing its distinction, and, two millennia later, it facilitates the New American interest in simultaneous coexistence, Duncan's notion of the ensemble (as discussed in the previous chapter), and perhaps by extension collage methodologies. The second idea from Aristotle is his theory that the plot of a narrative is ultimately of greater significance than its characters in terms of shaping effect and meaning ("Poetics" 2317). The modern autotelic, individualist, and confessional orientations of poetry are all swept aside by this observation. For, as Robert

Duncan noticed, Aristotle insinuates the hermetic correlation between form and content through this approach to plot (*The H.D. Book* 383). The third idea is Aristotle's faith in the underlying laws and structures that govern the universe and that these superstructures ought to be extended to cultural practices, including especially poetry.

While the New Americans were outspoken critics of exaggerated Western notions of reason and rationality, their comfort in articulating laws of poetry and issuing dicta on its ideal form echoes Aristotle's categorical approach. As Olson argues, "[t] here are laws, that is to say, the human universe is as discoverable as that other. And as definable" ("Human Universe" 53). Furthermore, many of their laws of poetry have a direct precedent in *The Poetics* and other works by Aristotle. For instance, consider Aristotle's declaration that every event portrayed, and every action taken in a text, must be a logical progression from previous events:

> The right thing, however, is in the characters just as in the incidents of the play to seek after the necessary or the probable; so that whenever such-and-such a personage says or does such-and-such a thing, it shall be the necessary or probable outcome of his character; and whenever this incident follows on that, it shall be either the necessary or the probable consequence of it. From this one sees that the dénouement also should arise out of the plot itself, and not depend on a stage-artifice. (15–16)

The linear movement of a text must respond to internal workings of the text itself. This dictum finds a comfortable corollary in Olson's maxim (borrowed from Edward Dahlberg) that "ONE PERCEPTION MUST IMMEDIATELY AND DIRECTLY LEAD TO A FURTHER PERCEPTION" ("Projective Verse" 17). For both, writing demands an internal unity so that the writer connects to a broader harmony of the universe that is positively embodied in the structure of the form of the text. The task of tracing all of the links and divergences between the New American poets and Aristotle's poetics, or even between the Vancouver authors and Aristotle, is beyond my intentions herein, so I defer and point to contemporary critics like Edna Rosenthal[1] and Pericles Lewis,[2] who have already initiated a systematic study of Aristotle's persistent centrality to modernist aesthetic debates in the twentieth century.

My task, in contrast, is to explore the connections between Aristotelian and New American poetics just enough to illuminate and extrapolate the division that

---

1 See her book *Aristotle and Modernism: Aesthetic Affinities of T. S. Eliot, Wallace Stevens, and Virginia Woolf* (2008).

2 See his book *The Cambridge Introduction to Modernism*, in particular his discussion of Aristotle as a central figure in the emergence of modernist theatre (178–180 in particular).

Vancouver poet and editor bill bissett announces in his long-running critique of this kind of aesthetics, which began with the very first issue of *Blewointment* magazine in Vancouver 1963, shortly after the VPC. I seek herein to question whether *Tish* and by extension the New American poets were indeed Aristotelian – asking to what extent this is a useful, however hyperbolic, provocation, and in answering this question work toward some sense of the transition to *Blewointment*'s aesthetics that it implies.

The VPC was a key moment in both the mythology and the narrativization of New American writing, but it also provides a much less narrativized but equally important demarcation point between *Tish* and *Blewointment*, for it marks the point at which the *Tish* editors concluded their first editorial period, as discussed in the previous chapter, and it coincided with the establishment of *Blewointment* magazine just a few months later (though the idea of the zine, and possibly proto-versions, were already circulating). Furthermore, inasmuch as these period terms are useful and not overly prescriptive, Vancouver 1963 marks the beginning of the end of late modernism in Canada and the onset of postmodernism. In this distinction, I am following Tyrus Miller's invitation to consider the ways in which late modernist writing fits into the narrative of an emergent postmodernism (7). While late modernist writing "offers no embracing vision in which the contradictions of modern life would be resolved" (11), it has not yet embraced the postmodern sense of inventing rather than disclosing the world. It is coexistent, overlapping, and interactive with its precursors; it maintains the modernist sense that form equals function, but with a scepticism and hesitation about "the efficacy of high modernist form" (20).[3] *Blewointment* ushers in, to borrow from Jameson, the "empirical, chaotic, and heterogeneous" impulse of postmodernism (1), latent and suggestive in *Tish* and New American writing though never fully manifest.

Interest in New American writing on the campus of the University of British Columbia began in 1956, when Warren Tallman was hired at the school. Tallman introduced UBC students to writing from San Francisco, where he and his wife, Ellen, were integrated into the literary scene that would become known as the San Francisco Renaissance. His connections to that network of writing manifested in the flesh a few years after his arrival when he organized the first of many visits from his American poet friends. On 12 December 1959, Robert Duncan read poetry and discussed poetics in the Tallman's basement on West 37th Street in Kerrisdale, not far from the UBC campus (and, by sheer coincidence, across the street from my family home). Forty people paid fifty cents each to attend. The event helped a group of young Vancouver poets focalize their literary ambitions onto poetry, and even more specifically onto the idea of starting a poetry magazine. The event also, however, had a significant impact on Duncan. As Lewis Ellingham and Kevin Killian note: "He was astonished and revitalized by their interest in new poetry" (267).

The interest was rewarded with abundant access. Duncan returned to Vancouver in the spring of 1961 for the first Festival of the Contemporary Arts, organized by

Figure 2.2 Fred Wah in 1959. Photo by Karen Tallman. Used with permission.

the Fine Arts Group at UBC. They paid him a substantial wage ($200 plus $125 plane fare) for his work there. Three months later, on 22–24 July, he came back again, this time to give three evening lectures. After the final night, the students gathered in the Buchanan Building on UBC campus and held a reading of their own, though only the male writers of the group were invited to perform (see Fong and Shearer xvii–xviii). By this point, the Vancouver students were assuredly enthusiastic about the New American writing and wanted even deeper access. Thus, in 1961, students Fred Wah and Pauline Butling drove down with their professor and his wife to San Francisco, where they met Jack Spicer, Stan Persky, and George Stanley. Intriguingly, of this trio of American poets, all three tried to relocate up to Canada. Persky and Stanley did, in fact, immigrate to Vancouver, and Spicer was set to take up a post at Simon Fraser University just before he died in August of 1965. That job went to fellow San Franciscan and New American poet Robin Blaser. The September after Wah and Butling returned from that auspicious visit south, a mixture of undergraduate and graduate students at UBC launched *Tish*. It was one of four literary magazines in the city at the time, but the only one devoted exclusively to a specific aesthetic. It was the only magazine west of Toronto even remotely interested in the New American mode.

The connection between *Tish* and the New Americans has never been disputed, but is it possible that both were shaped by a residual Aristotelianism? To begin such an assessment, it is necessary to recognize that the Black Mountain poets and the San Francisco Renaissance poets took regular public stands against Aristotle's legacy and used their difference from his poetics to articulate their own. This approach pre-dates the movement to their formative influences, back at least to Louis Zukofsky's early interpretations of Pound's poetry in the 1930s as the articulation of "the concentrated locus which is the mind acting creatively upon the facts," in contradistinction to the "Aristotelian expansive unities" (24–25).[4] Pound, himself, invited the comparison with his 1917 translation of "The Twelve Dialogues of Fontenelle," a series of imaginary conversations, including one between Aristotle and the poet Anacreon "the wise." Anacreon is presented as a Bacchanalian wit and drunk and given the upper hand in the conversation, which concludes with a sharp rejection of Aristotle's ethics/*Ethics*: "Can one hold in one's laughter at the sight of people who preach the contempt of riches, for money?" (58).[5] The sense of reacting against Aristotle to express their own poetics surfaces in essays by Jack Spicer, Robin Blaser, Robert Duncan, and Robert Creeley, most prominently in their embrace of simultaneous multiplicity disrupting the fold of categorical experience.[6] Olson, in his essay "Human Universe," argues that the difference between their project and Aristotle's philosophy depends upon the distinction between the Aristotelian sense of language as enclosing the universe versus the notion of language serving as an instrument for "discovery" and "extension" (53).

In a 1951 letter to Creeley, Olson further clarified that while the surface vocabulary had remained the same between himself and Aristotle, the "vision of reality" had shifted the significance of the borrowed terms (Letter 213). One example of this semiotic shift is with the idea of harmony, a key term borrowed from Aristotle but self-consciously modified in its recurring deployment. The New American poets embraced his general idea of simultaneous contrariness, and even of the importance of form's relation to content, but rejected its specific role in Aristotle's fully developed

---

3 Miller's sense of late modernist resistance to the more utopian ambitions of modernist form is expressed by Duncan's "the end of masterpieces [...] the beginning of testimony" (*Fictive Certainties* 90).

4 Pound, as was his wont, shifted the vocabulary to his own idiosyncratic form: he, thus, divided aesthetic harmony into logopoeia (language), melopoeia (sound), and phanopoeia (image), the last of which he defined as "a casting of images upon the visual imagination" ("How to Read" 25). Phanopoeia, of course, became the foundational concern of the Imagist movement.

5 In Pound's *Guide to Kulchur*, he clarifies his distance from Aristotle's ethics and its use as a guide to proper behaviour for young men in an extended and close analysis of Aristotle's *Ethics* and its various translations. Pound concludes with a note on Aristotle's value, but also that "I am merely indicating the insufficiency of our philosopher as guide [...] Arry is not fit to clean the boots of Confucius" (325, 326). Pound does not, however, dispute Aristotle's call for clarity in poetry and the exclusive use of current or proper words ("Poetics" 3.22).

6 Olson reminded Creeley of their shared difference from Aristotle in a letter on 1 December 1951: he writes somewhat vaguely, "At a certain point there was a profound departure" (Letter 213).

cosmology. Creeley, for instance, decidedly blurred its implications with his redefinition: "Harmony is just like what your ear says like" (*Collected Prose* 351). Notice, though, how that simple phrase melds all three of Aristotle's definitional components of poetry: language, music, and harmony.[7]

The disputations were profuse to the point of being excessive. Duncan's poem "Electric Iron" begins with a pertinent rejection of Aristotle's definition of tragedy in *The Poetics* because "a single thing, / potent in its electric thingness, / gives expectation of every kind of pleasure" (177). Duncan, who was actually much more invested in the mystical hermeneutics of Plato and especially the Neoplatonists and their pursuit of henosis (the union of the spiritual with the quotidian), captures here an important tension in Aristotle's aesthetic principles: namely, that genre and categorical distinction oppose the unifying energies of harmony and greater aesthetic unity. It is through this tension that we can understand the New American poets' interest in Aristotle; for while they discard specific tenets of his poetics, particularly his closed-universe model – Olson would add that such Western "anthropomorphism [...] make[s] mush of, any reality" ("Mayan Letters" 112) – they make a vigorous case for the relevance of his sense of literary form as the natural correlative of content.[8]

Aristotle's harmony is worth pausing on, too, for he writes of harmony in a manner that should be familiar to Olson's readers: "in using the word 'harmony' [...] the most proper sense is in relation to the magnitudes which motion and position, where harmony means their being compounded and harmonized in such a manner as to prevent the introduction of anything homogenous" ("On the Soul" 650). This sense of the dynamic play of contraries echoes freely across New American writing. It can be found throughout Olson's manifestos, in his appeal to "certain laws" of praxis intended to open up poetry to "some several forces just now beginning to be examined" ("Projective Verse"16), in the holistic consciousness of composition by field, and in Creeley's dictum that "FORM IS NEVER MORE THAN AN EXTENSION OF CONTENT" (qtd. in "Projective Verse" 16)[9] The links proliferate to the

---

7 Following Pound's lead, it is striking how frequently the New American poets invoke Aristotle, even if most frequently to dispute his categorical rigidities. He crops up in the essays, the letters, and even in the poetry, as in Blaser's poem "Departure," which works from a quote by Aristotle about the natural desire for knowledge ("Departure (envoi-commiato)" 239). Duncan and Levertov, the more mystically charged of the New American poets, embraced some of the cosmological implications of Aristotle's sense of form as harmony: indeed, "the form of the whole can be felt emerging in the fittingness of each passage," as Duncan says (*Fictive Certainties* 31).

8 See Duncan in *The H.D. Book* 79, 383, 642.

9 Further, it supports the notion of amalgamated contrariness that orients Olson's idea of America as a place that unifies magnitude and "malice" and that privileges projective magnanimity over agreeable passivity. As Philip argues, Olson rejects Whitman's "good news" version of America for Melville's recognition of the darkness lurking in the heart of the American empire (Phillip 296). When I say harmonious, then, I conjure up Olson's multilayered vision of America's best and worst tendencies simultaneously manifest. Levertov, for her part, works directly from Aristotle's *Poetics* in pursuit of a poetry that will "resemble a living organism in all its unity" (3.23).

point that an entire study is more than merited: Donald Allen and Ben Friedlander, for instance, note an unpublished 1965 essay by Olson that directly connects his interest in the projective to Aristotle's work on parataxis and succession (Olson, *Collected Prose* 424n239).

In Vancouver, the much younger *Tish* poets fervently embraced and examined all of these ideas as best they could, and especially the notion of a poet writing in harmonious contrariety with a particular locus. Davey's essay "One Man's Look at 'Projective Verse'" extends the implications of the Aristotelian harmony in the work of the New American writers by reconnecting them to a universal, even mythical cosmology: "Each poet has a giant feeling for the world, universe, man, and the timeless processes that operate in and thru them – a feeling which is largely religious (with the small 'r') [...] a feeling for an eternal order behind the transitory sense of objects" (101). "The poet must," Davey continues, "listen to the music of the universe as it is played within himself, and [be] able to sing his own song in harmony with it. The song/poem must always be natural" (103). Harmony here assumes its full Aristotelian sense by representing the functioning, dynamic state of contrarieties in the universe: the law that makes the universe move. Davey's embrace of this harmony, shared by the other *Tish* writers, connects them to, in Davey's words, a "universist line" of Canadian poetry who "tend to see the universe as vast, divine, mysteriously structured" (Introduction 10). Ironically, the same tension that Duncan identified in Aristotle, that the divisive application of genre and distinction opposes the unifying energies of harmony and greater aesthetic unity, resurfaces in Davey's sense of his own poetics: he divides Canadian poetry into exclusive camps and puts himself in the one that recognizes a universal harmony unifying all things – unifying all, that is, except Canadian poetry.

The *Tish* group of primarily poets focused on the experience of the individual in the environment and wrote from the perspective of a single consciousness navigating the complexity of the world, responding creatively to the facts. This follows from Olson's own law of the universe: "If there is any absolute, it is never more than this one, you, this instant, in action" ("Human Universe" 55). The writing is clean, compressed into raw kinetic energy, and classical in the sense of its distance, calmness, and intellectualization of the events described.[10] Layton wrote to Creeley to praise his poetry's "crispness and honesty [...] they are direct without being simple [...] whittled down to bare white sharpness" (qtd. in Faas and Reed xxii). Ideally, form and content are balanced, growing organically one from the other in a symbiotic and enabling

---

10 Davey, writing in 1975, argues that *Tish* 1–19 be recognized as belonging to the "universist line" of Canadian poetry (Introduction 10), which he defines in a way that contradicts my and Bowering's characterization here. While this is largely a semantic contradiction, brought about by incompatible binaries, *Tish* aesthetics are discussed in more detail in chapter 1.

relationship.[11] There is no hint of lush baroque or rococo excess in the pared-down words, no intended excess of materiality ("sprawl," they called such surplus). In George Bowering's terms, writing in *Tish* in 1963, and shortly after the VPC, "[t]he *Tish* poets have striven for accuracy and clarity, and have turned their attention upon the factual things that make up the world, men included among them" ("The Most" 423). Thus, the pages of the magazine abound with expressivist lines such as this beginning stanza of Frank Davey's poem "Of the North Shore":

> Skirting the shore again
> the Lions Gate Bridge is a
> n'empirical fact
> strung north-
> > eastwards
> > I have crossed it before.
> > > (139)

Similar stylings are met in Fred Wah's poem "The Grass," which reads in its entirety: "hewn, cut, sewn / no matter / the mown lawn / meets the nose / like the smell of summer" (*Tish No. 1–19* 234). While some of the writing in *Tish* 1–19 breaks out of this mode, especially in contributions by John Newlove (see "Vancouver-Spring-Dawn-List (2)" 317–18) and David Dawson (see "Tentative Coastlines" 266–8), most of the writing does not trouble the relationship between the words, their insights, and their speaker. *Tish*, in their advocacy of this singular aesthetic, rejected eclecticism in their magazine and almost exclusively published the narrow band of projective verse privileged by their sense of New American poetics. It was a thin band of poetry that ran between traditional verse (poetry by metronome, as Olson quipped) and revolutionary political poetry, which Davey dismissed for being human-centric and ultimately rationalist (10). One of those so characterized, mischaracterized I would offer, human-centric rationalists was bill bissett, the Canadian-Lunarian avant-garde poet.

2 Disharmony: bissett, Collage, and Another Vancouver 1959–1983

All of this seeks to contextualize bissett's 1972 protestations against the Aristotelian streak he continued to witness in the poetics of his contemporaries in Vancouver. In his delightfully, revealingly titled *RUSH: what fuckan theory*, bissett's most developed

---

11 Davey wrote a rash editorial in *Tish* 10 privileging content, particularly "testimony" (201), over form, but was promptly and widely scolded for the position. Denise Levertov's rejoinder, published in the subsequent issue, argues that he has made "a dangerous mistake" in his understanding of testimony (223). Davey responded in the same issue, humbly, and sincerely, thanking her "for correcting my ambiguity" (224–5).

Figure 2.3 Cover of *Blewointment*'s "Fascist Court" issue (1970). Source: Private collection of the author. Used with permission.

articulation of his poetics, he explicitly describes the reliance on categorical approaches to literature as an extension of Western imperialist logic; it is time, he writes, to go "byond the ol war/lord purposive aristotul categorees" (89). Pound would not have disagreed with this critique, for he too described Aristotle dismissively as the "[m]aster of those that cut apart, dissect and divide. Competent precursor of the card-index" (*Guide* 343). bissett's criticism is directed not just at evaluative modes of writing or academic interpretations, for he also connects Aristotle to the breath line and to the sequential orientation of projective verse: "i do not accept any significant correlation between one instant and the next ' ' but a poem can be tension of rejecting accepting this [at the] same time since no events 'really' occur at the same time tension achievd" (*RUSH* 44). The point he is making is subtle and slightly unhinged; by rejecting plot and the sequencing of events, he rejects all categories of human knowledge for being arbitrary and systemic rather than natural, inevitable, and *catalogueable*. He does acknowledge the appeal of Truth and meaning and its use value in art, but these are tensions, not absolutes or laws. A new kind of art, predicated on incoherence rather than coherence, emerges: Zarmsby Potsmurth writes (or is quoted) in *Blewointment* 1.2 to assert that "collage [...] the arrange- / meant that is pleasurable / because there is no / arrangemeant not a pictorial / corresspondence to a / supposed absolute" (n. pag.). This model of a human universe is not structured by observable laws or by a sense of timeless order. Peter Culley observed "a vast reassessment of accepted formulations of the real that was occupying the entire culture. It was not categories that were in ques-tion, but the whole notion of 'category' itself. In the maelstrom of the sixties, what was held on to mattered less than enthusiastically surrendering to the flow" (193). Post-modernism emerged in this categorical renunciation.

bissett's rejection of Aristotelian plot, laws, and systems includes a rejection of harmony and its underlying predicate of universal unity. His position marks a shift away from a mythological reading of texts, a universal determinist view of writing, to a more politicized, materialist approach: one that, in step with the postmodern-ism emerging a continent away, thinks about how writing reflects ideology, supple-ments action and being, and somewhat arbitrarily invents the world we all live in. Consequently, bissett's poetics (or anti-poetics) is one that invites radical difference and discontinuity. This difference of *Tish*, with its exclusive, categorical approach to poetics and its investment in universal harmony, from *Blewointment*, with its radi-cal openness and investment in eclectic disharmony, is emblematic of the transition between late modernism and postmodernism. In direct contrast to *Tish*'s editorial exclusivity, bissett published anything that was sent to him, prompting bpNichol's witticism that the magazine was "more interested in the news than in preserving great literature" (qtd. in Reid, "The Pome" 23).

The magazine also disrupted other publishing habits: some issues of the magazine excised author names from texts, while others included complex collages of vari-ous people's writing. Spelling and grammar were never standardized. bissett often stapled or pasted individually handcrafted textual objects of varying sizes inside and outside his magazine or even hand-painted on the covers. *Blewointment*'s radical openness – what Tim Carlson calls its "pure provocation" (43) – anticipates Barthes's 1974 attention to the "function" of the text within the "infinite play of the world" (5). *Blewointment* was a concerted attempt to re-imagine writerly communities outside of oppressive ideologies, to reconceive the function of the author, the publisher, and the reading community at large. Barthes posits that the "goal of literary work (of literature as work) is to make the reader no longer a consumer, but a producer of the text" (4). In like manner, bissett sought to open texts up, energize and radicalize readers, and create communities open to possibilities beyond transnational capi-talist imperialism. Stephen Voyce's recent work on alternative community forma-tion in avant-garde movements suggests a similar globalized consciousness within the founding motivation of Black Mountain College. bissett was never shy about

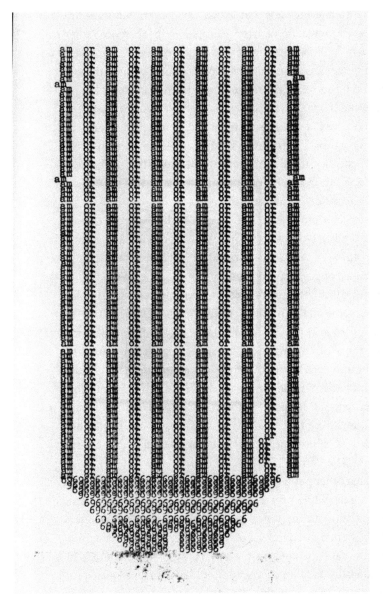

Figure 2.4 bill bissett's "Untitled," *Awake in th Red Desert* (1968). Source: Private collection of the author. Used with permission.

admiring the New American authors, but also attempted to extend their resistant spirit into more direct action and radical politics. His own response to the "I am that I am" self-assertion discussed in the previous chapter might be a 1968 visual poem depicting a massive column comprised of the repeating words "am or am or am or am." The oscillation between presence and doubt evokes an erotics of self-abnega-tion, opening a space within *amor*, which leads to a frenzied collapse at the end of the phallic column in a heap of "69"s (Untitled 23). Vivid sexuality in bissett is less about mastering another than dissolving selves into unadorned bodies.

Back in the first editorial of the first issue of *Blewointment*, published in October 1963, two months after the VPC, he had already identified his response to Aristotle's notion of harmony. Harmony reconciles the conflict between contraries in a grander union that encompasses both and inevitably acclimatizes or stabilizes opposing forces. For bissett, writing during the Vietnam War, living poor, and constantly facing the possibility of eviction and the perpetual police harassment of his downtown community, including his own arrests, there was no value and many dangers in such reconciliation to a greater union.[12] More essentially, difference, he realized, does not need to be overcome. In his first editorial of his new magazine, bissett praises filmmaker Léonard Forest's documentary *In Search of Innocence* for including "splits and retreats and paranoia" in his film ("About" 105) rather then attempting to create an artificial illusion of unity and coherence. bissett's stance as a writer and a publisher involves confronting difference and allowing that difference to stand unreconciled. Thus, bissett contests writings like *Tish* in which "th language is still correct nd teachabul nd backd up with troops by th fort knowx" (*RUSH* 38). It is no wonder, then, that the only featured poet from the VPC to publish in *Blewointment* was Margaret Avison, the author of "ancient science fiction," as Milton Wilson once put it, and the champion of those "[w]hose call is to the outer utter darkness" (Avison, "Geometaphysics" 319).

While *Tish* looked backwards to wrestle with its romantic and modernist inheritance, *Blewointment*, in issues such as "Fascist Court," "The Oil Slick Speshul," and "The Poverty Issew," confronted the present juggernaut of what Hardt and Negri would much later term Empire: the twentieth-century fusion of transnational capitalism with global governance. Recognizing the enormity of the phenomenon, bissett's poetics reacted against *Tish* and the 1963 VPC by embracing otherness, and consciously attempting to break apart and disrupt any vestige of exclusionary power in language, including on grounds of gender, sexuality, anthropomorphism, race, and more. These codicils of aesthetic shift were clearly palpable in the sprawling experience of the VPC, as evidenced by the collaged journal issue of *Tish* 21 discussed in the previous chapter. The *Tish* opening was blown wide open, and a huge range of voices were suddenly heard. While the *Tish* poets spent a great deal of energy celebrating the margin of the page as the site of their avant-garde conquest, bissett countered that "yu dont need the margin" (*Rush* 46) because "yu are already here" (42). Years later, the Language poets would highlight enforced complicity in capitalist violence through the compulsion of using a complicit language: as Steve McCaffery would quip, "Capitalism begins when you open the dictionary" (*North of Intention* 178).

---

12 Duncan, for instance, reconciles Hitler and Mae West as reflections of "the very nature of Man himself [...] Over and over again men disown their commonality with living things in order to conquer a place, exterminate the terrible or rise above the vulgar" (*Fictive Certainties* 115).

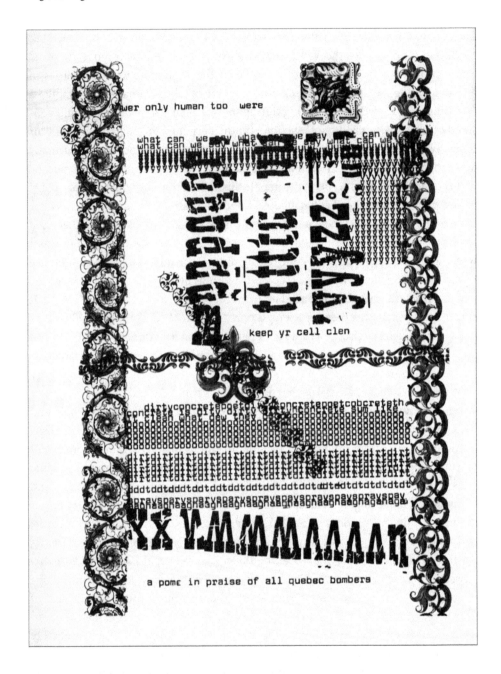

Figure 2.5 bill bissett's "a pome in praise of all the quebec bombers," from *pass th food release th spirit book* (1973). Source: Private colleagrievection of the author. Used with permission.

In defence of his laws in *The Poetics*, Aristotle argues, "Everything irrational should, if possible, be excluded" (3.23). In contrast, bissett built *Blewointment* as a space for, in McCaffery's words, "an exploration of both language and anti-language and an awareness of the forces that refuse textualization" ("Bill Bissett" 93). This combination of irreconcilable contrarieties is arranged without an appeal to harmony. For while Olson argued in favour of harmony, that "every element in an open poem" should act as "participants" ("Projective Verse" 25), bissett sought a space paradoxically open to nonparticipation. Indeed, he embraced discontinuity and the explosion of social codes and Western mores, even including famously writing in praise of Quebecois terrorists (from which the phrase "dirty concrete" was taken). Incorporating noise and irrationalism consciously evacuates systems, shatters the movement of plots, and claims disharmony as a necessary step in overcoming the rationalism at the core of Western logos.

3 The End of Categories: The Vancouver Litter-rary Collage

Despite whatever differences there may be between the aesthetic outputs and ambitions in their foundations, there were no firm or fixed social boundaries between the various aesthetic communities in Vancouver. People moved freely between them, and the social circles all overlapped and collapsed into one another. Still, the distinction between the university and the downtown poets is instructive for beginning to map the intellectual and artistic transitions underway in Vancouver in the early 1960s. It also helps to explain the different responses to the aesthetics privileged in the VPC, including bissett's establishment of a materialist/collagic magazine and Carol Bergé's sneering response to the Canadian acolytes (see *Vancouver Report* passim). Judith Copithorne emerged from the event inspired, but toward visual-literary connections and aesthetic crossover work that were decidedly not part of the curriculum. bissett and Copithorne both disconnected themselves even further from the university milieu and became central figures in the group already identified as the "downtown poets," a network that included poets like Gerry Gilbert, Maxine Gadd, Lance Farrell, Bertrand Lachance, Hart Broudy, and Martina Clinton, as well as primarily visual artists like Jack Shadbolt, Roy Kiyooka, Pierre Coupey, Ian Wallace, Gary Lee-Nova, Edwin Varney, and many others. It was not exactly an antagonism or even necessarily a rivalry that ensued between the downtown poets and the university poets, but a marked difference was clearly established. Michael Turner, for instance, notes the striking visual difference between the primary publishing vehicles of the two groups, noting the "clean and neatly-typed affair, filled with poems of a 1950s modernist bent," of *Tish*, and the *Georgia Straight Writing Supplement* with its "generic notions of literary writing – what [Ian] Wallace alluded to when he spoke of the explanatory and the expressive" styles that developed out of it. In juxtaposition, Turner positions the radical, messy avant-garde style of *Blewointment* magazine, *radiofreerainforest*, and *Circular Causation* ("Expanded" n. pag.). The downtown poets became more involved in local Vancouver politics, and were in fact instrumental in establishing the *Georgia Straight* as a downtown community newspaper in May 1967. By the time the *Georgia Straight* newspaper arrived, however, the first generation of *Tish* poets and editors had dispersed and been replaced by a group much more sympathetic with the downtown crowd, even if the radical eclecticism was not their preferred aesthetic. The lines between the communities were decidedly blurred.

Consequently, bissett established the *Blewointment* press and magazine as an explicitly eclectic venture, more likely to publish around specific contemporary interests and anxieties (poverty, Tantrism, end of the world, and so on) than strict aesthetics. It was this spirit of openness, montage, and honesty that allowed writers as diverse as Nellie McClung and George Bowering to publish work alongside Margaret Atwood and Judith Copithorne. (*Tish*, in contrast, would reject a poem that they could openly acknowledge was better than what they were publishing if it didn't fit their model aesthetic.) What the *Blewointment* venture suffers in editorial coherence and polemical focus, it makes up for in the optimism generated by the community's diversity. It took a stance against the habitual erasure of colonial Canada and made a space for everyone.

From this vantage, recognizing the arrival of Blew Ointment Press and *Blewointment* magazine and the editorial transition underway at *Tish*, the VPC looks much less like a genesis moment in Canadian avant-gardism than the ultimate note of an aesthetic that quickly established a new aesthetic orthodoxy in Vancouver, and that helped to subsequently provoke the radical heterogeneous imaginations of the next garde. As I will discuss later in the next chapter, bissett used the *Blewointment* experiment to apply the ethos of collage to publishing and community-building alike. Thus, the *Tish* authors freely published their New American poetry in bissett's magazine, alongside the exuberant collages and incoherent experimental riffs of the downtown writers. The "selfish and pretentious" nature of *Tish* ("Two Retrospects" 424), to quote Davey, was almost instantly rendered a relic of the past, set aside for the collegial utopia of unlimited potential and intermedial experimentation. As bissett himself describes the story, the magazine grew out of fighting with "editors who didint cudint see what we wer dewing so we decided to start our own publikaysyun [...] we wer talking abt how we had nowher to publish / n thats what we all wanted not ambishyun access [...] nowun cud evr stop us xcept ourselvs a great faith" (Introduction 7).

The break from traditional closed verse to open verse corresponds to a remarkable shift in opinions on the value and importance of technology. The university poets, following the interests of the New American poets, wrote about typewriters, radios, and cars as an extension of their interest in techne, theory, and poetics. Ginsberg's compositional method focused on intersection of the breath and tape recorder (integrating the human body into technology). Spicer saw in the typewriter a portal to access the Muse, and Olson revelled in the mechanical precision of the typewriter. Olson's vigorous interest in the writing machine caught McLuhan's attention:

> Poets like Charles Olson are eloquent in proclaiming the power of the typewriter to help the poet to indicate exactly the breath, the pauses, the suspension, even, of sylla-bles, the juxtaposition, even, of parts of phrases which he intends, observing that, for the first time, the poet has the stave and the bar that the musician has had.
>
> (*Understanding Media* 227–8)

In this way, through this technology, an alignment (a harmony) between writing and sound, speech, and music was realized.

George Bowering acknowledges an important divide in the avant-garde that is worth considering in this context: "The European theoreticians, Barthes and Ben-veniste, for instance, have taught their subscribers to pay attention to the written more than the oral use of language, to the discourse without the moment of uttering" ("Vancouver" 106). Against this error, he holds up Olson, for whom language was primarily and most potently oral and sonic: "Poetry that races to elude the author-ity of the poet herself. Not poems made to express the poet's point of view. Poems trying to trace their own autonomy" (109). In fact, however, the binary between writers interested in expression versus autonomy was irrelevant to those who were inspired by or connected with the European theorists he mentions. While Olson and especially Ginsberg were instrumental in challenging the contextual repressive limitations on what could and could not be said at the time, and offered instead a cry of freedom, a jubilant celebration of the sayable, as the 1950s folded into the 1960s, artists like bissett, Gerry Gilbert, Phyllis Webb, and many others began to question the possibility of autonomy (aesthetic or otherwise). Technology began to feel like something of a trap, and not necessarily liberatory.

In his investigation of the interface, and the limits of representation, contempo-rary media theorist Andrew Galloway marks a poignant distinction between artists invested in "a coherent, closed, abstract aesthetic world" – pre-existing or fashioned by them – versus "the disorientation of shattered coherence" that "makes no attempt to hide the interface" and "turns the whole hoary system into a silly joke" (39). I am reminded of a line from a letter written to me from Talonbooks founding editor Jim Brown on concrete and visual poetry: "In the sixties it was a fun part of writing poetry. Nobody took it seriously. We all had fun with it in one way or another" (Email correspondence n. pag.). This space of not taking it seriously (which he contrasts to the serious writing of Olson, Duncan, Bowering, and so on) is actually a gateway to a disturbing and systemic alienation from language and expression. Nichol, when asked of this kind of sentiment, retorted: "Many people don't realize that play is seri-ous. [...] Games demand work and involvement" (Jukelevics 133). Galloway writes that the melding together of form and content, such a core principle in the New

Figure 2.6 George Bowering and Allen Ginsberg in 1974. Photographer unknown. Source: Collection of the Estate of George Bowering. Used with permission of the Estate of George Bowering.

American poetics, "aims to remove all traces of the medium" as a barrier to representation (46). In contrast, dirty, messy, sprawling, deliberately incoherent works – such as we see in bissett's concrete poems, and throughout *Blewointment* – objectify "the necessary trauma of all thresholds" and stage "the upheaval of social forms" (46). Making the page visible shatters sayability: the ink spreads like a dark silence (like nothingness), the joyful autonomy of language overwhelmed by its materiality.

Judith Copithorne's poem "Famine," from the second issue of *Blewointment* in December 1963, articulates this consciousness of inarticulatability:

> So much moves by in cold and emptiness
> The silence of only oneself.
> And the voice in ones head far back
> as in a cathedral or a machine
> far away.
> One is often frightened because – last
> time – or the time before remembered
> when there was a famine
> What happened then

Never will the famine go
For leaving is a time.
There is no leaving
Coming is a misleading word
perhaps. [...]
Hear you all hear you tell us listen
Receive all receive I am trying to
listen to the famine.
The page flips You were flipping
the page when we came.
We want you to listen. Listen.
They are all mad and in so much pain
that I don't know what to do.
To protect them and myself.
    (n. pag.; reprinted with permission)

The poem achieves a liminal ground between a debilitating fear of inexpressibility and recognition of the dire need to both hear it and speak through it. This famine is a prophecy of the collapse of meaning and the recoil of language. In the same issue, bissett writes, "We are not the same as we were inside THE BODY, or as we were coming to it or taking our departure. We have become outside remembrance and forgettings, its illusions and skills, outside time" ("we are haunted" n. pag.). Such harrowing alienation belies the preternatural confidence of the *Tish* drive to overwrite, maximize the world.

At the risk of incomprehensibility, the downtown poets (and later the KSW [Kootenay School of Writing] Language poets[13]) shunned the romance of the typewriter as a technology endowed with special representational power, or as a force for autonomy, for forgetting the materialist and ideological contest from which such an interface had emerged. The political implications of the material world implied a disturbing complicity with a system bissett was actively fighting. As he wrote to Diane di Prima in 1971:

yr struggle is to bring down th pentagon – ours is to keep it out. its 1812 all ovr again & its 1850's red river & we th long hairs the metis again – peopul here who nevr done time for innocence talk uv hopeful change thru the existing govt – I don't know. (Letter n. pag.)

---

13 Bowering makes the delightful link between the "gambits of the Language poets" in Vancouver, done in order to reveal ideology behind expression, with the "purpose and effect of Brion Gysin's (who did not stay to construct Edmonton) famous cut-up method of the Beat days" ("Vancouver" 15). Clint Burnham, in a similar vein, describes the KSW aesthetic with reference to collage, which he defines as "work that operates with a high level of disjunction," and more specifically social collage, defined as "a critique of the hegemonic role of meaning in late capitalist society" (37).

It follows that dirty concrete poet bissett's exploration of the use of the typewriter was antithetical to the mechanical precision celebrated by Olson. He produced grimy and ambiguous texts wherein letters crash upon other letters, overlap, distort, obscure, and prevent reading. Such works connect less to a classical music metaphor than to Marinetti's letteral and sonic depictions of war. But whereas the Italian Futurists had extolled the cleansing violence of war, bissett's typewriter art functions as a libidinal eruption of repressed drives: highly sexual, openly revolutionary, and logically disturbing. Ink spills over the words, even the letters, darkening communication by its black fog. There is a spirituality at play in this destruction, but it begins with a slag heap of culture, with the recognition of famine and the page.

More generally, the downtown poets were ambivalent in their aesthetic use of technologies, aware of their role in transnational hegemonies, but drawn to the euphoric potential in mixing media and experimenting with machines. There was a simultaneously self-effacing and mystical-*cum*-spiritual organicism that decried machinery for a nascent environmentalist equilibrium that yet allowed them to glom on to new technologies (video, tape recorder, radio, film, mimeograph, photocopier, and so on) and repurpose those machines. Gerry Gilbert's poem "Thought for Penny" highlights the fact that this ambivalent position on technology includes writing and language itself:

the pen hits hardpan right on top of the paper page here
you'd naturally expect the pen to sink deep into the paper
like the paper was strange albino moss saturated with invisible waters
which would dissolve all inks so that all writing meets
& all pages are perfectly clear

                                                            (n. pag.)

The erasure of text, and the reconnection of paper technology with the ancestral forest, is not a nihilistic vision, but one entwined with what Galloway might describe as "radical alterity, the inhuman [...] We shall call it simply *truth*" (50; emphasis in original). Gilbert, in writing this poem, violates the *histoire*, the illusion of reality-making in literature, for *discours*, the self-conscious artifice. His breach of silence is the allegory of this rupture. Roy Kiyooka – whom Bowering called "the first Vancouver postmodern poet" ("Vancouver" 113) – similarly breaks silence by speaking to the importance of silence: finding nothing in art, literature, and even conversation is connected to overcoming artifice and the hollowness of Western culture; "what we come to in our solitude is the recovery of our / singleness defined, by s i l e n c e . // to recover our solitude the immeasurable silence that lies / at the heart of things is to define the future of Art" ("miscellaneous" 66). Recovering from the alienation of internationalist structures, embodied by so many technologies, begins with recognizing technology's complicity in the global violence of transnational capitalism,

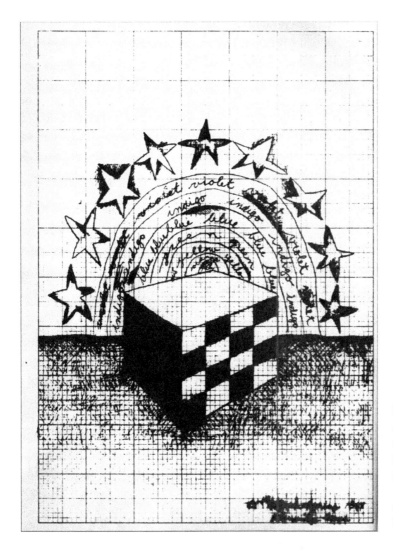

Figure 2.7 One of Gary Lee-Nova's untitled visual poems in *Blewointment* magazine 9.1 (June 1967). Source: Private collection of the author. Used with permission.

a systemic structure that connects poetry to transnational global conflict. Thus, Kiyooka continues: "any definition of a masterwork (whatever moves you) must / answer to The Silence it commands [...] the BOMB continues to grab the headlines. So also the Space/Cadets, Vietnam & Gerda Munsinger [...] no one pays for silence." A new art, or a new role for art, emerges in careful defiance of the noise of the contemporary moment, of its mass media and spectacle, which are entwined with war and global conflict. Smaro Kamboureli notes that Kiyooka's book *Transcanada Letters* evokes an "unimaginable community" undoing the constitution of locus through an excess of incommensurable details (x).

So, while cameras and printing presses, radios and televisions could be recruited into the revolution of sensibility, the service these were all pressed into was, ideally, the unravelling of transglobal, capitalist consciousness. Pierre Coupey admits that "the war in vietnam is also a result of the paint flowing from my fingers" ("An Allegory of Love" n. pag.). Unlike the first *Tish* poets who seemed surprised to find themselves almost instantly within a national and international conversation, these artists were extraordinarily aware of their proximity, of their art's proximity, to the levers of powers that shaped the world; thus the repetition of the importance of finding nothing, which functioned something like a mantra for the avant-garde of the period. Similarly, bissett's 1971 book *IBM (saga uv th relees uv human spirit from compuewterr funckshuns)* drew attention to the commonality in the dual implications of the acronym for International Business Machines and Intercontinental Ballistic Missiles: a deadly paragram. Copithorne, that same year, expressed a similar sentiment in her richly illustrated *Miss Tree's Pillow Book* when she wrote, "IBM / YES NO / ZABSURD [...] THE CURTAIN GOES UP IN THE COLONIAL MAGIC THEATRE" (n. pag.). This mistrust of technology can be connected with the proliferation of handwritten poems and hand-drawn visual poems, especially among women, that sought to re-inscribe the material presence of the body into the text. This gestural basis for Vancouver's visual poetry helps to distinguish the work emerging there from the international concrete poetry movement that harvested its aesthetic, however parodically, from corporate advertising models. It wasn't just external technologies that concerned these writers, however. While many writers sought an organic basis for the alphabet, such as McCaffery and Nichol in their interest in Alfred Kallir, who posited the origins of the alphabet in the sexual anatomy of humans, bissett recognized *language as technology*, culturally embedded and complicit in contemporary ideological antagonisms. In one of the most authentic and unique political gestures in the history of Canadian literature, upon recognizing this complicity, bissett proceeded to alter the orthography, refashioning the very DNA, of all his writing – including in poems, prose, essays, and correspondence – to a very free and flexible phonetic approach. Echoing the second De Stijl manifesto of 1920, whether consciously or not, bissett articulated his departure as part of an ongoing language revolution. Here is what Theo van Doesburg, Piet Mondrian, and Antony Kok proposed, fifty years before bissett:

THE WORD IS DEAD ...
THE WORD IS IMPOTENT [...]
is influenced by an individualism fearful of space
        the dregs of an exhausted era [...]
the word must be reconstructed
        to follow the SOUND as well as
        the IDEA
if in the old poetry
        by the dominance of relative and
        subjective feelings

the instrinsic meaning of the word is destroyed
we want by all possible means

> syntax
> prosody
> typography
> arithmetic
> orthography

to give new meaning to the word and new force to expression

(11)

Nichol would echo these exact sentiments in his 1971 book of concrete poetry *ABC: The Alpeh Beth Book*. bissett, much less prone to manifesto and theoretical expostulations, sought an unprecedented embeddedness in his poems, a total sensorium of full-body experience outside of language but touched by ink. This accords with the De Stijl call for a new kind of writing that "will not describe events / it will not describe at all / but ESCRIBE / it will recreate in the word the common meaning of events" (qtd. in McCaffery, *Carnival* n. pag.)

The progression toward postmodernism ushered forth an increasing biopolitical awareness of the material conditions of the surrounding environment, including its technologies. The New Americans poets wrestled with issues of proprioception and with the body as a means of extending the modernist fascination with precision technology and the power that illuminates and accords to the self. The body was outside the environment, and, accordingly, "angels," "muses," and meditations on how to connect daily life to a harmonious universe inspired poetry from this orientation. The downtown poets, in contrast, recognized the body within the material world and consequently wrestled with the material limitations of art in terms of both its particular mediums and its complicitous relation to the general society, including its worst acts of violence. These are both materialist orientations that highlight some of the contiguities between modernism and postmodernism, at least in this transitional phase in Canada.

THREE

Blew Collage

I'm beginning a magazine called "Spanish Fleye" – a philtre of new literature and i would like to have some of your work for the first issue. The magazine is dedicated to poets who are not generally seen because of their socalled "esoteric characteristics" or their newness (a poet like yourself), in whom i believe (and i believe you to be THE figure in canadian poetry).

David W. Harris (aka David UU) to bill bissett, Letter 88 (18 August 1966)

Collage is the archive of radical juxtaposition, the scholar's act of paratactic cutting and pasting. It establishes a montage of differences where the putting side by side illuminates those differences at the same time that it spotlights commonalities. Ideally, collage is a non-hierarchical act of comparison, a joining that illuminates both commensurabilities and incommensurabilities.

Susan Friedman, "Periodizing Modernism" (493)

[T]he extraordinary contribution of collage, is that it is the first instance within the pictorial arts of anything like a systematic exploration of the conditions of representability entailed by the sign.

Rosalind Kraus, The Originality of the Avant-Garde and Other Modernist Myths (34)

1 At the Margins of the Garde

Let us consider the alchemical swirl of *Blewointment* press and magazine and recognize how it unified a number of disparate interdisciplinary energies in Vancouver, and how it helped to accelerate each by collecting them into a shared forum. These energies included authors exploring the shared boundaries of literature and music and visual art and film and photography. Over the course of the 1960s, the individuals involved in the early years of the magazine – including bissett, Martina Clinton, Judith Copithorne, Jack Shadbolt, Gerry Gilbert, Al Neil, Lance Farrell, Jack Mawhinney, Beth Jankola, Gregg Simpson, Scott Lawrance, Curt Lang, and many others – became a scene and gradually coalesced into a broadly bohemian downtown community that had a significant impact on art in Vancouver, Canada, and even the world. The conceptual photographer Ian Wallace, a contributor to *Blewointment*, has said of those

Figure 3.1 Front cover of the first issue of *Blewointment* magazine, which appeared in October 1963. Source: Private collection of the author. Used with permission.

early days that "[n]ot only were the 1960s an amazing period of cultural transformation worldwide, but Vancouver was a great place to be at the time and remains so in my view. I have described it as the 'frontier of the avant-garde'" (Janssen 138). Hardly lost to the margins, as in the old narrative of the city, the beatnik-*cum*-hippie scene was prominent enough to attract the attention of the National Film Board of Canada, who released two documentary movies of the group: one on the scene in general, *In*

Search of Innocence, directed by Léonard Forest in 1963 and filmed in the style of the French New Wave cinema, and one focused on bissett in particular, *Strange Grey Day/ This: bill bissett Vancouver painter & poet*, produced and directed by Maurice Embra in 1965. It was in this milieu, serving that frontier, that bill bissett began publishing *Blewointment* and founded Blew Ointment Press, a magazine and a small press book publisher that specifically catered to the specific needs of the bohemian, beatnik, and hippie cultures emerging in Vancouver's downtown.

bissett, as both a poet and painter, experimented with abstraction and collage in his early works. He was a transformational figure in Canadian literature for developing new ways of integrating collage into poetry, for disrupting the lyric voice with error, for self-conscious materiality (the over-inked mark of a typewriter, unexpurgated deletions, and deliberate errors, for instance), and for giddily abandoning stylistic consistency. The first editorial of the first issue of *Blewointment* praises Forest's film for its use of a "gestalt of montage" (bissett, "About" 103) and focuses upon his method of stark juxtaposition as the necessary aesthetic for representing the contemporary moment: "had you done anything else i wud have turnd from you" (104). In 1971, he concluded his House of Anansi book of selected poems *Nobody Owns th Earth* (edited by Margaret Atwood and Dennis Lee) with a "bare bones biography" that foregrounded the collage form in his authorial identity: "collage makr i do poetry readings" (93). In the biography, he added that he prays "that th world be mor open as what is possibul that ther be less imperial isms" (n. pag.). Given his interest in what Rachel Farebrother describes as "the subversive potential of collage" (190), it is worth considering how the eclecticism of his magazine and press performed a collagic function – the archive of radical juxtaposition that Friedman describes in this chapter's epigraph – in the literary world of the time.

It is a fact, and very unusual for any publication, that bissett accepted and published anybody who submitted work to *Blewointment*. With the limited distribution of the magazine and its limited print runs, access was limited to those in the know, meaning that the authors included were much less than a random sampling of the full scope of Vancouver and especially Canadian literati. Nonetheless, it still presented a radically incongruous array of writers that extended far beyond bissett's local Beat or hippie scenes. What emerges across the magazine's issues and books is a polyphonic spectacle of open-minded authors who were committed, each in their own way, to a community of exuberant eclecticism: the writing is wildly uneven, from rank amateur to some of the most polished verse Canada (and beyond) had to offer at the time, but that unevenness contributes to a portrait of a holistic, multiplicitous network of artists. Unlike its exclusionary predecessors in Europe (let alone Vancouver), it was an astonishingly welcoming avant-garde. Given bissett's open-door publishing, it becomes instructive and often surprising to consider who self-selected to get involved and who chose not to participate in such an experimental publishing venture. Earle Birney, for instance, the establishment poet of Vancouver and acclaimed scholar of medieval Anglo-Saxon literature, surprised many by becoming

Figure 3.2 Detail of Maurice Embra's *Strange Grey Day/ This* (1965), an NFB documentary about bill bissett and his bohemian community in Vancouver in the early 1960s. Source: Private collection of the author.

an enthusiastic contributor – even connecting his call for collaborations between poets and painters (see "Poets and Painters") to bissett's exploration of concrete and visual poetries. Atwood was in, Ondaatje was in. Al Purdy and Milton Acorn were in. Most of the *Tish* poets and editors published at least once with bissett, but Frank Davey, however, did not publish anything with *Blewointment* in its twenty-year run.

If we think of this assemblage in the magazine as collage, it is worth reconciling the relationship between visual art and publishing in the exploration of the form as it became manifest in Vancouver in the 1960s. Collage, derived from the French word for "a pasting," is the name given to art that physically incorporates the work of another onto a canvas. The term was coined in specific reference to objects glued onto a canvas but also provides a categorical function for works that stage the juxtaposition of voices in more diverse ways. It is in the more generic sense that I am using the term herein. As Herta Wescher writes, "[i]t has been customary to apply the term 'collage' to all works in which components belonging to separate intellectuals or perceptual categories are combined, even when, as in many instances, nothing has been pasted or glued" (qtd. in Adamowicz 14). In this way, "collage" is the root term that connects photo montage (the combination of multiple images into one photo), assemblage (the sculptural combination of found or made objects), cut-up, found, and appropriative writing (the use of copied text in a literary work), bricolage (the creation of a work of art from a range of things at hand), exquisite corpse (the Surrealist game of collaborative writing, often where each contributor is limited to seeing only the previous line), and so on. Each of these predominantly twentieth-century methodologies opened the work to a multitude of creators and in doing so shattered the romantic notion of the self-contained and perfect (unified or harmonious) work of art. Of collage, art historian Diane Waldman writes, "By its very nature collage connotes the temporary, the ephemeral [...] The technique of collage was ideally suited to capture the noise, speed, time, and duration of the twentieth-century urban, industrial experience" (11). With this in mind, it is possible to recognize bissett's *Blewointment* experimental publishing venture as the embodiment of a collage aesthetic in dissemination for including radical difference in stark juxtaposition, for making the seams of its own production visible, and for privileging the contemporariety of its authors and their willingness to participate. *Blewointment* presents, in this way, a radical democracy in literary form, a privileging of nonhierarchical modes versus the monological restriction of ideolects. As its recurring interest in time-limited political issues (for instance, Elizabeth Coleman begins a poem, "In the month of March, reports on Lsd ..." ["War with LSD" 9.1]) makes clear, it aimed toward activism within an ephemeral frame rather than, to contrast it with *Tish*, a literature reflecting the preciousness of an eternal universal – not that *Blewointment* restricted universalist or precious modes of writing.

bissett's vision for his own writing, and his orienting aesthetic, was informed exactly by this notion of the integration of disparate energies. He explained what he was working toward in a letter to Margaret Atwood in 1971, sent while she was editing the selected edition of his work for *Nobody Owns th Earth*: choose and arrange the poems, he wrote, "so that thru th threding almost heer in thinking abt it like thru a needul eye social/politikul/personal/ situation/thery/fact/loss/ feelingsatisfackshun all bcum plausibully part uv th same concern" (Letter 2). His poetry was a maelström of causes and affects swirling into a giant alchemical vortex of unfettered energies. His correspondence with Atwood about the selected works carefully maps out how to maintain that disparate yet unified force across a selection of incongruent writing. By 1971, certainly one of the peak moments of avant-garde activity and especially of collage-literary collaborations in Vancouver, bissett had become something of an expert in that pursuit. This collagic spirit, which was indeed a rising force in the global avant-garde from the 1950s through the 1970s, animated Vancouver's downtown arts community and helped to foster a diverse array of interdisciplinary experimentation. The artists recognized within their interaction the possibility of something widely significant unfolding: they were using their art to help fuse a new model of individuality that posed an important challenge to the categorical constructs of Western culture and, perhaps, by extension, to the very idea of individuality. Though collage is most usually regarded as exclusively the domain of the visual arts, *Blewointment* demonstrates that collage was also a central dynamic of mid-century radical poetics.

Back in 1951, McLuhan was already meditating on the broad sociological significance of collage in art and literature. His work connected these forms to a much more widespread shifting consciousness than just avant-garde literary or art circles. In fact, he traced the shift in consciousness to the rise of electricity and the advent of the modern technological and mediated landscape, including, most prominently in quotidian experience, the collagic model of the newspaper:

> To the alerted eye, the front page of the newspaper is a superficial chaos which can lead the mind to attend to cosmic harmonies of a very high order. [...] This situation is a major feat of modern news technique. Hot spot news with a vengeance. What a thrill these men must have got from being on the inside of a big inside story. Participating in their own audience participation, they were able to share the thrill of the audience that was being thrilled by their imminent death. (*Mechanical* 4)

For McLuhan, audience participation in the creation of culture was a defining hallmark of contemporary "electric era" culture. The Vancouver art community acutely registered McLuhan's message. But it was this message, of using technology to draw people together in the production of a new consciousness and culture, that led the organizers of the Festival of the Contemporary Arts to hail McLuhan as the leading philosopher of their efforts toward interdisciplinary activity. Indeed, the 1965 FOCA (organized by Helen Goodwin, Takao Tanabe, Iain Baxter, and Arthur Erikson) was devoted specifically to the exploration of McLuhan's aphorism "The medium is the message" and coincided with the establishment of the Sound Gallery, a remarkably open institution that "provided a focal point for experimental collaborations that combined music, poetry, light shows and film" (Wallace 30). The primarily art world engagement with his work is beyond the purview of this study, except where it aligns with the literary communities that shared their interest and pursued the democratic participatory models of electric intermedia experimentation. The Sound Gallery, of course, anticipated the emergence of the Intermedia Society in 1967, Vancouver's first artist-run centre, which crystallized McLuhan's influence.

As its name suggests, Intermedia was devoted to interdisciplinarity and evoking new possibilities out of media through the juxtaposition of tools and techniques and practitioners. In Felicity Taylor's words, Intermedia was "a site where McLuhan's notion of the sensorium could interface with the countercultural idea of altered consciousness [...] the radical potential of Eros was a powerful means to politicize McLuhan's insight that shifts in communications technologies would affect human spatial awareness" (9). With significant federal funding (a shocking $40,000 from the Canada Council), they bought some basic equipment (most notably tape and video recorders) and established a radically open space for meeting and working. People generally supplied their own technology, and it was generally accepted that the rules of art production were deliberately shattered. Poet Maxine Gadd describes the ethos of the place: "There was the idea of public participation and the idea that everybody was an artist, everybody was a musician, anybody could paint, anybody could take photographs, anybody could play the flute or whatever [...] there was a suspension of standards [...] it was the last gasp of anti-specialism" (qtd. in De Courcy, "The Intermedia Catalogue" n. pag.). The role

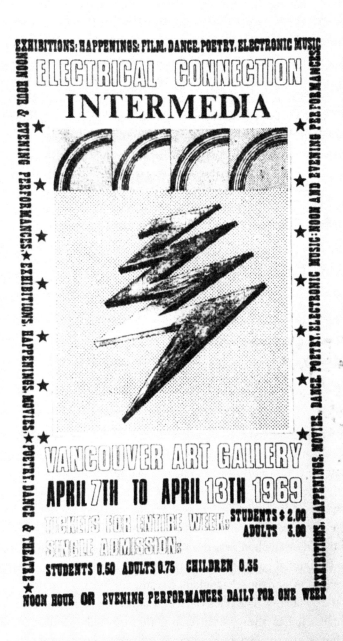

Figure 3.3 Poster for the Intermedia Society's *Electrical Connection* exhibition at the Vancouver Art Gallery, 7–13 April 1969. Source: University of British Columbia Rare Books and Special Collections, Intermedia Society Fonds, A4 B3 2–8 1518.

of the individual as the principal agent of change was discarded in the celebration and exploration of what happens when people (and arts) merge and intermix freely, with abandon, and without direction: artistic activity, as Keith Wallace adds, in the Intermedia scene was "less about authorship or careers than about collective achievements" (31–32). We encounter in this radical democratization a resemblance to McLuhan's sense of the foundational intent of the avant-garde, one key aspect of which he defined as the "delegation of authority from centre to the margins" (*Gutenberg Galaxy* 106). Such a shift of power away from stabilizing centres included disempowering competitive individualism and the aesthetic discourse of mastery and masters, and most importantly involved blurring the line between production and consumption of culture. The power to define what is art, even, was opened to all. People rushed into this opening.

By the mid-1960s, Vancouver was awash in this collectivist, indeed radically open spirit. Even a lyric poet like Patrick Lane caught the attitude and embraced it wholeheartedly:

> the voice of now is where we are
> in Vancouver and the west is
> tripping by itself on itself
>   catching the sunflower's yellow
> beautiful whispers and the poems
> the thing no style no way of writing
> no school no group NO THING is
>   ("(Auto)" 54)

Nothing, then, was arrived at as a peak aesthetic experience. It, *no-thing*, was pure, open, inspired, and unmitigated. Lane included a gorgeous concrete poetry collage by bissett on the cover of his most experimental book, *Letters from the Savage Mind* (1966; see Figure 3.4). *Blewointment* magazine reflects this radically open spirit in various ways, including page design, typography, and the use of random inserts of inexplicable advertisements, notices of publishing news, poems, stories, and more slipped or tipped or stitched between the covers – all of which foreground ephemerality and communal participation in the aesthetic project over individual efforts, tidiness, perfection, and the self-contained aesthetic object. If you hold *Blewointment* carelessly, things fall out. The book object itself has been remade to resist closure.

Though bissett has always been enamoured of Hollywood and the gorgeous spectacle of celebrity, literary star culture was distinctly eschewed in his magazine: shockingly, considering how things have changed, no author biographies were ever included in the entire run of the magazine. Indeed, a number of issues go so far as to strip authorial designation from the poems in the magazine (see issue 9.1 and the "End of the World Speshul" issue). An intentionally cumbersome index at either the front or the back of the volume reconnects the texts to authors, but the

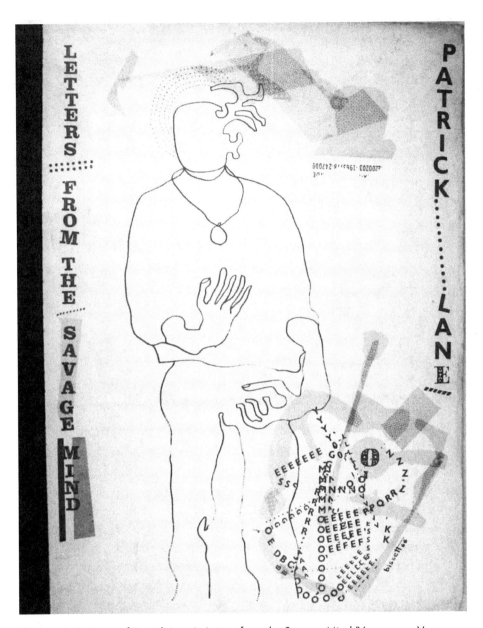

Figure 3.4 Cover of Patrick Lane's *Letters from the Savage Mind* (Vancouver: Very Stone Press, 1966).

inconvenience of this method speaks to the desire for the poems to be understood communally, as participating in a shared project, rather than individually in discrete perfection. Issue 4.1, meanwhile, includes various author attributions, but only for approximately half of the poems. The rest, all published on pages of various sizes and colours, are simply left unattributed. An answer to the question of who wrote the

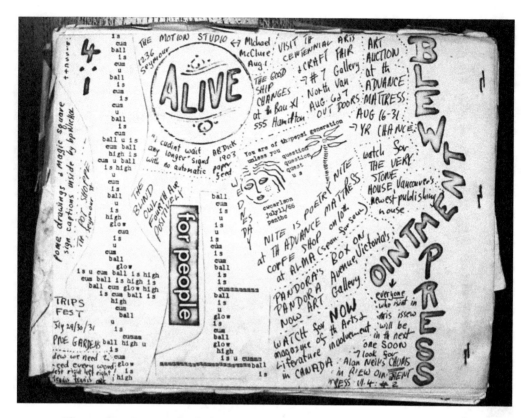

Figure 3.5 Front cover of *Blewointment* 4.1 (1966). Source: Private collection of the author. Used with permission.

poems in this issue might be provided by the French avant-garde poet Lautréamont: "Poetry must be made by all. Not by one" (qtd. in Blanchot 184). The magazine used authors as juxtaposed elements sometimes literally pasted into its pages as collage.[1]

Not coincidentally, Lautréamont's line became an important slogan and a motto for the mid-century avant-garde, especially as manifest in the *Poetry must be made by all: Transform the World!* exhibition at the Vancouver Art Gallery in July 1971, organized by Ron Hunt, who was then a visiting professor at UBC. One of the most radical and celebrated exhibitions in Europe in the sixties, it was first mounted at the Moderna Museet in Stockholm in November 1969 and featured a history of radical art from the Russian Constructivists, the Situationist International, and even the Black Panthers alongside free jazz performances and sculpture. The theme of the travelling exhibition was the interaction of advanced art and radical politics, documenting the

---

1 The Poem Company, a collective network of poets associated with Intermedia, would advance this collective anonymity by dropping even the index of their contributions to the group's books.

political-aesthetic fusion of the Situationist International and May 1968. It was, in the words of art curator Hans-Ulrich Obrist, "an attempt to link revolutionary politics to avant-garde artistic practices" (113). In the Vancouver version of the show, Hunt invited *Blewointment* contributor and photoconceptualist Ian Wallace to present an untitled slide show of eighty photographs taken on a walk from the Vancouver Art Gallery through the downtown: showing the scene/seen of Vancouver, if you will.

2 Blewointment

What was *Blewointment*? Let us materialize the discussion by focusing on the objects that substantiated the press. Over the course of twenty years, bissett published seventeen issues of the magazine, featuring a total of 314 different authors, 1,099 text poems, 125 visual poems, and 50 prose pieces. Though bissett was the only named editor of the magazine throughout its entire run, there were two distinct editorial phases of its production. The first period, 1963–8, involved the regular publication of numbered issues, staple-bound and marked by what the *Encyclopedia of BC* describes as "crude mimeograph" design ("blewointment" n. pag.). bissett signalled his growing impatience with the standardized regularity of the zine by perverting the issue numbering beginning in the second year: the second volume begins with issue 2.2 (April 1964) rather than 2.1, issue 4.1 (1966) announces content that will appear in issue 4.2 even though it actually appears in 4.1, and issue 9.1 (June 1967) appears between issues 5.1 (1967) and 5.2 (August 1968). Issue 5.2 is the last issue of the first editorial period, and the last numbered issue of the magazine. bissett ceased publication for all of 1969, during which time he was imprisoned (for two weeks) in the Oakalla regional prison in New Westminster for marijuana possession and suffered a major brain injury after falling at Alvin Balkind's house at the party celebrating the opening of the Concrete Poetry Festival at UBC. When the magazine resurfaced in 1970, with the onset of the second period, the issue numbers were replaced by named anthologies, often with overtly social or political themes. The production quality shifted as well: "What Isn't Tantrik," "End of the World Speshul," and "Th Combined Blew Ointment Picture Book nd th News" are all perfect bound, rather than staple-bound mimeographs. It is debatable whether these anthologies should be lumped in with the book publications or with the magazine, but the first examples – "Fascist Court" (1970), "The Occupation Issew" (1970), "Oil Slick Speshul" (1971), and "The Poverty Issew" (1972) – maintain a consistent design and content appearance with the previous magazine issues (note too the punning use of "Issew" in the titles of the collections). Editorially, the biggest difference is the orientation toward specific themes or "issews," tenuously sewn together approaches to specific issues. The first four of these second period issues are highly political, marked by a frustration that almost becomes cynical, while the last issues return to more esoteric terrain, albeit

without the euphoric mysticism of the 1960s issues. I do not include the two retrospective tribute anthologies, *The Last Blewointment Anthology* volumes 1 and 2
(1983), in the number calculations as these were produced after bissett had sold the
press to David Lee and Maureen Cochrane and were published in Toronto by their
small press, Nightwood Editions. In some respects, these retrospective anthologies
are the equivalent of the twentieth issue of *Tish*, and might have started a new period
were they not also the self-conscious finale of the previous moment.

The magazine was a veritable meeting ground of Vancouver literati: bissett published
representative editors from most of the magazines operating in the city, including *Tish*
(George Bowering, Fred Wah, and Jamie Reid from the first editorial period, and David
Cull, Gladys Maria Hindmarch, Stan Persky, Daphne Marlatt, and Robert Hogg from
the second editorial period), *Circular Causation* (Scott Lawrance and Jorj Heyman),
Georgia Straight Writing Supplement (Stan Persky), *Prism* (Lionel Kearns), representative editors from most of the presses operating in the city, including Very Stone Press
(Pat Lane, Seymour Mayne, Jim Brown), Returning Press (Judith Copithorne), Talonbooks (Jim Brown, Karl Siegler), Intermedia Press (Ed Varney, Henry Rappaport), and
representatives from most of the intermedial art organizations in the city, including
the Image Bank (Vincent Trasov, Michael Morris, Gary Lee-Nova), Intermedia (Gerry
Gilbert, Ian Wallace, Jack Shadbolt), and the Western Front (Henry Greenshow, Trasov, Morris). He published established older poets (Earle Birney, Dorothy Livesay, P.K.
Page, Milton Acorn, Nellie McClung, F.R. Scott) alongside the rising luminaries of the
next generation (Al Purdy, Margaret Atwood, Michael Ondaatje, Dennis Lee, bpNichol,
Pat Lowther, Gwendolyn MacEwen), and, of course, all of these historicized authors
appeared alongside multitudes of forgotten writers who never published again. He set
disintegrating visual poems alongside traditional rhymed and free verse, sophisticated
collages alongside juvenile hand-drawings, poems (with standardized spelling) alongside pomes (with phonetic or deviant orthography). He published hippies, feminists,
Red Power advocates, socialists, communists, environmentalists, and anyone else, even
squares, who wanted to be heard in that dynamic community. Admittedly, he published
no overt capitalists and no Irving Layton (or Frank Davey).

Blewointment magazine by the numbers

Total number of issues – 17
343 poems by women versus 756 poems by men – 31%
0 reviews of work by women versus 4 reviews of work by men – 0%
70 works of visual art by women versus 155 works of visual art by men
  – 31%
17 prose works by women versus 33 prose works by men – 34%

Figure 3.6 Ian Wallace's untitled collage from *Blewointment* 5.2 (August 1968).
Source: Private collection of the author. Used with permission.

Despite this astonishing national eclecticism, *Blewointment* was *prima facie* the literary publisher of the downtown community and, by this focus, helped to make
important connections between the literary and visual art worlds. bissett was (and
remains) both a poet and a painter, and it follows that the magazine is rife with

experiments in disciplinary crossovers. It was a place to try. *Blewointment* published poetry by the acclaimed painter Jack Shadbolt, short fiction and poetry by the acclaimed jazz musician Al Neil, and textual "cut-outs" by photographer Ian Wallace. The formal openness of the magazine is disorienting and astonishing: end-rhymed poems appear alongside concrete poems, children's cartoons alongside New American serial poems, confessional lyrics alongside political doggerel. Over the course of its twenty-year run, the magazine functioned, in many respects, as a geomantic core sample of literary activities of the period in the city.

Blew Ointment Press's book publishing began in March 1967 with the publication of Michael Coutts's *march 67 othr pomes* – "with inside drawing suitable for framing by cliff foreman plus original prints in each copy!" (9.1). As the promo copy of Coutts's book indicates, the new venture for the press began with a concerted focus on visual-textual intersections, including books by concrete poets David UU, d.a. levy, and Lance Farrell and *A Collage Portfolio of Easter Be-In* by Gary Lee-Nova.[2] That same year, bissett also self-published five of his own books, including *Th Gossamer Bed Pan*, *Gregorian Chant*, *Meth means death*, *Mantras: Direct Line to God*, and *What Poetiks*. Over the next sixteen years, bissett proceeded to publish a total of 104 books, chapbooks, and broadsides before, as previously mentioned, selling the press to Toronto-based poets David Lee and Maureen Cochrane in 1983. They renamed the press Nightwood Editions, but revived the *Blewointment* brand as an imprint series starting in 2005. Before they changed the name, though, but after the press relocated to Toronto, twelve additional titles were published under the Blew Ointment Press moniker, including titles by *Blewointment* regulars Cathy Ford and Steve McCaffery, and the two-volume tribute anthology by regular contributors mentioned above. For the same reason that the *Last Blewointment* anthologies were not included in the numbers I'm using in my calculations for the magazine, these books that were published in Toronto are not included in the numbers for the book publishing side of the operation. As with the magazine, the books bissett published represent a range of interests and styles – from d.a. levy's *Zen Concrete* (1967) poetry to Gwen Hauser's second-wave feminist poems in *the fascist branding pomes #2* (1974), from long, spiralling lyric poems to terse epigraphs, serial poems, and haikus, and so on. While the experiment with diminutized author functions did not carry over into the book operations of Blew Ointment, the interest in collage, collaboration, and community carried on apace. The vast majority of titles came directly out of the downtown Vancouver scene, including multiple books by Bertrand Lachance (three), David UU (three), Ken West (three), Michael Coutts (two), Lance Farrell (two), D.R. Wagner (two), Maxine Gadd (two), P.X. Belinsky (two),

---

2 Lee-Nova published *Cosmic Comics* in 1971 with Blew Ointment Press, but I have not been able to confirm that this other title did in fact appear.

Rosemary Hollingshead (two), Cathy Ford (two), Gwen Hauser (two), Beth Jankola (two), Martina Clinton (two), and Gerry Gilbert (two). Another thirty-nine were self-published books by bissett (plus one collaboration between bissett, Bertrand Lachance, and the photoconceptualist Christos Dikeakos). bissett or other visual artists in the city illustrated many of these books.

As the intermedia community matured, Vancouver art increasingly privileged direct experience, engagement, and, what Wyndham Lewis might call, romantic knowledge. Lewis's discussion of the lingering romanticism in modern art, which he likens to the "popular, sensational, and 'cosmically confused'" (35), is particularly useful in highlighting the mistrust of positive science and technology that became a common concern of the group, even as they embraced the utopian, McLuhanesque potential of new media. The imperialist war in Vietnam, the rise of environmentalism in Vancouver (Greenpeace was founded in the city in 1971), psychedelics, and the emergence of communal lifestyles all contributed to a deep sense of mistrust in Western notions of technology-led progress. McLuhan's theories of the increasing "tribalization" of citizens of the electric age, the denizens of the global village, also offer some insight into why science and rationalism were no longer deemed sufficient. He argued that electricity created environments that were reprogramming the sense ratios away from the detachment of the visual system in favour of the more immersive auditory system. The shift presaged a decline in rationalism and individualism as people experienced themselves within environments rather than detached from them. In this way, the electric age privileged multiplicity over singularity, communalism versus individualism, conversation over lecture. McLuhan, who now functions as the prophet of the digital age (at least as declared by the masthead of *Wired* magazine), was then read as a prophet of the Age of Aquarius dawning in the city. The downtown artists became emphatic followers and celebrated his theories of emerging multiconsciousness and his deployment of an anti-scholarly mosaical prose form. McLuhan lectured at the New Design Gallery on Pender Street in 1959, and later at the 1965 Festival of the Contemporary Arts. The latter event was subtitled "The Medium Is the Message" in tribute to his rising influence (see Michael Turner's "Expanded Literary Practices").

bissett, for one, worked to incorporate McLuhan's ideas into his writing. In the preface to *We Sleep Inside Each Other All* (1966), he explains the collection as a direct response to McLuhan's sense of epochal change:

Marshall McLuhan sz we are poisd between th typographic individualist trip the indus trial revolution & th electronic age we have been in for sum time, between a unique dis tance and alienation privacy well now iullbe in th study for th rest of th night with my nose in a boo k & th corporate image tribally we are a part of out extensions do reach now have been reach thruout all time th historical jazz consumd in th greater fire of mo view t v & lo ve. ("what ium doing in these pomes" n. pag.)

Figure 3.7 Terrance Loychuk's *Media Cluster*, four McLuhan-inspired posters. Source: The Estate of Terrance Loychuk. Used with permission.

McLuhanism, acid, jazz improvisation, anti-imperialism, anti-individualism, mysticism, and the emergence of new publishing technologies (the mimeograph and the typewriter especially) all facilitated the sudden prominence of collage experimentation in the city. Indeed, Vancouver was arguably the most fertile ground in the country for intermedia collage, and especially intersections between visual art and literature. *Blewointment* was the veritable epicentre for that endeavour. Building from this intersection of the visual arts and literature, the rest of this chapter will contextualize that Vancouver moment into broader, international contexts.

3 Collage into Canada

To understand the shift that took place in literature in the 1960s, one has to situate the sudden attention to the visuality of language within the context of the emergence and sudden dominance of the collage visual art technique. While collage in Europe has its own history that can be traced back to the eighteenth century (and beyond), collage in Canada has its roots in the composite photography of William Notman's photographic studio of the mid-nineteenth century.[3] Montreal-based Notman rose to international acclaim – "the first [Canadian] to have an international reputation," notes Ralph Greenhill (56) – for pioneering a manipulation method that allowed photography to produce the bustling, large-scale images associated with the art world traditions of outsized history paintings and towering *trompe l'oeils*. His studio

---

3 Biographical notes taken from http://collections.musee-mccord.qc.ca/scripts/explore.php?Lang=1&tableid=4&elementid=00016__true

Figure 3.8 One of William Notman's revolutionary painted composite photographs, *Skating Carnival, Victoria Rink*, Montreal, QC (1870).

business began in 1856 with the making and selling of portrait prints of royalty and celebrity. Before photography, portraits of luminaries were enormously expensive and laborious. Notman's relatively affordable studios helped to popularize the display of famous portraits with the general public. Business expanded rapidly, and he quickly opened up new studios across Canada and into the United States, until he controlled, in fact, the largest photography company in North America. The staff he hired was trained in retouching the negatives and colourizing the prints. Such expertise in photo manipulation led, indirectly, to large composite photographs of portraits, each of which were taken separately but were then stitched together into iconic or amusing scenes. Up to three hundred individual portraits, often of identifiable people, were cut up and then pasted onto a painted background – a skating pond, a marketplace, a city square, and so on. The images were subsequently copied, printed, and sold on the open market. The popularity of Notman's composites attracted significant attention, enough that he was officially declared "Photographer to the Queen" in 1860 after duly impressing a visiting Prince of Wales. His son, William McFarlane Notman, maintained the family business and toured Canada to track and photograph the progress on the Canadian Pacific Railway, arriving in Vancouver in 1887. He made nine trips to document the city, including in 1901 as the official photographer of the Duke and Duchess of York's Canadian tour.

The history of cameras and photography extends all the way into the ancient world, but the modern technology was effectively invented in 1839 in France. The device was still a new technology in mid-century but was already displacing painting as the dominant tool for capturing and representing the world: as French painter Paul Deroche declared, "From this day forward, painting is dead" (qtd. in S. Watson, "Art" n. pag.). The visual objectivity of the camera was its primary appeal in the early manifestations, and its success in this area helped to trigger art's crisis with representation a few decades later (for instance, Cézanne's first solo exhibition was not until 1895; Picasso's invention of the modernist collage was not until 1911). It is striking, then, that Notman's popularity arose precisely by his artistic manipulation of photographic realism. Indeed, the composite photo established something new in the negotiation of modern aesthetic technologies: it was an art that was made of the seamless integration of disparate elements into a unified composite image. To be clear about the historical context of his innovation, the Parisian photographer Hippolyte Bayard, roughly simultaneously with work by British photographers Oscar G. Rejlander and Henry Peach Robinson (UK), had pioneered small-scale and limited composite photography prior to Notman. Notman developed from their work by cutting out complete images and rearranging them into new compositions in a manner, as Diane Waldman notes, "that prefigures twentieth-century photomontage" (14). The unapologetic departure from realism in Notman's large prints makes the composite image a direct precursor to the defamiliarizing juxtapositions of collage. Collage was part of the reinvention of the visual arts following the crisis of representation in the modern period, utilizing the unfettered freedom to create imaginary worlds. In a similar way, and anticipating the stark, unnatural juxtapositions of modernist work, Notman's composites create impossible landscapes, phantasies in the Freudian sense, that insist upon their nonrepresentationality. It is all the more striking that these early photo manipulations were enormously popular, as they helped to create the positive conditions for the later experimentation in the visual and literary arts. The direct link between nineteenth-century photographic experiments and the European avant-garde, however, comes not from Notman but from another unlikely source – Hans Christian Anderson, whose paper-cuts and photographic collages in the 1890s were cited as influences on a wide array of avant-garde artists, including Max Ernst and Joseph Campbell.

The rising interest in collage and its transformation into "a viable medium in the context of fine art" (Waldman 8) bespeaks its connection to the broadly imaged cultural shift we now call modernism. Modernism was once generally understood through reference to the influence and invention of a handful of exceptional individuals – figures like Ezra Pound, T.S. Eliot, F.T. Marinetti, Virginia Woolf, Pablo Picasso, James Joyce, Gertrude Stein, and so on. In the context of this study, though, the idea of modernism is a highly differentiated one in which multiple styles and aesthetics are connected but not presumed to be in any way uniform or determined by singular points of origin. Instead, a more multi-nodal, geomodernist approach considers how various points of influence were distorted and adapted in local contexts, in this case in Vancouver. Such an approach is consistent with the modernist work in question, which also began to incorporate differentiation, multiplicity, and variant perspectivism into individual works of art. For instance, in British Columbia, Victoria-based Hannah Maynard (1834–1918) took inspiration from Notman's commercial experiments, including with photomontage. She was one of the first women, if not the very first in North America, to operate an independent photo studio. Her photos dating from the early 1860s incorporate photo-sculpture, multiple exposures, composite images, and cut-and-paste montage in an attempt to capture motion, disrupt the objectivity of the photographic object, and expand the aesthetic boundaries of the medium. She depicts herself having tea with herself, or four versions of herself attending herself while she drafts a letter. The images are different from the gleefully radical European avant-garde in how they maintain Victorian decorum all while shattering the technological limitations of her medium. She was doing something new, totally idiosyncratic, and delightfully British Columbian.

Modernism, from this vantage, is a global wave of art and literature that first responded to, sought to harness, or developed out of the enormous social and technological changes underfoot around the dawn of the twentieth century. It happened unevenly in different contexts and can be differentiated by the local forces at play in the spread of modernity and industrialization. In *Everybody's Autobiography* (1937), American novelist and poet Gertrude Stein, who was a pioneer in adapting geometrical Cubist painting methods to literature, uses the Eiffel Tower as a metaphor for the industrial oil wells she witnessed across the United States from Oklahoma to Texas to California. Her book looks back on the first wave of modernist literary production in North America and explores the quintessentially modernist theme of the paradox of individual isolation and alienation in an age of mass communication and mass transit: "since the earth is all covered over with every one there is really no relation between any one" (99). Like the oil wells that Stein found across the North American prairies, the harsh metallic Eiffel Tower cutting into the low-lying, flowing streets of Paris symbolized a break between the new technologies and the natural landscape, a break between people and their environment, and for some even the conquest of humanity over nature. Others found it nothing but an affront to good taste.

From the populist composites of the late nineteenth century, the avant-garde increasingly incorporated related alienating art techniques into their most utopian projections. At the turn of the century, Russian avant-gardists used photomontage to demonstrate their support for a new and progressive world order. Shortly after, the Italian Futurists embraced collage for its harsh, violent – hence vibrant! – juxtapositions. Dadaists used collage, photomontage, and assemblage to create enormously disruptive repudiations of institutionalized art practice. The Surrealists explored

Figure 3.9 Hannah Maynard's photomontage *Trick photography, self portrait* (1893).

collage to access and represent the subconscious. As Elizabeth Finch writes, for the Surrealists, "[c]ollage-making was about looking, about locating the dream image in the everyday" (116). It was through the influence of the Surrealists that French Canadians began experimenting with collage with that different but related form called the exquisite corpse (where a text or image is passed around obscured but for the last contribution and everybody adds a line, image, or deviation to the collaborative work). Alfred Pellan is credited with bringing the avant-garde parlour game to Quebec after he returned in 1940 from studying and working in Paris for nearly two decades. Proselytizing the Parisian avant-garde, in 1946 he led a group of artists (including some of the future Automatists) to experiment with texts combined with drawings. These artists included Pellan, Jean Benoît, Mimi Parent, Simone Jobidon, and Françoise Sullivan (Ellenwood 128). Automatist artist Jean-Paul Mousseau produced his first collages in 1947, but as with the rest of the Automatists shifted away from collage to explore non-figuration. Claude Gauvreau, however, continued to experiment with "verbal collage," clichés transformed through superimposition and disorienting linguistic blends, into the 1950s and 1960s (Bourassa 146).

From the outset of the twentieth century, North American modernist writers took up the collagic spirit and embarked on a similar trajectory of experimentation with harsh juxtapositions and perfunctory shifts in consciousness. The group of expatriate artists and writers in London and Paris who self-identified as part of the "Cult of Ugliness" (Pound, "Serious" 45) filled their writing with violent and jarring imagery and marked it with complex stylistic features, including collage, bricolage, and fragmentation. For these writers, especially Pound, Eliot, and Lewis, collage was a useful new form to depict the modernist despair at the fragmented remains of Western civilization; to register the alienation, the despondency, and even the however remote possibility of a new consciousness. Eliot's *The Waste Land* (1922), with its collage of multiple voices, highlights the dissolution of order into fragmentation. Indeed, the working title of the poem was originally *He Do the Police in Different Voices*.

Though the poem surveys the bleakness and spiritual violence of modernity, it does conclude with the invocation of sacred traditions as a possibility of redemption (or, less generously, the memory of the possibility of redemption). Such a nostalgic heralding of the redemptive structures of history is not anathema to the practice of collage. Indeed, art historian Blanche Craig argues that nostalgia is endemic to and materially embedded in the practice of collage: "By ways of its multiplicitous nature, collage is often perceived to both signify the spirit of contemporary culture (particularly in relation to its continual hybridization), and a desire to preserve cultural signs and nostalgically nod at a 'better,' less chaotic past" (7).[4] The nostalgic undercurrent underscores the widespread interest in so-called primitive cultures by modernists and avant-gardists alike. In like manner, Allen Ginsberg glossed a relevant section of his 1954 poem "Howl" in an interview and elucidated the plight of the hipsters he depicts: "They are 'looking for an ancient heavenly connection to the starry dynamo in the machinery of night,' meaning that they are looking for a connection back to nature from the hyper-industrialized urban high-tech slum" (Ginsberg and Le Pellec

---

4 In 1963, in the second issue of *Blewointment*, bissett writes an ekphrastic response to Picasso's *Still Life with Chair Caning* that addresses the appeal of nostalgia and how collage (Picasso's collage) evokes and disrupts such desires: "cube margins bloat, distend / shadows of coil / a vast green / we keep house / to yearn for calm / understanding [...] and the trumpet / is nostalgia / that cameos / must sometimes satisfy" ("We Paint the Mirror" n. pag.). The poem proceeds self-consciously, speaking against the possibility of a calm understanding that is yearned for: "reference turns / upon itself / an infinite mirage." It can be contrasted to Carol Bergé's ekphrastic yet lyric response to "Still Life" discussed in chapter 2.

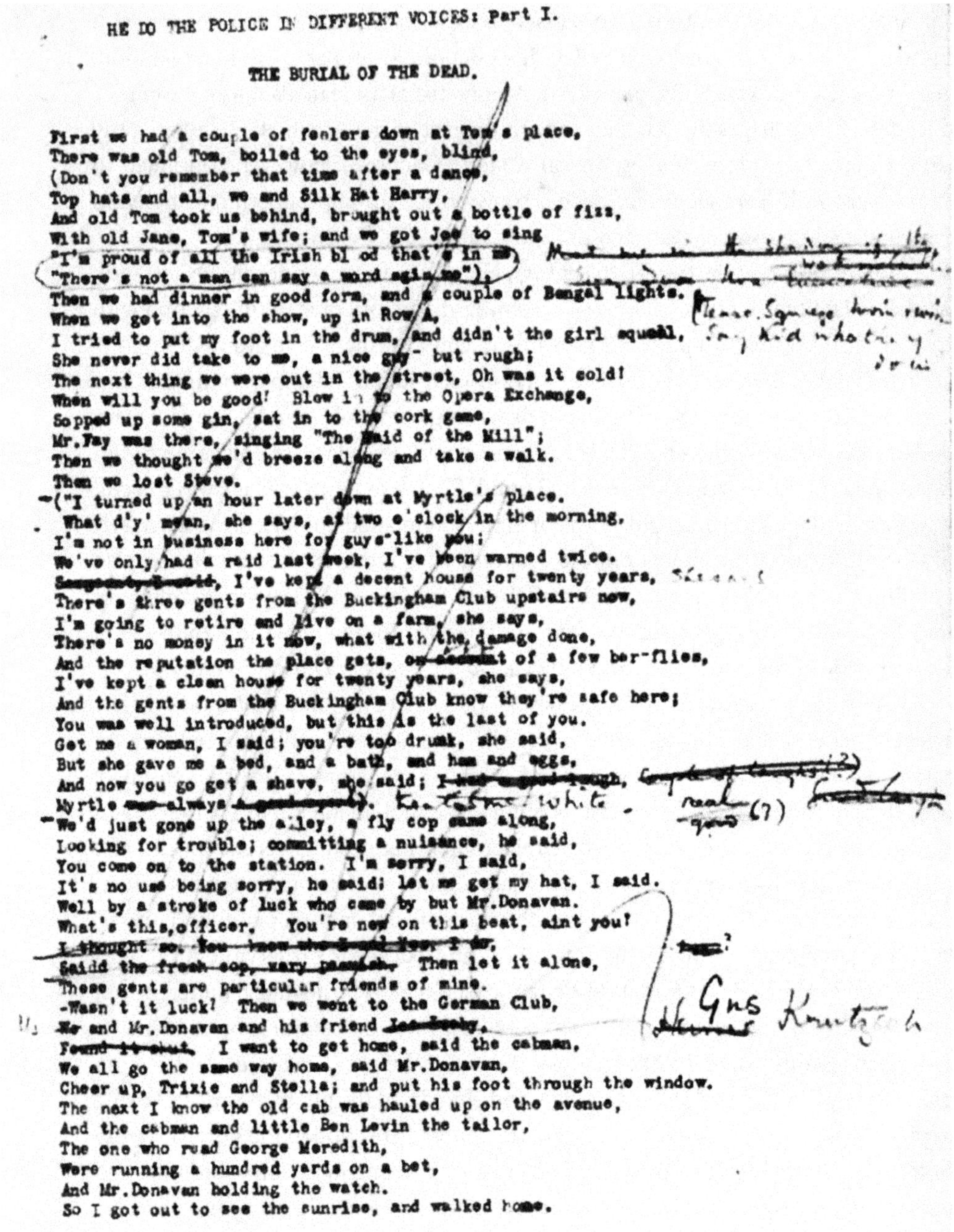

HE DO THE POLICE IN DIFFERENT VOICES: Part I.

THE BURIAL OF THE DEAD.

First we had a couple of feelers down at Tom's place,
There was old Tom, boiled to the eyes, blind,
(Don't you remember that time after a dance,
Top hats and all, we and Silk Hat Harry,
And old Tom took us behind, brought out a bottle of fizz,
With old Jane, Tom's wife; and we got Joe to sing
"I'm proud of all the Irish blood that's in me,
"There's not a man can say a word again me").
Then we had dinner in good form, and a couple of Bengal lights.
When we got into the show, up in Row A,
I tried to put my foot in the drum, and didn't the girl squeal,
She never did take to me, a nice guy but rough;
The next thing we were out in the street, Oh was it cold!
When will you be good? Blow in to the Opera Exchange,
Sopped up some gin, sat in to the cork game,
Mr. Fay was there, singing "The Maid of the Mill";
Then we thought we'd breeze along and take a walk.
Then we lost Steve.
("I turned up an hour later down at Myrtle's place.
What d'y' mean, she says, at two o'clock in the morning,
I'm not in business here for guys like you;
We've only had a raid last week, I've been warned twice.
Sergeant, I said, I've kept a decent house for twenty years,
There's three gents from the Buckingham Club upstairs now,
I'm going to retire and live on a farm, she says,
There's no money in it now, what with the damage done,
And the reputation the place gets, on account of a few bar-flies,
I've kept a clean house for twenty years, she says,
And the gents from the Buckingham Club know they're safe here;
You was well introduced, but this is the last of you.
Get me a woman, I said; you're too drunk, she said,
But she gave me a bed, and a bath, and ham and eggs,
And now you go get a shave, she said; I had enough tough,
Myrtle was always a good sport.
We'd just gone up the alley, a fly cop came along,
Looking for trouble; committing a nuisance, he said,
You come on to the station. I'm sorry, I said,
It's no use being sorry, he said; let me get my hat, I said.
Well by a stroke of luck who came by but Mr. Donavan.
What's this, officer. You're new on this beat, aint you?
I thought so. You know who I am? I do,
Saidd the fresh cop, very pleasish. Then let it alone,
These gents are particular friends of mine.
Wasn't it luck! Then we went to the German Club,
Me and Mr. Donavan and his friend Joe Leahy.
Found it shut. I want to get home, said the cabman,
We all go the same way home, said Mr. Donavan,
Cheer up, Trixie and Stella; and put his foot through the window.
The next I know the old cab was hauled up on the avenue,
And the cabman and little Ben Levin the tailor,
The one who read George Meredith,
Were running a hundred yards on a bet,
And Mr. Donavan holding the watch.
So I got out to see the sunrise, and walked home.

Figure 3.10 Manuscript page from a draft of T.S. Eliot's *He Do the Police in Different Voices*, which would be renamed *The Waste Land*.

97). In that interview, alluding to Eliot, he would explain that "Howl" and his poem "America" were written in a deliberately alienating, shifting consciousness: "It's all a collage of different voices!" (103).

From these avant beginnings inside and outside of literature, the form became increasingly central to the evolution of twentieth-century art. Of the more immediate precursors to the Vancouver activity, and one with significant connections to Black Mountain College, Robert Rauschenberg created "combine" paintings, assemblages of painting and found objects. His "Black Paintings" series, in particular, in the early 1950s combined text from newspapers with objects and thick gobs of black oil paint. Diane Waldman argues that his combines and collages revitalized collage in the North American context and set the stage for the pop art explosion that followed shortly after (15). Rauschenberg, whose works were included in the 1964 Festival of the Contemporary Arts in Vancouver, came back in July 1967 to exhibit a series of collages and assemblages at the Douglas Gallery. Ian Wallace reviewed the show for the *Vancouver Sun* and declared it "a momentous occasion then, when a local commercial gallery takes the initiative to exhibit a major example of recent American printmaking by such an internationally renowned artist as Robert Rauschenberg" (qtd. in Griffin, "In Vancouver" n. pag.). It is a poignant reflection on the advanced state of Vancouver art that Wallace added in his review, somewhat wryly, "This [work] would not be radical now, but it was in the fifties, and the implication of this attitude are still being felt today." Avant-garde art is, after all, not always avant-garde.

Things had developed from Rauschenberg's groundbreaking work with collage. Waldman highlights Rauschenberg's influence on Jasper Johns in particular, who invented collages built of *fake* found objects – objects manufactured to look like ready-mades:

> He thus took the Duchampian concept of the found object one step further, beyond acknowledging the found object as a valid subject in art to creating the appearance of the found object, often using traditional means of painting and sculpture. In doing so, Johns comments on how objects are formed and makes a powerful statement on how we perceive them in the world. (56)

Such a manipulation of the benchmarks of reality and realism proved enormously popular in Vancouver in the 1960s, where the altered or manufactured ready-made, like the misheard found poem, the doctored composite photograph, and manipulated landscapes, were widely used.

At present, there is no convincing or satisfactory survey of collage or related forms in Canada, such that details of its usage and origin are diffuse and ambiguous. The best overview of collage in Canada appears in the short introductory essay in Joan Murray's 1997 exhibition catalogue *Canadian Collage*. The forty-five objects in the exhibition, however, are primarily contemporary rather than historical examples,

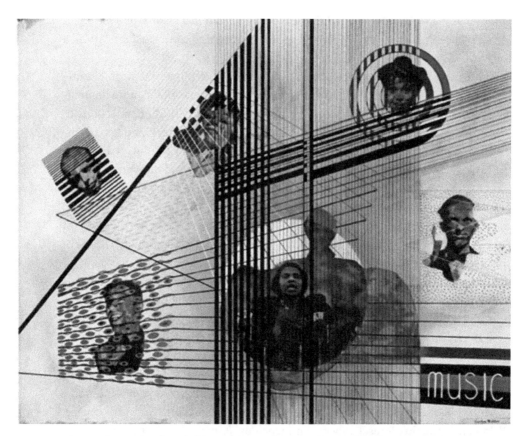

Figure 3.11 Gordon Webber's photocollage and gouache *Music* (1942).

and skip from Gordon Webber's groundbreaking collage gouache from 1939 straight to mid-1950s work (9–13). With regret, I set aside the task of a proper history for someone else, but note that the first documented collage in Canada used photography in the manner of László Moholy-Nagy's "photo-sculptures," whose form can be traced back to the early experiments pioneered by the likes of William Notman. What is immediately clear is that Canadians have been consistently experimenting with collage since the 1930s – starting with Gordon Webber's Bauhaus-inspired collages in the 1930s[5] and extending through the Cubist collages of Marian Scott in the 1940s and the Surrealist works in Quebec mentioned above. By the mid-1950s, artists like Michael Snow, Harold Town, Jack Bush, Dennis Burton, and Tom Hodgeson in Toronto and Douglas Morton in Regina were producing complex series of collages. By the 1960s, in the wake of Marcel Duchamp's return visit to Toronto in

---

5 Webber's recently discovered hand-painted films from 1940s offer a poignant model for the interdisciplinarity of Vancouver's 1960s. See http://cinematheque.qc.ca/fr/un-film-inedit-de-gordon-webber.

1961 (he first came to Canada in 1927), artistic engagement with collage had multiplied exponentially: Gordon Rayner, Louis de Nivervile, Les Levine, and Paterson Ewen all experimented aggressively with collage, but the names are too numerous to explore meaningfully in this context. Needless to say, from that point on, collage activity was rife and rich and widespread. Duchamp's visit also directly inspired Richard Gorman and Dennis Burton's 1961–2 exhibition in Toronto, *The Sign of Dada*, signalling the official arrival of that garde and even "Neo-Dada" into the city.

Even Marshall McLuhan became actively involved in collage-making when the Indian artist Panchal Mansaram immigrated to Canada, largely to work more closely with McLuhan. Mansaram painted several pictures for McLuhan (including a portrait), designed the covers for two of his books (*Voices of Literature* part 1 and part 2), and even "created collages on the old furnace in McLuhan's house" (Kuskis n. pag.). Between 1966 and 1972, Mansaram worked on a series of McLuhan-inspired works called "Rear View Mirror" (exhibited at the Picture Loan Gallery in Toronto in 1972). Not shown at that exhibition was a collage piece now titled *M&M* created by the two of them that incorporated pasted images, handwritten text, and stencils of McLuhan's aphorisms. It was for good reason that McLuhan was a guiding philosopher for the collage-oriented artists and writers in Vancouver, as so much of his media philosophy and social commentary articulated the radical shift posed by a collage-based media. As he explained to *Playboy* magazine in a 1969 interview:

> The day of the individualist, of privacy, of fragmented or "applied" knowledge, of "points of view" and specialist goals is being replaced by the over-all awareness of a mosaic world in which space and time are overcome by television, jets and computers – a simultaneous, "all-at-once" world in which everything resonates with everything else as in a total electrical field, a world in which energy is generated and perceived not by the traditional connections that create linear, causative thought processes, but by the intervals, or gaps [...] which create synaesthetic discontinuous integral consciousness. ("Playboy Interview" 258)

4 Literature into Collage (in Vancouver)

In Vancouver in the 1950s and early 1960s, downtown painters and sculptors like Jack Shadbolt, Roy Kiyooka, and Toni Onley were the principal investigators of collage techniques. Their canvases increasingly integrated mixed-media objects and elements. While each of these artists also worked as writers, in the years that followed the lines between painting, sculpture, performance, and literature became increasingly blurred as elements of each were drawn into the maelström of a new kind of intermedial art. The period of peak literary-visual art interaction spans the years from 1964, with the almost purely visual art exhibition *The*

Collage Show at the UBC Fine Arts Gallery (featuring the work of Jerry Grey, Roy Kiyooka, and others), to 1975, when Ian Wallace produced two literary-themed, large-scaled photoconceptualist narrative works, *Summer Script* and *An Attack on Literature*. During those eleven years, the city was rife with a significant amount of intermedia and collage activity in which literature, especially poetry, played a prominent role.

Visual art–literary collage interaction gained significant momentum in 1967. In that year, bissett, Joy Long, and Gregg Simpson launched the Mandan Ghetto Gallery on 4th Avenue, a space specifically dedicated to the fusion of art and literature.[6] Reminiscent of the equally short-lived Vorticist Rebel Art Centre (which lasted just five months), the gallery operated for only a brief seven-month period. The gallery had been created through an "Opportunities for Youth" grant from the federal government and disbanded when the money ran out (Simpson Correspondence 26 August 2015). During that brief moment, however, they hosted a series of groundbreaking events, including a Surrealist-inspired collage show (*Collage Show*, 1–14 February; organized by bissett, David UU, Ian Wallace, and Lance Farrell) and Canada's first international concrete poetry exhibition in the first two weeks of April. Between these two events, there was another literary collage show with Dada-inspired work by Pierre Coupey, Ian Wallace, Gregg Simpson, and Ken Christopher. While the gallery was ostensibly geared toward visual art collages, these works were marked by a significant amount of textual material, as in bissett's integration of comic-book dialogue and Ian Wallace's newspaper cut-ins (poignantly modifying the template of Brion Gysin's cut-ups). Wallace was employed by the gallery through their federal grant.

Out of the gallery collective emerged Th Mandan Massacre, a short-lived improvisational music troupe led by bissett. Others involved included Roger Tentrey (flute), Terry Beauchamp (guitar), Wayne Carr (keyboards), Ross Barrett (tape loops), Gregg Simpson (percussion), Harley McConnell (percussion), Ken Patterson (percussion), and Martina Clinton (percussion). Their activity led to the release of a vinyl LP, *Awake in th Red Desert* (1967), featuring fourteen tracks based on bissett's book of the same name that was published by Talonbooks. The band seems to have dissolved around the same time the gallery shut down.

In 1971, Chris Dikeakos and bissett organized another *Collage Show* at the UBC Fine Arts Gallery, featuring a remarkable array of representation from the Vancouver school of photoconceptualists (Jeff Wall, Ian Wallace, Chris Dikeakos), Vancouver Surrealism (Gary Lee-Nova, David UU, Gregg Simpson, Gilles Foisy, Edwin

---

6 The year of this exhibition is listed as 1967 by Grant Arnold (318).

Figure 3.12 Poster advertising the *Collage Show* in 1968 at the Mandan Ghetto Gallery. Source: Private collection of Gregg Simpson. Used with permission.

Varney), and *Blewointment* regulars (bill bissett, Al Neil, Mike Rhodes, Terry Reid). Of course, all of these artists were aligned through the Intermedia Society – indeed, Intermedia Press published the catalogue – and many of them were actively publishing poetry, prose, or some combination of the two. Of these interactions between literature and the visual arts, Wallace makes a compelling case to think of them as a

Figure 3.13 Cover of Th Mandan Massacre's LP *Awake in th Red Desert* (Allied, 1967). Used with permission.

unique kind of art production particular to the time and place in which they were being made:

> All that "stuff," conceptual art, idea art, documentary earthworks, etc., makes more sense when it is read as a literature of images rather than confronted as works of art to be gallery promoted, even magazine promoted through gallery devices [...] We are now thinking of the public location of this art. I think that it is being publicly misled and misread. It is essentially "page" stuff that is plugging into the media power of the present gallery (commercial and institutional) setup. ("A Literature of Images" n. pag.)

Poignantly, Wallace argues that objects in visual art should be treated and read as "free words" and words in public treated as objects. Unfortunately, such concerted blurring of art and life was unenthusiastically received by the living public, who failed to invest in the form, and critics were also rather decisively negative: as Richard Simmins wrote in his review of *The Collage Show*, "This is creative, artless collage. It uses the media without comment and it, too, can be thrown away at the end of the show" (n. pag.). It is worth noting, though, that the one-issue *Free Media Bulletin*, in which Wallace's essay above was published, represents a significant moment of avant-garde activity in its own right: published by Jeff Wall, Ian Wallace, and Duane Lunden, the forum aligned an emerging photoconceptualism with radical literary arts – advancing Earle Birney's 1957 call for collaboration between the visual and literary arts considerably. Wall, Wallace, and Lunden also situated themselves within the international avant-garde by publishing their works alongside unauthorized reproductions of essays by Arturo Schwarz, Richard Huelsenbeck, Marcel Duchamp, Alexander Trocchi, Antonin Artaud, and William S. Burroughs. Lara Tomaszewska describes the journal as part of a zeitgeist of "the investigation into language and the desire to free poetry from narrative limitations" (28). From an art historical vantage, she describes it as "the *culmination* of vanguard activities that had already taken place in Vancouver during the 1960s" (191; emphasis in original). It captured the intersection of the Burroughs/Gysin literary avant-garde with the advent of experimental visual collage. Dikeakos continued publishing his "Serial photo-collages" in literary milieus like *The Capilano Review* until 1973, well into the era of conceptual art, alongside the likes of bill bissett, Gerry Gilbert, Gladys Hindmarch, and George Bowering (in an issue that begins with an epigraph from Charles Olson's "Human Universe").

Remembering the popularity of Notman's work, visual/literary collage in Canada maintained a similar lowbrow populism through its use of ephemeral media sources (newspapers, comics, rock art, and so on) but coupled this with a radical politics that rejected the hierarchical distribution of power in so-called late capitalism. Such a fixture is a commonplace element in avant-garde circles, and Canadian collage definitely integrated the European avant-garde politicized collage style, especially as deployed by the Futurists, the Dadaists, and most directly the Surrealists. The underlying assumption of the politics in the aesthetics in Vancouver is that increased material consciousness in art and literature reflects an increased awareness of and commitment to environmental responsibility and social justice. For beneath the pervasive bleakness of the modernist consciousness, there is still an inherent optimism. The violence and existential alienation depicted in these modernist works often provides or performs a kind of cleansing, cyclical ritual. The violence of our cultural failings that led to that precipitous moment opened up the possibility of reintegrating and reconnecting with the material world. Birney concludes his "Vancouver Lights" poem on just such an optimistic note: "Yet we must speak [...] we conjured these flames hooped these sparks / by our will From blankness and cold we fashioned

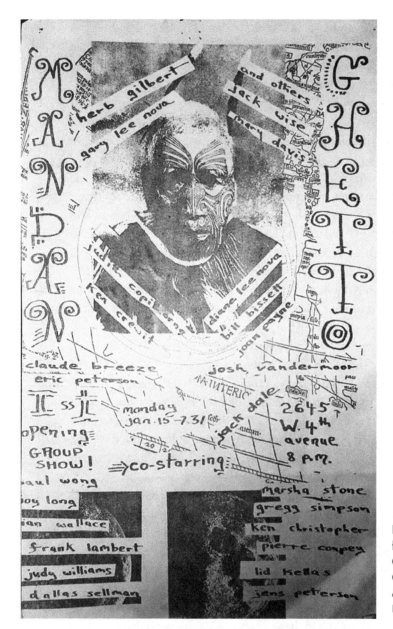

Figure 3.14 Poster for the Mandan Ghetto Gallery. Source: Collection of the Estate of Gregg Simpson. Used with permission.

stars / to our size" (72). In "Notes Toward a Supreme Fiction," Wallace Stevens writes that nature "expelled us and our images" (402) and it was our subsequent lot to reinvent the world through imagination.

Vancouver collage must be recognized as emerging out of modernist despair and awakening toward a new attitude of artistic liberty. McLuhan added to this material-oriented consciousness an elevated sense of the potential cultural contribution

Figure 3.15 Gerry Gilbert, George Bowering, and Allen Ginsberg in 1974. Photographer unknown. Source: Collection of the Estate of George Bowering. Used with permission.

of collage. He argued that "the medium is the message," which most people assumed broke with common consensus and simply re-ranked the technology that delivered the content above the content it delivered (a TV show is secondary to the impact of the TV itself, for instance). McLuhan went further, though, by addressing the *élan vital* of the technology, its role in the dynamic evolution of human cultures, and evaluated the broad socio-political impact of content produced by manual power versus electricity. He tracked the technology of writing from script to press to contemporary electric media as a development with implications far beyond each particular medium. In his estimation, the shift from hand-script to letter press, for instance, that followed Johannes Gutenberg's invention of moveable type in (approximately) 1439 was the singular invention that shifted European culture from the Middle Ages to the modern world. The difference between the flowing, interconnected letters of cursive script and isolated, strictly linear, and orderly type precipitated a shift in individual consciousness and gave rise to the modern conception of the discrete individual. Readers had to learn how to see the discrete letters on the page, which altered their perception of the world around them: each figure was separated from the ground (many critics have noted that Sheila Watson's 1959 novel *The Double Hook* explores this insight from McLuhan). All of the laws and cultural realignment that followed from the emergence of the modern individual can, as a result, be understood as the ultimate content or message of the printing press – including the very notion of authorship, ownership, personal liberty, civil rights, and so on. When McLuhan came to Vancouver in 1959, his lecture addressed the impact of electricity, and especially electric models of communication, via radio, television, and telephone, and how they were already undoing the legacy of Western individualism. Electric forms of communication created immersive, total environments, he argued, and thereby raised the possibility of a new model of individuality emerging through the reconnection of figure and ground. The literary age was falling to the electric age.

McLuhan further inspired the Vancouver crowd with his prediction that the shift elicited by the emergence of electronic communication was destined to be as impact-ful as the print revolution. Unlike the orderly isolation of type, electronic media are interdisciplinary, overlapping, and defined by an "all-at-onceness" that presages a new mode of consciousness. Life in the electric age demanded a total cultural shift to accommodate the shift in consciousness already underway. He was cautious, even concerned, about the new age; increased tribalism, he noted, was often associated with increased violence. His readers in Vancouver, however, were enthralled by the possibility of a dissolved individual reintegrated into the environment. As many scholars have noted, McLuhan's scholarship on the transition into a new mode of consciousness was manifested in his own writing method. Donald Theall argues that McLuhan revolutionized academic writing by disrupting the linear through-line (*The Medium* xiv; *The Virtual* 77). He was, in fact, pioneering a collage-style essay form.

Coming from the humanities (the department of English, in fact), McLuhan focused his cultural commentary on modernist arts and especially modernist litera-ture by attending to the work of James Joyce (especially *Finnegans Wake*), T.S. Eliot, Ezra Pound, and British-Canadian Wyndham Lewis in relation to their techno-cultural milieu. Such a cross-disciplinary approach helped to facilitate the interac-tion of artists who were interested in manifesting the new age he prophesized, and (ironically considering his notion of the end of the literary age) helped to give a special prominence to literature and especially poetry in the zeitgeist. He never wrote about Brion Gysin directly, but he did write about William Burroughs's cut-up method as

> a paradigm of a future in which there can be no spectators but only participants. All men are totally involved in the insides of all men. There is no privacy and no private parts. In a world in which we are all ingesting and digesting one another there can be no obscenity or pornography or decency. Such is the law of electric media which stretches the nerves to form a global membrane of enclosure. ("Notes on Burroughs" 89)

Is it useful to think about the explosion of confessional literature and lyric poetry in the mid-century in relation to this externalization? The advent of film and television had certainly prepared people psychologically for seeing themselves projected out-side of themselves, reflected back. For Joan Murray (writing in a chapter called "The Medium Is the Message"), Canadian collage was distinctly involved in the projection of the self into the surrounding world: "collage is a rich interweaving of personal experience and social values, an inclusive, open-ended medium that both expresses and challenges the two-dimensional picture plane as it provides messages both pri-vate and public" (*Canadian Collage* 13).

The collage shift in Vancouver literature, orchestrated by the likes of bissett, Judith Copithorne, David UU, Gerry Gilbert, Scott Lawrance, Ian Wallace, Roy Kiyooka, Edwin Varney, and many others, extended the boundaries of the self paranoically to include random samplings of cultural detritus and (sometimes fake) found objects of speech. Reminiscent of Jasper Johns's work, one of Gil-bert's recurrent techniques was writing deliberately misheard speech from his sur-roundings, letting words warp with paragrams and spoonerisms. Kiyooka added to this a sense of the environment as historically charged: "History as I practice it and it ought to be insisted upon that 'you' have a hand in its shaping begins with everything you already know brought to the thought of the work to hand" (qtd. in O'Brian 10). The spirit of total interaction among these artists was enhanced by their shared commitment to formal experimentation and aesthetic disruption and their interest in radical politics. They were impatient with McLuhan's passive observations they took to be absolute fact, and rushed into the environments he described. They collaborated on a sudden coalescing of their respective disciplines and facilitated a poignant nexus point wherein the visual, musical, and literary arts met with a shared sense of broader cultural impact by swallowing that culture and its forms into their work. bissett's visual poetry is rife with Hollywood starlets draped in overflowing text. Copithorne has an untitled visual poem in her collec-tion *Arrangements* (1973) in which a telephone "rings its changes" over copies of Blake (marking the visionary integration of text and image), Anaïs Nin (marking the extreme externalization of private life into text), and Karl Marx (marking the core of the revolution). In this work, modes of communication overlap with key visionary authors who transfigured the potential of what literature can do in the world (and with the material world). The Vancouver literary collagists were pio-neers of a new society and recognized their work as participating in and advancing an amorphous cultural revolution. It was disruptive, inventive, political, and fun and incorporated wholeheartedly into their poetics. By 1973, though, the faith in the possibilities of change had dimmed considerably. Copithorne concludes *Arrangements* with a meditation on the challenges of orchestrating change: "oh they came to us with love & found hate, / fearful greed, defoliation, / mass slaugh-ter, poisoned skys, / bodies changed beyond recognition, / a never opened mind. [...] What we have done then, / was the best we could do. / There should be more [...] will be" (n. pag.).

The literary possibilities of the collaborative energy of the intermedial and col-lage explorations are well demonstrated by David UU's *Gideon Music* (published by Blew Ointment Press in 1967), which includes hand-drawn illustrations by Gordon Payne, visual poems and two collages by UU, and front and back cover collages by bissett. Moreover, the text itself performs a kind of collagic engagement with and response to contemporary pop music. The fifteen poems at the core of the book each respond to one side of one album by popular bands of the era, as follows:

"side 1 – BMI" resamples "Heart of Stone" from *The Rolling Stones, Now!* (1965) by the Rolling Stones.

"side 2 – BMI" resamples "Pain in My Heart" from *The Rolling Stones, Now!* (1965) by the Rolling Stones.

"side 3 – Left Banke" resamples "Pretty Ballerina" from *Walk Away Renée/Pretty Ballerina* (1967) by the Left Banke.

"side 4 – BMI" resamples "Ruby Tuesday" from *Between the Buttons* (1967) by the Rolling Stones.

"side 5 – BETWEEN THE BUTTONS" resamples "Let's Spend the Night Together" from *Between the Buttons* (1967) by the Rolling Stones.

"side 6 – 2:20" resamples "Yesterday's Papers" from *Between the Buttons* (1967) by the Rolling Stones.

"side 7 – CAPITOL/MARTIN" resamples "Strawberry Fields Forever" from *Sgt. Pepper's Lonely Hearts Club Band* (1967) by the Beatles.

"side 8 – ROYAL ALBERT" resamples "I've Been Loving You Too Long (To Stop Now)" from *Got LIVE If You Want It!* (1966) by the Rolling Stones.

"side 9 – REVOLVER" resamples "For No One" from *Revolver* (1966) by the Beatles.

"side 10 – NEW SYNDROME" resamples "Lookin' at a Baby" from *The Collage* (1968) by the Collage.

"side 11 – ST 2576" resamples "Tomorrow Never Knows" from *Revolver* (1966) by the Beatles.

"side 12 – ASCAP" resamples "Love Minus Zero/No Limit" from *Bringing It All Back Home* (1965) by Bob Dylan.

"side 13 – TAMLA" resamples "You Really Got a Hold on Me" from *The Fabulous Miracles* (1963) by (Smokey Robinson and) the Miracles.

"side 14 – 33 1/3" resamples "Take It or Leave It" from *Aftermath* (1966) by the Rolling Stones.

"side 15 – DERAM" resamples "A Whiter Shade of Pale" from *Procol Harum* (1967) by Procul Harum.

Here we encounter a literary parallel to the extension of Rauschenberg's assemblages by Jasper Johns in the form of distorted, manipulated found texts. The poems are at once filled with immediately recognizable lyrics from some of the most popular music of the time, but UU has subtly and insistently morphed the original lyrics into original configurations: "strawberry fields for / ever straw / berry fields un/real for / ever ever but / you know & i / know & its a / dream mis/understanding all / i see" ("side 7" n. pag.). Such reshuffled plunderings of the iconic lyrics are glossed by stanzas that respond to the themes and sounds of the poem: "& now / you a new / love a new / lady of / my words / a woman of / reality & / dreams." The self of the speaker is externalized, projected back to him in dreams as the music he hears, which is then selected and contorted. It is an art of the moment in which the self is intermingled with everything in the environment surrounding it. As a poignant fact informing this particular collage work, by the mid-1960s the Beatles and the Rolling Stones had both fallen into the orbit of Brion Gysin and experimented with his cut-up and collage techniques in their music (see Warner 350–99). Furthermore, the Beatles' track "Tomorrow Never Knows," which UU samples in "side 11" of his fifteen-sided album, mixes in tape loops that are based on methods and techniques introduced to McCartney and Lennon directly by Gysin and Burroughs (Savage, "Brion Gysin").

While Copithorne's caution mentioned above highlights an abstracted perspective on the possibilities of change, in the mid-60s the motivation was more driven toward opening the imagination and senses as widely as possible. *Apocolips: Poems*

Figure 3.16 Front cover of David W. Harris (UU)'s *Gideon Music* (1967). Source: Private collection of the author. Used with permission.

and Collages (1967) is an example of the euphoric disruption of literary and visual arts conventions by their intermediation. The collection includes five collages by Gregg Simpson, eight poems by Scott Lawrance, and two exquisite corpses by Scott Lawrance, Gregg Simpson, and Richard Anstey (the bass player from the Al Neil Trio). The collages include impossible technologies (a piano opens up to reveal a lake scene), nature-technology perversions, cross-cultural juxtapositions (a doe-eyed cherub is crushed in a printing press), scale distortions, and bodily dismemberment (floating lips, distorted limbs). Similarly, Gary Lee-Nova's *Cosmic Comics* (1971) features a series of eleven collages that combine vintage linocuts with images of astronomy and electronic technology. The juxtapositions jarringly imagine earthly technology on a cosmic plane, while revelling in the humour of such strange pairings.

The legacy of collage in Vancouver goes beyond the dreams of a new consciousness emerging and has secured a place in the art history of the city, the nation, and even

Figure 3.17 Cover of Blew Ointment Press anthology *Apocolips: Poems and Collages* (1967). Source: Private collection of the author. Used with permission.

the world. It was within the context of a permissive intermedial environment, honed by these experiments in collage, but alas too far beyond the purview of this current study for extended consideration, that the Vancouver School of Photoconceptualism emerged. The figures of this group met at UBC, where Ian Wallace had been hired in 1967 to teach art history. At the university, he supervised Jeff Wall's thesis on Berlin Dada, as well as taught other key figures in the group, such as Rodney Graham and Dennis Wheeler (Augaitis 318). The Vancouver School pioneered several alienating effects in their photographic exploration of collage, montage, and assemblage. Like William Notman, they were interested in depicting landscapes through a kind of photography that resisted realism. Thus, Ian Wallace juxtaposed photographic images with occluding stripes of paint. In these disruptions in Wallace's work, the French philosopher Jacques Rancière found the core crisis of modernism and modernity: "What we call modernity has its origin in this dual separation between figure and action, between art and the expression of a people. This dual separation forms the ground of aesthetic experience as the experience of a new sensible community, open to all and prefiguring a freedom to come" (103). Julia Polyck-O'Neill takes up the question of the aesthetic foundation of the Vancouver School of Photoconceptualists, including their association with conceptual schools of writing that followed, in her 2021 dissertation "Rematerializing the Immaterial: A Comparative Study of Vancouver's Conceptual Visual Arts and Writing." She positions the emergence of photoconceptualism as a distinctive response to modernism that overcomes Clement Greenberg's model of avant-gardism for an aesthetic that "is both critically and materially engaged with the social, cultural, political, and economic histories and realities of Vancouver" (2). In this way, they present an important anticipation of the avant-garde mode in the era that follows this study.

While the emergence of the photoconceptualists provides an excellent link between the work that follows this study and the work Notman did with experimental photography, the role of the intermedial space of Vancouver in accelerating visual experimentation, especially as facilitated by *Blewointment*, cannot be overlooked. The first exhibition of work by the Vancouver School was in the UBC Fine Arts Gallery in 1971. Appropriately called *The Vancouver School of Collage*, the exhibition featured work by internationally acclaimed photoconceptualists Jeff Wall, Ian Wallace, Christos Dikeakos, Gilles Foisy, and Gary Lee-Nova alongside regular *Blewointment* writers like Bissett, Al Neil, Terry Reid, Ed Varney, David UU, Michael Morris, and Vincent Trasov. It is true that "nothing sold" at the collage exhibition (David UU, 30 June 1971 Letter 116), but despite this fact the artists each and all pushed deeper with their experimentation rather than retreat. This comfort with isolation is one of the consistent hallmarks of avant-gardism: as literary critic and poet Donato Mancini argues, "The aesthetic conscience of the vanguard won't let them be satisfied with half measures, with inherited forms, nor with conditions as they are. The duty of a vanguard worth the badge is to pursue the logic of a social-aesthetic proposition

do you know what's happening in west coast poetry

Figure 3.18 Page detail from Talonbooks' 1969 catalogue. Source: Private collection of the author. Used with permission.

right to its explosive end" (84). Energized by the recognition that they were on the verge of a significant aesthetic breakthrough, they redoubled their efforts in pursuit of the almost magical energy achieved through collage. Already in the summer of 1971, David UU and Pierre Coupey immediately set to work on organizing the International Exhibition of Visual Poetry, also known as *Microprosophus*, which took place at the Avelles Gallery in September.[7] Dikeakos, meanwhile, supplied collage work to Lance Farrell's Blew Ointment Press book of spatialized and proto-concrete texts *Ten Pomes*, published in August 1971.

Here we arrive at a significant peak of avant-garde activity in a city awash in performance art, be-ins, happenings, week-long intermedia nights, contemporary

---

7 UU writes to bissett in the summer of 1971: "im putting together another visual poetry show calld MICROPROSOPHUS at avelles gallery sept 8 to 28th" (Letter n. pag.).

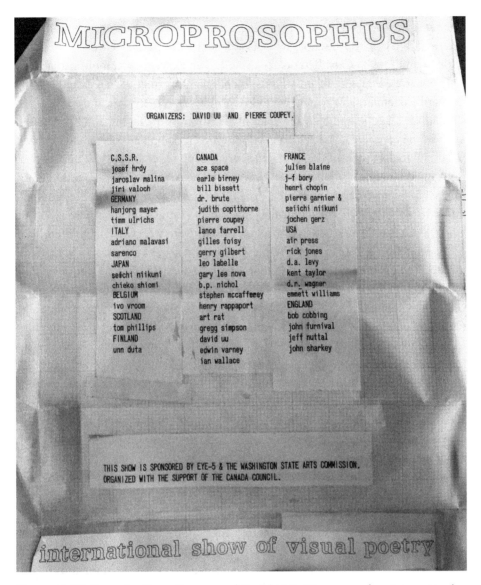

Figure 3.19 Poster for Pierre Coupey and David UU's *Microprosophus: International Exhibition of Visual Poetry*, September 1971. Source: Private collection of Pierre Coupey. Used with permission.

arts festivals, concrete poetry festivals, sound poetry, experimental music, and an abundance of receptive and supportive institutions. It is no surprise, then, that interest in literary extensions of collage continued to expand in the early 1970s and with increased institutional support. Poets who had been aesthetically otherwise inclined were drawn into the vortex. In 1972, for instance, the Canada Council gave a significant project grant to Pat Lowther for her literary experiment with collage called

Canadian Mosaic. Following on the emergence of poetry performance art by the likes of Judith Copithorne and Maxine Gadd, her textual performance was proposed to be "a multimedia Canadian poetry thing [...] an experimental multimedia show [...] conceived as a sort of post-modern collage" featuring samplings of work by Leonard Cohen, Tom Wayman, Milton Acorn, Margaret Atwood, and Emily Carr, slide images, and sound recordings all mixed together (Wiesenthal 334). Though ambitiously conceived, it was held in a modest coffeeshop and "only about a dozen people" actually attended (335). Lowther was disappointed by the low turnout, but undaunted.

That same year, bissett published "The Combined Blew Ointment Picture Book nd th News" (1972), a collection that included twenty-six items of visual/collage work by eighteen different artists (nine of whom were women). The text portions of the works invoke an array of hippie-*cum*-spiritualized optimism, offering tributes to "The Promised Land" (B. Shaw n. pag.), "th endless spirit singing th endless spirit singing" (bissett n. pag.), and the "heart land sutras / [that] pulse thru blud" (Lawrance, "blood sutra" n. pag.). Jorj Heyman, co-editor of the collagist magazine *Circular Causation*, writes of "another vision of love awaiting / our reaching grasp to make it real / and active, standing – / another few moments peace / & growing strong // now it is anew / spirit, culture / to take hold of this life" ("Ghost Dance" n. pag.). Offsetting the unbridled spiritual optimism of these works are contributions by Nellie McClung, George Bowering (who translates a poem by Roberto Sosa from the Spanish), and bissett himself that draw attention to the real-world political forces actively working to prevent the change in global consciousness the rest of the book advocates. Impervious to those forces, though, bissett never stopped pursuing the revolution through aesthetic experimentation. He even began to work with Shirley Gibson, the editor of Anansi, on "a buk uv th collages only" (Letter to Gibson n. pag.) – something that has not yet come to pass.

Meanwhile, the small audience for Lowther's one-time performance of *Canadian Mosaic* did not dissuade her either from continuing work in this direction, and her next project pushed even deeper into intermedial experimentation and collage. *Infinite Mirror Trips: A Multi-Media Experience of the Universe* was an enormously ambitious endeavour to connect poetry, music, song, a light show, and images projected above the audience in a planetarium. It was presented in August 1974 at the H.R. MacMillan Planetarium and praised in the *Vancouver Sun* as "a seamless composite of star show, music, and Lowther's poetry" (qtd. in Wiesenthal 337). Without compromising her background in radical politics, Lowther turned her attention to the material universe and marvelled at the magnitude of its orchestration. Her text is an oscillation of scale, jumping from the "farthest galaxy" to the "fine-spun" hair of a baby ("Infinite" 110). Her interest was not mythical or mystical, or even universalist, but rather scientific, conceptual, and decidedly in-the-world: "Light has shaped itself / into this mechanism, / all parts meticulous, / functional" (109). We humans

Figure 3.20
Photograph of Pat
Lowther and Fred
Candelaria in September
1975.Photograph by
Kate Bird. Used with
permission.

are the by-products of stars, of light itself, and are therefore "still inside" the visual
spectacle of the universe (104). Shown only five times, this show, too, suffered from
low audience numbers and was quickly shelved by the planetarium.

Lowther is most commonly celebrated as one of Canada's foremost lyric poets,
working, as Pablo Neruda did, in that smart combination of sharp personal insight
with a radical political consciousness. These two experimental projects, however,
demonstrate that she was capable and interested in exploring formal experimentation beyond the individual speaker's voice. Indeed, especially with *Infinite Mirror Trips*, Lowther takes poetic form to an avant-garde extreme by representing the

irrational, the random, and the counter-intuitive concepts of the material universe through literary form. Her interest in the quantum order of physics, which posits the basis of matter and reality as paradoxical rather than constant, including a fundamental instability of things and knowledge, aligns her project with Alfred Jarry's 'pataphysical extravagances. Her work must not be confused with 'pataphysics, however, because it is not satirical and does not gleefully abandon the truth as understood by science, but it is a parallel gesture inasmuch as it reaches through materialist consciousness to uncover a realm of irrational literary possibility. In this context, it is worth noting that Lowther published three uncollected experimental poems about Vancouver street life in Canada's chief pataphysician bpNichol's magazine *Ganglia*, appearing in the 1966 issue #3 alongside downtown Vancouver poets like Judith Copithorne, Scott Lawrence, Martina Clinton, and Patrick Lane (plus international avant-gardists like Ian Hamilton Finlay and d.a. levy). Her "Scatter Poem" is one of her most spatialized and typographically free poems in her oeuvre.

In 1974, Varney's imprint the Poem Company orchestrated *5 B.C. Poets*, a galvanizing anthology of poets and painters working in visual modes, especially collage (published by Intermedia). The collection includes significant sections (ironically called "monographs," because they had been previously published as such by the Poem Company) by each artist, Judith ("Judy") Copithorne, Gregg Simpson, Richard Snyder, Tim Lander, and Jim Carter. Copithorne's section, as discussed above (later published as a stand-alone book called *Arrangements*), is a collection of textually rich collages of images and poetry, works that emerge in the interface of text as object and object as text. However, not all of the works in the anthology are interdisciplinary: Simpson's are pure visual art collage, and Richard Snyder's are conventional lyric poems of individual alienation. The first section, however, called "Reading," is the most intriguing and conceptually/formally rich and demonstrates the unique formal achievement of Vancouver's literary-collage crossovers. The forty-page section is comprised of a melange of text, image, photocopy, poem drawings, and rubber stamps in a dense collage of work and words by Jim Carter, Jeremy Newsom, W. Somerset Maugham, Steve Jackson, Cheryl Druick, Jone Pane, Ash Harvey, Ed Varney, and Bruce Singer (presumably with permission from all of the contributors). Like the most experimental issues of *Blewointment* magazine, the attribution of authorship is deferred to the end and almost impossible to reconnect to specific texts. This is a collaboratively produced collage of work that speaks to the impossibility of arrival: poignantly, it begins with an illustrated epigraph that reads, "[T]here is a great silence in saying things" (n. pag.). Toward the end, a love poem is cut into a photo of Charles Manson, followed by an image of a "Void" sticker that has itself been voided. Every page is a unique experiment in typography and design.

Despite the great work being done in Vancouver to realize the formal and aesthetic possibilities of the collage form, some of its revolutionary potential seemed to have slipped by 1974. As David UU wrote to bissett in August of that year, he was "discouraged at the quality of what's happening now, how it has slipped into such mundaniety really an anti-climax to all the discovery that occurred in the late 60's" (Letter n. pag.). Donato Mancini's work on contemporary and postmodern poetics in Canada offers some insight into the grim reality UU was confronting back in the seventies: "'Innovative' artistic strategies, such as the diverse compositional strategies in postmodern poetics, are constructed as specific sites of discursive resistance to unconscionable social contradictions. New poetry enacts new formal strategies as interventions into actual hegemony" (84). In embracing a revolutionary ambition to their exploration of collage, writers like bissett and UU were in fact confronting an actual hegemony and seeking to change it through art and literature. Actual hegemony, however, is insidious in its insistence on ideological conformity and perverse in the relentlessness by which it maintains itself. The revolutionary impetus of collage, facing a diverse barrage of resistance, had decidedly abated. *Blewointment*, though, can be recognized as a postmodern vanguard for insisting upon the fundamental value of diversity, or relinquishing control over models of aesthetical and intellectual closure and imagining the radical extension of literary form as the alteration of consciousness and socio-political structure. This radicality has its roots and clearest manifestation in the formal dynamics of collage. As bissett writes in "a study uv language what can yew study" (1971):

> a pome that frees yu from any chains
> talks uv is uv th desire to see is as sacred
> as yr next meal [...]
> langwage is really molecular not parts
> uv speech so yu don't need all th rules
> that cum thru generashuns uv bargain
> wars th right to say th space on the papr
> yu can use it all [...]
> poetry is changing thousands uv ways all ovr th world [...]
> poetry now knows no boundaries that is its potentshul anyway can pass
>   thru th blocks xpress thru collage structure big lettrs what
>   we make words from standing up th isolashun uv whun or
>   few letters
>   (93, 95, 96)

FOUR

A Line, A New Line, All One: Variant Narratives of Concrete Canada

1 The Concrete Liturgy

The habitual narrativization of concrete and visual poetry maps a trajectory from the spatialized poetry of Stéphane Mallarmé and the pattern-poem calligrammes of Guillaume Apollinaire (1897–1918), through the riotous *parole in libertà* of Italian Futurists, the transrational speech of the Russian Zaum poets, the "Konkrete kunst" of Hans Arp and Max Bill, the textual collages of the Dadaists, through the expressively shaped work of American E.E. Cummings and Italian Carlo Belloli, and finally arriving in its formal self-realization with the coincidental intersection of Swedish poet Öyvind Fahlström's "Manifesto for Concrete Poetry" (1953) and the Noigandres poets in Brazil adopting the same name for their visual poetics in 1955. Concrete poetry developed from the desire for a self-consciously international culture that would, in Hans Arp's words, "transform the world. It wants to make life more bearable" (524). A central concept to the movement – its revolutionary mandate, if you will – was that an entirely accessible global culture could emerge from the fusion of visual and literary arts, modelled on but subverting the aesthetic of international corporate advertising. A world shaped by the reversal of monolithic culture would be an improvement to the current mess. Thus, Jiří Kolář's "evident poetry" in Czechoslovakia in 1961, to take one example, sought to invent visual forms that aimed to be instantly and universally readable (Spatola 17–19). Similarly, the Noigandres group in Brazil, led by the de Campos brothers, Décio Pignatari, Wlademir Dias Pino, Ferreira Gullar, and Ronaldo Azeredo, described the concrete poem as "an object in and by itself, not an interpreter of exterior objects and/or more or less subjective feelings" – hence "[c]oncrete poetry: total responsibility before language. Thorough realism" (70–72). Jamie Hilder surmises, "[T]he international anthologies of concrete poetry that came out in the mid-to-late sixties and early seventies enact the poets' project of international connectivity in a way that anticipated the spatial turn of the internet" ("Concrete Poetry and Conceptual Art" 582). In accord with various international scholars, he muses that the concrete poetry movement lost its avant-garde cachet around 1970 ("Concrete Poetry: From the Procedural" 115).[1] That was the end of the endeavour to create an international culture through the genre. This survey is intentionally terse: this liturgy is repeated far more often than it is ever interrogated.

---

1 Michael Turner, more attuned to the Vancouver and Canadian contexts, surprisingly dates this earlier, in 1968 ("Visual Poems" 142).

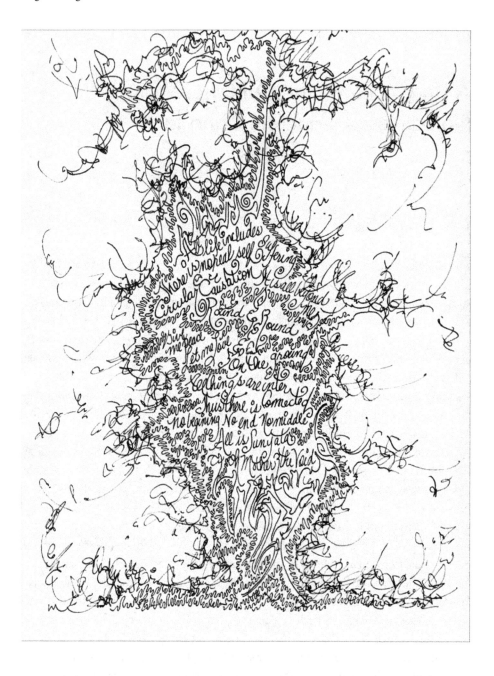

Figure 4.1 Judith Copithorne's untitled visual poem from *Circular Causation* 2 (1969).
Source: Private collection of the author. Used with permission.

2 Canadian Concrete

The liturgy of concrete poetry's Canadian connection continues from the international context: once it was established as a genre unto itself, rather than an offshoot of another movement, it proliferated across international borders. Canada, by 1965, had become an important zone of concrete activity. bissett and his downtown community began experimenting with more than spatialized poetry, discovering the openness of the full page. Having relocated from Vancouver to Toronto, bpNichol wanted to establish there a beachhead of the kind of visually oriented writing he had witnessed out west. Nichol, in particular, acknowledges Pierre Coupey, Earle Birney, bill bissett, and Lance Farrell as influences on his development toward concrete (Interview with Nicette Jukelevics 128–9).[2] He established Ganglia Press and swiftly connected with poets in England, France, Czechoslovakia, Japan, America, and of course Brazil. He established himself as, in George Bowering's words, "Canada's most famous concrete poet" ("Cutting Them" 18). In fact, though, in distinction from the international concrete movement, the bulk of Nichol's visual poetry bridged comic and typewriter arts, and would expand into increasingly pataphysical and conceptualist directions. In Vancouver, bissett's *Blewointment* magazine and book publishing venture continued to focalize the intermedia energy of the city's arts community into a concerted exploration of visual-literary intersections. He used the term "dirty concrete" to articulate the deliberate messiness of his visual-textual experiments and revelled, as Steve McCaffery argues, in the fleshy, libidinal materiality of language ("Bill Bissett" 93). McCaffery, himself, became a significant progenitor of concrete after he arrived in Canada in 1968 from Sheffield, England, and quickly befriended bp. In his study of Canadian visual poetics, Stephen Scobie (another visual poet) adds in the names of Judith Copithorne, David UU, Ed Varney, and himself (33). Caroline Bayard deepened the historical lineage in her 1989 study when she acknowledged Martina Clinton, Lance Farrell, Rob Smith, Hart Broudy, David Aylward, and Andrew Suknaski (106–8). Neither Bayard nor Scobie acknowledge Colleen Thibaudeau, who was, in fact, the author of the first book of shaped or pattern poetry in Canada – a fact that Frank Davey, who had relocated to Thibaudeau's hometown of London, Ontario, in 1990, acknowledges in his 2012 biography of Nichol (*aka* 72).

Had they known of it, scholars of visual and concrete poetry might have begun their surveys with the first visual novel in Canada, *Southern Cross: A Novel of the South Seas* by Laurence Hyde (1951), told wordlessly through a stunning set of 118 wood engravings. If the trajectory of experimental poetry in Canada has been to

---

2 In that interview, when asked if "concrete in Canada started on the West Coast," Nichol replied, "In a way it started with Earle Birney. Earle Birney was interested in specific notations, that is to say the rise and fall of the line on the page which approximates the human voice, or which approximates the action of something falling. It's simple in a sense" (128).

Figure 4.2 Page detail from Laurence Hyde's *Southern Cross: A Novel of the South Seas* (1951), which uses only images to tell its story of colonial violence in the South Pacific. Source: Private collection of the author.

increasingly engage with our colonial heritage, and to reverse the erasure and silencing of the violence of that history, Hyde's work represents an important stage in the transformation. It does not emerge from the same lineage as concrete poetry, but, using silence and wordless images, it tells the story of the colonial and ecological disaster caused by American nuclear testing in the South Pacific.

Another important precedent for Vancouver's visual poetry is the asemic semiotic work by Graham Coughtry in 1960 (and that was published in the *Tamarack Review*). Coughtry's work has a minor if still important place in the annals of Canadian literature for his gorgeous front and rear cover illustrations of Kenneth McRobbie's *Eyes without a Face* (1960), a beautifully designed book by Jay Macpherson's Emblem Books. Poignantly, McRobbie's book of spatialized poetry contains one of the earliest pattern poems in Canadian writing, "Blastoff," in the shape of a Martin Marietta SM-68A/HGM-25A rocket (35). The poem acknowledges the first successful test firing of a Titan I intercontinental ballistic missile in February of 1959 at Cape Canaveral. It is curious, too, that this remarkable book also contains a long poem, a "martyrology of Toronto," called "Serenade to the Queen City" (52), anticipating the marytryology life-project that bpNichol would initiate in the later sixties to complement his own pattern and concrete poetry. Even more than these connections, though, Coughtry's non-signifying language series, begun in 1960 and published in 1963 in the *Tamarack Review*, captures the essence of the dirty concrete aesthetic that would emerge a decade later.

Nichol, for his part, unabashedly reminds people of the "purely canadian roots" of his visual poetry (*Ganglia Press Index* n. pag.). His initiation came through Pierre Coupey's visual-textual "The Alphabet of Blood," which was published in *Delta* (#24) in 1964 – shortly before Coupey moved to Vancouver from Montreal in 1965 (after a year in Paris) and launched the *Capilano Review* two years later. Coupey notes, however, that his welcome in the city was initially rather muted, though he did manage to connect with Seymour Mayne, who would proceed to publish a series of concrete

Figure 4.3 Graham Coughtry's "Quotation" (1960), from a series of visual works exploring language and grammar from 1960–61. Source: The Estate of Graham Coughtry. Used with permission.

works with Very Stone House. Indubitably, under Nichol's and bissett's tutelage, aided by key contributions from Birney and Coupey, visual poetry slowly but surely flourished in Canada, most prominently in Toronto and Vancouver. Nichol edited the first anthology of concrete poetry, *The Cosmic Chef Glee & Perloo Memorial Society Under the Direction of Captain Poetry Presents … An Evening of Concrete* (1970), a boxed anthology containing work by thirty-one Canadian visual poets, including fifteen poets with roots in Vancouver: Birney, bissett, Bowering, Broudy, Jim Brown, Copithorne, Gilbert, Lionel Kearns, Martina Clinton, Seymour Mayne, Nichol, Andrew Suknaski, UU, Varney, and Phyllis Webb. It is worth acknowledging, though, that of the Canadian practitioners only Brion Gysin and bpNichol were included in Emmett Williams's foundational and internationally rich *Anthology of*

Concrete Poetry (1967), and only Nichol appears in Mary Ellen Solt's 1968 anthology *Concrete Poetry: A World View*. Canadians, especially bp and McCaffery, became mainstays of the mode shortly thereafter,[3] but Vancouver's contributions to the form have been almost totally overlooked in the international context.

Too often unheeded in the international context are the two groundbreaking exhibitions of international concrete poetry that took place in Vancouver: *Brazilia 73* in 1967 (organized by David UU as part of the Canadian Biennial of Contemporary Art at the Mandan Ghetto Gallery), followed by the Concrete Poetry Festival in 1969 (organized by painter Michael Morris and curator Alvin Balkind at the University of British Columbia). The *Brazilia 73: An Exhibition of International Concrete Poetry* show ran from 1 to 15 April and featured the work of bill bissett, Pierre Coupey, Gerry Gilbert, David W. Harris (UU), bpNichol, and Stephen Scobie alongside that of international concrete poets like British Ian Hamilton Finlay and Dom Sylvester Houédard, French Henri Chopin, Austrian Ernst Jandl, and American d.a. levy. The event, while a landmark on any scale, has been almost completely ignored by historians of the form. Still, despite the blanket of silence that fell swiftly on the event, it prompted Edwin Varney to draft an enthusiastic short essay called "Concrete Poetry" to meditate on the significance of the genre. He notes that for "some reason, perhaps the truly seminal McLuhan in Toronto, Canada has become a center for the new poetry" (n. pag.).

The latter event, Balkind and Morris's Concrete Poetry Festival, remains one of the most ambitious avant-garde literary events the country has ever seen. Like the VPC, it consisted of three weeks of programming, from 28 March to 19 April, including an exhibition, readings, and a remarkable exhibition catalogue that included new essays on concrete writing and correspondence art by Michael Rhodes, Ed Varney, Ian Hamilton Finlay (with Stephen Scobie), and Ian Wallace. The catalogue was published in a jackdaw envelope, drawing together the wealth and spread of ideas and events associated with the exhibition in unbound, somewhat messy (though not *Blewointment* messy) materiality. In his contribution, Ian Wallace highlights the radical medium-consciousness proposed by the form:

> The power of literature as a creative activity has traditionally treated language as a transparent medium so that the content is revealed in a direct reading of "what is said." Recent movements in literature, concrete poetry explicitly, treat language as an opaque medium, which throws content back into the realm of literature as "something to say" rather than "what is said." ("Literature – Transparent and Opaque" n. pag.)

---

3 In fact, Nichol was included in the 1966 anthology *Concrete Poetry: Britain, Canada, United States* as well as the 1970 reissue of Mary Ellen Solt's *Concrete Poetry: A World View*.

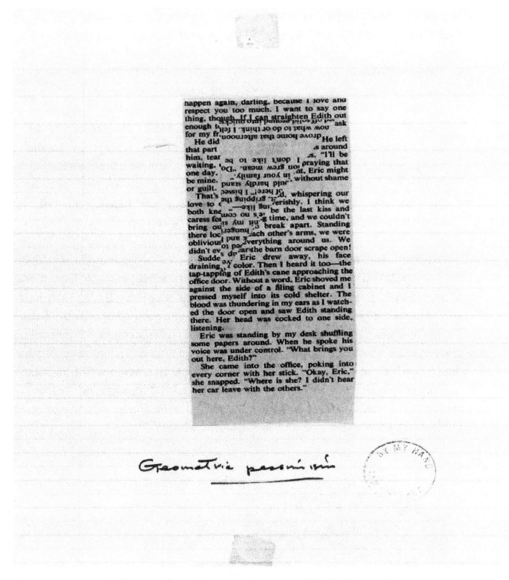

Figure 4.4 Ian Wallace's collage *Geometric Pessimism* (1969). Source: Private collection of the author. Used with permission.

Wallace mocks the "pathetic clichés of greatness" of expressive literature for being "powerless to affect the dominating forces of our society, which are not spiritual or of the imagination, but rather are technological and economic." Against all self-satisfied, traditionally bounded forms of literature, Wallace posits concrete poetry as a totem of contemporary awareness without religion, a "revolutionary flair" upending intellectual and creative sterility in literature. In this way, the exhibition can be understood as a salvo against the established orthodoxy of the 1960s, whose "art is already beginning to look old-fashioned, its pretensions and involvements [...] becoming increasingly distant or irrelevant" (von Meier n. pag.). Against this heritage, Kurt von Meier proposes the "mosaic patterns, new models for an alternate culture" as embodied by concrete poetry. Wallace's *Geometric Pessimism* (1969) embodies the disruptive energy of concrete poetry by cutting into dominant cultural habits. As he writes,

> this seemingly very marginal work is in fact the prototype for a whole series of works that involves cutting into a text and reversing the verso page and reinserting it into the recto page so that the logic of the text is interrupted [... it] is so titled because it is about an incident of marital infidelity from a novel by anais nin titled *a spy in the house of love* – the last line at the bottom is the give-away [...] and by coincidence (or not) this cheap paperback novel was given to me by al neil. (Email correspondence)

As if to insist on the contiguity between collage, concrete, and intermedia, the exhibition was composed of four parts: a selection of recent concrete poems by international poets, twenty-four "letter drawings" by Michael Morris, nineteen collages by Ray Johnson, and a melange of film, slides, and recordings of sound poetry. The essay by Michael Rhodes positions the Vancouver event as the culmination of the concrete liturgy, noting that despite its advanced state, and its full arrival within Canada, "[c]oncrete poetry has not yet reached the Canadian popular press" (n. pag.). The event was the manifestation and culmination of Morris's interest in what he called "illiterature," which is to say writing at the intersection of drawing, collages, and photography – surface-oriented production without expression (qtd. in S. Watson, "Mirrors" 78).

Figure 4.5 bill bissett's *The Vancouver Mainland Ice and Cold Storage* sculptural collage contribution to the Vancouver Concrete Poetry Festival, organized by Michael Morris. Source: Private collection of the author. Used with permission.

A third important event, the previously mentioned *Microprosophus: International Exhibition of Visual Poetry*, took place in 1971 at the Avelles Gallery (see Figure 3.19). Curated by David UU and Pierre Coupey, the month-long exhibition included work by Gregg Simpson, Sarenco, Jochen Gerz, Air Press, Josef Hrdy, Art Rat, David UU, Pierre Coupey, Jaroslav Malina, Earle Birney, bill bissett, and many others. The *Microprosophus* show also travelled to Evergreen College in Tacoma, Washington. Selections from the show were featured in a special section of the very first issue of the *Capilano Review*, edited by one of Canada's first practitioners of concrete poetry, Pierre Coupey.

3 Other Narratives of Concrete Poetry

Jamie Hilder's recent essay "Concrete Poetry: From the Procedural to the Performative" seeks to clarify the parameters of the genre more precisely. In doing so, however, he is working against the variegated networks of formal features and other movements that coalesced into the specificity of some types of concrete work. There are other considerations that make the narrative of concrete poetry less singular and more complicated, less housed in the authority of select men and women. Concrete poetry, unlike, say, the Vorticists or Surrealists, was never a closed coterie. Somewhere between a method and a worldview, it was a disruptive current that spread widely and quickly and internationally, *as it was intended to do*. This current, like all moving waters, began from various trickles, such as the thin but significant tradition of pattern poetry in English literature dating from George Herbert's seventeenth-century work (thin only in its canonicity: Dick Higgins proves the international wealth of the tradition in his verdant anthology *Pattern Poetry* [1987]) and Lewis Carroll's nineteenth-century games with typography. It emerged from the confluence of pattern poetry and Imagism: the Noigandres group, of course, took their name from a deeply ambiguous passage in Ezra Pound's *Cantos*. Pound was no concrete poet, but he was interested in the Chinese ideogram as an example of "phanopoeia" (which he defines as "a casting of images upon the visual imagination" ["How to Read" 25]) and for its grammatical ambiguity (to a non-Chinese speaker especially) as a potential source of imaginative poetry. His interest in Asian literary forms, including the haiku, the hokku, and Noh theatre, helped to establish the central tenets of the Imagist school of poetry (which he famously named). The Imagists were not visual poets, but their condensation of literary expression down to raw, unadorned imagery extended Mallarmé and Apollinaire's resistance to the habitual structuring devices of verse form – especially the organization of end-rhymes, the syllabic patterns of the meter, and other carry-overs of traditional verse forms. The Imagist paratactic poems, even as they foregrounded the objective expressive capacities of language, looked different on the page, as linguistic images were jammed next to each other without regard to traditional meter. Eugene Gomringer (who had worked as a secretary for the "Konkrete kunst" Dadaist Max Bill) was captivated by

Pound's attention to the multilayered visual properties of language, as both literary image and ideogram, and worked from that ground to develop concrete poetry. The Noigandres group also acknowledged Mallarmé, Apollinaire, Joyce, and Cummings by name as wellsprings for their work.

But even this dynamic individual-centric linearity is not enough to capture the maelström of forces at play in the emergence of the form. As Jukelevics writes, the shift in avant-garde aesthetics in the mid-twentieth century toward visual and concrete forms "is a clear indication of the need that began to be felt by poets and artists to re-evaluate the function of poetry, to re-examine the meaning and the value of words, and to develop new methods of composition" (5). The arrival of mass media technologies in the early twentieth century, especially the television and the cinema, accentuated visual spectacle, while an ever-maturing advertising culture worked consciously to disrupt through visual means the habits of the past. Some of the earliest concrete poems played off of the visual-linguistic culture of advertising, such as Décio Pignatari's "LIFE" and "beba coca cola" (both in 1957), and the clean aesthetic of such work firmly echoes the normative aesthetics of period advertising. Is it just a coincidence that concrete poets emerged in response to modern visual culture at the same historical moment that Marshall McLuhan inaugurated the practice of performing literary close-reading exercises on advertisements and mass media – something he begat with his 1951 book *The Mechanical Bride*? No – the Brazilian concretists were, in fact, translating McLuhan figuratively but also quite literally; in 1969, Pignatari published a translation of *Understanding Media*. (Also of note is the fact that both the Brazilian concrete poets and McLuhan were deeply influenced and inspired by Pound and Joyce.) The avant-garde were concentrated in the visual arts, where one of their signs of radicality was the inclusion of linguistic fragments within their canvases – such as Picasso's "JOU," discussed in chapter 3, such as Marinetti's onomatopoeic works or Kurt Schwitter's newspaper collages, such as Brion Gysin's asemic calligraphy paintings that evoke language but deny semiotic meaning, hence evoking what Barthes might call the unrepresentable structurality of language. In 1972, McLuhan commented on the explicit connection between newspaper's mosaical "juxtaposition of items without connection" and "poésie concrete" (*Culture* 146). Hilder captures something of this general *weltanschauung* when he notes that "[l]anguage is tied to ideology and produces subjectivities, which is why the concrete poets felt that they had to adapt: they created designed words for a designed world. Recognizing that language was producing new, global subjects, the poets aimed to intervene" ("Concrete Poetry and Conceptual Art" 591). Herein lies the anti-environmental ambition of visual writing: to defamiliarize public language enough that readers might learn how to see what it is doing to them in a capitalist environment.

There were many further overlapping entanglements in the emergence of concrete poetry. The modernist crisis of representation in the arts led to an increasing aesthetic meta-consciousness and a concerted investigation into the material properties of tools of art production. Wassily Kandinsky's kind of investigation into the semiotic properties of colour and shape arrived in Canada in the 1920s, when artists such as Bertram Brooker and Marian Scott began experimenting with geometrical shapes and colours as representative of tone and sound. Brooker brought his material consciousness to play in his experimental theatre but focused his poetry and novels on spiritual and cosmic veracities instead of geometry and page space[4] – with the exception of various unpublished studies in his notebooks, including "The Romance of Trade Marks" (see Figure 4.6), that attend to the visual allure of capitalist cultures. In the 1940s, the French Canadian Automatists continued the exploration of the material properties of art, especially the visceral qualities of paint, in a manner that anticipated the American abstract expressionists a decade later. The Automatists challenged the expressive limits of theatre and the material dimensions of fashion. They wanted to revolutionize Canadian consciousness and break the hold of the Catholic Church on Quebecois society, so they embraced the Surrealist call for irrationalism and conscious re-evaluation of the expressive limits of all forms of art. This kind of self-consciousness and self-referentiality was extended to literature, where the poet Claude Gauvreau made an art of the sounds of letters and the sensuality of syllables. While not visually oriented, Gauvreau's linguistically disruptive work in poetry and theatre marked the arrival into Canada of language use governed by material consciousness rather than semantics. In his own words, as translated into "English" by Ray Ellenwood: "Breachclout – bobo / Agaïante ipluche / Mutton-chops masturbating on the two cheeks of the English lord / Lord lard / Heuh-Hi-Heu-ouh" ("The Oval Mayonaisse" 137).

Concrete or, more generally put, *visual* poetry began surfacing in Canadian little magazines, including *Alphabet* (December 1962), the *Tamarack Review* (1963), and *Delta* (December 1964). While *Blewointment* was not the first publication in Canada to publish spatialized poetry, it was the first that was aesthetically invested in the terrain of concrete and visual poetics as a loosely coordinating aesthetic. This experimental praxis was influenced by the convergence of abstract visual art, Surrealist Automatism, and, more specifically, the multimedia experiments of Kenneth Patchen, who was connected to Vancouver's art and literary scene primarily through his experimental melding of poetry and music.[5] Patchen's illuminated works, with his flowing handwritten texts, exude a spiritual confidence in the dissolve of the

---

4 Brooker also, as I address in *Avant-Garde Canadian Literature*, regarded advertising as a revolutionary force that could, with artists at the helm, overcome the cloistered consciousness of the Church.
5 Patchen began touring and performing his jazz poetry around British Columbia in the late 1950s with Vancouver's Al Neil Quartet, ultimately leading to their 1959 album *Kenneth Patchen Records with Jazz in Canada*.

Figure 4.6 Bertram Brooker's "The Romance of Trade Marks" (c. 1912–15). Source: Courtesy of the Robert McLaughlin Gallery (collected by Adam Lauder). Used with permission.

categories of humanity and individual consciousness into the world. His 1967 collection *Hallelujah Anyway* compiles works produced from the early 1960s that reject the techno-utopianism of modernism. His flowing handwritten aphorisms divest the self of individual autonomy and reject the singularity of human consciousness. In one of the works, he writes: "The World is nothing that can be known / in the shadow we shall see the color of god's eyes again / beyond love there is no belief" (n. pag.). For McLuhan, too, the relevance of the individual was disappearing into a generational moment characterized by multiconsciousness and the accelerated extension of the individual beyond their typewriter-grid individualism. So inspired, an emerging collective of experimental writers in Vancouver wrote against the self in part as a political gesture of solidarity and sympathy with the global oppressed. As bissett declared in 1965, "we are thru with the absolute / we are thru with the known" (Untitled, *Blewointment* 3.1 n. pag.). They manifested this shattering of traditional order in verse form in visual, dynamic use of the page space. Accordingly, Nichol acknowledged Patchen (and the Chinese ideogram) as an early and important influence on his visual work (Interview with Nicette Jukelevics 133) and dedicated one of his first typewriter concrete poems, "Pome for Kenneth Patchen," to him in his 1967 book *Konfessions of an Elizabethan Fan Dancer*.

Figure 4.7 Cover of Kenneth Patchen's *Hallelujah Anyway* (1966). Source: Private collection of the author.

```
o  o  o  o  o  o  oXo  o  o  o  O  oeuoooeo  o  o  o  o  o  L O V E   X X
o  o  o  o  o  o  oXo  o  o  U  o  Oooooeooo  o  o  o  o  o          X X
o  o  o  o  o  o  oXo  o  o  oOoOoeoooeooo  o  o  o  o  o            X X
o  o  o  o  o  o  cXo  o  o  o  O  oeuoeooo  o  o  o  o  o           X X
o  o  o  o  o  o  oXo  o  o  u  o  ooooouoco  o  u  o  o  o          X X
o  o  o  o  o  o  oXo  o  o  o  o  ooooeooeo  u  o  o  o  o          X X
o  o  o  o  o  o  oXo  o  o  o  o  oouooooeo  u  o  o  o  O          X X
u  o  o  o  o  o  oXo  o  o  o  o  ou_ooooooo  o  o  o  o  o         X X
U  O              x                 o  o  o  e                o    X X
U  O              x                 o  o  o  o                o    X X
O  O              x                 ooooooou                 o    X X
U  O              x                 o  o  o  o                o    X X
O  O              x                 o  o  o  o                o    X X
U  O              x  x  x  x  x  x  xoxuxoxox X x x x x xOx x x x x x x x
O  O              x  x  x  x  x  x  xoxoxoxoX x X x x x xOx x x x x x x x
O  O              x  x  x  x  x  x  xoxoxoxoxXxXx x x xOx x x x x x x x
O  O              x  x  x  x  x  x  xoxoxoxox X x x x xOx x x x x x x x
U  O              x  x  x  x  x  x  xoxoxoxox x x x x xOx x x x x x x x
O  O              x  x  x  x  x  x  xoxoxoxcx x x x x xOx x x x x x x x
U  O              x  x  x  x  x  x  xoxoxoxox x x x x xOx x x x x x x x
O  O        E V O L x  x  x  x  x  x  xoxoxoxox x  x x x xOx x x x x x x x
```

Figure 4.8 bpNichol's "Pome for Kenneth Patchen," from *Konfessions of an Elizabethan Fan Dancer* (1967; image from the second edition in 1969). Readers of Nichol's work will notice the parallels to "Blues," perhaps the most famous Canadian concrete poem, which also appeared in the same book. Source: Private collection of the author. Used with permission.

The poems in the first issues of *Blewointment* are almost all spatialized works that spread out across the page in dramatic, visceral form. One poem by bissett in the second issue ("whilst waiting") pushes further into pattern poetry as letters droop into subsequent stanzas:

now where do i
go from there i a
    m
   not a
    r
     e
      e
       t
        irud count of milk
        ing anything i
        dont even have my cross
          with me o ignobul
             end
                 (n. pag.)

Where does he go from there? He animates the language, lets its spatial existence interfere with its linear telling. McCaffery would describe such visual interruptions in bissett's writing as "spontaneous variations in margin which melt the hard lines of the poem's iconicity" ("Bill Bissett" 99). The poem becomes a site of rupture and vitality, rather than well-wrought perfection. In the same issue, Lance Farrell's "well her name is paranoia" includes lines that drop suddenly vertically straight down the page and concludes with a swerving wave of text that washes over the square margins of the rest. It stages the interruption of fixed voice for the flow of an identity in motion. One of the final poems in the issue, bissett's "In Other Words The Food of the Soul," is structured entirely around its visual pattern and geometric shapes in a manner that would become characteristic of bissett's poetry for the rest of his career.

The first work that pushes beyond spatialized and pattern poems appears in the September 1964 issue (2.4), wherein Judith Copithorne publishes a neatly hand-drawn image of a stylized nude woman with cursive text integrated into the design. The text, in ostensibly the first work of Vancouver visual poetry, concludes with the poignantly prophetic line: "I never knew what I had done" ("This was drawn" n. pag.). Another visual poem from the same issue, also by Copithorne, provides a suitable answer by including the text: "actually / a poem writes itself." From this point forward, visual-textual experimentation would come to proliferate in the magazine and then throughout the city and beyond. Visual-textual crossovers took many forms, with the distinctly poetic variety (there is, in fact, no formal definition of visual poetry that perfectly delineates poetic visual work from visual artists' use of language) appearing as typewriter art, cut-ups (and cut-outs), comics, collage, photography, occultic symbology, hand-drawn work, and more, using technologies such as photocopiers, cameras, shredders, mimeographs, typesetters, Letraset, etchings, computers, and rubber stamps. Thematically, this melange of stylistically diverse texts explores everything from strident manifestos for the language revolution to light-hearted puns and jokes, but a consistent theme of this work is the failure of language to adequately reflect or represent experience in the world, a concept constant in avant-garde literature at least since Mallarmé despaired at the degraded language of the tribe. Such an attitude has pervaded the visual poetry community to the present, where Vancouver poet Donato Mancini defines poetry (in an essay on visual poetics) as "[l]anguage looked at with a certain misrecognition" ("The Young Hate Us" 64).

In considering the various manifestations of concrete poetry, Jamie Hilder distinguishes between "mechanical and clean" procedural work and "manual and excessive" performative work ("Concrete Poetry: From the Procedural" 116). Building from the dirty-versus-clean-concrete distinction that is prominent in North American avant-garde discourse, Hilder proposes thematic and political implications to the shifting styles: for whereas rationalist procedural works are invested in "issues of economic blocs of power and culture, and the influence that advertisement had on the shifting of a readership bound to a national language into a viewership that operated in a much wider cultural sphere," performative works are those that "turned [their] scope inward, toward the composing subject's dependency on language. [Their] international character was less concerned with the effect of current technology or geopolitical structures than it was with the site/sight of language" (121). Such a depoliticized, nonrevolutionary aesthetic might make sense of Steve McCaffery's dirty performative works (*might* – Hart Broudy would have probably been a better, if less celebrated, exemplar. I discuss the politics of McCaffery's visual work in my essay "A Postmodern Decadence"), but they make little sense of the overt socio-political orientation of bissett's dirty concrete work. Similarly, Hilder describes clean procedural work as "a generally masculine technique" (123), not recognizing how the female concrete and visual poets in Vancouver turned away from what Copithorne acknowledges as "the mechanical or more male dominated forms" (see textbox "Judith Copithorne on Vancouver Concrete") and made their concrete art political, formal, personal, and international at the same time.

And indeed, while men overwhelmingly dominate the narrative of concrete and visual poetry (which has been told many times in a way that continues to foreground the work of male practitioners), there were a significant number of female writers and visual artists in Vancouver who found access to concrete especially by exploring handwritten visual poetry. As with the openness of *Blewointment*, the emergence of a new aesthetic space allowed previously silenced voices to find purchase. Georgia

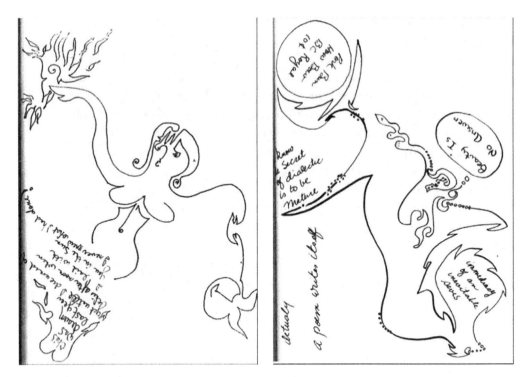

Figures 4.9, 4.10 Two untitled visual poems by Judith Copithorne in *Blewointment* 2.4 (September 1964). Source: Private collection of the author. Used with permission.

Brown, Laurren Radunz, Deirdre Ballantyne, Carole Itter, Sandra Cruickshank, Susan Musgrave, Marsha Stone, Martina Clinton, Phyllis Webb, and Lynn Ruscheinsky all published a limited few examples of visual works in literary magazines and books that blur the border between visual art and poetry. What value is there in denying the proximity of these works to the concrete poetry moment? Carole Itter's *Word Work* (1966), however, published by Intermedia Press as the first of their "Poem Company Supplement" imprint series, presents visual games with the words "work" and "word," pairing them in hand-drawn cartoonish plays with the visual and semantic implications of the words. They would have been perfectly at home in bpNichol's *The Cosmic Chef* concrete poetry anthology, or as a publication by his press Ganglia.

Related to these overtly concrete experiments, Carole Itter's gorgeously designed, visually rich book *The Log's Log* (1972) ought to be acknowledged, as should her 1982 artbook *Location Shack*, which contains a series of layered poems. Though falling after the period proper of this study, the latter poems meditate on the story of a girl's return to her home and the rush of familiarity after a long trip away. The first layer of the page is a typewritten text on gridlines. The gridlines swerve, though, and strike through the first-person text. Above that, photocopied and disintegrated images of

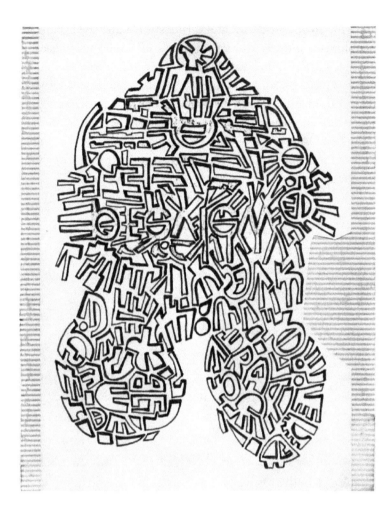

Figure 4.11 Early visual poem by Carole Itter from her multimedia "Preview" series in 1967 (not 1961 as listed on the Vancouver Art in the Sixties website). Source: Private collection of Carole Itter. Used with permission.

farm tools further occlude the text. Above these two layers, and spilling out freely into the margins of these blocked sections, Itter's handwriting celebrates the "manifold possibilities" and "inspirational" thought of "observing, observing so closely as to be totally awake of what surfaces – to a surface somewhat less multi-channeled, somewhat less straddling all the dimensions" (n. pag.). She is not celebrating harmony between the layers of the text, but the sudden freedom she has discovered in handwriting over and alongside the occluding collage. Such handwriting embodies the liberating material consciousness of concrete writing, while yet radicalizing the dimensionality of the page. Many other women explored similar visually charged textual terrain. The contributing members of the Poem Company collective, for instance, published an eponymous collection in 1972 rife with visual and concrete work. Fifteen women contributed to the collection – Judith Copithorne, Maxine Gadd, Alison Dale, Pamela Yenser, Martina Clinton, Lorla Wasmuth, Kay Holm,

Anne Griffith, Rhoda Rosenfeld, Lesze Bechtold, Janice O'Conner, Beth Jankola, Laura Nyro, Anne Waldman, and Iris Murdoch – but as the individual entries in the book are not attributed to any individual, it is impossible to tell, now, how many and which ones were produced by female contributors. Beth Jankola, in the 1980s, would publish two key texts of visual poetry that embrace many of the themes I outline below, though her work falls beyond the purview of this study. It is Copithorne, however, author of the first visual poem in the city, that stands as the best example of a female artist-*cum*-author exploring the visual, sensual, and expressive qualities of language simultaneously.

Judith Copithorne on Vancouver Concrete, email interview, 27 October–14 November 2013

As for concrete or visual connections with writing, the field is actually so huge and goes back as long as one cares to look and in Vancouver there was also all that Chinese signage available to stir analysis and imagination. And then there are the Dada and people such as Paul Klee who my mother was particularly fond of. Vancouver was also on the circuit in the twenties for theater, ballet, opera, music and so forth that started in London or Paris and traveled through New York, other places such as New Orleans, and then San Francisco, Seattle and here. I believe that the depression stopped a lot of that and then WW2 but before that there was perhaps more access to such things as the newest in design which took quite a while to start up again after WW2. I got to see The Ballet Ruse when I was 6 and their stage sets were inspiring.

I only saw asemic (although I only have the slightest image of it far back in my brain if in fact i do remember this) work or/and strictly abstract by Gysin and by the other people I saw at that time. I was looking for more links but I didn't get them here although I could extrapolate from what I had read but there were no actual links available to me at that time although I wished at that time that there would be. I did have a small catalog of some of his abstract work at one time which I liked. So I mainly knew of Gysin's work because he was a Canadian who I had heard did experimental work perhaps related to visual writing and was connected to the Wm. Boroughs crowd. And then I must have read something by him, perhaps a bit later in the City Lights Journal which included a statement about literature being 50 years behind art. But I have always felt (and sometimes have actually been made to feel I have to say) some what separate from that masculinist strain of that group.

And course I loved Mark Toby and Morris Lewis. But my perhaps my main inspiration was the typographic and design material of my uncle's. He had died in 1933 in a mountain climbing accident and we had most of various projects and material's stored away. The 20's as you know was a great time of typographic exploration and I probably got a sense of this from his work as he designed such things as the Vancouver School of Art and Design's first and second prospectus.

Characteristically, in this poem, an untitled work from *Release* (1969), the writing takes place in the white space, the silence of the gaps in the rippling patterns. While Olson championed the page as latent grid for typewriter scores ("Projective Verse" 23), a maximalist extension of "the personal and instantaneous recorder of the poet's work," such hand-drawn visual poetics refute the machinic choreography of the typewriter for an intrinsic interest in the body and its organic extensions within the world. Copithorne, of course, was not alone in exploring hand-drawn visual poetry (Carlfriedrich Claus did so in his hand-drawn works in the early 1960s, for instance, and Patchen in his picture poems; her work is also published alongside hand-drawn concrete by Tim Lander in the Poem Company's anthology *5 B.C. Poets* [1974]), but the integration of language into an environment of form contradicts the more common concrete practices of harshly imposing text onto landscapes or of erasing all context of the language but the metallic grid of human technology. The hand-drawn works, in contrast, speak in whispers, find quiet safe nooks for voice, and always seem cognizant of the possibility of misrecognition, silence, and disappearance. Such works illuminate the failure of language to dominate earth, life, bodies, animals, and material forms, contest the presumption of a separation between subject and object, body and mind, and reverse the Cartesian separation privileged by Western culture since Aristotle. Daphne Marlatt developed such an aesthetic into a clear definition of poetry: "language in poetry plays with silence or its own absence: each word radiates multiple possibilities, pure potential in the silence surrounding it that is then closed down into manifest direction by that which follows it" ("Long Ongoing Line" n. pag.). The military procession of one perception marching directly into the next perception falters in the rupture of connotation and what Kristeva terms "signifiance" (*Revolution* 13). Like Copithorne in the poem "Famine," discussed earlier, Los Angeles poet Barbara O'Connelly's *There Were Dreams*, published by Nichol's Ganglia Press in Toronto in 1967, captures the anxious apprehension of language as a precise instrument slipping away. She depicts her protagonist trapped and suffocated by language (indeed by a language that flows out of her belly button like an emaciating umbilical). It does not affirm her voice or secure her identity: it denies her. Similarly, Copithorne's poem "How do you ever know? / You never do" concludes with the line: "what I am: a handful of mistakes, within this solid medium / memory of you and complex art" (19).

Copithorne's engagement with experimental poetics began when she attended a Patchen performance at bissett's urging in 1961. She dropped out of university shortly thereafter, inspired by the possibility of exploring non-normative aesthetics ("A Personal" 55). While exuding a similar spiritual intensity as Patchen, her texts are even more likely to reject the individual as a useful determining category of experience: "know that / that all life is impermanent / that there is no real self // all is emptiness / silence fluttering" (*Release* 10). She recalls her visit to City Lights bookstore in San Francisco and seeing visual-textual crossover work by Brion Gysin as a particularly formative moment in her development. Gysin's calligraphic works evoke the feeling and shape of language typically without semantic content (or with deconstructed words). Similarly, the text in what Copithorne calls her "poem-drawings" (the subtitle to her book *Release*) blends in with the shapes and patterns, threatening to undo whatever vestige of meaning accrues in the often disconnected, discontinuous text. The text – when there is text – is consistently shaped by a confessional lyricism lamenting the limits of verbal expression. Sometimes this lament is balanced by the prospect of other modes of communication, especially through the body and sexuality. One can also detect the mystical, illuminated influence of William Blake in such lines as: "There's another Order / to things [...] produced from / my body of bliss / growing / beyond / my mind // There's another Order / to things / in which we / perhaps unknowingly / live" (*Release* 7). Her 1971 poem-drawing collection *Miss Tree's Pillow Book* delves into the problem of living with magic, community, and art on a daily basis in a capitalist world, by noting that "Blake would certainly have had his doubts."

**Judith Copithorne on Vancouver Concrete,
email interview, 27 October–14 November 2013 (*cont.*)**

And then bill bissett and I had many conversations about experimental art and literature in those years especially when we were at ubc from 1959 to 1962. And you know I read the back, cultural pages of the New Statesman and Nation which my family got from 1950 to 1963 or so and although they certainly did not then talk about concrete poetry they did review many British and European cultural activities. And you know it was bound to come with the comics, crazy cat for example and movies and so on and in fact the biggest thing that puzzled me then and still does is how long it has taken (is taking) to spread it's influence.

I should also say that one of my reason's for using hand work in concrete poetry which was not the norm in those days was that I felt hand work being ignored in favour of type could be seen in part perhaps as a privileging of the mechanical or more male dominated forms over the hand made forms more often used by women.

It was not easy for Vancouver women poets in the early 1960s. Maxine Gadd has always been one of the very best poets around. Her work, her performances, her feminism, her imagination continue to fascinate me. Pat Lowther was another great and politically dedicated writer who was supportive of women; Beth Jankola and Anne McKay were each superb poets who offered me inspiration and friendship. There were other exceptional women, some of whom were writers and artists, some who had quite different interests. I met and became familiar with the varied and brilliant work of Phyllis Webb, Dorothy Livesay, Myra MacFarlane, Marya Fiamengo, Gwen Hauser, Joy Long, Daphne Marlatt, Nellie McClung and Skyrose Bruce. And, during this time women who came from outside the city – the inimitable Margaret Atwood, Diane Di Prima, who read with her company of performers, the Floating Bear, also gave exceptional readings here.

Each of these women's writing had quite different qualities. The work of some has been, for excellent reasons, well-remembered; that of others has been undeservedly almost forgotten, but their struggles with the complexities of society formed an important support web in those days – for many people, including me. Each of the women mentioned were strong and talented, commented on and explored the travails of women in our society, and were usually serious supporters of the ideas of feminism. As such, they were also involved in the battles being fought to forward the social and economic equality and physical and intellectual freedom of everyone. Feminism has always been an important facet of this movement and is almost inextricably intertwined with it.

Figure 4.12 Untitled visual poem from Judith Copithorne's *Release: Poem-Drawings* (1969). Source: Private collection of the author. Used with permission.

The dialectic of doubt and optimism is a central recurring feature of Copithorne's work, predicated on her recognition of calamitous violence in the contemporary world and faith in the possibility of its reversal. McCaffery noticed a similar dialectic in bissett's work in "the materiality of language [which] is that aspect which remains resistant to an absolute subsumption into the ideality of meaning" ("Bill Bissett" 105). For McCaffery, the tension in bisssett's work exposes a "libidinal" agonistic force that threatens constantly to undo the accumulation of power in language. The work becomes a thin veil of language covering a powerful undercurrent of anti-language that makes it impossible "to actually read Bissett" (102) because the writing strives "to expel the need to write" (106).[6]

Meanwhile, in Copithorne's visual work, gender helps to focalize and personalize the power that needs interruption – even as she also contends with what McCaffery terms "ultimately frustrated gestures against repression" ("Bill Bissett" 100). Mikhail Bakhtin suggests that texts bear the mark of both their resistance to and facilitation of epistemic violence (see *Rabelais and His World*), and Copithorne's work bears the hallmark of such a struggle: of how her voice might have been limited, but also how and in what way she resisted her own marginalization. There are occasionally blunt textual eruptions of frustration at the counter-revolutionary tendencies, the

---

6 Carl Peters takes exception to McCaffery's attempt to radicalize bissett, claiming instead a shamanic and spiritual mode operating within bissett's writing. Peters seems unaware of the commonality of the themes of self-negation and world-negation in the mystical traditions bissett explores. If anything, McCaffery gives bissett too much credit for simultaneously orchestrating an entire publishing venture as the embodiment of an aesthetic that fulfils the revolutionary spiritualism of hippies, mystics, and postmodernists alike. McCaffery's portrait of bissett hardly undermines bissett's value, but places him so far beyond anything comparable in Canadian and indeed world literature as a veritable vortex of linguistic revolution, a black hole of raw pressure disrupting the total shit-storm of the world.

habitual patriarchal stance, of the period's avant-garde. Though encoded differently, and often more subtly, the concrete writing from the period also raises poignantly gendered objections to any universalizing projections offered by the avant-garde. And indeed, it is precisely this plaint, this lyrical personalizing of experience and expression, that signals the gendered modalities of concrete poetry and that differentiates Copithorne's visual work from the broader ambitions of concrete poetry. In the Dutch De Stijl artist Theo van Doesburg's early articulation, the concrete movement sought explicitly to "exclude lyricism [...] for absolute clarity" because "[a]rt is universal" ("Basis of Concrete Painting" 520). Such a position misunderstands the ideology that flows through all products of human cognition, through all language. Mary Ellen Solt, in contrast, notes that even despite the anti-expressive orientation, individual personality and even national culture are still evident in concrete works.[7] This exception calls to mind Kenneth Goldsmith's recent recognition that even the most strictly anti-expressionist uncreative writing – plagiarized texts dutifully copied out verbatim from any source – still bears the imprint of the author's character and circumstance (*Uncreative Writing* passim).

While lyrical expression was permitted as an inevitable secondary characteristic of concrete work, the freedom to explore the *expressivist possibilities* of anti-expressive concrete poetry in Vancouver was decidedly imbalanced along gender lines. Thus, while Michael Turner and Stephen Scobie both note the lyrical inflections in concrete poetry by bpNichol and bissett, this politic is more observable in work by female concrete poets of the period and directly contradicts the universalist ambitions of the concrete poetry movement. It is not surprising, then, to discover that there were only three women out of the sixty-three poets represented in the 1969 Concrete Poetry Festival and none in the 1967 and 1971 shows curated by David UU and Pierre Coupey. The exclusion or marginalization of female concrete and visual poets from the marquee events in Vancouver extended the sexist problem highlighted by Robert J. Belton of women's Surrealist work being accepted only to the extent that it reflected male discourse (50). In this case, in concrete poetry, women's writing was excluded to the extent that it contested the illusory universalist ambitions of masculine discourse and experience.

Poignantly, this tension, and its attendant acknowledgment of the failure to become *universalized*, becomes a dominant theme of the published visual poetry

---

7 "The Brazilian 'pilot plan' challenges the poet to a position of 'total responsibility before language' with the interesting result that although he is more concerned with the object he is making than with his personal-subjective motivations, his poems will express an individuality that is entirely his own. We hope to show by this limited selection that, despite its international outlook, concrete poetry displays both distinctively national characteristics and individuality, personal style. For example Gomringer's 'constellations' are lyrical and personal at the same time that they are objectified at a distance. And although the *Noigandres* poets wrote as a group, each developed in his own way despite the fact that Brazilian concrete poetry exhibits certain general characteristics which make it a distinctive school" (n. pag.).

Figure 4.13 Untitled visual poem from Judith Copithorne's *Release: Poem-Drawings* (1969). Source: Private collection of the author. Used with permission.

by Vancouver women: "Little girl, you've become / a fuss budget / a worry wart / a harried / house wife / Let it all go / Let it all go / Let go / fly free" (Copithorne, *Release* 5; see Figure 4.13). The image and the text contradict one another here: the visual is free, asemic, and vibrant, but the text still speaks of the gendered limitations to that freedom. The ambivalence of this lyrical misgiving contradicts the liberated assumptions of concrete poetry and apologetically fails the impossible ambition of, in the Noigandres terms, concrete poetry's "thorough realism" (A. de Campos et al. 72). More cynically, Martina Clinton's 1971 book *Yonder Glow* includes two concrete works that mock the masculinist Western tradition: the first is the word "crap" repeated and shaped in the form of a cross, and the second is a circular vortex of the repeating words "everything isn't crap" (n. pag.). In her second book from 1971, *Something In*, publisher bpNichol describes her as "one of the foremost radicals in the early stages of the Vancouver poetry renaissance" (back cover). Lynn Ruscheinsky's "Travelling in the United States of Male Supremacy" (1974), meanwhile, depicts a pigeon carting a female astrological symbol as an act of defiance against the masculine arts milieu that seemed unified in its hostility to women.

Looking at the published visual work by women is important precisely because these works survived the value-laden filter of the period just enough to become part of the public record. They become evidence of an ideological contest surrounding the expanded expressive opportunities for women with the arrival of modernism and concrete poetry in Canada, and open up the possibility of even further unsilencings. It could be argued that publishing these texts at all implies a self-criticism by the Canadian avant-garde in acknowledging women and contesting the forces that limited them, even though the writing claims their words cannot or will not be heard. Against this awareness and credit for self-criticism, I note Katie Degentesh's satiric article in the *Boston Review* wherein she acidly suggests that women have been encouraged toward confessional and lyrical poetic modes as a means of keeping them out of real power ("Legitimate and Illegitimate Poems" n. pag.). In this case, the lyrical and political orientations of women's visual writing separate this body of work from the more celebrated revolutionary-*cum*-universalist ambitions of the concrete poetry movement evidenced in men's work from the same period. Critics who limit their representation of women's writing to complaints against the inarticulate, inadmissible void that is women's subjectivity in patriarchal capitalism do little but maintain that silence. There was good reason for women's concrete writing to recoil from the universalizing gambit of internationalist concrete poetry, resisting the machinic fantasies of type that McLuhan argued triggered the emergence of Western individualism in the sixteenth century. While Canadian women produced important experiments with type, including Thibaudeau's pioneering work in pattern poetry, including Martina Clinton's pioneering work in spatialized and visual poetry, including the work of many of the anonymous women at Intermedia, the gendered modalities of Vancouver's visual work offer a useful repudiation of any impression of the concrete poetry avant-garde as a homogenous realm. It was an eruptive site of voicing where frustration against old ideologies did not get erased, even as it was being marginalized. The small number of works produced by these women introduces another narrative of concrete poetry in Canada and begins to break down the symbolic order imagined by a masculinist avant-garde that too often legitimizes itself at their expense, even as it contests the narrativization of a Canadian avant-garde that ignores them.

Building from Susan Stanford Friedman's notion of modernism as a creative response within and against modernity, and the avant-garde as a creative response within and against modernism ("Planetarity" 475), women's concrete and visual writing becomes an extension of this negotiation and stands as a counter-current to the universalist utopianism within twentieth-century avant-gardism. This is not a dialectical model, which never attends to the imbalance of power relations, but a dialogical resistance strategy. Marx and Engels wrote that, despite its limitations, the arrival of modernity signalled a dramatic increase in the potential for liberation. The avant-garde too increases the potential for liberation and emerged in response

to modernity as part of what Hardt and Negri term "the multitude's desire for liberation" (*Multitude* 39). The idea of the avant-garde consequently reflects a globalized
imagination of modernity even while it participates in a transnational struggle to
harness the liberatory possibilities of globalization. It does so, however, by limiting the possibilities of the local and the individual, which explains in part its common resistance to individual, lyrical work. Concrete poetry fits this kind of model
of resistance, inasmuch as it articulates a "utopian element of globalization" working
"to forge a counterglobalization, counter-Empire" (115). Women's visual writing in
Vancouver in particular evidences an important ambivalence about the utopian possibilities of a counter-Empire. It is, indeed, a writing outside writing, one that helps
to establish the impossibility of women's writing (let alone political revolutionary
writing) especially in the context of the masculinist, Eurocentric narrativization of
visual poetics.

4 Coda: The Visual Roots of the Alphabet

Beyond the habitual history, even beyond the inclusion of women in that history,
there is another way to narrativize the genesis of concrete poetry that reverses
many of the value-laden assumptions about international culture. Though it does
not develop it to any great extent, the exhibition catalogue to the *Concrete Poetry*
exhibition acknowledges an alternate history of language that is grounded in primarily visual experience, as a sensory orientation. For instance, the slides used in
the exhibition include eight pre-modern examples of hieroglyphic, petroglyphic,
and runic texts. Similarly, Ed Varney's typographically experimental essay on
concrete poetry included in the catalogue connects Chinese ideogrammatic language with Egyptian hieroglyphic symbols, concluding that "concrete poetry / is
form as content / medium as message / poem as object / (Is this phase 1 of a pure
visual language?).". In fact, rather than a new phase of language, in this lineage,
visual poetry represents a return to the origins of language use, a rediscovery of
the inherent connection between mind and body in human experience, and a
rejection of all cultural edifices built upon the separation of form and content.
bissett's collage work "Evolution of Letters Chart" (see Figure 4.14) from the
exhibition, also published in *The Cosmic Chef* and later reprinted in *The Poem
Company* (1972), offers a poignant interruption of the very Eurocentric history
of the evolution of our Phoenician letters with an image from *A Staircase of
Stories* (1920) by Louey Chidholm and Amy Steedman. The cut-in text depicts a
boy riding on the back of Quatta, a "broken-hearted" chimpanzee devastated for
being cut off from her roots (85). After Quatta and other stolen monkeys burn
the ship that stole them, a sympathetic sailor travels with her to help her return
home. The parable, while enshrined in colonialist logic, presents a sentimental

Figure 4.14 bill bissett's "Evolution of Letters Chart," as published in 1969 in bpNichol's anthology of concrete poetry *The Cosmic Chef* (1970). Source: Private collection of the author. Used with permission.

interruption of that violence. To interrupt a Eurocentric evolution of language with this image, as bissett does, draws a poignant parallel between Western language and history.

Correspondent with the rise of visual poetry is the rise of a branch of archaeological linguistics that sought to establish the very roots of human language. One of the earliest popular market successes of this variety was a best-selling book by a Canadian, Richard Albert Wilson (the popularity of which was no doubt boosted by the delightful preface supplied by George Bernard Shaw). Wilson's book on the sonic roots of language and the visual roots of the alphabet begins with the premise that our language and our world were at one time melded:

> It is the one unique human instrument which man has designed for the purpose of elaborating within his own mind an actual mental picture of the material world of space and time in which he lives. By means of these designed symbols of language he has built up, and is still building up within his own mind a space-time picture of the space-time world; and since the space-time mental picture elaborated by language is the approximating image or counterpart of the actual space-time world, there must be a close correspondence between the structure of language and the structure of the world which language images. (4)

The roots of language are, he concludes, fundamentally visual:

> In every known case, so far as the records have come down to us, when man first felt the need of a written record to preserve a present experience for a future time, or to transmit it to someone at a distance from him in space, he began by pictorial representations of natural objects that were seen and known. (183)

Other similar theories of language's symbolic origins abound: of particular interest to Canadian visual poetry is Alfred Kallir's argument that they are sexual and psychogenetic, which inspired bpNichol and Steve McCaffery (Nichol, *Meanwhile* 56–68), and Toronto poet Nick Drumbolis's claim in his alphabet origin story *Myth as Math* that they are based on the cycles of the moon.

American visual poet and scholar Johanna Drucker maps out the transition from pictures to ideographs, which were still spatial representations of spatial things (i.e., not full representatives of the space-time experience of human consciousness). The visual element started to dissipate in the transition from ideographs to phonograms, where written language moved from pictorial symbolism to representations of spoken sound. Before that break, however, human culture was rife with a rich visual symbolism in alphabets, including runic languages, hieroglyphs, and petroglyphs. In the Canadian context, considering the petroglyphs in the context of a discussion of avant-garde poetics offers an opportunity to destabilize the logic of settler colonialism that runs rampant through our literary histories. Indigenous scholar Neil McLeod writes about the importance of the petroglyphs that are found across Canada as cultural markers: "When you look at the petroglyphs, you can see layers of drawings. The image is always changing, depending on the angle, direction, and flow of light. There are literally hundreds of archived iconic memories housed at this spot, along with endless interpretations throughout the generations" (7). The language used to describe such works is also revealing: "hiero" means "sacred," such that hieroglyphs are a form of sacred writing; "petro" means rock, such that petroglyphs are a form of rock writing – or, if you return to the root of the word, "actual, solid," hence concrete. In other words, concrete poetry is not an invention so much as a recovery (a salvaging) of something that we lost in the world. As McLuhan suggests in *The Gutenberg Galaxy* (and throughout his writing), humans became detached from the material world, from the earth, and our language encodes and expands that distance. While concrete and visual writing is certainly a manifest response to modernity, it is more broadly also an attempt to realign us with our past, and correct the mistakes that have been made. Certainly, any history of visual poetics that does not acknowledge petroglyphs, hieroglyphs, or runic work, or that does not acknowledge the international proliferation of visually impacted literary forms, such as Magha's *Shishupala Vadha* with its palindromes and Chitra-kavya visual language wheels, is a false history of the form, intrinsically local (in Canada's case, ultimately Eurocentric), and of increasingly diminishing value.

Edwin Varney, "Concrete Poetry" (1968)

Concrete – actual, real, immediate to experience, not abstract or general, the thing itself; as poetry, the graphic union of word as symbol for meaning and the poem as object. The poet's craft consists in somehow suspending the flux of experience as it eddies around him. The jewel in the whirlpool then, the poem itself must be placed before the reader's eyes like an explosion. "how can the poet reach out and touch you physically as say the sculptor does by caressing you with the objects you caress?" asks bpNichol who, answering goes on to say that the poet "creates a poem/object for you to touch and is not a sculptor for he is still moved by the language and sculpts with words."

The poem as object, sculptural or graphic, is as old as writing, Oriental pictograms, as well as Egyptian and Babylonian hieorglyphics [*sic*], are, to our eyes, just that – pictures which speak as language does. These early languages make sense through the eye's understanding, English mainly through the ear. [...] Concrete respects the integrity of the poem as object. The original itself must be the source for all reproductions. Language is treated as design as well as the medium for ideas. Just as each poem is a separate hieroglyph, a whole new language is built out of the totality of a poet's work; each poem is the basis for a new alphabet.

But since concrete poetry depends upon immediate reaction, it excludes the whole realm of myth from poetry. Since it is not linear there can be no sense of progression, no plot or story, no structuring of time elapsed. Concrete consequently eliminates the high voice, the diction of moral purpose and piety which has characterized most great western poetry.

Nichol, in a discarded afterword on bissett's poetry that was to be included in *We Sleep Inside Each Other All*, arrives at a similar insight:

> Poetry often seems nothing more than an attempt to give back to language the rich pictorial texture it had prior to the creation of the phonetic alphabet, or, rather, an attempt to keep alive those qualities which were sacrificed to make way for the phonetic alphabet's creation [...] Bissett is reactionary in his attempt to bring the language back to its pictographic base. But Bissett's reactionary behaviour is the kind that brings renewal and gives rise to new possibilities for in lines like the following he has repeatedly stated how we have trapped ourselves by stifling language and how it is only thru its liberation we have a chance of growing & taking our proper place in the world:

> > "to let fly high/let
> > that bird go, see how yur hand
> > takes up the space so itself
> > without the bird crampd in it."

> ("The Typography" n. pag.)

McCaffery, for his part, goes even further than this acknowledgment with his enormously provocative anthology *Imagining Language: An Anthology* (co-edited with Jed Rasula), which tracks an alternative history of international alphabets and poetic experiments that foreground visuality. Similarly, in 1975, *Tish* editor Fred Wah published *Pictograms from the Interior of BC* with Talonbooks, a book of literary translations of the pictograms the BC author John Corner had photographed in 1968. While these readings are reminiscent of Pound's deliberate mistranslations of Chinese ideograms, and appropriate Native voices with sincerity but still with a casual disregard, the project helps to bridge the gap between European and non-European visual literary cultures.

Integrating such a linguistic-evolutionary consciousness into this particular localized and chronologically bounded history of visual poetry in Vancouver in 1959–75
helps to explain the revolutionary undercurrent within such work at the outset, as
well as the deep political frustration that girded it through the 1970s, but ultimately
pulls the narrative far beyond the purview of this present study. It also threatens to
impose a teleological frame on contemporary works, especially works by Nisga'a
poet Jordan Abel that have begun to integrate Indigenous aesthetics and politics
into the genre. His books *The Place of Scraps* and *Un/Inhabited*, in particular, appropriate non-Indigenous texts and pull them into exquisite visual patterns that rebut
their toxic colonialism. To be clear, while the visual poetry that I have highlighted
in Vancouver was distinctly political, it did not operate in the "oppositional sub-
version or utopian transformation" modality of historical avant-gardism (Drucker
101). Increasingly in the present, an intersectional politics informs the visual poetry
that is emerging in Canada that seeks to contest various manifestations of oppression, especially settler oppression of Indigenous cultures, as a means of addressing
our own history as colonial agents. The practitioners in the 1960s were attuned and
awakening to this latent potential, even as the colonial violence continued to rage
around them.

Indeed, while the historical avant-garde had a problematic relationship with some
of the darkest tendencies of European imperialism, fascism, and hegemony, a new
avant-garde in Canada is emerging through a combination of art and politics specifically oriented to advancing anti-imperialism, combatting fascism, and rethinking the
racist underpinnings of Western capitalism.[8] In particular, a growing set of authors
are mapping out a necessary re-imagining of settler–Indigenous relations, thinking

8 In thinking about the intersections of Indigenous decolonization and the avant-garde, it might be
  instructive to think of the avant-garde as a kind of pun, pointing backwards to that legacy and century-
  long tradition as much as forwards to the work that remains to be done. The pun hinges on the difference
  between "avant" and "avant": the French adverb for "earlier" or "before" and the French adjective for
  "forward" or "in front." If the avant-garde are those in front, the future-oriented soldiers of a better
  tomorrow, the avant of Canada also refers to those who came before Canada – including the begetters
  of the colonial legacies of British and French settlements and then also the Indigenous populations who
  long preceded and coexisted alongside them. If we take an honest look into the future of Canada, and
  especially Canadian art and literature, is it easy to imagine that the legacy of those who came prior to
  the country itself, those outside of it, buried by the legacy of violence that defines European settlement
  and Canadian administration, those historically disenfranchised, will become increasingly a priority of
  the national imagination. This is not the moral question of the day; it is a question of the integrity of the
  national project itself. The before-Canada and the avant-garde met for the first time in the eighteenth
  century, when the conscripts, derelicts, and convicts of the new colony were compelled to fight on behalf
  of the European powers. The earliest use of the term "avant-garde" in Canada that I have found dates
  back to 1704, in reference to the *coureurs de bois* and *des Sauvages*, Natives, Métis, and French Canadians
  sent to battle *avant of* the French military. They were the sacrificial lambs of battle, the first soldiers sent
  into hostile territory, those most likely to be killed. The before-Canada and the avant-garde meet again in
  contemporary times when the legacy of those European revolutionaries intersects with the politics and
  poetics of decolonization.

about new ways that settlers in Canada (those who came since the first settlements in 1604) can inhabit the land without erasing the Indigenous peoples and cultures who preceded them. The turn to the past contradicts the natural orientation of the avant-garde, which, as Tyrus Miller has noted, is "constituted and defined by *anti-historical impulses*" (88; emphasis in original). This garde lacks the hubris and the ego of the historical avant-gardists, who positioned themselves as the revolutionary prophets and front-line soldiers of a redeemed potential future. These contemporary Canadians, in contrast, explore the possibilities of decolonizing themselves and their texts, and by challenging the basic assumptions of daily life in the country extend that decolonizing to all of Canada. Decolonizing literature, in this context, re-imagines the past and revitalizes the present – including especially the contemporary avant-garde. Decolonization from an Indigenous perspective means, as the Cree poet Neal McLeod recently wrote, a "return to our own conceptions and frameworks, and rage against simple conventions of mimicry" (4); the clearest reasons for decolonization are to "deal with our collective trauma as experienced in residential schools and the spatial diasporas from our own homelands" (5–6). As we turn in the next chapter to the Surrealists in Paris, London, and British Columbia, we can recognize a much deeper and more mutually interested relationship between avant-garde aesthetics and Indigenous decolonization.

Decolonized (and decolonizing) visual poetry reacquaints language use with its visual roots while disrupting the political status quo in the present. Even though it was published well after the period in question, I want to conclude this section by looking more closely at contemporary Vancouver poet Jordan Abel's *The Place of Scraps* (2013), a book that plunders the writing of official state ethnographer and founder of Canadian anthropology Marius Barbeau, taking from him as Canada (under Barbeau's watch) stole the totem poles from Abel's ancestral villages in northern British Columbia. Such an appropriation takes and plagiarizes historical Canadian texts in a way that is intended to be read as analogous to the greater theft and appropriation of Indigenous land and cultural artefacts by European settlers. As Shane Rhodes remarks:

> Living in a settler society means your history and present are built upon radical discriminations that we are lulled into believing don't exist [...] colonization [...] has shaped every part of my thinking, what I have been taught, the stories I hear, and making some questions and some facts almost unseeable. ("X" n. pag.)

This recognition, and confession, implicates all authors in Canada, Indigenous or otherwise, in the ideology of colonization and proposes a new metahistorical orientation for avant-garde literary production as a means of enacting a new possibility of decolonization. When Abel first visited the Royal Ontario Museum in Toronto, he didn't even notice the grand totem pole at the centre

Figure 4.15 Collage work from page 17 of Jordan Abel's *The Place of Scraps* (2013). Source: Private collection of the author. Used with permission.

of the gallery space. When he returned a few years later, he refused to pay the admission price to see the same pole that had been stolen from his people on the Nass River in British Columbia. He makes his art in relation to that transition in historical consciousness: waging creative plagiarism against violent appropriation.

Abel carves his poems from Barbeau's work, exposing the raw material and speaking back to Barbeau's role as an appropriator. As Pauline Wakefield writes, "[f]rom Barbeau's ambivalent colonialist perspective, the 'passing' of 'the Indian' was a *necessary* tragedy, justified by the supposedly inevitable progress of Western culture and its burden to civilize North America. For Barbeau, therefore, the vanishing Indian was a figure of colonial poesis" (58; emphasis in original). While Abel acknowledges Barbeau by name in these pieces, his defacement of Barbeau's texts in his plunder-verse poetry excises Barbeau's authorial control over his work and reverses the spectacle of the vanishing subject. For Abel, therefore, the vanishing ethnographer is a figure of *decolonial poesis*. Finding nothing in Barbeau, and his claims to those objects, by proxy Canada's claim to the land that held those totems, means asserting a space of Indigenous agency and sovereignty. What is striking is precisely how Abel's objectification of Barbeau's writing, Abel's use of it as the raw matter of his own textual sculpting, asserts the ongoing vitality of Indigenous subjectivity. This reversal is the task of the decolonized Indigenous author: as Lee Maracle writes, "[B]eing colonized is the internalization of the need to remain invisible. The colonizers erase you, not easily, but with shame and brutality. Eventually you want to stay that way. Being a writer is getting up there and writing yourself onto everyone's blackboard" (qtd. in McLeod 45).

In the book, Abel contrasts sparse letterscapes with a series of tightly woven collages of Indigenous art mixed with heavily repeated text that speak back to the author's decolonizing shift in consciousness: "a feud over this pole" (3), "transported to Toronto" (17), "removal of Sakauwan Pole from Nass River" (29), and "R.O.M." (57). Some of these texts are taken from Barbeau, but others, such as "wooden spoon" (95), highlight poignant scenes and images from Abel's self-reflexive narratives of his expanding consciousness. The wooden spoon, for instance, refers to a gift he is given by friends of his absent father (97). That his father carved the spoon prompts Abel to reassess "the validity of the past" (105) and strikes him with the cultural disconnect of the wooden spoon sitting on a display shelf. Like the totem poles in museum galleries, the spoon is stripped of its utility and function in the performance of culture for the "uncontrollable nakedness of spectacle." The place of scraps, where culturally functional things are discarded as waste, and waste gets repurposed into art, signals a problem with our detached model of art: it is bound up in the spectacle of erasure and emptiness. In the unused spoon, mark of the absent father, Abel confronts the idea of an alternative model of culture wherein art and life are realigned.

The full political and revolutionary legacy of concrete and visual poetry is still being uncovered. The utopian potential of this art lies in how it can disrupt such historical errors and colonial failures (in the double negative, a space opens). Indigenous scholar Glen Coulthard in an interview in 2015 explains the need to disrupt the ongoing racialized violence experience by Indigenous people in Canada: "These violences are unmasking that originary violence that Marx referred to as primitive accumulation. It's showing, through blood and fire, its original tactics in order to reproduce our colonial and deeply racialized present" (n. pag.). The hope is that the idea of historical narrative can be re-encoded to disrupt the inevitability of Indigenous abjection. As Benjamin writes, "[t]he awareness that they are about to make the continuum of history explode is characteristic of the revolutionary classes at the moment of their action" (395). And this moment is rife with action in Canada. The post-postmodernist avant-garde shift connects to a wider intersection and sudden interaction of activist moments in the realm of economics (focalized through the Occupy movement), environmentalism (focalized through the pipeline/tar sands resistance – which is combatting the expansion of the oil fields in Alberta, often called the most environmentally destructive project on the planet), and Indigenous rights (focalized through the Idle No More movement – a protest movement that rose up in 2012, led by Indigenous people in Canada seeking justice and recognition). Visual poetry in Vancouver has rushed into this politicized moment, self-conscious of the failures of the historic avant-garde yet determined to rethink the political possibilities of writing in the present. If the form had a key moment of heightened activity and achievement that peaked somewhere between 1968 and 1970, the fuller story of cultural work in Vancouver and British Columbia demonstrates that that was only a single wave in a much older and still moving body of water.

FIVE

The Triumph of Surrealism: Magick Art in Vancouver

Gleaming diamond
Vancouver
Where the train white with snow and fires of the night flees the winter

Guillaume Apollinaire, "Les Fenêtres" (29)

and they gatherd here to
behold the forces now
the magick heart shall speak

David UU, "page 177" (n. pag.)

1 Vancouver Deformance

While the rush of intermedia art in Vancouver helped to trigger a diverse array of experimentation across the arts and led to the emergence of Canadian schools of conceptualism, collage, concrete poetry, and sound poetry, the interfusion and explosion of avant-garde art also inspired various writers and artists to investigate the history of continental avant-gardism and attempt to revive and extend various precedents. In this pursuit, the Vancouverites participated in a recurring habit of the arts and letters in Canada. Rather than look back and develop from their own literary past, Canadians have long been especially adept at revisiting and recuperating old gardes from Europe and America, particularly in the avant-garde context, as witnessed by the resurgence of Aestheticism and Decadence in the 1920s and 1930s, Surrealism and Vorticism in the 1940s and 1950s, and Dada and 'pataphysics in the 1960s and 1970s. Part of this tendency can be explained in the colonial terms of delayed access and exposure: something or someone arrives in a Canadian city belatedly and helps to introduce and spread the aesthetics of a waning foreign garde. To a colonized imagination, it feels more real and relevant if it comes from elsewhere (especially America, England, or France). Conversely, another aspect of the phenomenon is simply the inevitable process of education, influence, and general cultural literacy; a small group of Canadians encounter a declining node or network of aesthetic production and learn it by imitation but distort it by challenging it and attempting to customize it to their locale. Transnational cultures flow into spaces, but are never received passively. Though this may be an aesthetic version of the dead-cat-bounce, it is at least a more postmodern approach in that it recognizes the imbalanced spread of modernisms around the globe and into (and out of) Canada, and the dialectical nature of their reception.

Despite the presence of Group of Seven painter Frederick Varley, as well as pioneering photographers John Vanderpant and Harold Mortimer-Lamb, a sense of belatedness was certainly felt in Vancouver in the 1930s, where, as Lorna Farrell-Ward writes, "European avant-garde movements or trends held little interest. The outlook was that of a colonial community without an efficacious centre, but with standards that were imported or artificial" (14). Sheryl Salloum reports that there was little to offset the favour of Anglo-European work; the city didn't even have a civic art gallery until 1931 ("John" 41). In the Vancouver of the 1960s and 1970s, however, something more vital than these models of delayed access emerged in the avant-garde investigation of interdisciplinary, intermedial arts. The mish-mash, free-to-discover zeitgeist established an aesthetic milieu conditioned to what Jerome McGann would describe as "deformance": *deformance* art exudes a false sense of unity and continuity with past models by reordering, isolating, altering, and adding to what came before (117). Consequently, in their spirit of openness and discovery, the Vancouver artists turned to the past and previous gardes to learn about existing precedents and use them to open up new directions and extend present ones. When I speak of a Vancouver Surrealism, then, in this chapter, it is intended to reflect not a colonial, delayed imitation of a forty-year-old continental aesthetic, but a deformed aesthetic built of the shards of avant-garde precedents almost collaged together into something new. The standards of previous Surrealisms were less held up as models of an abstract ideal to imitate (the usual trap) than they were plundered, smashed together with clues from other gardes, other experiences, reduced to a series of anachronistic tools and techniques that could be used and customized for new productions suited to the time and place. The complex philosophies and ideological aspirations of the previous gardes were easily shucked from the forms – to the chagrin of critics and purists – inasmuch as they were deemed not useful to the present moment and place.

In his quick sketch of Vancouver in what he calls the "[c]lassic period in collage" ("The West Coast Surrealist Group: A Chronology 1965–2014" n. pag.), namely 1967–9, Gregg Simpson suggests that previous gardes were instrumental in orienting the kinds of intermedial experimentation underway during the period:

> Lee Nova and [I] made collages from etchings, influenced by Max Ernst and also made dada/pop style photomontages; Al Neil made complex, totemic, junk assemblages which evoked Kurt Schwitters and Dada; bill bissett continued doing a combination of the mystical and satiric in his photomontages and mixed media work. Film makers at this time

in Vancouver used techniques like juxtaposition and quick cut editing to achieve a dissociation of the senses. Poets david uu and Gerry Gilbert and [I] all made dada-inspired home movies in 8mm at the same time as filmmakers Al Razutis, Dave Rimmer, Al Sens, Gary Lee Nova and others made more elaborate statements combining abstraction with cosmic imagery.

As if to demonstrate their awareness of and localized investment in the European movements, Simpson's 1968 film *Life with Dada* alludes to several iconic Dada and Surrealist images restaged in and around the city by Gerry Gilbert and Roger Tentrey (see Figure 5.1). Despite the premise, the film is not itself a Dada work of art: the French New Wave cinema, a more *au courant* garde, instead shapes the aesthetics of the film. Dada imagery provides the content, such that, as per McLuhan's notion of displaced technologies providing content for new technologies, an old garde is reduced to the content of a new garde in the latter's emergence.

In Europe, the anti-art codices of Dada helped to release the revolutionary ambitions of the Surrealist group. So, too, in Vancouver did the avant-garde probings of Dada weirdness quickly open up new Surrealist terrain. "Surrealism was Dada with wings," exclaimed Gregg Simpson in 1970 ("The Quest" 4). This transition coincided with a shift by Vancouver avant-gardists to more concentrated and focused ambitions, though the terms and conception of that focus were distinctly different from what the Surrealists had envisioned. Indeed, one of the most regularly asserted first principles of the Vancouver Surrealists was a self-conscious (perhaps gleeful, perhaps callous) violation of the doctrines of previous Surrealisms. Yves Laroque suggests that the transformation away from European models toward establishing their own Anglo-Canadian heterodoxy happened "little by little" ("Cours général" 415), but, in fact, the difference was articulated and accentuated with the founding documents of the movement. When we speak of Surrealism in Vancouver, then, it is worth conceptualizing it as an intentionally *deformed* Surrealism. For Natalie Luckyj, the West Coast Surrealists emulated the Parisian movement and discovered therein "a genuine alternative to Abstraction and Realism" (19). Many, including Laroque and various figures in Vancouver, describe this emulation through the term "Neo-Surrealism" and date its activity from properly 1964 to the present. Such a declaration suggests that what emerged in Vancouver was but one thing, when in fact there were at least three different manifestations and orientations of Surrealist activity in the city, which I characterize as anarchist, Hermeticist, and individual liberationist. Some effort will be spent in the paragraphs that follow in sorting out the differences between these threads.

With all of the activity in multiple directions, and various other intermedia interests coalescing into Surrealism, by the end of the decade Surrealism had become one of the dominant modes of avant-garde production in the city. As Joan Lowndes writes in the *Vancouver Sun*, it was "[a]s though through some time-warp surrealism

Figure 5.1 Still image from Gregg Simpson's 1967 film *Life with Dada*, starring Roger Tentrey and Gerry Gilbert. Source: Private collection of Gregg Simpson. Used with permission.

Figure 5.2 Gregg Simpson in the 1960s. Photographer unknown. Source: Private collection of Gregg Simpson. Used with permission.

has returned, along with the alchemical visions, pop, eroticism, political satire and protest in the free-wheeling spirit of the West Coast" (qtd. in Simpson, "The Vancouver School" n. pag.). By that point, various Surrealists in Vancouver had collected into a self-conscious group devoted to the exploration and advancement of the movement. The emergence of this focus, as with *Tish* before it, had the inadvertent effect of producing schisms in the city.[1] It is particularly striking, in this regard, that the Surrealism that emerged in Vancouver was primarily affiliated with and influenced by nonrevolutionary British rather than outspokenly revolutionary and much more cliquish Parisian Surrealism. The difference helps to underscore the institutional locus of West Coast Surrealism and the general aversion to groupthink, both of which were common traits shared with the British variety. Though there were aesthetic conflicts in the Vancouver Surrealist community, there was nothing approximating Breton's purges of deviant, impure, or bad Surrealists.

Surrealism in Vancouver was, at its outset, deeply embedded within the biggest institutions of the city. These institutions included the University of British Columbia (especially the creative writing program, where Michael Bullock, Murray Morton, and Hosea Hirata taught, and whose art gallery organized the 1973 *Canadian West Coast Hermetics* exhibition of Vancouver Surrealist art), the Vancouver School of Art (where Roy Kiyooka and Rob Stonier worked), the Emily Carr Institute of Art and Design (where Martin Guderna worked, the editor of two Vancouver Surrealist magazines), and the Vancouver Art Gallery, where a series of directors, including Richard Simmins (1962–6), Doris Shadbolt (1966–7), and Tony Emery (1967–74), worked consciously and diligently to democratize and expand the repertoire of the gallery to intermedial experimentation, including Surrealism. Indeed, from the first year of his tenure, Emery gave the city's main gallery over to Intermedia every spring for a festival of events that "stemmed directly from McLuhan's insights on the cross-fertilization of disciplines made possible through the electronic revolution" (Lowndes 144). Emery was ousted in 1974 by the board of directors, but not before, as he says, "[w]e had pioneered North America's first truly open public gallery, open to artists and all the arts and open to the public, free of charge. [...] I had alienated

---

1 In this case, though, the splintering of the avant-garde created a division between the Surrealists and the Vancouver School of Photoconceptualism that has not yet been reconciled or fully investigated (and is far beyond the proper purview of the current study). The early proximity and then division between these two groups have gone largely uncommented on by scholars of the period. For instance, Daina Augaitis and Lara Tomaszewska document the rich intersections between photoconceptualism and the Vancouver literary communities but omit Ian Wallace's connections with the Vancouver Surrealists who emerged out of the same avenues (Wallace even produced one Surrealist-inspired collage). However, the emergence of the Vancouver node of Surrealism corresponds to the emergence of the Vancouver School of Photoconceptualism, which achieved swift notoriety and acclaim for their fusion, especially in Wallace's case, of photography and painting. This division offers a small premonition of the political and aesthetic divides that would swamp the Vancouver scene throughout the 1970s, as idealism shifted into recognition that the revolution was no longer imminent or had failed.

the old social elite of Vancouver but had 'pandered' to another elite of young, dirty, hairy people who had no money" (qtd. in Griffin, "An Era Ended" n. pag.). It is worth noting that many Surrealist/Hermeticist practitioners, such as David UU, Gregg Simpson, Gary Lee-Nova, and Edwin Varney, remained outside of these institutions professionally, though worked and collaborated with them regularly.

This paradoxical institutional-avant demonstrates a dramatic shift in art culture in Vancouver in the early 1960s away from any residual provincialness or colonial conservatism toward exuberant and empowered experimentalism. Lowndes traces this moment to 1966, when "Vancouver turned on. Gifted artists, imaginative curators, money, and a supportive art press came together to make a scene" (142). The shift was palpable and widely recognized: that year, the Canada Council awarded the Vancouver Art Gallery the biggest operating grant in the country after the head, Jean Martineau, declared it the "most progressive in Canada" (qtd. in Lowndes 142). Indeed, the avant-garde had taken control of the institutions and suddenly had the resources and the support to create the kind of aesthetic nexus envisioned in the UBC Festival of the Contemporary Arts. It gave rise to an astonishing optimism about the efficacy of art in real-world politics: as Iain Baxter writes, "In the sixties we thought that art could change life; change the environment, change Vancouver. A lot of artists got involved with looking at art as a way of living" (qtd. in Farrell-Ward 135). Alvin Balkind, the director of the UBC Fine Arts Gallery, and Abraham Rogatnick, an instructor at the UBC School of Architecture, made enormous efforts to ensure that UBC became a nexus of contemporary experimental arts. They also worked together to establish the New Design Gallery, the first commercial gallery of contemporary art in Vancouver. This was the much-less-repressed aesthetic milieu that gave rise to the Surrealist initiatives of the mid-sixties and seventies.

Consequently, the town-and-gown divide that had kept the *Tish* poets isolated from the vital downtown scene was no longer a problem: the institutions were now intrinsically integrated into the many and numerous emerging downtown scenes, and the poets and artists deeply connected with each other. The West Coast Surrealists (also known variously as the West Coast Hermeticists, the Divine Order of the Lodge, and the Melmoth Group), working both inside and outside institutions, emerged as a kind of culmination of many of the avenues of formal investigation and thematic interests of the decade. They commandeered whole or special sections of magazines like the *Georgia Straight Writing Supplement* and the *Capilano Review* in Vancouver and *grOnk* in Toronto to promulgate and disseminate their works, published extensively in eccentric little magazines like *Circular Causation* and *radiofreerainforest*, and presented strange performances of what they called "Ritual Theatre" in multiple venues around the city. Literary presses (especially Intermedia Press [founded by Edwin Varney with Henry Rappaport] and Blew Ointment Press) in the city began publishing Surrealist poetry, fiction, and collage work. Eventually, they began publishing their own magazines, including *Lodgistiks*,[2] *The Vancouver Surrealist Newsletter*, *Melmoth*, and *Scarabeus*. Even the rather maligned magazine *Prism* published Surrealist work, including a translation of the French Surrealist Marcel Béalu.[3] Meanwhile, various galleries, including the Vancouver Art Gallery, the Bau-Xi Gallery, the Avelles Gallery, and the Move Gallery, began exhibiting Surrealist work as early as 1967, activity that led to the international touring exhibition of 1973 that travelled across Canada as well as to London and Paris. As Yves Laroque writes, there was a genuine vibrancy from this avenue of exploration: Surrealism helped bring about the "occasion of a first convergence of young artists practising the same language. They were interested in esoteric matters, occultism, Eastern mysticism, and First Nations culture (Mandan was an Indigenous nation), the components of their vocabulary and, in juxtaposition and transmutation, their syntactic element" ("Cours général" 417).[4] By 1970, in a manifesto published in the *Georgia Straight*, Simpson had declared the ascendency of Vancouver Surrealism: "Forty-six years after the publication of the first draft of the Surrealist Manifesto by André Breton, we are pleased to announce the absolute triumph of the surreal and magical consciousness" ("The Triumph" n. pag.).

The "magic artists" in Vancouver that Simpson celebrated were a group that included a diverse array of intermedia activists with a shared interest in avant-gardism and the occult. They were a network of poets and painters "who know and use the various procedures for probing fantasies, dreams, visions and intoxications with the purpose of rendering the results in some formal way, with no moral preoccupation, or comment on the nature of what comes out, no matter how startling they are" ("The Triumph" n. pag.). The key figures in pursuit of Hermeticist Surrealism included Gregg Simpson, Al Neil, Roy Kiyooka, David UU (David W. Harris), Gilles Foisy, Gary Lee-Nova, Ed Varney, Robert Davidson, Michael Bullock, and Jack Wise. bill bissett, erstwhile publisher of all avant-gardes, was well attuned to the embrace of magic and held wide open the doors for this initiative: "release yr magical powrs," he chants invitingly ("a pome" 52). However, as Jamie Reid argues, bissett's sense of magic was less occultic and more about creating eruptive networks across cultures and geographies and very much in the world: "The ends may be magical and devotional, but the means are strictly physical and earthly" ("one man" n. pag.). His figurative/magic realist work on the conceptual

---

2 Even after editor David UU moved to Kingston, Ontario, in 1975, *Lodgistiks* was still heavily dominated by Vancouver Surrealists. Issue 3, for instance, includes work by Gregg Simpson, Gary Lee-Nova, and Ed Varney, among others. In 1976, UU reactivated Derwwydon Press and published two books, *Luminous Desires: collected writings* (1977) by Vancouverite Gregg Simpson and Bob Coleman's *Improvisations* (1977). He also published Simpson's *Earth and Sky Changes: drawings* (1981). Derwwydon also published a reprint of Plato's *The Banquet* (with an introduction by Percy Shelley).

3 That is, "The Water Spider," translated by Michael Bullock, published in *Prism* in the summer of 1976.

4 My translation. The original French reads: "C'etait l'occasion d'une premiere convergence de jeunes artistes pratiquant un meme langage. Ils trouvaient dans l'ésotérisme, l'occultisme, le mysticism oriental et amérindien (Mandan était une nation amérindien), les composantes de leur vocabulaire et, dans la juxtaposition et la transmutation, leurs element syntaxiques."

planet of Lunaria might be a significant exception to his materialist consciousness. As the West Coast Surrealists moved from the 1960s through the 1970s and into the 1980s, the radical interest in practical magic dissipated into less disruptive and more literary strains of magic realism. The focus shifted from the revolutionary disruption posed by alchemy to individual liberation and especially to the imaginative freedom of the artist. The unique alignment between radical politics and experimental arts dissipated. The group expanded to include more people and more diverse engagements with Surrealism without any prerequisite attachment to notions of revolution or radicalism. People from the second phase of Vancouver Surrealism included Julie Duschenes, Hosea Hirata, Françis Thenard, Judi Smith, Ladislav Guderna, Martin Guderna, W.D. McKinlay, Cornelia Jone Trieys, Ted Kingan, Paul Montpellier, Kiyoshi Nagahama, and Rose-Marie Tremblay.

As with any renaissance of a previous art movement, and especially one that appears in a totally new context, the new group inevitably introduced significant differences in both aesthetics and politics from their forebears. These differences included the sublimation of what had been core tendencies coupled with the acceleration of forms, themes, and ambitions of the original garde. Thus, in Vancouver, while many of the familiar Surrealist tropes reappeared, such as the interest in the unconscious mind, liberating the repressed imagination, and creating an improvisational art that exceeds the interpolated ego, the West Coast Surrealists also infused their work with McLuhanesque notions of technology, mediation, and multiconsciousness, a more open (less homophobic, less misogynist) and graphic sexuality, as befitted the 1960s sexual revolution, and an even more pronounced engagement with the esoteric arts. Media self-consciousness, graphic content, and magic are all common Surrealist tropes in Europe and Canada, but the Vancouver writing is more self-conscious about its own production and much more likely to be sexually graphic, almost pornographic in articulating their collective ambitions: as David UU writes, "lawrence proved one can fuck an ideal as the greeks gave cunts to their goddesses / weere back to the golden road" ("Note for Aurea Mediocritas" n. pag.). The Parisian Surrealists were, of course, deeply invested in notions of magic, mystical symbolism, spiritual rituals, and esoteric practices (to say nothing of erotica), but this interest in magic was often treated metaphorically, as in Breton's description of the boundaries of reality that "certain magical practices momentarily permit us to entertain but which we can never overcome" (*Nadja* 111). The Vancouver Surrealists, in contrast, admitted no such hesitation about the limits of reality and orchestrated public performances of magic rituals in the hopes of shattering these boundaries. In that hope, UU declared: "All art is magic. [...] We are the first to realize this in our art and our lives. [...] We are upon the moment of gods meeting their goddesses. This is the meaning in our lives and in our art. There is no other" ("Magic and the Goddess" 11).

The earlier Surrealists' hesitation about the reality of magic can be traced back to the initial orientation of the movement, which had been biomedical rather than anarchical or mystical. Growing out of the First World War, Breton and others reacted with horror at the ease with which European civilization could descend into total violence. They sought psychological explanations and remedies for war and believed that strategic irrationalism (as per Freud's theories of art and culture) could be used as a tool to restore balance. Magic and occult practices provided key alternative knowledge horizons, and offered a potent, delightfully scandalous means of staging irrationalism. It should be clear, however, that in the early years of Surrealism, their embrace of magic was more metaphorical than devotionalist, attempting "a profound revolt and even a moral insurrection against conventional manners of thinking and feeling" (Breton, "Taking Stock" 18). Though much has been made of Surrealism as a Romantic rather than classical or rational school of art, there was still a decidedly logical and reactionary instrumentalism in Breton's use of irrationalism as part of his search for systemic structural alternatives to capitalist biopolitics. This search was effectively abandoned following his 1930 call for "THE PROFOUND, THE VERITABLE OCCULTATION OF SURREALISM" ("Second" 178), Surrealism's denunciation by the Communist Party in Russia in 1933, and Breton's subsequent embrace of Alfred Jarry's 'pataphysics. Jarry, similarly, had turned to Satanism and esoteric practices in the nineteenth century as part of his rich satire and general denunciation of the overly Christian Western rationalist imagination.

It is worth acknowledging that other Surrealists beyond Breton explored magic and occult knowledge systems more overtly, and perhaps more faithfully. Max Ernst's work in the early 1920s has been connected to the esoteric pursuit of alchemy, and the rich occultist symbolism in his paintings generally reflects his interest in mystical and especially Rosicrucian symbolism (Warlick 80–85). His work followed from the close alignment between the occult and the avant-garde in Paris since at least the turn of the century. Joséphin Péladan, a sincere occultist, launched the Salon de la Rose+Croix in 1892 with the acclaimed avant-garde musician Erik Satie acting as the official composer (see Figure 5.3). The revived Rosicrucian group, with their devotion to real magic in Paris, demanded a didactic art that represented their interests and ambitions faithfully, cultishly, which at once put them at odds with more anarchically inclined avant-garde arts and artists. The connections lingered, however, as in Apollinaire's attitude as recorded in *The Poet Assassinated* that encourages modern magicians to collaborate with science and the plastic arts in order to help achieve a universal perspective and general consciousness raising. For Apollinaire, magic was "a valid system of creative knowledge" (Choucha 30). Picasso, on the other hand, acted more in the spirit of the Surrealists by exploring the African use of fetishes "not to be slaves of the spirits any longer, to become independent" (Samaltanos 19) – indeed, his use of African masks in these works were said to be paintings of "exorcism," symbolically purging the irrational.

To be sure, the discourse of magic was deeply embedded in the Surrealist self-consciousness from the outset. In 1924, after Breton published the first Surrealist

Figure 5.3 Carlos Schwabe's poster for the first Salon de la Rose+Croix (1892).

manifesto, the Surrealists searched out related techniques and technologies that would foster their pursuit of "the Secrets of the Magical Surrealist Art" ("Manifesto" 29). They discovered many parallels between their interests and occult practices – especially the similarity between their use of automatic writing and the speech acts of mediums in séances. In 1925, Breton penned a "Letter to Seers," in which he offered lavish praise to such mediums, calling "these young women [...] the only guardians of the Secret" ("A Letter" 197). The next year, Antonin Artaud wrote his own "Letter to the Seers" (which he dedicated to Breton) also praising the magic of a medium who revealed to him a "magnificent absolute. I had no doubt learned to get closer to death. This is why all things, including the most cruel ones, appeared to me in their most balanced aspect, in perfect indifference to any meaning" ("Lettre à volante" 16).[5] The language of the occult crept over into the Surrealists' description of formal artistic techniques: Ernst thus described collage as the "alchemy of the visual image. The miracle of the total transfiguration of beings and objects with or without modification of their physical or anatomical aspect" (12). The Vancouver Surrealists' interest in alchemy and collage can be traced back to this initial linkage.

Even despite all this saturation in esoteric concerns, book-length studies of the association between Surrealism and the occult by Mircea Eliade, Nadia Choucha, and Ruth Brandon all arrive at the same conclusion: that the turn to magic was far more literary than literal, symbolic rather than indicative of a serious ideological stance.[6] The interest in the occult and the public embrace of such things as Satanism, spiritualism, and even insanity were shaped by a desire to *épater les bourgeoisies* – to shock the bourgeoisie out of their presumptions of acceptable practices and beliefs – and to jar themselves out of inherited rationalism. As Eliade writes: "To conclude, from Baudelaire to André Breton, involvement with the occult represented for the French literary and artistic avant-garde one of the most efficient criticisms and rejections of the religious and cultural values of the West – efficient because it was considered to be based on historical facts" (53). Furthermore, while Breton and Soupault's *Les Champs magnétiques* (1919) mimics the verbal automatism of spirit mediums,[7] both authors understood the source of the automatic words to be the unconscious mind of the medium rather than any veritable spirits or deities communicating through the medium: as Brandon writes, they worked "with Freudian rather than occult intent" (158). Breton himself confirmed, in 1930, that "Surrealism believes Freudian criticism to be the first and only one with a really solid basis" ("Second" 160).

Though the Surrealists would increasingly experiment with spiritualism and séances, and contemplate the parallels between automatism and mystical mediums,

5 My translation. The original French reads: "Un magnifique absolu. J'avais sans doute appris à me rapprocher de la mort, et c'est pourquoi toutes choses, même les plus cruelles, ne m'apparaissaient plus que sous leur aspect d'équilibre, dans une parfaite indifférence de sens." Thanks to Prof. Catherine Parayre for help with the translation.

6 McLuhan, for his part, dismissed such occultism, and Eliade particularly, as childish irrationalism (*Gutenberg Galaxy* 77).

7 Using automatic methods to unlock the mysteries of the deep brain provided many transformative moments for Breton, as if giving him access to a secret source of knowledge on the mind through its unconscious machinery. He quickly extrapolated this metaphor of a hidden occult source of knowledge into broader significances about the workings of the human mind and even our consensual notion of reality itself. Unlike occultists, who believed incantations, rituals, and acts of magic could transform the external, material world, Breton used the term "magic" to describe the ability of the mind to access this unconscious pool of knowledge: "nothing we say or do has any value except when we obey this magic dictation" ("Les Mots" 12).

the core orientation of Surrealism remained primarily psychological and intellectual.[8] The discourse and practice of magic provided both the rhetoric and spectacle of revolt: like eroticism, it offered "a path towards both the scandalous and the transcendent" (Brandon 238). As Mireille Bellefleur-Attas writes, magic and the occult joined forces with automatism, dreams, objective chance, and myths in later Surrealism because "they proved useful in generating images which, at their best, possess the quality of what Breton has defined as the 'marvellous' – or, in other words, 'convulsive beauty'" (20–21). While scholars like Justin Vicari argue that Breton "unambiguously enlists fortune-tellers as shock troops in the aesthetic, social and political revolution" (57), the sincerity of the Surrealists' exploration, perhaps exploitation, of the esoteric arts, even after the shift to increased occultation of the movement, remains a question. In *Le Surréalisme en 1947* exhibition at the Galerie Maeght, for instance, Breton used steps of the gallery to pair images of the enlarged spines of favourite Surrealist books with cards from the tarot arcana (for instance, the Emperor was paired with James Frazer's *Le Rameau d'Or*). While this seems to celebrate a history of occult engagement by avant-garde artists, the effect is less devotional than it is rather comical and almost parodic.

In 1952, Breton wrote an article assessing the state of Surrealism in Canada, primarily the work of Paul-Émile Borduas and the Montreal Automatists. His essay notably strays from that topic to address the relationship between Surrealism and the esoteric arts:

> Previously, in *Arcane 17*, which I wrote in Canada, I expressed the conviction that the process of artistic discovery is enfeoffed in the form and in the means of advancement of high magic. To-day it is well established, we have proof of it, that esoteric thought strongly attracted or influenced most of those who embraced surrealism, such as: Hugo, Nerval, Bertrand, Fourier, Baudelaire, Lautréamont, Rimbaud, Jarry, Roussel, Kafka. [...] We know that surrealism began with the systematic recourse to the unconscious; in the so-called reasoned phase of its activity it occupied itself in applying the benefits of the results of its exploration to consciousness [...] Only unconscious action is natural; only it is capable of accomplishing physical and chemical operations that cannot be translated in terms of reason. ("Taking Stock" 87–88)

Even in the context of praising the value and role of esoteric interest in Surrealism, Breton attends to its part in the history of thought rather than to the contributions

---

8 When Breton demanded a "profound and true occultation of Surrealism" in 1930 ("Second" 178), his efforts produced a wholesale revolt: Jacques Prévert, Raymond Queneau, Robert Desnos, Georges Bataille, and several others joined forces to produce *Un Cadavre*, a bitingly satiric text that declared, "How could the revolutionary opinions of a Breton be anything other than a joke?" (Ribemont-Dessaignes et al. n. pag.).

or actuality of the esoteric arts. The article continues to assert the primacy of psychological over magical forces.

For a period in the 1960s and 1970s, the Vancouver Surrealists reversed this sense of magic's subordinate role to psycho-biological processes. They were not the first avant-garde artists in Canada to do so. In the first decades of the new century, it was the artists, poets, playwrights, and mystics I have referred to as the Cosmic Canadians who invested most heavily in spiritism, going so far as to publish complete transcripts of séances and conversations with the dead. The embrace of spiritism was widespread inside and out of avant-garde circles and entirely sincere in both of those contexts. One of the most anthologized poets from the set (who has since fallen far out of favour) was Albert Durrant Watson, who published multiple books of transcribed conversations and poems from long-dead literary figures. At the end of his life, Watson tried to publish a long transcript of a discussion he had had with Jesus Christ through a medium, proposing it as a new sacred text for Christians. The text was quietly blocked at the embarrassed insistence of friends, family, and the church, demonstrating the limits of permissible discourse on the subject at the time. Canada's first truly avant-garde figure, Bertram Brooker, won the country's first Governor General's Award for Literature for his novel *Think of the Earth*, on the psychological burden of cosmic consciousness. Of course, like the other Cosmic Canadians, Brooker believed that he, too, had made the evolutionary leap and was, accordingly, mystically endowed.

Vancouver had its share of Cosmic Canadians, and the influence of the occult and magic ritual on modernist writers like A.M. Stephen, Malcolm Lowry, Charles Stansfeld Jones, Robin Skelton, and Anne Charlotte Dalton has been richly documented (see Karen Meijer-Kline's *Secret Wisdom of the West Coast Esoteric and Occult Practice in British Columbia* as a decent starting point). The Theosophists established their first lodge in the city in 1897, and became, as Grant Hurley documents, central to the establishment of the Vancouver Poetry Society.[9] The iconic British occultist Aleister Crowley visited Vancouver in 1915 and selected the city as the North American headquarters of the Ordo Templi Orientis (O.T.O.) to teach and practise his particular brand of esotericism. The devotees of the O.T.O., including Charles Stansfeld Jones (aka Frater Achad) and Wilfred Talbot Smith (aka Frater 132), were integrated into the arts community and helped to facilitate the spread of spiritualism in the city. Stephen Cain's essay on Breton's time in Canada includes a list of Canadian authors who explored the use of the tarot in their poetry, including Vancouver poets George Bowering and Frank Davey, as well as their Toronto compatriots Gwendolyn MacEwen, Margaret Atwood, David Aylward, and Victor Coleman (52). The evocations of occult practice Cain alludes to, however, in contrast to the activities of the O.T.O., were more formal exercises or

9 See his MA thesis, "The Lyric West."

Figure 5.4 Tarot cards designed by Gregg Simpson. From top left, the Magus, Transformation, Beauty and the Beast, the Witness, the World, and Fortune. Source: Private collection of Gregg Simpson. Used with permission.

playful allusions to the dark arts and were in no way sincere engagements with magic ritual. Stephen Collis, for instance, connects Bowering's engagement with the tarot to what he "does with the serial poem" rather than any esoteric pursuit ("Of the Dissolved" 4). While I don't want to erase the humour or tongue-in-cheek aspect of parts of their investigations of magic and alchemy, the Vancouver Surrealists, in contrast, explored this popular general interest into even more openly occultic pursuits, explicitly seeking a hidden gnosis that could recondition the world. In 1971, Gregg Simpson produced a tarot suite of his own (see Figure 5.4), published by the Divine Order of the Lodge, that functionally aligned the intermedial exploration of collage with the emerging ambitions of the Vancouver Surrealists. His tarots combine text and images and demonstrate a useful intersection between the formal experiments underway in Vancouver and the avant-garde interests in Surrealism.

2 The Surreal West Coast

Though the influence of British Surrealism was the most prominent, the dialogue between Vancouver and Parisian Surrealism was significant and stemmed from a long history that is worth mapping out in more detail. Yves Laroque, Dawn Ades, Natalie Luckyj, Joan Lowndes, and Gregg Simpson have all helped to establish and advance the field of scholarly consideration of Vancouver Surrealism, and they, in turn, have built upon the voluminous research on the Surrealists in Paris and Britain. What becomes clear is that the Surrealists were attracted to Vancouver and British Columbia as a point of access to Indigenous and especially Inuit and Haida art. It is also striking that, despite Breton being the most frequently cited Surrealist figure, the Vancouverites' principal point of contact with European Surrealism came through the British rather than the French. British Surrealism, like Canadian Surrealism, appeared belatedly in response to the continental movement and accentuated individual difference and variety over the homogeneity of the group. They were, as a general rule, more comfortable working within institutions than without. As Michel Remy writes, British Surrealism "took place in university magazines," without the "desire for total rupture" (32). The British Surrealists, it turned out, were far more interested in the psychological and medical applications of Surrealism than in any esoteric or radical politic suggested by the work. Accordingly, the art produced there was much more invested in precise representation of dream states and imagery than were the more discordant, messy, and gleefully irrational automatic Surrealist arts. It should also be remembered, at this point, that the first Canadian Surrealists in Quebec pursued the exact opposite trajectory from the British in their belated engagement with Surrealism. The French Canadian Automatists rejected Parisian Surrealism for the aesthetically compromised use of dream imagery. They argued that the only sincere power of Surrealist techniques lay in the art that accessed the unconscious mind (rather than art that symbolically depicted the unconscious). They pushed deeper into Surrealist methods, rather than pulling back into more literary terrain. We have, then, in these two branches of Canadian Surrealism in Montreal and Vancouver a stark embodiment of an essential cleavage in European Surrealisms.

The dividing lines were not absolute, of course. For instance, like the Parisian Surrealists, British Surrealists saw in Indigenous art forms an ideal fusion of psychological projection, representational form, and unselfconscious aesthetic production. There was an enormous Eurocentric cultural pretension informing such an assessment of Indigenous cultural production, even if it came out of genuine interest and begat a sincere cultural exchange. As Colin Browne writes in his review of Surrealist engagement with Indigenous art in British Columbia: "Where some see a profound appreciation for the ceremonial art of indigenous peoples, others find misguided Eurocentric amateurism, or, even worse, an ignorant, paternalistic form of appropriation, the familiar utopian projection of social, political and religious renewal onto North American Native culture" (248). Setting that concern aside for the moment (it will return), it was the proximity to Indigenous art that helped connect Canada's modernist and nascent avant-gardists with their European (including British) counterparts. Indeed, in the first decades of the twentieth century, there was a widespread interest in Indigenous art forms and techniques among Canadian artists and Canadian art institutions alike. This investigation, while deeply problematic for sustaining the colonial appropriation of Indigenous cultures, and notably empowered by the settler-colonial apparatus bent on destroying that same culture, had the inadvertent effect of connecting Canadian art to the front lines of the European avant-garde, especially the Surrealist group in Paris. For while the European avant-garde of the twentieth century was initially inspired by the vast difference of African art from Western models, the Surrealists were the first group to really glom on to West Coast Indigenous art (Jonaitis 240). The timeline and source of that interest are a little murky, but evidence of the interest abounds right from the outset of the movement. In May 1927, for instance, three years after the founding manifesto of Surrealism, the catalogue of Yves Tanguy's exhibition at the Galerie surréaliste included reproductions of Haida carvings (supplied by Breton) and a Tlingit totem pole (supplied by Paul Éluard) (Ades 31). The interest was confirmed in 1929 with the publication of the Surrealist world map, called "Le Monde au temps des surrealists,"[10] in a special "Surrealism in 1929" issue of the Belgian magazine *Variétès* (see Figure 5.5). The map is a playful representation of the planet reflecting the interests and disinterests of the Surrealists: North America is reduced to Alaska, the Queen Charlotte Islands (also known as Haida Gwaii) in British Columbia, and Labrador. England, France, Canada, and the United States are entirely absent. As a post-war provocation, Paris appears as the capital of Germany. Likely drawn by Yves Tanguy (Roediger 172), or perhaps Éluard (Wood 199), the map humorously codifies Surrealist interest in the non-Western world – especially the Pacific isles, Soviet Russia, Mexico, and China. The traditional homelands of the Inuit people (Alaska, Labrador, Greenland, and Russia) dominate the map.

While no North American Indigenous artist became officially affiliated with the Surrealists, or was welcomed into that fold, the interest in West Coast and Inuit art never abated. In 1931, the *La vérité sur les colonies* exhibition documented the hardships caused by French and European imperialism and included both Surrealist and Indigenous art side by side. In 1936, the *Exhibition of Surrealist Objects* at the Galerie Charles Ratton staged Surrealist work, including the launch of Meret Oppenheim's fur-covered teacup, alongside examples of "primitive art,"

---

10 Now commonly known as the "Surrealist Map of the World," though a more direct translation is "The World in the Time of the Surrealists."

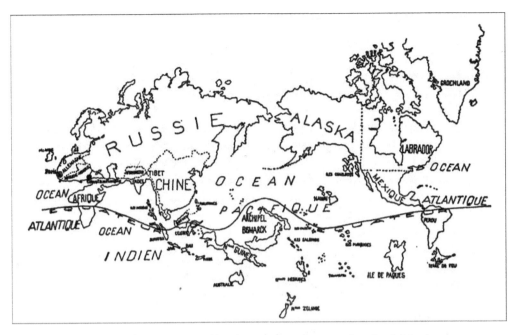

Figure 5.5 The Surrealist Group, "Le Monde au temps des surrealists," published without attribution in 1929 in Belgium.

including African tribal masks and Oceanic art. As the sculptor Isabelle Waldberg wrote of the period: "We threw ourselves into the poetic atmosphere of the Eskimo masks. We breathe in Alaska, we dream Tlingit, we make love in Haida totem poles. Carlebach's on Third Avenue has become the place of our desires" (qtd. in Le Fur 240).

In the 1930s, Surrealist attention to Indigenous art translated into institutional interest. The Swiss Surrealist Kurt Seligmann, for instance, was commissioned by the new Musée de l'Homme in Paris to visit British Columbia and Alaska to witness and purchase monumental totem poles and other Indigenous art forms. The success of his trip in bringing Native art to Paris inspired the Austrian Surrealist Wolfgang Paalen to make a similar excursion. Paalen travelled from Ottawa to Jasper by express train, over to Prince Rupert, down to Seattle, up to Alaska via the British Columbia coastline, and then back down to the Queen Charlotte Islands (Neufert 230). He wrote enthusiastically to Breton in 1939 about his adventure: "I believe I am attaining a new perspective on this art – an art certainly greater than all the assumptions that are made about it in Europe" (qtd. in Lederman n. pag.). Beyond just a fascination with the Indigenous art styles, the Surrealists were fully cognizant of the political implications of opening European culture to non-European influences. As the French and Belgian Surrealists wrote in their shared manifesto "Revolution First and Always," the Imperial European imagination was a violent repression on a global scale, metonymic of the psychological blocks they were trying to undo within the individual imagination: "we vigorously and in every way reject the idea of this kind of subjugation" (Aragon et al. 202).

It was during this trip, in September of 1939, that Paalen and his wife, the painter Alice Rahon, met the Canadian modernist painter and author Emily Carr (Carr, *Dear Nan* 194). Carr had established herself at that point as one of Canada's leading modernist painters primarily for her vivid depictions of West Coast forests and Indigenous cultural artefacts. Though she described the visit as "refreshing [...] he is so modern," Carr was rather baffled by both Surrealism and their interest in her work: "I can't get the surrealist point of view, most of their subjects revolt me [...] To my surprise Mr. Paalen was very enthusiastic about my work. I felt like a hayseed but he found something in it" (195n6). Despite her self-deprecating bafflement, Carr was in fact familiar with Surrealism. In 1939, just prior to the Paalens' visit, she delivered a series of lectures on contemporary art that made reference to the CNE (Canadian National Exhibition) exhibition of Surrealist art in Toronto, a touring version of the infamous 1936 London International Surrealist Exhibition. The Toronto version of the show came complete with a catalogue that included a definition of Surrealism by British Surrealist Herbert Read that Carr found useful (160). Stressing the biomedical over the magical, Read writes, "Superrealism in general, then, is the romantic principle in art. The modern movement known as *surréalisme* is a reaffirmation of this principle, but on the basis of a wider and more scientific knowledge of the psychological processes involved in the creation of a work of art" (12). John Vanderpant, Vancouver's first modern photographer and art patron, had also lectured on Surrealism in the 1930s for the Vancouver Poetry Society (Salloum, "John" 48). He was instrumental in convincing the Vancouver Art Gallery to purchase the eccentric-for-their-time (in that context) works by Carr, as he himself had done.

The Surrealists' interest in Carr's work stemmed from a shared or common aesthetic; Carr's confusion over their interest was because of a fundamental disconnect in their respective understandings of Indigenous cultures. For Carr, in contrast to the Surrealist belief in their contemporary revolutionary relevance, the Indigenous relics that she painted were evidence of a waning civilization, akin "to us Canadians," as she wrote in a lecture delivered in 1913, to what the "ancient Britons' relics are to the English" (*Opposite* 203).[11] Though many scholars have made the case that Carr was sincere in her exploration of Indigenous culture and sympathetic to the people she encountered, she did not value their art and living culture as a radical challenge to the gross presumptions of Western imperialism. Indeed, though her

---

11 It is a striking parallel, then, that the Surrealists and Emily Carr both began exhibiting their work alongside Native art in 1927. Following the significant Surrealist exhibition in London, England, in 1936, Carr's work was featured in the Century of Canadian Art exhibition in 1938 at London's prestigious Tate Gallery alongside Haida carvings, various totem poles, and two Chilkat blankets (Dawn 406fn7). Vancouver painter Jock Macdonald was also represented in the London exhibition.

canvases are gorgeous carnivals of colour and celebrate the astonishing achievements of Indigenous art, there are no people in her works, only decaying vestiges being overrun by wilderness. She writes, "Only a few more years and they will be gone forever into silent nothingness, and I would gather my collection together before they are forever past" (*Opposite* 203). For Carr, these totem poles were artworks in ruin, not portals to a reimagined future. Her confusion at the Surrealists' interest in her work stemmed from the fact that she, herself, was not invested in the revolutionary discourse of the avant-garde, for whom Native art signalled the vitality of non-European traditions.

For the Surrealists, in particular, the First Nations and Inuit art represented a challenge to the colonialist violence of capitalist and imperialist Europe, the extension of which was the subjugation of Indigenous people in North America. This politicized engagement with Indigenous art connected to the Surrealists' exploration of and commitment to communism, which actively contested the logic of European colonial domination around the globe. In 1931, for instance, the French Communist Party, the Anti-Imperial League, and French Surrealists organized an exhibition called "The Truth of the Colonies" that directly opposed the logic of European imperialism (Bate 216). The entrance to the gallery was dominated by a quote from Lenin: "Imperialism is the last stage of capitalism." One third of the exhibition was devoted to the "[e]xploitation of Indigenous Peoples" and included detailed maps and graphs of the violence and horror of European colonialism alongside totem poles and ceremonial masks and other objects. As Bate writes, "[a]ll the objects were accompanied by short quotes to contextualize them; for example, one described the destruction of art by colonized peoples by European missionaries who, for the sake of 'Christian progress', had collected and burnt what they considered 'fetishes'" (218–9). The Surrealists devoted another third of the event to their own work. Participating Surrealists, including Breton, Éluard, Benjamin Péret, Georges Sadoul, Pierre Unik, André Thirion, René Crevel, Louis Aragon, René Char, Maxime Alexandre, Yves Tanguy, and Georges Malkine, produced a text for the exhibition called "Boycott the Colonial Exposition,"[12] which was later republished in their magazine *Le Surréalisme au service de la revolution* (194–5). The essay spends more time rejecting the politics of colonialism than advocating aesthetic alternatives: "The dogma of French territorial integrity, so piously advanced in moral justification of the massacres we perpetrate, is a semantic fraud; it blinds no one to the fact that not one week goes by without someone being killed in the colonies" (qtd. in Bate 221).

Modernist and experimental artists in Canada were much less invested in the moral ambiguities of colonial expansion and violence. While the European avant-garde was contesting European imperialism from within, and saw their art as part

---

12 My translation. The original French reads: "Ne visitez pas l'Exposition colonial."

EXPOSITION COLONIALE INTERNATIONALE — PARIS 1931

219 GROUPE D'INDIGÈNES

Figure 5.6 Original postcard promoting the *Exposition Coloniale Internationale* in Paris, 1931. The Surrealists organized their protest exhibitions and events in response to its colonialist themes.

of that contestation, their Canadian counterparts were celebrating links between settler culture and the Indigenous communities it had displaced. An important exhibition in 1927 at the National Gallery of Canada called *Canadian West Coast Art: Native and Modern* staged work by white settlers like Emily Carr, Edwin Holgate (the eighth member of the Group of Seven), and other non-Native Canadian art next to work by Indigenous artists,[13] subsuming both under the moniker of the nation. In the catalogue, Marius Barbeau used the pairing of the art to proclaim the triumph of the emerging nation: "this aboriginal art for us [...] is truly Canadian in its inspiration" (qtd. in Harrison and Darnell 231). Barbeau, discussed in the previous chapter through Jordan Abel's response to his work, was a complicated ethnographer, involved in the collection and preservation of Indigenous lore and works but also wholly complicit in the forced appropriation of art from Indigenous

---

13 Tellingly, the Native art was assembled by the Museum of Man (now the Canadian Museum of Civilization), not the National Gallery (Whitelaw n. pag.)

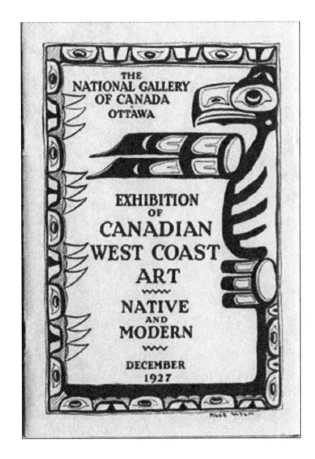

Figure 5.7 Exhibition catalogue of the 1927 *Exhibition of Canadian West Coast Art: Native and Modern*. Source: Private collection of the author.

communities. Despite the nationalist embrace in the exhibition in Ottawa, by the 1920s the Canadian government had adopted a policy against Indigenous culture that is now recognized – by the Truth and Reconciliation Commission – as "cultural genocide" (*Honouring the Truth* 1). Indigenous people were strictly forbidden from maintaining their own cultural practices, including using their own languages, holding traditional dance ceremonies, and producing the kind of sacred religious objects (such as totems and ceremonial masks) that were on display in the National Gallery in 1927. Residential schools were established to explicitly break the continuity of Indigenous culture being passed down to the next generation. Carr's work proceeds from the passive assumption of the inevitable domination of Canada's genocidal cultural policies. The Surrealists, in contrast, while abstract from the particular Canadian political landscape, were far more sympathetic to and invested in a politics of resistance against such acts of violent colonialism. So, while Carr's work contains echoes of Surrealist themes and caught the attention of visiting Surrealists in the province, their hopes for producing a revolutionary art

Figure 5.8 Photo of the 1927 *Exhibition of Canadian West Coast Art: Native and Modern* installation. Source: Private collection of the author.

of post-colonial resistance was not served by what they encountered in the art of Canadian modernist settler culture.

3 Precursors and Early Forays: Surrealism in Vancouver

These early intersections and exchanges with continental Surrealists, however, led to more sustained engagement with Surrealist art in Vancouver by the early 1940s, triggered by the wartime exile of European avant-gardists to the continent. Most significantly, Dr. Grace Pailthorpe and Reuben Mednikoff, both members of the British Surrealist group, came to and temporarily settled in Vancouver at the end of a cross-continental tour (Bellefleur-Attas 40). Pailthorpe gave a public lecture on the CBC called "Surrealism and Psychology" on 10 July 1944 in conjunction with an exhibition of her and Mednikoff's surrealist work at the Vancouver Art Gallery (13 June to 2 July 1944). It was one of three public lectures on Surrealism she delivered in the city: the first was organized by the Vancouver Ladies' Auxiliary; the second was at the Vancouver Art Gallery (Remy 261). In her talk on the CBC (on a lifestyles show called *Mirror for Women*), Pailthorpe discussed the ongoing role of Surrealism after twenty years of activity:

> The work of Surrealism will go on, for the liberation of man is an emotional urge within each one of us, and one that in the end cannot be denied. As we become more emotionally and creatively conscious we bring the day of our deliverance nearer. The creative urge is within each of us [...] Surrealism is but one of the many indications of the ever-mounting insistence on the liberation of man, for the freeing of mankind can only come through the releasing of the creative spirit within each one of us. (qtd. in A. Wilson 37)

Despite the rhetoric of liberation, as a committed psychologist, Pailthorpe believed that Breton's groundbreaking work on psychology and repression had been fore-stalled by his forays into revolutionary social action (Remy 261). The lectures and the exhibition were well received, no doubt enhanced in part because of her distance from the revolutionary politics of the first-wave Surrealists and her scientific credentials, and, as Remy hints, because she and Mednikoff were both British – the preferred ethnicity in British Columbia at the time (263). They returned to England in March 1946, after four years in the city (Laroque, "Grace" 35). Brion Gysin, Canada's only member of the Surrealist group in Paris before the war, also happened to be serving in the Canadian army in Vancouver during the time of Pailthorpe and Mednikoff's residence, but there are no records of his interaction with either of them or of his attendance at their exhibition.

Before they left, though, Pailthorpe did visit and consult with the painter Jock Macdonald about his work. He had already experimented with Automatism as early as 1934 (Luckyj 13) and was thus open to Pailthorpe's encouragement to press on with it (J. Murray, *Confessions* 132). Her backing led to a significant shift in his style. Shortly after her visit, Macdonald produced a series of "automatics," paintings begun in Surrealist fashion without premeditation but, as he was not a formal purist, developed and finished less spontaneously. He exhibited these semi-automatic paintings at the Vancouver Art Gallery in 1946, and then again in California at the San Francisco Museum of Art in 1947. He moved to Toronto in 1947 and became a prominent member of the group that would be called Painters Eleven.

In keeping with the British Surrealists' comfort with institutions, one of the most celebrated figures in Canadian art was actively orchestrating these intersections and appearances of Surrealism in Canada: Lawren Harris, the founding member of the Group of Seven and a champion of the occultist Cosmic Canadians. Harris was one of two members of the Group of Seven to relocate to Vancouver in the 1940s, along-side Frederick Varley (who would proceed to found the short-lived British Columbia College of Art with Jock Macdonald). Peter Larisey notes that Harris was, in fact, the chairman of the exhibition committee that had approved the Pailthorpe-Mednikoff

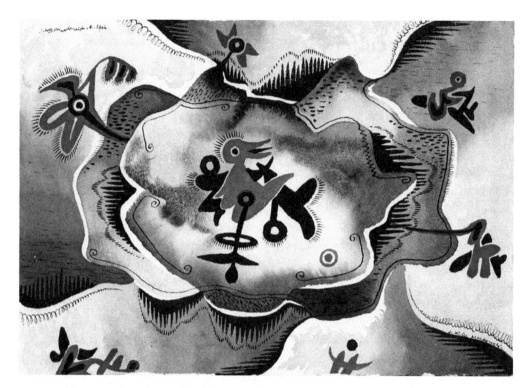

Figure 5.9 Jock Macdonald's *Orange Bird* (1946).

show (166) – indeed, Jack Shadbolt quips that Harris "practically ruled" the board during the period ("A Personal Recollection" 41). Despite his reputation as a nationalist landscape painter, Harris's interest in avant-garde work was no coincidence or aberration. He had, in fact, coordinated the first and most important early exhibition of avant-garde art in Canada in Toronto when he brought the International Exhibition of Modern Arts to Canada in 1927. The show was curated by Marcel Duchamp, Katherine Dreier, and Man Ray and had stops in Brooklyn and Buffalo before arriving in Toronto.[14] Harris was the only Canadian painter to exhibit in the show (although he recused himself from the Toronto event), appearing alongside avant-garde stalwarts like Pablo Picasso, Marcel Duchamp, and Man Ray and Surrealists like Jacques Villon, Salvador Dalí, and Francis Picabia. As a poignant point of serendipity, Harris also arranged Emily Carr's 1927 exhibition in Ottawa, discussed above, where her work appeared alongside Indigenous art. His influence on early Canadian avant-garde visual art was enormous.

---

14 For a full account of Harris's work with the IEMA, see the first chapter of my *Avant-Garde Canadian Literature: The Early Manifestations*.

After leaving Toronto in some controversy, Harris attended the "Fantastic Art, Dada and Surrealism" show at the Museum of Modern Art in New York City in December and January 1936–7, and then proceeded to join the Transcendental Painting Group in New Mexico with spiritual abstract painters like Raymond Johnson, Emil Bisttram, and Agnes Pelton. Harris moved to Vancouver in 1940 and became deeply ensconced in the local art scene, including becoming a key partner of Jock Macdonald's in promoting experimental and avant-garde initiatives in the city. Harris, like Macdonald, experimented with Surrealist methods and eventually integrated modified versions of automatic painting methods into his own work (Larisey 166). He describes the results of these experiments in his 1954 book *A Disquisition on Abstract Painting*:

> Surrealism is automatic painting, wherein the whole process comes from and is controlled by the unconscious. Whereas the process of abstract painting is a creative interplay between the conscious and the unconscious with the conscious mind making all the final decisions and in control throughout. This leads to quite different results in that it draws upon the full powers of the practitioner and therefore contains a much fuller range of communication and significance. (8)

Harris makes the poignant distinction between the art of the "pure" Bretonian Surrealists, who practise automatism, versus the "Fantastic Art" of those still invested in representation. The abstracts Harris produced in Vancouver represent an enormous departure from his earlier, more famous landscape canvases by including more overt reflection of his esoteric interests and beliefs. Harris worked diligently with Harry Täubel, another mystic who had recently arrived in Vancouver, to spread Theosophical beliefs and the ideas of Rudolf Steiner and other European gnostic philosophers within the city's art community. Shadbolt, who was ostracized for being, in his own characterization, rather godless compared to such company, notes that a "wave of interest in the occult among converts in the art world of Vancouver seems to have risen then" ("A Personal" 38).

Though Shadbolt was less invested in the occult, he was another BC painter who experimented and integrated aspects of Surrealist methodology (if not philosophy) into his work in the 1940s. While living in New York City in the 1930s, Shadbolt encountered Dalí's work at the Julien Levy Gallery. The experience was transformative and inspired a rigorous education in Surrealism and European avant-gardism, especially through writing by Breton and Lautréament (Bellefleur-Attas 42). Back in Vancouver, he began experimenting with dream imagery, especially as a means of probing and relieving the psychological impact of the violence he had witnessed first-hand in Europe in the Second World War. The impact on his art was immediate, and he acknowledged both Cubism and Surrealism as points of origin for his cycle of nature paintings produced between 1949 and 1955 (see Fleming *passim*). He also fell under

Figure 5.10 Lawren Harris's *Abstract No. 7* (1939). Source: The Estate of Lawren Harris.

the influence of British Surrealist painter Paul Nash and his experiments with abstraction (Nasgaard 131).

Echoing the Surrealist interest in West Coast Indigenous work, Shadbolt began exploring Indigenous art and responding to their cultural artefacts in his own work. Belleflour-Attas describes Shadbolt's exploration of Indigenous myth in his Surrealist works as "the most significant aspect of his art" (45). Scholars like Laurie Ricou, Marjorie Halpin, and Paul Duval defend Shadbolt's exploration of Indigenous themes as moving beyond cultural appropriation by "making it possible for people inhabiting different worlds to have a genuine and reciprocal, impact on one another" (Ricou 301). Like Carr, however, Shadbolt's use of Indigenous work did not engage in the revolutionary post-colonialism of continental Surrealism,[15] instead borrowing imagery and techniques as if from an absent or fading subject – in fact indigenizing himself at their expense. Rather than engage with the politics of his cultural appropriation, his interests were "more formalist, concerned with the spatial and

---

15 It is well to keep in mind, though, the productive and *avant* implications of this engagement, despite its inherent colonialism. In 1947, for instance, Doris Shadbolt wrote "Our Relation to Primitive Art," a short primer on the importance of Native representations of myth as the expression of a shared collective unconscious that argued that such myths helped artists (*qua* Surrealists) overcome "any intellectual hesitations" (15). This vein of investigation led to a series of "fetish" exhibitions in Vancouver in the 1970s, which included a return to figuration.

Figure 5.11 Cover of Jack Shadbolt's *In Search of Form* (1968). Source: Private collection of the author.

compositional rhythms within the picture" (Nasgaard 131). As he grew increasingly integrated into the jazz community in Vancouver, his paintings shifted away from Surrealist automatic methods and Surrealist exploration of mysticism and primitivism to focus on free improvisation and on representational methods that explored links between urban spaces, human technologies, and the natural world. He was becoming, in other words, integrated into the nascent Beat scene in downtown Vancouver explored in chapters 2 and 3. It has not been documented, but it seems likely that his experience and interaction with Surrealism helped to steer that community toward those interests. In 1968, he published *In Search of Form* (a title with a distinct echo of Léonard Forest's *In Search of Innocence*, and a cover text/image reminiscent of Graham Coughtry's early investigations of visual poetry) and began experimenting with collage.

4 Canadian Literary Surrealism

Literary Surrealism arrived in Vancouver with the foundation of the Neo-Surrealist Research Foundation of Vancouver in 1964. Established by Murray Morton, the

Figure 5.12 Cover of the first issue of Murray Morton's *Limbo* (1964).

Surrealism of the Neo-Surrealist Research Foundation was decidedly oriented toward anarchism and absurdism, with some revolutionary rhetoric but no commitment to radical politics. Morton was a lecturer in the English department at UBC, where he believed that "[a]ll the senses should be stimulated in teaching literature. Or perhaps classes could be taught in art galleries with background music" (Cawsey 1). The foundation's activity was focused on the publication of a literary journal called *Limbo*, edited by Murray Morton with Frances Robinson, John Doheny, and William Martyn, that lasted for eight issues published between 1964 and 1967. The first issue of the magazine, divided into two booklets, is ambitious and reminiscent of Wyndham Lewis's Vorticist magazine *Blast*: the cover of Morton's twenty-eight-page founding manifesto even shares the iconic puce of the first issue of *Blast*. The manifesto, which "does not attempt to set down a set of laws [... r]ather it seeks to evoke and inspire" (1), includes a giddy array of contradictory exclamations about art, literature, politics, and the future course of the magazine. It is by turns silly, euphoric, and earnest. It does, however, map out a modus operandi for the future issues:

Limbo

intends to publish works

which cultivate

a joy in the zany

a sense of wonder [...]

a desire to cultivate the creative, positive moods, moments, activities, works in the face
of the hundreds of millions of Eichmanns all around us who are so willing to be
accomplices in the preparations now being made to exterminate everyone for the
sake of ideals and/or greed.

Dada	was	destructive
Surrealism	was	destructive and constructive.
Neo-Surrealism	IS	absolutely constructive.

(iv–v)

While this historical positioning is helpful in situating the ambitions of the magazine, it equally obscures the actual orientation of the publication. As the reviewer for
Canadian Literature noted in a response that highlights without a note of generosity
the inconsistency and frivolity of Morton's critical approach, "there is nothing surrealist about his 'neo-surrealism.' It is just another way of spelling Murray Morton"
(Burns 77). It is rather comic-tragic that English Canada's first collective foray into
Surrealism was so heavily blasted *for not being Surrealist enough*. To be fair, though,
Morton (like *Blast*) includes a long list of preferred writers, almost none of whom
are or were Surrealist (Herbert Read being the sole exception). Vorticists and *Blast*
contributors, meanwhile, are especially prominent by name, including Ezra Pound,
Wyndham Lewis, and Rebecca West. Why, then, was this collective not rather
framed more suitably as a Neo-Vorticism? Lewis's unpopularity following his very
public flirtation with Nazism (before Hitler's rise to power; he published extensive
apologies for the error after the Nazi horrors became apparent), and Pound's work
on behalf of Italian fascism (*after* Mussolini's rise to power, and during the Second
World War), is likely enough explanation, although questions remain.

The second part of the first issue, being the actual magazine itself, includes a remarkably strong and diverse coterie of authors from across Canada, the United States, and
England. There is another eight-page editorial on the first principles of *Limbo* (later
followed by an additional nineteen pages of editorial content, for an overwhelming
total of twenty-seven out of sixty-four pages – also reminiscent of *Blast*) and strong
essays by American poet A.J. Hovde and British Canadian anarchist-critic George
Woodcock. The rest of the issue contains a poem by and an interview with Roy Fuller
(British), poems by Charles Edward Eaton (American), John Glassco (Canadian), L.W.
Michaelson (British), and Guy Gauthier (Canadian), and prose by Sweeney Chisholm
(Canadian) and Emilie Glen (American). The magazine was not directed toward

Vancouver audiences, but to "readers who are conscious of living in one world-city" (2) – a McLuhanesque nod to the global village. While the issue includes poems by the notorious outlaw Bonnie Parker (of Bonnie and Clyde fame), surely a Surrealist (or Vorticist) gambit, the lack of specifically Surrealist content signals the natural orientation of the magazine toward late modernist masculinist modes instead. Woodcock's excellent short essay on British Surrealism, for instance, titled "Elegy for Fur-Covered Motor Horns: Note on Surrealism in England," rejects all but the anarchist bent of the movement. His notion of a movement "influenced by, rather than adhering to, surrealism" (51), while attuned to the British distance from the "organized church" of Parisian Surrealism (49), summarizes well almost all of the English Canadian examples of the kind. Other issues include work by Ewart Milne (Irish), Joan Finnegan (Canadian), Anne Lewis-Smith (Irish), Robert Bly (American), and Kenneth Burke (American) – none of whom had any connections to British or Parisian Surrealism; indeed, both Burke and Bly had taken public stands against Surrealism.[16]

The momentum for these nascent threads seemed to gain even more speed when in March of 1964, the London (Ontario) Public Library and Art Museum curated an exhibition of forty-four painters who "never subscribed thoroughly to European Surrealist doctrine" but were yet directly "influenced" by the movement. The exhibition went to three cities in Ontario and then to various points in "western Canada" (*Surrealism in Canadian Painting*) Surrealism was on the march in English Canada.

5 Super-natural British Columbia: From Lawren Harris to David W. Harris

The West Coast Hermeticists, the full blossoming of Surrealism in Vancouver in the 1960s, grew out of the intersection of the scattered, growing Surrealist strains in the city and the interdisciplinary and experimental nexus created by the likes of Shadbolt, bissett, Al Neil, Gary Lee-Nova, and the rest of the downtown artistic community. Michael Bullock, Roy Kiyooka, Hosea Hirata, Martin Guderna, and others teaching within Vancouver's universities and colleges also helped to orient and organize the diverse strands of experimentation into a more coherent group manifestation. They called themselves "Hermeticists" at first, then "Surrealists," but is it fair to describe the work as Surrealist proper? They began working as a group forty-five years after the initial thrust of Surrealism in Paris, and over twenty years after the first Surrealist movement in Canada. Surrealism had been declared dead dozens, if not hundreds, of times before the Vancouver scene began. Indeed, French Surrealist Jean Schuster officially announced the death of Parisian Surrealism on 4 October 1969, just as the

---

16 See Burke's *Surrealism* (1940), and Bly's interview with Francis Quinn, "Time at Harvard," from the April 2000 edition of the *Paris Review*.

Vancouver group was coming into its own. Furthermore, while Michael Bullock was connected to British Surrealism, there appears to have been little attempt to formalize the Vancouver group's affiliation with the existing Surrealist movements on the continent or elsewhere (though these links would happen in the 1980s and beyond) or to produce analogous group manifestos. Instead, it is far more accurate to describe them as a Surrealist-inspired collective, or perhaps *post*-Surrealists,[17] a distinction that recognizes their interest and freedom in exploring Surrealist ideas and methods without any of the burden of purity that divided so many Surrealist practitioners.[18] Their work with Surrealist methods and forms set the stage for what Bradford Collins calls "a late flowering of Surrealism" in Vancouver (92), though the idea of their belatedness undermines the value of the difference they achieved. A further complication in the case of Vancouver Surrealism is the diffusion of Surrealist influences that arrived all at once, including the multiple generations of continental Surrealisms without all of their decades of intricate battles and personal foibles; French Canadian Surrealism, more properly known as Automatism; and the proliferation of North American Surrealisms that had already taken root by the late 1960s. They were free to pick and choose – or *deform* – elements they found useful, and ignore the debates and politics surrounding the history of each of those choices as much or as little as they wanted. The first manifestation of the literary side of the Vancouver Hermetic Surrealists occurs in *Blewointment* issue 5.1 (January 1967), where David W. Harris (before he became known as David UU) published three poems responding directly to French Canadian Surrealist work: "Composition (after pellan)," "Maquette Pour Une Fontaine (after louis archambault)," and "Une Famile (after archambault)." Harris was living in Toronto at the time and was presumably responding ekphrastically to French Canadian Surrealist[19] work – the poems are dated and located as having been written in the Lang Gallery in August of 1966. I have not been able to locate any specific details of an exhibition, but that year, Archambault had been commissioned by the Government of Ontario to produce a sculpture for the Macdonald Block of the Ontario legislature buildings that visually connects to the images in UU's poems. The piece, *Man and Woman*, is, for instance, abstract and vaguely anthropomorphic and combines sharp geometrical shapes with meandering automatic detailings. The woman is represented by a hollow enclosure ("thewomb / a sanctuary") with a hovering circle within – perhaps a breast ("i reach

---

17 Michael Bullock, for his part, described himself as a "neo-surrealist, in that I base my work upon the free play of the imagination without, however, sacrificing clarify of expression" (Chevalier 122). "New Surrealism" does not, in my estimation, adequately reflect the apolitical, nonrevolutionary orientation of Morton's or Bullock's Surrealism.
18 Borduas, for instance, refused to sign Breton's 1947 declaration because of Surrealism's acceptance of figurative representations of automatic and dream imagery, as by Matta and Dalí.
19 In that same issue of *Blewointment*, by useful coincidence, the links to French Canadian experimentation advanced with publications by Pierre Coupey, having only recently arrived in the city.

up and / touch the softness / of your breasts") or else a womb proper. Regardless of origin, the poems meditate on the Surrealist themes embedded in the work and serve as the first published salvo of the second manifestation of literary Surrealism in Vancouver. Harris's first two poems establish a gender binary as the basis of his sketch of a new poetics: men, being trapped within their machinations, "weave" a complex pattern of interrelation and interdependence between themselves and their technologies; women, being the source and embodiment of human origin, provide "a sanctuary" that provokes longing and nostalgia. The third poem posits a man, woman, and child "all sitting in / their roles / waiting for / the shutter / to / click." The technological consciousness draws attention to the performance, rather than essential characteristics, of gender roles. Art and technology are, in this manifestation, essential to the process of Surrealist liberation and individual becoming in the contemporary moment. Harris/ UU brought his rising interest in Surrealism to Vancouver when he moved to the city the next year, 1968.

Une Famile (after archambault)		Composition (after pellan)	
UNIT		Man	
THE MAN			the machine
	CHAIR	the machine	
THE WOMAN			/ an extension
	WOMB		of man
THE CHILD			Weaving
	SAPLING		with time
	all sitting in		the complexities
	their roles		which trap
	waiting for		the machineman
	the shutter		
	to	i	
	click	the poet	
		weave too	
		a more complex	
		pattern	
			delicately finding my way
			in the crystal maze of my
			invention

Two poems by David UU (Harris), composed at the Lang Gallery, Toronto, 8 August 1966.

That also happened to be the year that Michael Bullock arrived in Vancouver, the author whom scholar Neil Querengesser describes as "a grand master of contemporary surrealism" (180). He was fifty years old and already an established Surrealist when he came to Canada as a Commonwealth Fellow at the University of British Columbia to teach a course on translation. Bullock had attended the 1936 International Surrealist Exhibition in London and had integrated himself into the local Surrealist community there. From the outset of his arrival in Canada, he was an unabashed advocate of the avant-garde movement. That first year, he had his students produce translations of André Breton's *Poisson soluble* (1924), a radically experimental text published in the same year as the founding manifesto of Surrealism. Bullock, overenthusiastically described by George McWhirter as "the last, living, orthodox surrealist" (48), became a permanent fixture in the community when he joined the UBC creative writing department in 1969.

After all the forays and experiments with Surrealism, here finally was the first member of the group to permanently settle in the city. He brought his connections to the original pre-war British Surrealists with him and maintained regular correspondence with the likes of Herbert Read, David Gascoyne (author of the first British Surrealist poem), and Conroy Maddox (Green, "Remembering Michael Bullock" n. pag.) as well as other avant-gardists like Man Ray, Oscar Dominique, and Roland Penrose (Varney, "Remembering Michael Bullock" n. pag.). It was, in fact, Read and T.S. Eliot who encouraged Bullock to stop painting and focus on his writing (Cartwright, "Michael Bullock The First Fifty Years and Family" n. pag.). UU and Bullock, though wildly different in temperament, both arrived in the city in the same year and joined forces with the Vancouver intermedia artists to unleash a concerted exploration of Surrealist techniques and themes. The difference between them helps to explain the unusual and very distinctive reconciliation in Vancouver between esoteric magic practice (which UU favoured) and less radical magic realism (which Bullock championed).

At the outset of this Surrealist turn, collage was the dominant form of experimental visual and literary work. The spirit of collage allowed the Vancouverites to splice themselves together in a kind of aesthetic alchemy of their various interests in the history of esoteric practices, twentieth-century avant-garde art, and modern technology. When the Quebec artist Gilles Foisy came to Vancouver (also in 1968), however, the range and intensity of these experiments broadened and increased. He and UU together formed the Divine Order of the Lodge (DOL), an arts collective that was devoted to the occultation of Surrealism. Their esoteric name and practice were a self-conscious attempt to resurrect Joséphin Péladan's Salon de la Rose+Croix in Vancouver. With the establishment of the DOL, Vancouver Surrealism became increasingly devoted: they began to call their Surrealist collages "Co-Lodges" and developed an occultic variant of performance art they called "Ritual Theatre." It was fun, weird, and pointedly unsettling, much in the manner of Parisian Surrealists' use of magic, but did push beyond their continental forebears. Gregg Simpson, for instance, penned a series of short stories focused on the foibles of historical alchemists and other magical figures, but without any of the usual Surrealist techniques of irrationalism, magic realism, or otherwise. Likewise, there is something strikingly earnest about his integration of Erik Satie's composition *Sonneries de la Rose+Croix*

Figure 5.13 Ritual theatre performed by the Divine Order of the Lodge. Photographer unknown. Source: Private collection of Gregg Simpson. Used with permission.

into his magical theatre project *Theatrical Evening* as an attempt to bridge the avant-garde and occult worlds once again (*Luminous Desires* 60–61).

The movement arrived in the public eye with the June 1970 publication of *Splendor Solis* (Latin for "the splendour of the sun"), an art supplement included in the *Georgia Straight* weekly newspaper. The section had been approved by Barry Cramer, one of the founding editors of the *Georgia Straight*, eventual director of the Intermedia Society, and original owner and programmer for the Cellar cooperative jazz club. Alongside hosting the Al Neil-Kenneth Patchen collaborations, Cramer had orchestrated avant-garde theatre at the Cellar, including productions of work by Samuel Beckett. The *Splendor Solis* supplement reached Toronto, where bpNichol duly noted it in his *grOnk* literary newsletter:

> gregg simpson sent along the georgia straight art supplement for june from vancouver which was devoted to the magic movement out there and includes manifestos state-ments & positions by al neil, david uu, gregg simpson & allan alchemy as well as pho-tos, collages and paintings by gary-lee nova, jack wise, gregg simpson & others. gerry gilberts smiling face peeked thru. (Late October grOnk Mailout n. pag.)

The title of the supplement acknowledged both the esoteric and psychoanalytical interests of the group (above emancipatory politics), as it echoed the 1532 illumi-nated manuscript *Splendour Solis* by the acclaimed German alchemist Salomon Tris-mosin, which had been cited by Carl Jung in *Psychology and Alchemy* (1953). The Vancouver publication was edited by Gregg Simpson and combined Surrealist draw-ings, photographs, and collages with alchemical, mystical, and revolutionary writ-ings. Al Neil contributed a short essay assessing the state of revolutionary discourse and activism in the city at the time, and the value of tantric energy-shifting to the movement: "I believe the only art that is revolutionary has always sprung from these states" ("Guess Work" 12). He lambastes social realism and Aristotelian thinking and looks to primitive music forms as the source for a new art:

> Only the earliest man, unhampered by subject object predicate one-way Aristo-telian fucked-up head space could have approach with his cry at the moon, the thinking processes (analogous, associative, total systems, world games) it is imper-ative to learn and fast in order to get out any art strong enough to counter the mind-boggling insanity we are being led to by the mindless freaks in power on this planet. [...] I'm atomically plugged full of holes, nobody's driving the spaceship, a bunch of madmen are trying to make an asteroid out of it, but still, still there is this, the most venturesome minds on the planet are fast converging to Point Omega where we will at last experience the workings of the Universe in our mind-body. An art moving from near to this point must strike all men with its unassail-able power, worked and king alike.

Neil's political criticism, while hardly orthodox Surrealism, is tidily integrated into a mystical-aesthetic conception of the evolution of human consciousness. Rather than biomedical or political, his concept of revolution is magical, mystical, and esoteric. Other contributors to *Splendor Solis* included UU, Gary Lee-Nova, Gilles Foisy, Ed Varney, Michael de Courcy, Jack Wise, Cathie Falk, and Glenn Lewis.

In September 1970, UU launched a series of special issues of Toronto-based *grOnk* magazine (issues 7.1–7.6) focused on magic, alchemy, and the general interests of the Isle of Avalon Society, the ritual theatre group made up of Vancouver Surrealists,

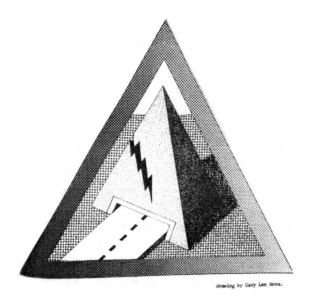

STRAIGHT ART SUPPLEMENT   JUNE 3–10, 1970

SPLENDOR SOLIS

drawing by Gary Lee Nova.

Figure 5.14 Cover of *Splendor Solis* supplement in the *Georgia Straight* for June 1970, documenting the West Coast Hermetic movement. Source: Private collection of Gregg Simpson. Used with permission.

designed by the Divine Order of the Lodge. The issues are unabashedly laden with esoteric symbols. The series begins with an unsigned manifesto of magicians that uses the occult, and the Divine Order's privileging of the role of hidden networks of knowledge over public revolution and dream symbolism, as a key point of the group's difference from the Parisian Surrealists. The manifesto also articulates the unique aesthetic freedom of deformance art:

> we take what we wish from the symbolists we take what we wish from the impression-
> ists we take what we wish from the surrealists we take what we wish

our art is drawn from spirits the process of incantation and dealings with the powers our magic is the true magic strong magic high alchemy

though we are the true brothers of the surrealists we do not deal with dreams we
deal with the forces that cause dreams the symbolists faild [*sic*] by creating a system of
symbolic references we talk with symbols in their animate and real forms are symbols
ourselves we live in pictures of the imagination we are not myth makers we are myths
we are like onto the gods knowing neither good nor evil

all magic is black all magic is golden

like the surrealists we are a way of life unlike the surrealists we strive to change
nothing but ourselves our art is secret and not meant for most eyes the works that are
our main concern will never be seen by the uninitiated we are a secret order and like
the alchemists dedicated to our own transmutation through out art

we like the spirit BETHOR are subject only to the will of GOD the will of the cosmos
and serve no other entities mortal or immortal we each have our cosmic territory to
observe some of us deal with OPHIEL some with PHUL at times we have been served
by all the spirits including PHALEG when the course of history is being changed

we are guardians of that which is sacred in the cosmos we uphold reverence we take
on the outward form of profanity to keep our secret our lives are pure and holy though
we are hidden we are among men though our knowledge is too dangerous to proclaim
we reveal such wisdom that will warn men against evil forces and provide them with
spiritual aid

we are the high magicians and being so our power is either our doom or our salvation

(UU, "The Magicians Manifesto" n. pag.)

The unsigned manifesto is remarkably closer in discourse and intention to the dec-
larations made by the likes of Aleister Crowley and the Vancouver followers of his
Ordo Templi Orientis than to the psychoanalytical and Marxist discourse of the
Parisian Surrealists. Gregg Simpson discusses studying Crowley, Manley P. Hall,
A.E. Waite, and Lewis Spence in advance of his Surrealist work ("Hermetic Series
1970–1975"), but it appears that the Vancouver Surrealist exploration of magic came
independent of the O.T.O. The practice of magic, however, helps to distinguish the
Vancouver manifestation from the Montreal-based Automatists, who abandoned
the conscious use of symbolism and rationalism and psychoanalytic theory. They
were focused on breaking the overly rational hold of the Catholic Church in Quebec
and saw representational art as sustaining Western appeals to logic. In contrast, the
cover of *grOnk* issue 7.6 (see Figure 5.15), designed by Gregg Simpson, presents
an eclectic but consciously arranged mix of linographic, photographic, and hand-
drawn occult images and symbols. The issues combine concrete and visual poetry
with extended meditations on myths, magic, and other esoteric concerns. There
is no engagement with the psychological or automatic interests of continental or
British Surrealism.

Figure 5.15 Cover image of *grOnk* 7.6 (August 1971), featuring a "Co-Lodge" by Gregg Simpson. The issue is the final issue in a series of six produced by the Divine Order of the Lodge. Source: Private collection of the author. Used with permission.

The embrace of magic raises an intriguing alternative to the irreconcilable division that Peter Bürger maps out in his essay on the avant-garde and the neo-avant-garde. He begins by isolating two principles at the core of avant-gardism: "the attack on the institution of art and the revolutionizing of life as a whole" ("Avant-Garde" 696). Both of these principles demand a renunciation of the autonomy of the artist, and a subjugation of the work of art to its utility in serving the creation of a "finally liveable world" (698). The problem with the utopian projections of the avant-garde, however, stems from its appearance within the context of a bourgeois society from whose ideological hold it can never break. The promised historical rupture, consequently, never happens. Accordingly, the failure of this avant-garde can be measured by the fact that anti-art objects are predictably subsumed and consumed by the market – and future gardists are forced to admit the "illusion that they were part of a revolutionary moment" (700). Rather than mimetically (or metonymically) reflecting the sovereign autonomy of the free individual, avant-garde art retains the ideological stamp of its contextual capitalism.

Gavin Grindon argues, however, that the provisional rejection of capitalist interpolation in the avant-garde art object successfully "forged a new political language of sovereignty" (84). The discourse of magic offers another language of provisional sovereignty, especially as occultist practice begins with the insistence that our knowledge and understanding of reality are limited and insufficient. The discourse of magic does not depend on the ideological autonomy of the work of art or the artist, nor does it gain agency through its relationship with a contextual bourgeois society and its various authorizing institutions. Gnosis is a portal out of the bourgeois quotidian, a counter-environment through which the boundaries of capitalism might be imaged and accordingly delimited. Conversely, in this discourse, the unknown itself becomes a fetishized commodity that registers the alienation from socio-political power, while insisting on alternative sources of power that must remain protected within the hermetic circles, rituals, and groups with ancient lineages. Unlike the public revolutionary model that Bürger critiques, occult devotees and initiates are only gradually exposed and permitted access to the alternative set of reality's coordinates. The avant-garde, from this perspective, becomes a point of access to an ancient tradition that extrapolates the subject out of their ideological fold and into an alternative space of consciousness.

For some of the Vancouver Surrealists, magical discourse and ritual theatre were no doubt just far-out pranks and playful weirdness in tune with the contextual psychedelic Age of Aquarius. Conversely, David UU, Jack Wise, and Gilles Foisy were all rather emphatic about the metaphysical and even physical transformations rendered by alchemical consciousness. As Foisy writes:

> there exists a way to manipulate matter so as to produce what modern scientists would call a "force-field." This "force-field" acts on the observer and puts him in a privileged situation towards the universe. From this privileged position, the alchemist has access to "realities" that time and space, matter and energy veil from us ordinarily. This is what we call the "great work." (n. pag.)

Foisy is not speaking glibly, but with an ambition of developing the practice of alchemy into an aesthetic: the role of art, he argues, is to create a "theatrical feeling" that relaxes the conscious mind (arguably the site of ideological interpolation) and opens up a point of access to the collective unconscious. Every compromise in the name of "freedom, ethics, trends, even culture itself" diminishes the radical potential of art to open up artist and audience to a new vision of cosmically aligned creation: "The alchemical system of symbols is complete in itself." This perspective breaks out of linear models by skipping over the historical avant-garde and projecting a self-unified para-tradition both forwards and backwards in time. The Vancouver Surrealists' establishment of a "Lodge" and a "Society" rather than an institute or foundation speaks to the essential religiosity and radicalism of their ambitions with magic. Bürger's model of avant-gardism registers only their disappointment when the evolution of esoteric consciousness did not expand, and not their abiding faith in a para-tradition they sought to protect, sustain, and revitalize.

What does Surrealism have to do with such a holistic, atemporal para-tradition? The historical avant-garde offered a means by which the contemporary mind could be opened up to such alternative possibilities. As Salvador Dalí once said, "I believe the moment is near where a thought process of an active, paranoid, character can [...] raise confusion to the level of a system and contribute to the total discrediting of the real world" (qtd. in Bürger, "Avant-Garde" 702). More to the point, and making the connection between the avant-garde and anti-colonialism, in Kurt Seligmann's interview with a Tsimshian man, published in *Minotaure* in 1939, the man describes the Canadian government's response to West Coast totem poles, and how they think "of them now like heraldic poles, stripped of all magic. For our young people they are outmoded objects and have lost their power. The magic of bicycles, cinemas, railways, seems infinitely more attractive to them, and they speak with little respect of the older people who know and jealously guard the ancient secrets" (222). For Bürger, the central concern is the shifting modes of fashion and taste that pass over the avant-garde and sweep away its relevancy. The loss of interest and continuity from one generation to the next includes losing power through, in this case, the intervention of the colonial state. For the religious-minded, however, the garde are the ones who protect alternative ritual knowledge and resist the present every bit as much as any futurist. The totems and the real magic they evince are not works of the past, but a radical, almost impossible intervention against the contemporary milieu. As Leonard Cohen writes in *Beautiful Losers*: "Magic never died. God never sickened. Many poor men lied. Many sick men lied. Magic never weakened" (414).

In his artist's statement in the 1973 *Canadian West Coast Hermetics* exhibition catalogue, David UU invites his readers into the great work on the other side of the discredited real world: "i hold yu as vision wonders of the veil" (*Canadian* n. pag.). Here, and in UU's sound and visual poetry as well, language becomes marked by the transmutation, becomes a deformative symbol where the second-person declarative reaches through the shards of a shattered culture, pulling his readers into the verity of the magical extrapolation: "beyond what is cognizant fire rise the escaping essence form is gatherd as realized sphere passd through solid space there beyond reflection eyes darkness obscured in matrix of season is final is infinite [...] of this vision there is one tradition."

Figure 5.16 Mr. Jupiter's (Gregg Simpson) outdoor sculptural installation piece called *Lightning Bolt* (1972). Source: Private collection of Gregg Simpson. Used with permission.

When UU chants, or breaks language in his visual work, he is working toward a rupture in the category of the real that concludes only at the arrival of the devotional act. Chanting, thus, becomes aligned with prayer or, as in the text that follows, the vocalizations of the gods themselves:

yyyyy
nnnnn
ööööö www [...]

Figure 5.17 Gregg Simpson's collage *Jou Jouka* (1973). The Master Musicians of Joujouka collective was prominent in the 1960s for the master improvisational Sufi musicians that Brion Gysin popularized among the counterculture. Source: Private collection of Gregg Simpson. Used with permission.

Dn-nnnnnnnnnnnnnnnnnnnnnnnnn
Dun-nnnnnnnnnnnnnnnnnnnnnnnnn
Oooooo- Dnnnnnnnnnnnnnnnnnnnn
Dooooooooo – nnnnnnnnnnnnnnnnn
thE- EEEEEEEE-OOOOOOOOOOOOOO
thE- EEEEEEEE-DNNNNNNNNNNNN
eeeeeeeeeeeeeeeeeeeeeee-DON-NNN
OOOOOOOO – DONNNNNNNNNNNN
INNNNNNNNNNNN EEEEEEEEEEE
DON – NNNNNNNNNNNNNNNNNNNN ("The ODinity" n. pag.)

This text UU describes as "the sound of bells volcanic ice behind his voice over the sea shine as guard the holy palace" (n. pag.); the cycles of disintegrating language invoke the Germanic god Odin and then attempt to sound through him.

The fourth *Lodgistiks* issue[20] contains a collection of writing by UU that maps out the Surrealist group's transition from a logical Western consciousness into an

---

20 *Lodgistiks* 4 (1976), Editor: David UU, Lodge South Editor: Gregg Simpson, Lodge Correspondent: Patricia Garrett, Production Assistant: Dame Isadora Lodge.

alternative magic mode. Accordingly, the first of three sections is "Sleep Descending," which contains examples of concrete poetry and automatic, improvised irrationalisms – disruptions to the linguistic foundations of consensual reality. The second section, "Before the Golden Dawn," continues the disorienting effects by beginning with chapter 7, page 1, skipping to page 5, and then following with page 2, a second page 5, and page 9, followed by chapter 0, page 176, and finally page 177. These "pages" are stand-alone poems, but their scrambling and deliberate incompleteness suggests disorder and omissions. Gnosis is here evoked by the absence of a key to the chaos; only the initiated may decipher the glimpses of disordered texts. The third section is "Advent of Heliocentrum," wherein UU engages with the mystical experiences of transformation and visitation. The texts are filled with occult symbols, such as the sea goddess with the "rosy cross on her breast" (n. pag.). As in the text above, UU crescendoes with a glossolic poem but here makes the connection to prayer explicit: "olo shone idi-en / tilshn iss neplt ashen / grevver nonld kaff / gloriab delsibalf / in the name of the lord of lords / amen" (17). Readers might notice in passages such as this a comparable use of both glossolalia and standard diction as discussed in the work of Claude Gauvreau earlier in this chapter. The remarkable accomplishment of UU's Surrealist poetry, whether grounded in visual or sonic effects, is the marriage of the discourse of occult practice with the automatic methods of Surrealism (and rhythmic improvisation of jazz and Beat culture). Neither confessional, nor epiphanic, nor limited to a singular perspective, the speaker of his writing is incantatory and speaking from within the awakened magical consciousness:

> the holy black heart sings as
> music of the spheres rise angelic aether flow in
> the holy grail wash bless vision of her form to
> receive as earth womb of the star seed mystical
> realm through passage of the moon this veil as holds
> yur form beyond the dream of flesh
>
> is goddess key through the guardian mist at the
> cries of midnight carried in its claws the sacred
> stone of the fiery cradle manifestation of the high
> priest who stands above the oily smoke calls of
> the element form advances to the circles edge
>
> of this vision there is one tradition glows as fluid
> vapour come up the holy tone diamonds as the
> Nordic sea rise in hearts full voice of aethers
> knowledge shine through all death wonder [...]
>
> ("The ODinity" 41–43)

The use of present tense in this passage is not narrative-based plot but sign of a constant timelessness. These things did not happen; they are always happening. Though the strange juxtaposition of images and disjunctive grammar might suggest the chance-based effects of an Automatist work (or Gysin cut-up), the careful and limited selection of images from the occult tradition suggests a more rhythmically oriented, non-linear composition method. Call it ecstatic, or even romantic, but the focus of such writing is unquestionably gnostic.

Through the alchemy of the magic Surrealists, the diverse strands of sound, concrete, collage, and intermedia experimentation in Vancouver align. Thus, Ed Varney's seven-fold definition of art, offered as his artist's statement for the 1973 *Canadian West Coast Hermetics* exhibition catalogue, is: "1. Collage as the manipulation of ideas. 2. Collage as thinking. 3. Images as thoughts. 4. Images as archetypes, as people. 5. I am the subject of my work, my world. 6. Man in the world landscape. 7. Woman" ("Untitled" n. pag.). Along with all of the biographical intersections between the Surrealists in Vancouver and all other avant-garde communities and initiatives after *Tish*, the movement can also be linked to the story of collage in the city, as discussed in chapter 4, and the challenge against gender norms, as discussed in chapter 6.

The 1973 Hermeticist touring exhibition was the result of a proposal by Gregg Simpson to Alvin Balkind at the University of British Columbia Fine Arts Gallery in 1971 to collect and present an array of the most accomplished Vancouver Surrealist work. It was a functional representation of the visual art accomplishments of the Surrealist activity in the city. Titled *Canadian West Coast Hermetics: The Metaphysical Landscape*, the exhibition ran from 9 to 27 January 1973 and featured contributions by Lee-Nova, Wise, Simpson, Foisy, UU, and Varney. Reactions to the exhibition were mixed. Carol Cram reviewed the exhibition as "a mosaic of dream-like tableaux and hard-edge symbolism" (36). Bradford Collins, on the other hand, reviewed the exhibition and evaluated it based on how well they fulfilled the mandate of the original Surrealism: "Other words and statements, however, seemed incompatible with the aims of that movement and the spectator was left with the suspicion that the surrealistic quality of the show was often merely apparent. [...] Two distinct purposes are evident: the one surrealistic, the other relating more to Eastern mysticism" (92, 93). He dismissed their exploration of magic and alchemy as "fadism and elitism" even though the "concern for the occult, however, is historically grounded in the development of Surrealism" (93). The difference he mapped out is between Freudianism (with the focus on the repressed desires of the individual, and the resulting trauma and sublimations of those unfulfilled desires) and Jungianism (with its focus on a collective unconscious and the shared imagination of the human community), the individual in pursuit of liberty versus the collective in pursuit of harmony: "this striving for communal unity is antithetical to the surrealist celebration of difference, diversity, individual inclination" (93). He missed

Figure 5.18 The installation of the exhibition *Canadian West Coast Hermetics: The Metaphysical Landscape* at the Centre Culturel Canadien in Paris. The show ran from March to April in 1973. Photographer unknown. Source: Private collection of Gregg Simpson. Used with permission.

the broader, more fundamental distinction between psychoanalytic and esoteric Surrealism, and offered the Canadian artists no room to develop their own version of the mode. The exhibition also appeared in London and Paris, before returning to Canada. Surrealist scholars, particularly French scholars like José Pierre and Yves Laroque, were interested in the new manifestation of what was presumed by then to be an exhausted movement. As Laroque writes: "Elle est peut-etre arrive trop tard, mais chez les Anglais le resultat ne s'était pas fait attendre" (465).[21]

Magick Surrealist Events and Exhibitions

The Great Mandrake Mission: An Evening of Ritual Theatre and Autocannibalism
East End Gallery, 17 January 1971
Performed by Isle of Avalon Society, directed by David UU

---

21 "It may have arrived too late, but the results in English were still surprising" (my translation).

Divine Order of the Lodge Exhibition #1
Avelles Gallery (1304 SW Marine Drive), 5–31 December 1971
Featuring: Gilles Foisy, Lord Jupiter, Gregg Simpson, Spade LaChance, Alan
Alchemy, Doctor Dog O.D., Mrs. Dog O.D., Anegton, Commander Venus,
Ingrid UU, and David UU

Microprosophus: International Exhibition of Visual Poetry
(Curated by David UU and Pierre Coupey)
Avelles Gallery (1304 SW Marine Drive), 8–28 September 1971
Featuring: Gregg Simpson, Sarenco, Jochen Gerz, Air Press, Josef Hrdy, Art Rat,
David UU, Pierre Coupey, Jaroslav Malina, and bill bissett
Microprosophus also travelled to Evergreen College, Tacoma, Washington.

"Tri-Solar-Pool" Ritual Theatre and Film Process
The Colonial Magic Theatre, 6 February 1971
By Gregg Simpson, Gilles Foisy, Paul Baird, Gary Lee-Nova, David UU
Performed by Tetractys (under the direction of Foisy and Isle of Avalon Society)
and featuring the voice of Doctor Dog

Canadian West Coast Hermetics: The Metaphysical Landscape
Fine Arts Gallery, University of British Columbia, 9–27 January 1973
Canadian Cultural Centre in Paris, France, 15 March–14 April 1973

Other Realities: The Legacy of Surrealism in Canadian Art
Agnes Etherington Art Centre in Kingston, 1978. Also travelled
to Paris and London.

West Coast Surreal: A Canadian Perspective
Museu Granell in Santiago de Compostela, Spain, 2005

6 Post-Revolutionary Surrealism

The year 1977 was the last important year for Surrealist advancements in Vancouver, highlighted by a series of key publications and events that demonstrate the increased institutionalization of the movement in the city and its turn away from devotionalist magic practices. David UU relocated to Wolfe Island, just outside of Kingston, Ontario. In 1977, he began publishing books with direct relevance to Vancouver Surrealism, including with occultic content, but his connections to the city's Surrealist group began to wane. That same year, the Move Gallery was established and became the headquarters of the newly labelled "West Coast Surrealist Group." The difference in personnel is striking: only Simpson and Varney carried over from the original group. New members included Michael Bullock, Ted Kingan, Davide Pan, Robert

Davidson, and Andrej Somov. Lori-ann Latremouille soon joined "as a very young woman" (Varney, "Lori-ann" 3), and Czechoslovakian Surrealists Martin Guderna and his father, Ladislav Guderna, joined shortly after they arrived in the city in 1980. Varney explains that the group "had no doctrine but it did place an emphasis on content designed to generate, evoke, and manipulate viewer response, forcing viewers to acknowledge the importance of the irrational, the symbolic, and the archetypal as the basis for culture's biases, motivations and world views" (3–4). As Cram notes, the orientation of West Coast Surrealism shifted away from their previous occultic concerns "to an increasingly organic form of spontaneous surrealism" (37). While Martin and Ladislav Guderna continued to include esoteric symbolism in their works, painters like Kingan and Simpson pushed deeper into automatic methods and away from occultism. Group exhibitions at the Move Gallery led to the creation of the *Vancouver Surrealist Newsletter*, which was renamed *Melmoth* after two issues. *Melmoth* published issues from 1981 through to 1984.[22] UU, for his part, exhibited in one Surrealist exhibition at the Move Gallery in 1980, but was never a part of *Melmoth*. The shift into the new phase, which is properly beyond the purview of this review, included a broadening of the focus of the group and a de-escalation of radical or revolutionary content. Accordingly, the first issue of the *Vancouver Surrealist Newsletter* begins with a long editorial explaining the new nonrevolutionary outlook of this reformed Surrealist group:

> After the war, a growing disillusionment with politics became widespread and surrealists were not immune to it. The result was a decrease in the emphasis on the possible contribution of Surrealism to social revolution and increased stress on its role in the self-liberation and a transformation of the psychological climate. [...] A concern with social revolution – in a narrowly political sense – gives birth to dogma; dogma brings with it orthodoxy and heresy, which in turn produce schisms and fruitless ideological conflicts. All of this becomes pointless once we agree that Surrealism is the product of a temperament and the expression of a state of mind, that is linked with an *intense individualism* and has to be both lived and given concrete form in works of art, rather than theorized over in hair-splitting exegeses. [...] Revolution, even in the name of freedom, unfailingly destroys freedom, and to the surrealist freedom is the highest good.
>
> (Bullock, "Surrealism's Janus" 1–3; emphasis in original)

Accordingly, Jack Stewart's book *The Incandescent Word: The Poetic Vision of Michael Bullock* (1990) accentuates the nonrevolutionary politics of Bullock's writing in

---

22 The West Coast Surrealist Group was renamed the Melmoth Group in 1981 as a nod to the recently defunct *Melmoth* magazine, published in London from 1979 to 1980. That British Surrealist magazine was itself a tribute to Charles Maturin's 1820 gothic novel *Melmoth the Wanderer*, an upriotous text widely admired and praised by the Surrealists (Rosemont xxxvii).

favour of a more neo-Romantic aestheticism. This program for the new orientation of the movement coincided well with the general tendency of British Surrealism and marked its ultimate triumph over the esoteric contingent in the contest of Surrealist aesthetics in Vancouver. The depoliticization of Surrealism brought Vancouver's work back into a shared ideological outlook with the British variant. In the words of E.L.T. Mesens (a Belgian Surrealist who relocated to London and eventually became director of the London Gallery): "I shall not be hypocritical enough to simulate the slightest hope in Proletarian Revolution. It is a little too late for the world. The proletariat and its leaders diacritically resemble their oppressors and their leaders" (qtd. in Remy 284).

Bullock's nonrevolutionary Surrealism is evidenced in his 1977 experimental novella *Randolph Cranstone and the Glass Thimble*. The text exaggerates magic realism to the point of discordance, but yet sustains a coherent first-person narrative style that belies the bizarre images and events depicted. Sea monsters rise out of the water and devour the narrator's housemaids, organic matter on walking paths spontaneously animates and chases the narrator, and underground worlds open up with private rulers, monsters, and gods. The narrator observes all of these occurrences with a kind of detached nonchalance, as if immunized from or habituated to the constant disruption all around him. The book thus follows the logic of dreams, though without automatic dislocutionary effects. Bullock, earlier in 1973, had been asked about his public embrace of the moniker of Surrealism to describe his writing. Hardly in the spirit of UU's 1975 poetic declaration that "surrealism existed before me and i firmly believe that it will survive me [...] and i firmly believe" ("Homage to Andre Breton" 17), Bullock genuflected before his own personal Surrealism: "What I understand by surrealism is partly a kind of protest against realism. I'm not sure whether I'm a surrealist in the strict sense as defined at one point by André Breton who made the essence of surrealism the use of automatic writing. I don't think my writing is really automatic [...] by surrealism I almost mean anti-realism" ("An Interview" 5, 6).

Kiyooka's *The Fontainebleau Dream Machine* was also published in 1977 and offers a more evocative fulfilment of the intersection between Surrealism and Vancouver collage, as well as the shift from revolutionary esotericism into personal liberationist practice. The book presents eighteen collages with a recurring balloon theme in which the progression of Western art and science collapses into a crushed heap of dream, desire, and failure. Kiyooka provides an endnote that explains that the book "incurs within the body of its own forebodings, the notion that Language-as-Rhetorick is, itself a terrifying dream, the [*Fontainebleau Dream Machine*] is, among other things, my ofttimes bemused Homage to the whole domain of European Art" (n. pag.). The recurring balloon imagery becomes akin to the speech balloons of dreams, of the unconscious, and encodes a deep ambivalence in Kiyooka's "bemused" perspective on European art. Eva-Marie Kröller reads the collages less ambivalently as violent disruptions of

Figure 5.19 Front cover of *Melmoth* 2.1 (Autumn 1981). Source: Private collection of the author.

European art, as Kiyooka's collages highlight the "forced [...] fantastic synchronicity and contiguity" (48) in the combination of verbal and visual collages, a kind of violence that at once both rejects and marvels at the "debris of western art." The poems connect their rejection of inherited cultural forms with linguistic disorder:

aphasia	a cross	the frozen stubble
aphasia	of his	Famine
aphasia	the drifting	snow-mantl'd pasture brok n
aphasia	down the huge hole	
aphasia Black.root	*pie* in the sky	
aphasia		

(n. pag.)

»Fontainebleau«
DreamMachine

Figure 5.20 Front cover of Roy Kiyooka's *The Fontainebleau Dream Machine* (1977). Source: Private collection of the author. Used with permission.

In the end, the text proceeds to a familiar Vancouver reconciliation of worldly antagonisms and short-sightedness in the trope of silence: "step quietly but firmly thru / the door way of your incredulity where all the dreams / 'death remainders' lie in the folded Silt under a Mute's tongue" (n. pag.). Silence (more than esoteric ritual or Surrealist practice) opens up a space into which the unconscious can crash, and destroy and begin to repair its symbolic composition (let alone lived oppressions). As Kiyooka wrote in *Transcanada Letters* in 1975, "its the s-i-l-e-n-c-e at the core of our hapless desires that gives us the itch to shape things. And it's the whole biz of us artists to take with utmost seriousness both this silence and our assorted itches" (n. pag.). Such a project is, then, steeped in the forms and discourse of Surrealism, but at the same time is even further outside of its fold than Bullock's self-conscious discordance.

Other texts that appeared in the short aftermath of the transition away from radical Surrealism include Crescent Beach, BC, poet Bob Coleman's book *Improvisations*, which was published by David UU in Kingston. *Improvisations* is a suite of poems that, as the author's biography notes, "successfully carried on (out) the Beat tradition with the added refinement of the French Surrealists" (n. pag.). This, the author's first book, was written through an automatic or "intuitive" approach, creating texts that are rife with the "abyss of nocturnal journeys" and symbolic links between language and especially jazz music. Of course, by 1977 Surrealism and Beat poetry were both aesthetic anachronisms, and accordingly the book ends with an elegy for both movements. "The Beatnik's Farewell" depicts his out-of-timeness as a force that necessarily dislodges him from the world: "Artistic cancer is very serious, strikes the soul, sends you out man, out of the way man."

In 1979, Intermedia Press published *Contemporary Surrealist Prose* (edited by Ed Varney), with selections from Austrian author H.C. Artmann and American author Rikki Ducornet, and eighteen prose poems by Michael Bullock. Each section of the book is accompanied by the work of a different illustrator: Ernst Fuchs, Roland Topor, and John Digby, respectively. Even though it echoes the rejection of Surrealist radicalism, the book is the first clear publication to self-consciously situate Vancouver Surrealist writing in the context of international Surrealist production. After *Melmoth* ceased publication, Ladislav Guderna launched a new Surrealist magazine called *Scarabeus*, which included both writing and images from members of the group as well as from other Surrealists around the world. Things carried on in this way until the death of Ladislav Guderna in 1999, at which point the Melmoth Group drifted apart. Bullock continued working with Surrealist methods and eventually arrived at a technique he called Abstract Surrealism – the use of subliminal representation within ostensibly nonrepresentational works. It is, in many ways, the evolution of the biomedical origins of Surrealism, perfectly detached from the world-saving, anti-imperialist energies that birthed the movement.

7 The Colour of My Dreams

I turn to the Vancouver Art Gallery's staging of an enormous retrospective of Surrealist art called *The Colour of My Dreams: The Surrealist Revolution in Art* as a coda on the rise and demise of Vancouver Surrealism. Curated by Dawn Ades, the event gathered 350 works "by all the leading surrealist artists" (Bartels 12). Bartels's foreword to the catalogue incorrectly states that the exhibition "breaks new ground by exploring, for the first time in an exhibition, the Surrealists' intense interest in indigenous art of the Pacific Northwest." Of course, such pairings have been happening since the very advent of Surrealism as an art movement. Ades, herself, acknowledges Yves Tanguay's 1927 exhibition at the Galerie surréaliste, which included "sculptures and artefacts from British Columbia" (31). What was strikingly different, however, about the curation of Indigenous art in *The Colour of My Dreams* was the historicization of the Indigenous artefacts that circulated in European Surrealist circles. The works, in fact, were not timeless relics of a fading people, but handcrafted marvels made by contemporary Indigenous artists, who in many cases were most likely alive when the works were confiscated by government officials and sold into global art markets.

That their art reappeared out of context back in Europe as anonymous pieces of a timeless culture is evidence of the dehumanizing apparatus of settler colonialism and its inherent Eurocentrism. The Vancouver Art Gallery's show made a significant advancement by recognizing the agency and subjectivity of the Indigenous artists. What a shame, though, that the gallery chose not to also highlight Indigenous artists who have been influenced by Surrealism, including contemporary artists like Brian Jungen, Donald Varnell, Lawrence Paul Yuxweluptun, and Da-ka-xeen Mehner or a mid-century artist like Daphne Odjig, all of whom discuss Surrealism as an active and positive influence on their work. Their inclusion would have cemented the gallery's recognition of Indigenous subjective agency.

Furthermore, it is regrettable, and almost unconscionable, that Canadian Surrealist art was entirely absent from the show. This exclusion included not just contemporary Native practitioners and the Vancouver Surrealists from the 1960s, but also the Montreal Automatists, and the various widely acclaimed Canadians who were affiliated with Parisian Surrealism and exhibited as members or fellow-travellers there, such as Brion Gysin, Alfred Pellan, Jean Benoît, Mimi Parent, Jean-Paul Riopelle, David Silverberg, and others. Why were they cast out? Dawn Ades goes even further in the erasure in her introduction, where she discusses early "international exhibitions in Japan, England, Denmark and elsewhere" (15) without acknowledging that Canada, barely behind England, was one of those anonymous elsewheres. Finding nothing is an ongoing colonial erasure.

Surrealist art has appeared consistently in Canada since 1927. Surrealist literature has appeared consistently since the 1930s, especially in Toronto and Montreal. It is almost impossible to reason the deliberate, unfathomable exclusion of Canadian work, legitimate Surrealist production by any estimation, from such a show – except it isn't at all unfathomable and is all too predictable. In fact, my very first academic publication was a protest paper co-written with my mentor Ray Ellenwood called "Canada's Forgotten Surrealists: Joys and Sorrows of the AGO's Surrealist Summer." The essay was published in *Artfocus* in the winter of 2002 and addressed the glaring lack of Canadian content at the "Biggest Surreal Experience Ever," as the exhibition fashioned itself. We wrote, "This is not a flag-waving complaint about low Canadian content; it is a protest against almost total historical erasure" (7). We drew attention to a protest performance by William Davidson and Sherri Lyn Higgins, two contemporary Canadian artists in the Surrealist stream, that took place extemporaneously outside of the AGO. The artists performed a tableau inspired by Magritte in which they covered their heads with a lush white cloth. They were the anonymous, colonial backdrop against which the [sarcastic font] really important, relevant work from the imperial centre was staged [/sarcastic font]. They might well have reprised their protest in Vancouver in 2010. Though Canadians had broken free from the colonial mindset, and had discovered through Surrealism a means by which to advance and transcend the limitations of disruptive avant-gardism, the story that Canadian art galleries want to tell of the movement is insistently focused on the accomplishments of foreign climes and the successes they had there.

In the January 1975 issue of *Lodgistiks*, the last year proper of this survey, UU published his "Homage to Andre Breton," which is worth citing in full to demonstrate the emphatic sense of connection that existed between these Canadian artists and their continental forebears and the sense that the movement was shaped by but not limited to the charismatic individuals who made it:

> surrealism existed before me and i firmly believe that it will survive me
> surrealism existed before me and i firmly believe that it will survive me
> surrealism existed before me and i firmly believe that it will survive me
> surrealism existed before me and i firmly believe that it will survive me
> surrealism existed before me and i firmly believe that it will survive me
> surrealism existed before me and i firmly believe that it will survive me
> surrealism existed before me and i firmly believe that it will survive me
> surrealism existed before me and i firmly believe that it will survive me
> surrealism existed before me and i firmly believe that it will survive me
> surrealism existed before me and i firmly believe that it will survive me
> surrealism existed before me and i firmly believe that it will survive me
> surrealism existed before me and i firmly believe that it will survive me
> survival
>   existed before me and i firmly believe that it will survive me
> surrealize   survival
> surrealism existed before
>   and i firmly believe

                                                                (17; used with permission)

SIX

Performing Proprioception: The Birthing Story as Public Discourse

"What do you think a contraction feels like? asked Ruth, our birth instructor, last night. I dont know, I thought, I've read four books now, and I dont know. No one said anything. She waited. Well, what do you imagine? The two women who have had a child dont speak."

Gladys Maria Hindmarch, A Birth Account (66)

"learning to speak *in public* to write love poems for all the world to read meant betraying"

Di Brandt, "Foreword," Questions i asked my mother (n. pag.; emphasis in original)

Four books by Vancouver women from the 1970s recounted, in wildly different fashion, the story of a pregnancy. By doing so, they broke a significant veil of gendered erasure and made birthing part of the public discourse. These books functioned as a kind of negotiation with the boundaries of what could and could not be said about pregnancy and the subjective experience of the female body at the time. Male writers in the city were well accustomed to using birth and pregnancy as metaphors for their own work, but such appropriations obscured the particularities of female experience. Feminist scholar Della Pollock writes of the birth story as told outside of literature as an essential part of the (re)production of maternal subjects. In her book *Telling Bodies Performing Birth: Everyday Narratives of Childbirth* (1999), she documents the supplantation of "women's birthing culture" by medicalized spaces and discourses in which "birth became less a sign of women's power than a symbolic internment of female passivity" (12–13). The birth story, marginalized in women's experience by this medicalization of the body, was reduced to pejorative gossip, lore, and anecdote. Telling one's birth story stages a localized resistance to biopolitical interference that marginalizes women from the experience of their bodies; writing and publishing a birth story goes further and disrupts the codified silence. As part of Vancouver's experimental literary community undoing of the colonial culture of deliberate erasures, the persistent shroud of ideologically structured silences, these works register as avant-garde. Their disruptive energy not only challenges the literary status quo but comes to embody an alternative ethos with a rich web of sociopolitical and aesthetical implications.

The parameters of the boundary between maternal subjectivity and literature can be registered in the writing by these women's mostly male colleague poets in the city at the time, who were very excited about writing the body into literature but did so predictably through re-inscribed patriarchal notions of the body that limit women to the role of object-other or silent mother. George Bowering, for instance, specifically renounced the role of mother as a model for literary production: "A poet is neither a grader nor a mother. His job is to participate" (Editorial 17). I read these Vancouver pregnancy narratives, literary birthing stories, thus *Geburtsgeschichte*, if you will, as a direct public intervention against the neutralized and by default masculine body of the literary tradition. As Di Brandt has said of the 1970s, "none of the literary skills I had acquired so diligently as a student of literature, had anything remotely to do with the experience of becoming a mother" (3). If the birth story outside of literature can "operate in and against the silences" (Pollock 11), the birthing story inside literature is a form of public storytelling that overtly interrupts the boundaries of permissible discourse for women by opening up and establishing new narrative patterns. I believe this was a necessary intervention into the flow of Vancouver avant-garde aesthetics and began the shift toward identity-oriented writing that continues to play an ever-increasing role in contemporary experimental writing. Indeed, writing the birthing story involves creating a new genre for literature but especially for (cisgender) women.

In this chapter, I map out some of the formal features of this new genre and proceed to highlight the avant-garde implications of these innovations. To begin, the birth story is not just a depiction of child-rearing, or even the spectacle of pregnant bodies. It needs to be stressed that the basic plot form of these types of narratives differs from the normative, linear Gustav Freytag model for being structured around the insemination, the successful pregnancy, and the delivery: thus, literally, beginning with a climax and ending with a beginning. The meta-literary aspect of the text is also different from the *Künstlerroman*, in that most of the cases documented here end with the production of the book in the reader's hands. The *Geburtsgeschichte* texts insist that the writing be simultaneous with the pregnancy, an immediacy accentuated by frequent puns that indicate the intersection of writing and birthing. As Haggerty writes: "Come out and I will cut you from me by periods" (203). The general movement is away from the manifest world, toward an increasingly impressionistic linguistic space. The struggle to encode this space directly, honestly, and in a language that resists the normative valence of women's stories shapes the central conflict of the work. Haggerty again: "If only I could tell from what I have written where I must go, listening always for hints, imputing every bit of love and love I have to their cold connections as if words were larger vessels than they were ever meant to be" (206).

Literary form, like the body itself, is a public event marked by strategic and troubling silences. As the avant-garde networks in Vancouver continued to expand throughout the 1960s, this new genre opened the possibility of allowing women access to the public act of speaking themselves into being; these were maternal subjects, yes, but more broadly an elaborate metaphor, perhaps metonymy,[1] of the creation of literary sub-jectivity for erased voices. In order to write their birthing stories, the authors had to develop new literary techniques, rupture and expand the codes of realism to include maternal experiences, and, perhaps most importantly, accept that women's embodied experience was a legitimate source of literary material. As Brandt writes, registering this difference required writing against literary heritage: "the reality of my maternal body and transformed subjectivity were insisting their unmetaphorical otherness unpolitely into my consciousness" (4). It was this insistence, this new unmetaphorical maternal subjectivity that oriented and impelled the shift in storytelling by Audrey Thomas, Daphne Marlatt, Joan Haggerty, and Gladys Maria Hindmarch.

What of the broad impetus for such a new genre? The birth narratives are emotion-ally raw but yet politically strategic rebuttals to that recurring and historically lim-iting question: What is a woman? Ever since Artemis was supplanted by Zeus, and the matriarchal past supplanted by the patriarchal present, this question has been a recurring theme of Western literature: writers, thinkers, *men* have struggled to make sense of the "unspeakable, unrepresentable, unconscious" entity that is woman (Brandt 6). What is a woman? It, being an ontology that refuses as much as it is refused, is a question encoded with the assertion of difference, absence, silence, and inscrutability. It seeks essence and admits no difference between nature and nurture, between the biological experience of being born female and the sociological experience of being raised woman. "What is a woman?" also insinuates the more nefarious question "what is a woman *for*," substituting essence for utility. In such accounts, she is defined in rela-tion to masculinity; defined by her role, her difference, her service. Thus, for Emanuel Swedenborg, woman is "born subject to the will of the man, to serve" (76); for the more, shall we say, observant Jacques Lacan, she is a creature that lacks a penis – a fact that situates her beyond the symbolic, a powerless and denuded subject.[2] This absence (she looks down, finds "nothing") poses a serious problem for literary symbolism and literary subjectivity. Indeed, a recurring problem plaguing the answers to the question has always been men's inability to actually see women: "Most women have no charac-ters at all," wrote Alexander Pope in 1743 (248). This blunt dismissal is encoded into

1 This chapter will explore the relationship between the birth story and Della Pollock's sense of performative writing, which she defines as metonymic, *not* metaphorical.
2 Lacan has been criticized by feminist scholars for his theories of feminine difference that resolve through women's symbolic/phallic lack. His Seminar XX, however, while containing provocations such as "Woman cannot be said. Nothing can be said of woman" (qtd. in Barnard and Fink 3), does push into the more ontologically radical territory of disrupting the categories of knowledge through which the real of gendered experience can be perceived. As Barbara Freeman argues, woman's radical otherness in Lacanian theory "offers a site of resistance to, and the potential for a critique of, exclusively phallic notions of sexuality and sense" (120). See, also, Suzanne Barnard and Bruce Fink's *Reading Seminar XX* (2002) for more on Lacan and feminism/feminine sexuality. Žižek, for his part, defends Lacan's gender theories on the basis that Lacan's discussion is based on the distortion caused by a feminity that is reflective of a masculinity that is predicated entirely upon projections and desires rather than anything essential (2423).

the repetition and reproduction of female silencing, marginalization, and objectification that create the circumscribed female subject under patriarchy. Another problem
is that of women giving credence to such pompous absurdities: "The greatest wit in
her Majesty's Dominions," writes Virginia Woolf of Alexander Pope (*Orlando* 150).
Importantly, Woolf uses her character Orlando to add nuance to her praise of the great
author: "Wretched man," the character quickly comes to observe.

Woolf, as a great modernist writer, did not inherit literary habits passively. In fact,
she staged an intervention of her own into the habit of answering this perverse woman
question. In 1942, she wrote, "[W]hat is a woman? I assure you, I do not know. I do not
believe that you know. I do not believe that anybody can know until she has expressed
herself in all the arts and professions open to human skill" ("Professions" 1852). Not
only does such a stance name normalized masculinity as a barrier, but Woolf also envisions a space on the other side of that erasure, a place of speaking that is outside of
the boundaries of literature – the wider boundaries, if you will – built out of women's
experience; a space of apprehending women's multifarious experience directly, through
the direct vale of the senses and the faculties, as stripped of the silence that shrouds the
body, women's bodies; this she envisions as possible.

Simone de Beauvoir took up this challenge, this possibility, in 1949 with the
publication of *The Second Sex*. I include a quote from this book at length because
of how well it demythologizes the possible answers to the elemental question,
and how it furthermore demands a re-evaluation of the medicalized discourse of
pregnancy:

> But first we must ask: what is a woman? "Tota mulier in utero," says one, "woman is
> a womb." But in speaking of certain women, connoisseurs declare that they are not
> women, although they are equipped with a uterus like the rest. All agree in recognis-
> ing the fact that females exist in the human species; today as always they make up
> about one half of humanity. And yet we are told that femininity is in danger; we are
> exhorted to be women, remain women, become women. It would appear, then, that
> every female human being is not necessarily a woman; to be so considered she must
> share in that mysterious and threatened reality known as femininity. Is this attribute
> something secreted by the ovaries? Or is it a Platonic essence, a product of the philo-
> sophic imagination? Is a rustling petticoat enough to bring it down to earth? Although
> some women try zealously to incarnate this essence, it is hardly patentable. It is fre-
> quently described in vague and dazzling terms that seem to have been borrowed from
> the vocabulary of the seers, and indeed in the times of St Thomas it was considered an
> essence as certainly defined as the somniferous virtue of the poppy. (xix)

Beauvoir disturbs the essentialist position by noting the difference between biological
femaleness and sociological femininity, and, poignantly for our purposes, she notes the
lack of a public language open to the realities and complexities of women's experience.

She writes in defiance of the extensive prescriptions of acceptable female bodies and behaviours, and especially against those formulas designed to erase claims of femininity to deviant bodies.

Mid-century female authors took up this challenge to create just such a public language; the authors addressed in this chapter took up the problem of *tota mulier in utero*, of reducing femaleness to a woman's mechanical procreative function without acknowledging her own subjective experience of procreation. The birthing story as literary genre thus began with the turn to female subjective experience, which Pauline Butling and Susan Rudy characterize as a revolution of sensibility and rank its accomplishment alongside the most celebrated achievements of twentieth-century literature (20). The rise of female subjectivity, as a radical new literary stance, and as the impetus toward the creation of new literary forms (and by extension social arrangements), was certainly one of the most significant advances in Vancouver's avant-garde milieu. It began with the direct act of seeing, writing that directness, and then stripping away the barriers of ideology and the language of the seers as completely as possible. Consequently, the language that characterizes these early birth narratives is richly impressionistic, blunt, graphic, and highly biographical. The narratives are avant-garde examples of what Della Pollock describes as performative writing, a writing of "brutally chastened hopes for embodied, creative counterspeech" ("Performing Writing" 74). It is a writing that sees the resistance, reacts against the chastening of female subjectivity, and records the impossibility of the truly free speech act, even as it creates new possibilities for expressive subjectivity by the act of its expression. Hence, the birthing story as performative writing is *consequential*: it "subsumes the constative into the performative, articulating language generally as an operational means of action and effects" (95).[3]

What constitutes this new genre? For this, I turn to Audrey Thomas's *Mrs. Blood: A novel*. In this work, published in 1970, the narrator is divided into two points of view: the narrative begins with the demarcation, "Some days my name is Mrs. Blood; some days it is Mrs. Thing" (11). The story of the novel details the first-hand account of the experiences of a pregnant woman who ultimately miscarries (Mrs. Thing), complemented by the more physical, embodied, and psychologically penetrating experience of that miscarriage (Mrs. Blood). In the obstetrics ward, there are women all around her, including especially nurses whose daily lives are filled with pregnancy stories. The singularity of a pregnancy is thus structurally recognized as part of the broader wealth of stories of pregnancies. The novel, while recognizing the great dramatic potential of birthing stories, moves freely back and forth between the individual and the multitude. So even while it divides the singular consciousness of the narrator in two, it

---

3 Pollock's use of "constative" and "performative" follows J.L. Austin here in distinguishing words that do from other words that report what they do (a wedding vow versus a wedding announcement, for instance).

also recognizes a division between individual and commonplace experience. Such a narrative frame does not privilege the singularity of the protagonist but insists upon thinking of her as an example of the diversity within a broader collective. The novel's back-and-forth structure between these two creates a poignant common context for the personal experiences of Mrs. Thing. This relational aesthetic requires authors, readers, and especially *women* to acknowledge the stark realities of female experience and female labour (in all senses) beyond the veil of traditional silence. As one character admonishes: "You mustn't be so squeamish" (56). The nurses' stories are ribald and messy, marked by a gallows humour that helps to normalize the messiness of bodies, such as in the story of a homebirth where the family dog snuck off with the afterbirth. Despite the optimism and humour of this novel's first blunt looking at the female body, Thomas's story is harrowing and frank in its assessment of women's circumstance. One character acknowledges masculine privilege and confesses: "I would like to be a man sometimes. Women's genitals are mouths and tongues and eyes. Men's are tongues and fingers" (77).

Audrey Thomas (1935–) is a three-time winner of the Ethel Wilson Fiction Prize, the top literary prize in British Columbia. She has written eighteen books and won many awards. In avant-garde circles, she is most acclaimed for *Ten Green Bottles* (1967), an interwoven collection of experimental short stories. Born in the United States, she moved to Vancouver in 1959. She received the George Woodcock Lifetime Achievement Award and the Order of Canada in 2009.

The gendered crisis in the book provokes a crisis of form, of storytelling, that shifts the pregnancy from theme, or mere content, to formal structuring device. For rather than a birth, the book ends with a miscarriage, connecting the body to the general frustration and hesitation of women's experience – *something* prevents women from arriving into the fullness of their creative potential. This something – this *it*, again, an ontology that refuses to be named – also terminates procreation. In her hospital bed, Mrs. Thing resents her husband's additional freedoms, "the ease of his adjustment – I am the only one who has to suffer" (96). She looks inside herself and confronts a surprising depth to her silence from the lack of a shared language of experience: "Why can I not ask these nurses similar questions about themselves as women? What do you call periods, among yourselves? What do you feel about virginity, sex, contraception?" (83). These questions, which begin with the silences she finds within herself, quickly extend outward to acknowledge the gaps in a much wider frame of public

MRS. BLOOD

a novel by Audrey Thomas

Figure 6.1 Cover of Audrey Thomas's *Mrs. Blood* (1970). Source: Private collection of the author. Used with permission.

discourse: "Can you think of any mountains named for women?" (141). The silence she discovers is not innocent, but carefully constructed by those around her – including women – and by the secretive, furtive culture of bodies and pregnancy at the time: "I don't even remember seeing a pregnant woman when I was a child. Nor asking a question about sex. Where were all the pregnant women?" (163). The negation is doubled here: a silence encompasses female experience, and Thomas by naming it un-writes the veil over the unsayable. There is potential in this negation, but Mrs. Thing is harangued by the gossip and judgment of the local ladies, who sympathize with her husband and pathologize her through a poisonous yet freely available misogynistic public discourse. They borrow that language from the men in power, such as the hospital director who yells at her, "You're not insane, you're just promiscuous!" (158). Promiscuous: there is too much of her, too much voice, too much presence, too much body; therefore she must be reduced.

The book concludes with a more acute and wide-reaching probe of the public discourse surrounding women's experience: there are extensive quotes from newspapers (190–1), Bible passages (209, 212), and children's songs and poems (210, 214), until the entire narrative breaks down into a barrage of quotes, comments, clips, and scenes collaged together in scattershot disarray:

> I am a flower dying from the sun. The wind passes over me and I am gone.
> "Lie still."
> Monkey, Banana, Cocoyam Driver. Monkey Banana Coco-
> yam Driver. Monkey
>   banana
> cocoyam
>   DRIVER.
>   "Avez-vous du pain?"
>
>
> I am Zacharias.
> I am Number One
> Number One stole the meat from the cookin' pot
> Who me?
> Yes you
> Couldn't be
> Then Who?
> I am Zacharias. [...]
> "Dr. Biswas. Where is Dr. Biswas?"
> "Lie still."
> I am not what I am.
> A deed without a name.
>
> (214–15)

Why the meltdown in narrative voice? The collagic breakdown happens after the miscarriage and connects to the breakdown of self and body: the narrator begins repeating, like a chant, "I am not what I am" (215–8), echoing the similar destabilizing chant previously discussed by Brion Gysin that asked, "I am that am I?" The essentialist view of *tota mulier in utero* fails her for failing to acknowledge her experience: "And then they took my crimson soul and crimson lining. And then they let me go" (217). There is no traditional narrative model that accounts for the movement from repressed subjectivity to the loss of subjectivity caused by a lack of available public discourse.

Thomas, in a story published in 1977, revisits the *Geburtsgeschichte* and, with dark irony, represents the telling of this kind of story as a direct form of violence – indeed, as *rape* – against the patriarchal order:

> a reversal too – but ugly, unnatural. She had dominated him always, more and more, had emasculated his body and his soul [...] He remembered how she had told him, captive, everything about her labour during the birth of their third child. Had described

it in such detail he had sickened and begged her to desist [...] She had raped him –
truly – as the Vikings raped their conquered women. And she had desecrated him and
everything he dreamed of. That night, while he sat wretchedly with his head between
his knees, she talked of herself and the young doctor who assisted her as if they had
been lovers who created the child between them. ("Aquarius" 17)

To this male character, the mere act of hearing a birth story is a figurative form
of rape, a disfigurative violence to the ongoing performance of patriarchy and his
mental well-being. If the birth story represents an extreme form of ideological violence against the status quo, it must begin with the recognition and undoing of systemic violence against women and all the systemic mechanisms designed to silence
them. From such a linguistic crisis, the *Geburtsgeschichte* pushes deeper into a site
of ontological crisis – to borrow Kristeva's lovely image of the collapse of individuality after the rejection of the mother and motherhood: "Narcissus drowning in a
cascade of false images (from social roles to the media)" (172). Gaining control of
representation matters because false representations that circulate in patriarchal literatures prevent women from encountering themselves in art. To fall in love with
false representations is to drown as a perverted Narcissus. Thus, the collaged cascade
of public languages at the end of Thomas's book is entirely empty and emptying of
life, destroying a poisonous inheritance where acknowledging women's subjectivity
is registered as a violent act. The repetitions, remembrances, allusions, and citations
also introduce circularity into narrative structure, a recurring modality in birthing
stories. As Thomas explained in an interview with George Bowering, "giving birth
is an archetypal experience that you can know & remember, whereas the others you
cannot. Archetypal experiences are sort of circular experiences" (Bowering, "Songs"
21). While we can question whether this essentialist vision of maternity re-inscribes
constraining myths, it is worth acknowledging how this counter-myth of experien-
tial circularity helped to establish a positive space for the production of an erased
literary subject position and empowered a new narrative mode that gave voice to the
experience of one's erasure.

  Published in the same year as Thomas's novel, Daphne Marlatt's birth narrative *Rings* was released as part of the *Georgia Straight Writing Supplement*'s series
of book-length works. Neither prose nor poetry, Marlatt's text takes up a similar
symbolic circularity and also encounters a crisis in writing through the experience of motherhood. Marlatt asks, "Mother is inarticulate dark? / (Smothering)"
(83). This bleak question is her inheritance as a female writer and attests to the
legacy of that regressive question "what is a woman?" But Marlatt immediately and
emphatically rejects the insinuation of female silence and subjugation: "No," she
answers curtly. The text proceeds to struggle against the (historical) weight of that
violent silencing: the fractured language functions impressionistically, rendering
her physical environment and internal experience of that environment through the

Figure 6.2 Portrait of Daphne Marlatt. Photographer unknown. Source: Private collection of Daphne Marlatt. Used with permission.

Daphne Marlatt (née Buckle, 1942–) was a student at UBC when *Tish* first launched. She was invited to join the editorial collective at the outset but declined for various reasons. She attended the 1963 Vancouver Poetry Conference and became an editor of *Tish* shortly after. She is the author of thirty books of experimental poetry and prose, many of which (like *Vancouver Poems* [1972], *Steveston* [1974], and *Ana Historic* [1988]) are genuine classics of Canadian experimental literature. Between her writing and her extensive publishing and editing work, Marlatt's impact on multiple generations of Vancouver and Canadian authors cannot be underestimated. She was born in Melbourne, Australia, and moved to Vancouver in 1951.

broken grammar of a shifting consciousness carefully navigating each moment. As Fred Ribkoff writes,

> Marlatt applies the theoretical vocabulary of New American poetics to her unique female experience of pregnancy. [...] In "Rings" Marlatt does exactly this. However, she must come at this writing from the perspective of a s/mothering. She is so literally aware of herself as proprioceptive agent [... as] the ring through which another will pass and make contact with other rings/bodies. (n. pag.)

The struggle to uncover and thus embody (and embolden) the maternal subject from the weight of her absence is a breach in the cycle of her erasure and marginalization. Instead of linearity or ontological origin, the birth becomes a mark of maternal speaking and (potential) narrative form: "Like a dream. There is no story only the telling with no end in view or, born headfirst, you start at the beginning & work backwards" (n. pag.). Like Thomas, Marlatt is frustrated with her male partner's power and self-control, especially as her pregnant body and the social mechanisms of dealing with that unruly body seem to conspire to take away her power, self-control, and speech. Importantly, this imbalance is registered as a literary problem that Marlatt seeks to address by rethinking the nature of subjectivity through the combination of feminism and proprioception. As she wrote in a letter from 1975 to Warren Tallman, "Subjective insofar as it is proprioceptive & the body is ground, yes, self transmits" ("Correspondences" 14).

The eponymous rings that pervade the book begin with the ripples of a stone dropped in water and expand to include "screwy neighbours" (n. pag.) circling her house, the official authority of nations circumscribing movement by borders, the dense fold of mountains around Vancouver, the choking silence of female speech by masculine noise, and a score of other strangling frustrations. Unlike

Daphne Marlatt, email interview, 3 June 2013

just the exchange of what had been thought of as individual experiences & problems was huge because we began to see they weren't individual or personal at all. "the personal is political." we were still coming out of the 50s & early 60s (for my take on that period in which we were raised, see *Untying the Apron: Daughters Remember Mothers of the 1950s* [Guernica, edited by Lorri Neilsen Glenn]) so all sorts of tacit assumptions & borders were being undone in those C[onsciousness] R[aising] conversations. at the time, a few of us were also experimenting with communal living (there was a lot of interest in Marxist theory – in fact that was probably the origin of the term) & then the collaborative arts collectives like Intermedia and the Western Front were important places for the artists & writers in our particular group because so much was happening in them. this is what i mean by a large context: we were living it. & the influences came from across the continent – we were right about "consciousness raising" coming, as a term, from the States.

Thomas, however, Marlatt finds an opening in both narrative method and symbolism through the ring: for the ring is also the encompassing womb around her baby, and the circle of her vagina that will birth him. Poignantly, both of these circles are broken in the text, punctuated by birth and in the birth experience by episiotomy. The recurring symbol of a gap denying a closure becomes her opening to a new narrative form – the curtains that don't quite close, the countries with porous borders that open into new spaces. It is through such an opening that her child is born. She takes this image of ruptured enclosing back to classical roots to signal her break from the patriarchal tradition: "'It's a man's world,' she said. (Got to stand up.) [...] Trouble is, I stood up poked my head through the roof of the cave."

The image of a breach, of breaking out of Plato's cave (an image that is also reminiscent of Athena penetrating Zeus from the inside), out of this man's world, offers a poignant insight into Marlatt's literary career. She began writing immersed in the masculinist milieu of Vancouver's modernist poetry but evolved into an iconic radical lesbian feminist writer in the 1980s and 1990s. In the 1960s, however, she affiliated with the *Tish* group of poets. Frank Davey, in his memoir of the period, notes that she, Gladys Maria Hindmarch, and three other women were invited to edit the magazine in its first editorial period but all declined (*When* 113). Despite that purported inclusiveness, five men took over the mantel of the new magazine, with Davey elected to lead. As I've documented in chapter 2, she and other women were not exactly encouraged to join the young men in the magazine, though the male *Tish* authors frequently wrote about women and their experience of female bodies. Davey muses further, and somewhat weirdly, that *Tish* might never have happened at all but for his attempted but failed seduction of her: "Perhaps the *Tish* community, such as it is, should thank her" (124). Why not thank her for her writing, her decades of service on behalf of many literary communities? Despite this claim to her centrality, Marlatt's writing was never published in the magazine throughout the three years of Davey's editorship. If she was a muse to the magazine, she was kept a silent muse.

Within that unpromising milieu, Marlatt was deeply influenced by the ideas of literature endorsed by the *Tish* group, especially those that stemmed from Charles Olson. Olson rejected the rhyming, metrical line of traditional poetry and sought to bring more of the vital, living body of the poet into verse. He was interested in the rhythm of breathing as an organizing principle for poetry – the breath-line, he called it – and explored the possibilities of projecting the body onto the page – hence, projective verse. As he writes, "What we have suffered from, is manuscript, press, the removal of verse from its producer and its reproducer, the voice, a removal by one, by two removes from its place of origin *and* its destination. For the breath has a double meaning which latin had not yet lost" ("Projective" 22; emphasis in original). The extension of this interest in the physical producer and reproducer is the instruction or invitation for the poet to discover her own identity through the body; and for writing, to bring a consciousness of material realities into the work. However, despite the encouragement to engage with space and place through the discourse of the body, and the centrality of the pregnancy metaphor in Olson's poetics, women's subjectivity was conspicuously absent in public discourse in Vancouver literature. Marlatt, writing in *Ana Historic* (1988), would later write about the weight of the absence of Vancouver women and pause to wonder: "what would she say in all that silence?" (104). Ribkoff counters that Marlatt began mapping out an answer two decades earlier in *Rings* by presenting "a woman who is struggling to understand what it means to be a mother, to matter, to utter. By locating herself in her own body Marlatt is gradually able to utter the silences of her predicament" (n. pag.). She found (herself within) nothing.

Daphne Marlatt, email interview, 4 June 2013

my own sense of the "avant-garde" here (& that's such a contested term) is that it wasn't "unified" but worked as a loose network of closely or distantly affiliated arts groups who were interested in what other groups were doing & shared a similar politic re working to undo the entrenched conservative views and tenets of the establishment. these interests connected with other groups right across the continent, fuelled by anti-war, pro-civil rights, women's & gay rights movements, socialist & anti-capitalist thinking. well, a dawning greater freedom for women thanks to better birth control, provincially funded day care – all these vectors played a role. then there were the bigger philosophical/psychological questions that the gestalt movement, for one instance, & the use of psychedelics for another, raised. less bureaucratic regulation too, despite the police spying on "undesirable elements." an incredible time really, looking back on it from today's constraints!

more personally & locally, once i got together with Roy Kiyooka & we left Kitsilano to move into Strathcona in 1975 or 6 i grew more acquainted with groups on this side of town: so Gerry Gilbert's B.C. Monthly, Vancouver Co-op Radio & his Radio Free Rain-Forest show there, a group of inter-disciplinary women artist friends connected with Gerry & Carole Itter, Roy's Blue Mule gallery, Talonbooks where Paul de Barros & i laid out each issue of our prose mag periodics (our contributing authors were both Canadian & American), & of course the Western Front with its reading series (which Roy & i were attending & participating in earlier than our move). all of these were functioning through the 70s. so i can't say that i felt any collapse of avant-garde activity/interest in that decade.

Ribkoff offers a more extensive analysis of the formal and theoretical connections between Marlatt and the New American poets, but it satisfies the present purposes to note that the connection Olson identified between breathing and creating combined with the rise in feminist consciousness in Vancouver encouraged Marlatt to tell and write her pregnancy narrative. From this perspective, the *Geburtsgeschichte* can be read as a public intervention into the inheritance of a patriarchal literary modernism – that is, as breaking into (or out of) the closed ring of the canon. While literature in Vancouver and far beyond was overrun by masculinist modalities, the raw, unexpurgated birth story formalized a new literary space from the common practice of sharing pregnancy stories among women. To be clear, pregnancy scenes are common in literature, but appear in service to advancing other plot concerns. In the mid-twentieth century, however, writing by Margaret Drabble, Penelope Mortimer, Jean Rhys, Margaret Atwood, and Djuna Barnes, among many others, began exploring the birth narrative as a focal point in its own right, and thinking about the legacy of maternity. Through such a gendered genre, women could confront their own experiences, their own bodies, and from that experience develop new narrative models and new symbolic arcologies. This work also fulfilled the call for a proprioceptive writing that was responsive to the writer's time, place, and bodily processes. Furthermore, such work fulfilled Pollock's sense of the ambition of performative writing, where the "writing/subject puts his/her own status on the line [...] in the name of mobilizing *praxis*" (96; emphasis in original). While it was dialectical in writing against a disempowering tradition, it demanded the invocation and creation of new literary resources to make manifest. As Judith Butler writes, "a generation of feminist writing [has] tried, with varying degrees of success, to bring the feminine body into writing, to write the feminine proximately or directly, sometimes without even the hint of a preposition or marker of linguistic distance between the writing and the written" (*Bodies That Matter* ix).

Marlatt eventually became an editor of *Tish*, after Davey, Wah, Bowering, and the first wave of editors had mostly left Vancouver or that literary scene for other interests and pursuits. She helped to open that forum to increased female-driven content.[4] There, she was joined by one of her close friends, Gladys Maria Hindmarch, who also wrote a pregnancy

---

4 See chapter 2 for more details on the shift in *Tish* editorial periods.

Figure 6.3 Gladys Maria Hindmarch at the Western Front, 1975. Photographer unknown. Source: Private collection of Gladys Maria Hindmarch. Used with permission.

narrative of her own experience. Hindmarch's book *A Birth Account* was written in 1969 and 1971 but published only in 1976.[5] In her introduction she explains the motivation of the book in terms of public discourse: "I wrote the birth account to share my experience with others and to see if I could as closely as possible record what happened" (9). Following the Olson-*Tish* principles of projective verse and voice-based poetry, she invites her readers to "[p]lease read my work aloud. The rhythm, the sound, the breathing are all part of what it is. When you come to the third section of this book, breathe the breaths [...] You may find your consciousness alters" (10). Despite this shared sense of aesthetics, from the outset the difference of subject position from the masculinist *Tish* imagination is striking: the book begins, for instance, with a woman's observation of the pleasure in farting while fucking (15). The book's function as an intervention into public discourse is made overt through her rendering of such subjective, eccentric moments: "I laughed, and he didn't know why till I told him then he giggled a bit too." In the moment of disrupted coitus, her experience of her body, and her making that experience public, creates a new empathetic community between her, her husband, and a broader reading public. They laugh together.

Like Daphne Marlatt, Gladys Maria Hindmarch (1940–) was invited by the editorial board to join the *Tish* collective at the outset. She was a prose writer, however, and did not appear on the masthead until after the Vancouver Poetry Conference in 1963. She is the author of three prose works, *The Peter Stories* (1976), *A Birth Account* (1976), and *The Watery Part of the World* (1988). A video of the reading depicted above is available here: https://vimeo.com/139012771.

---

5 George Bowering published a version of the work as the third entry in his Beaver Kosmos Folios chapbook series. It was called simply *Sketches* (1969).

Hindmarch's book plays with the boundary between private, personal experience and the public, political experiences of the period. In an exaggerated, almost metaphysical use of the pathetic fallacy, her pregnant body echoes the public spaces around her: her miscarriage is followed by descriptions of political protests, the Kent State police murders, and the revelation that "the war is just beginning to come home" (28). After she has an abortion, and her dog dies, her experience with (public) language falls into crisis. She grows swiftly alienated from the people speaking around her: "I can make out the emphasis on syllables, like they're bigger than usual, yet I cant tell what the words are" (32). Her baby is born on May Day, and her husband and friends move back and forth between the maternity ward and local leftist protests. During the delivery, her husband says to her: "If you hurry up [...] I'll be able to make the demonstration" (99). Such a divided attention seems horribly unkind, except that the book depicts her telling of her subjective maternal experience as a radically political action against the oppressive politics of the world surrounding her. The delivery is of a kind with the demonstration, as both are public acts against the status quo; something new, some new consciousness at least, is being born. Her subjective experience of her own body thus informs her writing, which gains power and utility inasmuch as it helps to change the world: "I feel needed when I'm teaching [...] I'm lonely, teaching is public, I dont know, I just feel useless, and writing is useless" (21). Writing as a self-contained, aesthetic experience is useless until it claims a place in public discourse and seeks to change the power relationship therein. She surveys other books on pregnancy and comes to "resent" them, for the "mother is already placed in the mommy-role to her husband" without any thought on how to "accept who you are in the centre of this" (71). She sees a nurse writing down details about the delivery, but "[t]his has nothing to do with me. Nothing at all" (100). Her book, in contrast, begins with the radical acceptance that she is in the centre of her own experience.

Working from a combination of *Tish* and avant-garde methodologies, Hindmarch developed a new means of bringing her body and her breathing into literature:

Starting now: > > ><h<h<h   > > ><h<h<h
I am breathing   am completely open   he is stepping
towards my cunt   > > ><h<h<h   his fingers slip
in   > > ><h<h<h   but I don't feel them in
> > ><h<h<h   his touch is not like any I've had
before   > > ><h<h<h   the closest is a dentist in
a totally frozen wide-open mouth   > > ><h<h<h
in my head I know he's in, and only through my head can I
feel   > > ><h<h<h   he is smiling, a full faced
smile   > > ><h<h<h   good god, he says
his hand slips out   I feel it at the outer edge only
> > ><h<h<h   fully dilated, I hear his voice beyond
my breath   > > ><h<h<h   case room
> > ><h<h<h   no labour, I'm through the first stage,

I didn't even know it, through   > > ><h<h<h
he is giving her commands and leaving   > > ><h<h<h
the cot rolls next to me and I'm still   > > ><h<h<h
> > ><h<h<h   > > ><h<h<h   > > > >

(93)

This is the writing that, as she suggests in the introduction, could alter reader con-sciousness, especially if readers perform the work aloud, including the breathing. In correspondence, she told me that she developed this transcription technique with the assistance of the concrete poet Lionel Kearns (Interview 1), the most regular con-tributor to *Tish* magazine who was not an editor. The form thus allows the breath, represented mimetically on the page, to interfere with the narrative movement by its insistent disruption. It structures how long each thought can be, and by interrupt-ing dislocutes the linear movement of the narrative with the return to body focus via breathing – a genuine breath-line. The text itself is distinctly impressionistic, touched by the graphic madness of the body and the physical abstraction of medical discourse, struggling as if against language to maintain body focus. While the book ends with the birth of the child, this is the mother's account and not a reification of the child or essential womanhood. She discovers that she is not a womb, she is a pro-jective agent: "I come out of it happy. Know who I am. I'm Gladys, pushing" (105).

Figure 6.4 Joan Haggerty reading at the Western Front, 1975. Photographer unknown. Source: Private collection of Joan Haggerty. Used with permission.

Joan Haggerty (1940–) is the author of three novels, including *Daughters of the Moon* (1971), and one memoir, each of which attained prominence. Born and educated in Vancouver, she spent 1962–72 in London, England, where

Daughters of the Moon is partially set. Her most recent book, *The Dancehall Years* (2016), depicts the gritty vitality of Vancouver from the forties through the seventies.

The fourth novel that I want to address here is Joan Haggerty's *Daughters of the Moon*, a more conventional, popular-market narrative, yet one that also affirms the performative nature of the birthing story. Published in 1971, Haggerty's novel depicts the story of two women, both pregnant and married, who leave their husbands and seek solace in an exclusively female space. It is through their encounter with the feminized margin that the novel becomes performative, becomes both a reflection of gendered experience in the world and in its self-consciousness an attempt to re-encode and expand the possibilities of female experience. Or, as Pollock defines the performative, a "writing as the constitutive form of unrealized democracies [...] projects new modes of being and relating through its forms, constituting the very norms by which it will be read" (78, 95). The self-consciousness breeds a kind of self-reassessment and body consciousness: "I am a body. They prick me and my blood leaks" (Haggerty 146). It also encourages an awareness of the process by which the author writes the book being read: "I have no idea what to write or how I will find out" (Haggerty 149). Pollock describes performative writing as metonymic in the sense that the writing participates in but does not encapsulate the entire scene (82). This partiality, this sense of linguistic incompleteness, leads to rather striking moments of linguistic eruption during the birth scene in Haggerty's novel:

> One two blow. I've got to do one two blow. Get me over on my side. Spaces in between
> only . . . god . . . .
> . . . .
> . . . . words, what do they mean? Now nothing
> now, now nothing, now, owwwwwww. (298)

Poignantly, in the same discussion on the limits of language in performative writing, Pollock highlights an extreme use of punctuation to "mark the materiality of the sign with the use of a practically unspeakable, non- or counter-presential element of punctuation, an element intelligible only by reference to visual grammatical code" (83). The body and the experience overwhelm the telling, literally, figuratively, and through this performative punctuation symbolically. Similarly, Jordan Abel's *The Place of Scraps* begins his writing against the legacy of colonial erasure with pages of punctuation, reclaiming a sense of presence from colonialist erasure.

Haggerty's formal integration of pregnancy into the generic features of the *Geburtsge-schichte* includes using it as the structuring device for the plot movement. Her telling includes repetition with increasing intensity, Braxton Hicks false labours leading toward the birth as a kind of conclusive epiphany and self-discovery:

> The girl who'd come to write wanted to separate the relevant from the irrelevant [...]
> If only I can spend enough days away from him to give it a pattern, she thought; a beginning, middle, and recognize the last time I saw him as a part of the same episode, I may emerge ... (159, 161)

The self-discovery, a hinge for ontological probing, is thus intermingled with the emergence of the *Geburtsgeschichte* as genre. Content and form, cause and effect, are all unified in this novelization: *Daughters of the Moon* tells the story of two pregnant women, spurned in their own way by the men who impregnated them, seeking self-knowledge through their bodies and each other. Poignantly, they find each other by chance literally in the desert and become lovers, even learning to love themselves and their changing bodies. In the ninth month, however, Sarah leaves Anna to search for her man, hoping to nest in a traditional way. Anna dies in childbirth, alone. Sarah is spurned, again, but ultimately reunites with people who care for her. The ghost of Anna returns to haunt her, to warn her, "You'll have no rest until my story is told" (320). The book is thus a reckoning of the cost of patriarchal ideology and the doubt it renders in women. It recalls Samuel Taylor Coleridge's ancient mariner, whose rime is a curse warning hapless wedding guests against his tragic error. The error in Haggerty's text, though, is not the mariner's sacrilege or hubris, but rather Sarah's fear in the face of violating social decorum, and allowing her performance of gender norms to be policed internally. Her failure is the failure to realize the full implications and liberating potential of the genre her telling her birth story helps to create.

These texts are foundational works of a new order of female public intellectuals in Vancouver, intellectuals who spoke through the complexity of their experiences and against the shroud of masculinist silence. They participated in a broad construction of a language to accommodate female subjectivity, to make women feel at home as themselves in the world. Needless to say, they did not take place in a vacuum, but participated in a broad shift of available public discourse. In Vancouver, this shift can be measured through the emergence of specific forums for women to express themselves publicly, openly, and honestly. Such forums began with the pioneering writing of Dorothy Livesay and Phyllis Webb, and then accelerated with the women's liberation discussion groups that were inspired by Betty Frieden's 1963 book *The Feminine Mystique*. The success and proliferation of these meeting groups led Hindmarch and a small group of Vancouver women to propose a new magazine called *Canadian Woman's Monthly*. They assembled an enormous coterie of female public intellectuals from across the country all focused on imagining "what kind

Gladys Maria Hindmarch, "Women Etc"

WOMEN ETC

THE NEW YORK LIFE
LIFE OF JACKIE KENNEDY ONASSSIS
HER APT
WHERE SHE SHOPS
WOMEN WHO LOOK YOUNGER THAN THEY ARE
ETC

WOMENWOMENWOMENWOMEN
SHOP   SHOP   SHOP   SHOP
WOMEN LOOKYOUNGER
WOMEN LOOKYOUNGER
SHOP   ETC
SHOP   ETC
THEY ARE   ETC
THEY ARE   ETC
WOMEN THEY ARE ETC
WOMEN THEY ARE ETC
WOMEN ETC
WO . . . MEN . . . ETC
WOO . . . . MEN . . . . . . ET.CET.ER.AH

From Beaver Kosmos Folios #3, published as Gladys Hindmarch's *Sketches*. Used with permission.

of work would be done by a first rate female artist if she were free at last from the constricting influence of mediums and messages that have evolved out of a strictly masculine point of view" (Craden 6). Though their fundraising campaign failed to raise enough money to launch the magazine, it attracted letters of interest and support from male and female public intellectuals across the country. A version of the dream came to pass in 1975, with the launch of *Room of One's Own*, inspired by Virginia Woolf's 1929 essay of the same name. This Vancouver magazine, and the more radical-feminist *Tessera* magazine that evolved out of it, marked the shift in public discourse that these pregnancy narratives dared to imagine.

SEVEN

Avant Now and Then: Locating the Post-Avant

"City of death, city of friends."

George Stanley, *Vancouver: A Poem* (49)

"An event is the creation of new possibilities."

Alan Badiou, "The Idea of Communism" (5)

1 Hegemony and the Single Riot

In the aftermath of the 2011 Stanley Cup riot in Vancouver, author and musician Dave Bidini rejected the idea that the riots were just an aberration. In a column in the *National Post*, he wrote, "Vancouver is a tough city [...] It's a violent, stressful place, as uptight as it is free" (n. pag.). While most commentators recoiled at the political emptiness of that violence and insisted upon its exceptionalism and difference from the beautiful and scenic status quo, Bidini's was an early voice that sought to connect the directionlessness of the experience – to twist Gautier's motto, the violence for violence's sake – to the regulatory regime that governs capital flows in the local economy and that resolves into an extreme imbalance between poverty and excessive wealth. His reading suggests the violence was an extension of capitalist disaffection, or what Douzinas and Žižek characterize as a carry-over of the "defeat, denunciations and despair of the 1980s and 1990s, the triumphalist 'end of history,' the unipolar world of American hegemony" (vii). The kids were not fighting for anything, nor against any social ill, but their outrageous actions signalled a profound alienation from an environment laced with social dysfunction, and performed metonymically rather than antagonistically: inter-antagonistically, in fact, rather than agonistically. As Michael Barnholden writes in *Reading the Riot Act: A Brief History of Riots in Vancouver*, "[t]he Stanley Cup Riots are superficially sports riots that, upon closer examination, fit neatly within the realm of class riots as either a consumer or youth riot" (23).

This reading of the 2011 riot poignantly reverses the politics of the 1971 Gastown riot, the so-called Battle of Maple Tree Square, where youth also went wild on the streets of Vancouver. In that case, however, it was marijuana activists recoiling

Figure 7.1 The "Battle of Maple Square" Gastown marijuana riot, in which seventy-nine protesters were arrested. The Supreme Court would later describe the event as a "police riot." Photograph by Glenn Baglo (*Vancouver Sun* 1971). Used with permission.

panic-stricken from an attack by the police for protesting government harassment via the war on drugs, including undercover police operations, regular beatings, and trumped-up arrests in the hippie community. In that riot forty years earlier, the state violence was directed against the possibility of local social change, denying activists the right to agency and advocacy. After reviewing the details of the "police riot," Barnholden concludes: "The implications seemed clear: any threat to the hegemony of the city's power elite would be met with extreme violence" (939). The constant hassles and intimidation techniques directed at the hippies were intended to divide and break them and erase their provocation and were in fact largely successful in meeting this goal. As bissett wrote of the country at large, despite its internal tensions, "shes usually united / togethr enuff to put down any / radicul change" ("Canada" 137). It is poignant, indeed, that the techniques used against the Vancouver hippies were identical to techniques used in the state battles against communism in Canada from the nineteenth century through to the 1980s. The hippies, with their wildly idealistic projections of future utopias, were treated as another domestic front in the *longue durée* of the Cold War. Reg Whitaker, Gregory Kealey, and Andrew Parnaby document the surveillance techniques used by Canadian governments on their people and discover "an activist conservatism on behalf of capital against its perceived enemies" that has consistently included covert disruption, division, and defeat of leftist activity as a part of its mandate for well over a century now (12).

The local in both Vancouver riots serves as the point of crisis in the ascendance of transnational capitalism, and, as the point of crisis, the site of rupture in which the potential for revolution lies dormant, being either suppressed or sublimated. Reading the two riots as extensions of the general violence of transnational capitalism also highlights the change in literary responses to neoliberalism, including the transition from avant-garde revolutionary hubris to post-avant experimental stasis.[1]

I read these two incidents as the sociohistorical markers and contexts of parallel transformations that occurred in Canadian literature. The characteristic revolutionary spirit of 1960s and 1970s avant-garde literature disappeared, became swiftly outmoded, in part because it got worn down by the military precision and power of the state apparatus – as in the Gastown riot, as in the secret service political interventions on behalf of capital – and in part because of the rise of a disaffected culture resistant to resistance. Al Filreis's *Counter-revolution of the Word: The Conservative Attack on Modern Poetry 1945–1960* uncovers in American literature a direct connection between anti-communist government agendas and the resistance to experimental and avant-garde literary practices: what he calls the "cold war politics of poetic form" (288). He consequently identifies the lyric poem with the "postideological moment" that follows, or as Charles Bernstein writes, "[t]he intellectual heir of anticommunist antimodernism is a post- or neoliberalism that underwrites its defense of dominant aesthetic values as common sense. Critiques are dismissed as unjustifiable agonism (the ideology of the avant-garde), part of a struggle that is deemed outmoded" (63).

If things cannot change, and socio-economic disparities and violence are both endemic and systemic, then it should hardly be a surprise when young people erupt in cathartic aggression. Jameson anticipates as much in documenting the ultimate "indifference" of the "anarchism" of the 1960s that led to the cynical reasoning of postmodern consumerism with its turn to the consumption of consumption itself[2] (274). In this way, the empty expenditure of violence in the Vancouver hockey riot echoes not the militarized discourse of modernity, which at least has access to the fantasy of a countervailing militarized agency of the avant-garde and the hopeful discourse of revolution. Instead, it reflects a postmodern moment with its surface

---

1 The early Surrealist mandate of existing in order to serve the revolution – that is, explicitly the communist revolution – and that had important recurrences in Vancouver Surrealist schools in the sixties and seventies gave way to the so-called post-ideological end-of-history moment that concedes the immutability of capitalist hegemony and seeks to soften its blows.

2 Jameson proceeds to discuss the "misery of happiness" within an American consumer culture that no longer knows "itself apart from genuine satisfaction and fulfillment" (280). It is this alienation that permits the misrecognition of destruction as consumption, misery of happiness as happiness.

erosion of value masking a globalized spectacle of violence – and a moment that lacks any countervailing agency. Michael Hardt and Antonio Negri's *Empire* connects just such a sublimated, depoliticized violence of transnational capitalism with postmodernism directly: "Postmodernism is indeed the logic by which global capital operates. Marketing has perhaps the clearest relation to postmodernist theories, and one could even say that the capitalist marketing strategies have long been postmodernist, *avant la letter*" (151). Postmodernism, inadvertently, disarms resistance to the conditions of global capital and thereby helps pave the way for endless empty expenditure without dissent.[3] Part of the cost and consequence of this disarming is the loss of an avant-garde mode of resistance in exchange for a post-avant mode of experimentation without revolutionary hope. Though grim, this is how we conclude the story of Vancouver's avant-garde renaissance, not with a revolution but a riot.

2 Hailing *Taxi!*

The transition between these two points is suggestively mapped out in Helen Potrebenko's 1975 novel *Taxi!*, in which the somewhat idealistic protagonist grows increasingly jaded about the real opportunities for social change in Vancouver. Shannon, the hippie communist taxi driver and narrator of the novel, gradually confronts the ideological juggernaut her idealism is up against: "Only a few short years ago, I was out to save the world, and now I've been reduced to foraging for dimes" (56). The city in the novel is tough and marred by regular examples of extreme poverty and pollution alongside paralyzing experiences of racism and sexism. Shannon is constantly harassed and exposed to a powerful undercurrent of hatred that structures capitalist society: "Next after women, the [other] drivers hated people of races other than their own" (93), she observes. This hatred serves a broader purpose: "Hatred helped them survive and, at the same time, prevented them from improving conditions in order to escape the necessity for hatred" (94). The narrator gradually realizes that individual experiences and opinions reflect a shadowy structure that facilitates and depends on disparities and the attendant frustration of inequality: hatred, she observes, "is necessary for a loyal citizen of capitalist society" (49).

Global politics, particularly Cold War global politics, saturate the local space and severely limit the opportunities for local power to effect change. When a Russian dignitary arrives in Vancouver, Canadians en masse heave a sigh of relief and feel that the Cold War is over. The narrator, however, experiences this imagined end of the Cold War as "a traffic jam and nothing more [...] The war went on as before" (80). Given this

---

3 See Terry Eagleton's discussion on the political importance of essentialism and agency in *After Theory* (2003) – ideas that postmodernists have consistently debunked.

Figure 7.2 Helen Potrebenko, author of *Taxi!*, in her taxi in 1975. Photographer unknown. Source: Private collection of Helen Potrebenko. Used with permission.

decidedly cynical perspective of a class war operating above and abstract to the political conflict of capitalism versus state communism, which is itself above and abstract to the running street battles and petty hatreds that shape the lives of individuals in Vancouver, the possibility of radical restructurings – that is, change down to the very roots of a society – evaporates. It is from a similar vantage that bissett concludes in his poem on Canada and Canadians with the realization that the power brokers "dont figure wer big / enuff for freedom" ("Canada" 137). Any hint of idealism in Potrebenko's novel quickly transmutes into a similarly bleak finality that is suggestive of the end-of-history mantra that surfaces through the development of the postmodern condition. A conversation with a bartender from the West Hotel captures the transition:

> The world. You told me you were going to change it.
> Oh. Yeah. That was a long time ago. There is no hope.
> None?
> None.
> Did it take you all these years to learn that?
> I guess I'm pretty dumb. You're supposed to learn that on your first job so
> that you no   longer trouble capitalism with incipient rebellion.
>
> (55)

The systemic cynicism in Potrebenko's book is rather shocking when put in the context of 1960s and 1970s Vancouver avant-garde revolutionary optimism. Just three years earlier, for instance, in the wake of the Gastown riot, *Blewointment* released the iconic "Poverty Issew," with work by seventy-six different authors protesting and contesting the inevitability of socio-economic imbalance: "all th peopul stand!" wrote Bertrand Lachance. "all th peopul march!" ("frosting" 58). In contrast, her novel signalled the start of what would become a much more general and wide-spread rejection of avant-gardism for its futility in overturning the conditions it fights against (especially within its own manifestations).[4]

With Potrebenko's novel in mind, I want to revisit the rejection of the avant-garde, but not through the familiar debates of its military etymology, gender politics, or problematic teleological implications. I would like to address the failure of the avant-garde through a problem raised by Hardt and Negri's *Empire* that identifies the local, which has formally negotiated its sovereignty from the nation-state, as primarily subject to the new paradigm of international capital. The consequence of this transfer of subjugation is not the erasure of difference (the local is now encouraged to facilitate multicultural agencies and pluralized identities) but rather the erasure of liberating possibilities outside of globalized capital and its attendant violence. There is nothing to be found outside of global capital. It has been pointed out by many that, like postmodernism, the avant-garde also suits the smash-and-build mandate of capitalism with its requisite of constant change (though limited by the boundaries of transnational flows of capital). So, while specific avant-gardes might have proposed unique and complex alternatives to present-day multinational capitalism, their cumulative effect has been the extension of that very modality – effectively anticipating and establishing the ideological paralysis inherent to the postmodern condition. It was this realization of the avant-garde's complicity in oppressive networks of power, including sexism, racism, colonialism, and capitalism, that led to its widespread rejection on the grounds outlined above. In contradistinction to the 1960s Vancouver sense of a localized imagination as a potential site of liberation, Potrebenko's text represents an early confrontation with the juggernaut of globalized capitalism as a source of local and national disempowerment. Consequently, I read her book as a key indicator of the transition into a post-avant modality, of the end of an era in Vancouver. In her protagonist's words: "Behaviour is prescribed by economics, you know" (19).

3 Locating the Post-Avant

The post-avant, 'patalinguistically linked to postmodernism, is a temporal paradox by name that can be characterized by a self-aware writing that exposes problems of present-day multinational capitalism, including its own complicity, without the

---

4 Jameson connects the arrival of this widespread disillusionment with Reagan and Thatcher (*Postmodernism* 207–8), Derrida with the beginning of the fifties (15).

presentation of liberating alternatives ("We lack resistance to the present," write Deleuze and Guattari [108]). *Taxi!* presents the arrival of this post-avant disillusionment through its protagonist's gradual recognition of local subjugation to globalized forces. In a discussion with an American tourist, for instance, who struggles to understand American cultural imperialism in Canada, Shannon rebuffs his instruction to seize control of the local: "your army would come marching [...] destroy this city in minutes [...] You don't fight the ruling class at a time when it's certain they will win" (158). What hope for a local revolution against an imperialist superpower willing to use force to crush alternatives to its hegemony? Still, revisiting this text at the onset of post-avant experimental writing in Canada helps to re-imagine the disempowered local as a latent site of resistance to the new international paradigm. Hardt and Negri address something along these lines in their second book, *Multitude: War and Democracy in the Age of Empire* (2004), in recognizing the people at the core of class revolt and "the construction of new circuits of communication, new forms of social collaboration, and new modes of interaction [...] moving beyond the modern guerrilla model toward more democratic network forms of organization" (81). The full arrival of these new models into revolutionary space is kept distinctly vague in *Multitude*, as it operates more in its potential than its realization. Similarly, even after conceding defeat to transnational capitalism, Shannon the taxi driver still humours fantasies about life after the revolution. For these fantasies, she is openly mocked: "It sounds like a song, Bradley said. Everybody will carry their own luggage. And when you die you'll go to that great big highway in the sky where there's a flag on every corner and the traffic lights are always green" (157). Including this ironic mockery of revolutionary discourse as mere wishful thinking demonstrates Potrebenko's acknowledgment of the transition away from a revolutionary cultural moment, something Shannon herself concedes: "it didn't appear there was about to be a socialist revolution" (129). However, it also demonstrates that revolutionary fantasies persist despite that loss and, however hollow they may be, continue to provide comfort and hope to the protagonist. Derrida, in *Specters of Marx*, makes much the same point about Marxism after the so-called death of Marxism, arguing that it lingers like a phantom and persists as much by the desire to make it present as by the lingering echoes of Marx's influence.

In *Taxi!*, Potrebenko follows the general aesthetic trend of 1960s and 1970s Vancouver literature in focalizing her imagination onto her own time and space. She trains her language to engage with the local as directly and perceptively as possible. What she records, however, differs dramatically from the projective verse project, Surrealist eruption and feminist rising, and hippie antagono-idealism in her recognition of the ideological machinery employed to prevent change in the local. You cannot find yourself, or follow your bliss, while confined and defined by social determinants. The novel explicitly rejects modernism as represented by both James Joyce and Hermann Hesse for presenting, respectively, either a naïve depoliticized aestheticism or else an easily manipulated mysticism: both, in the end, are perfectly toothless dinosaurs deserving extinction. Instead, the novel anticipates the general disillusionment of the post-avant mode, which is often oriented toward exposing the inevitable compliance and complicity of localized nodes of individual expression, from names to grammar to individual words to oppressive superstructures. The post-avant begins in the discovery that dissent is unimaginable and contrary to Badiou's notion of an Idea, which he defines as "a truth procedure, a belonging to history, and an individual subjectivation" (3). What Shannon and other avant-garde idealists seek is a new Idea, a new truth procedure, the restart of history, and the creation of new liberated subjects. What the post-avant teaches, however, is that this desire, and the rebellions it provokes, is already anticipated and contained by the system that provoked it. History ends when no new Ideas are conceivable. Potrebenko's poetry presents a similar transition to a new truth procedure: in a poem from 1971, she muses on the defining characteristics of life in "the new society" that will emerge post-revolution ("The New Society" 3); by 1983, in contrast, her sense of revolutionary alternatives had decidedly soured: "Marxists support capitalism / in unity against farmers" ("Canadian Agriculture: 1946–1983" 49).

Though the time frame represented in the novel overlaps with the timing of the Gastown riot, Potrebenko opts not to depict or refer to that conflict in any way: perhaps the spectacle of young people fighting police for their rights was too loaded with positive modernist revolutionary symbolism for a novel about the disappointment of revolutionary fervour. Instead, she depicts another hippie outbreak from the period, a riot at a rock concert, that is more suggestive of the empty catharsis of the 2011 hockey riot. The Rolling Stones came to Vancouver in June 1972 for the first time, and, just as the concert began, a riot erupted outside of the Pacific Coliseum by a ticketless throng of thousands seeking to force their way in. While there might have been revolutionary inflections to the historical riot,[5] the politics are dismissed in the novel but for the bare fact that some "crazy hippies wrecked the stadium" (96). Shannon's defence of the hippies that follows the fact is said "without conviction" and leads her into a list of hippie hypocrisies, especially with regard to gender equality. Criticisms of hippie chauvinism became increasingly common in the early 1970s as women lost patience with the hypocrisy, appearing, for instance, in the poetry of Maxine Gadd, where she writes of the "haughty apes of gods that any woman can see their weakness though no concession made for hers till she lose her soul to keep her womb" ("the happy vision gone" 76), and Gwen Hauser, more directly: "What did the underground / ever do for women? // allow you to sleep / with some handsome young stud / and wash his dishes / to the yippee national anthem?" ("What Did the Underground Ever Do For Women" n. pag.). Though they don't address the

---

5 See Mike Culpepper's "The Rolling Stones Riot, Vancouver, 1972," http://shrineodreams.wordpress.com /2012/04/19/the-rolling-stones-riot-vancouver-1971/.

gendered contest specifically, Hardt and Negri recognize the common problem in which "the forms of domination and authority we are fighting against continually reappear in the resistance movements themselves" (*Multitude* 79).

The empty violence in Potrebenko's book signals her sense of the collapse of the revolutionary potential of the hippies, including her own identification with that movement. Historically, outside the text, the Rolling Stones riot was significant for redeeming the integrity and necessity of the RCMP (Royal Canadian Mounted Police), who had lost favour after the ugly violence of the Gastown riot, and for precipitating tighter rules and security in light of the dangerous hippie "mob." The RCMP superintendent Ted Oliver was reported on the front page of the paper the next day as saying, "I'm proud of every one of those bastards I had working for me. They were cool and they were very, very brave" (Honeyman and Bachop 1). The confidence in their rugged heroism completed their physical and discursive triumph over any nascent revolution from the hippie community. In the novel, Shannon explains the failure of the rebellion bluntly in the language of social determinism:

> The shrinking of the middle class accounts as much as the war in Vietnam for the student rebellions of the late 60s. The students saw their future being taken away from them and they were furious, but they lost and are now docile and suckhole a lot since so few of them are going to make it. The rest will be busted into the working class or learn to like LSD and heroin. (66)

Žižek's *In Defence of Lost Causes* (2009) examines an array of cataclysmic twentieth-century losses and failures by the Left in search of moments of political redemption from which to rebuild the crumbled resistance to neoliberal hegemony. His purpose in doing so is less about redeeming the leftist movements of the past than enabling the possibilities of imagining an alternative (which, if nothing else, surely registers how far the radical Left has fallen from power). He looks to the articulation of humanist values in even the darkest chapters of Stalinist Russia and Maoist China and finds encouraging evidence. Even more powerful than these rather obscene examples, though, is his insistence on the dire need to provoke, challenge, and contest the networks of oppression around the world. Without that challenge, the possibility of an event – that is, of the creation of new possibilities – will evaporate. Despite its cynicism, *Taxi!* also suggests a similar glimmer of hope in the midst of failure by describing the hardship of Vancouver as a sign of a "disintegrating society" (100), an assertion Shannon repeats throughout the novel. Change is coming, such a claim implies, because it is necessary. Hope remains a haunting presence, a spectre that is both present and absent, in the midst of hardness – barely there, only just enough to prevent despair. "Whatever happens," she says, "I think it will happen in Quebec first, but then they can't do it all by themselves either. I think taxi-drivers should get organized. I don't know what will happen in the end. There is no end" (159). bissett, too, after being arrested on trumped-up charges of marijuana possession, wrote "a pome in praise of all quebec bombers" ("a pome" 116). In this pique of frustration, terrorism was not beyond the pale.

Beyond Potrebenko's book, by 1975 the paralysis of aesthetic disruption had become widely recognized and increasingly embedded within the art of the time itself. During the October Crisis, seven activists in Vancouver were arrested for distributing FLQ (Front de libération du Québec) literature, revealing that even fundamental rights were subject to the whims of rulers – even a glamourous intellectual ruler like Pierre Elliott Trudeau. The war in Vietnam had not been affected by any of the many protests. War and capitalism marched ever on over the bodies of assassinated resistance figures. The revolution was not coming. A new spirit of jadedness and even cynicism circulated widely. The modernist crisis of representation, with its displacement of authority by the rise of mass cultures and machinated technologies of reproduction, had overwhelmed the role of individual artists, whom Lewis and Pound had once called the "antennae of the race" (Pound, ABC 73). In place of the individual artist leading society forward, the mass media, as Ian Wallace writes, "still reign[ed] as the authoritative model of reality. The avant-garde could only confront this dominance with a symbolic negation at the margins of the culture of the superstructure" ("Photography and the Monochrome" 171). In 1975, Wallace offered a compelling symbolic image of the negation of literary power in the form of two large-scale artworks called *An Attack on Literature: I* and *An Attack on Literature: II* (see Figure 7.3). The series of images in these works depicts a man and a woman balefully interacting with blank pages that have been tossed, presumably by the man. A typewriter sits on the floor, dividing the actors in the scene. The woman is Ingrid Bergman, collaged in from a still of Roberto Rossellini's *Stromboli* (1950). She is sheltering her eyes from the smoke of a volcano.[6] The author, or authors, is/are in despair. In 1968, Roland Barthes argued that literature since Mallarmé had effaced the role of the individual author to the point of its irrelevance, its death ("The Death of the Author" 1323). Appropriately, Wallace's images were conceived as a response to Mallarmé's 1895 essay "The Book: A Spiritual Instrument." But whereas for Mallarmé, the triumph of the world was its distillation into literary form, life for art's sake, if you will, in Wallace's canvases the pages of literature are hauntingly blank. This particular erasure of text signals an end to the possibility of rewriting the world through literature. Intermedia and experimental work carried forth into the new era, but the avant-garde aspiration of Vancouver's intermedial moment was over.

Of all the setbacks that happened in Vancouver in the early 1970s, the most disturbing for the literary community was unquestionably the tragic and brutal murder of Vancouver poet Pat Lowther in 1975. Her spousal homicide, which, as Christine Wiesenthal has well documented, has come to symbolize many things for many different

---

6 Wallace discusses this image in his interview with Stan Douglas (Douglas, "Interview" 111–12).

Figure 7.3 Installation view of Ian Wallace's *An Attack on Literature* (1975).
Source: The Estate of Ian Wallace. Used with permission.

people and groups across the country, also marks the utter shattering of whatever innocence and naïve optimism remained. Lowther was an astute cultural observer, though, and in the emergence of a post-avant moment had already begun re-evaluating the role of the individual author. Inasmuch as her shift away from revolutionary aesthetics triggered her jealous husband, her murder can be thought of as less a symbol for the onset of post-avant disenchantment than a consequence of her engagement with the literature of a new zeitgeist. He was not willing to concede the change, and this conflict of aesthetics (and paranoiac misreadings of her poetry) was at the core of the tension between them: as Wiesenthal writes, his trial "*was* about poetry in the sense that poetry was, inescapably, its main referential frame" (55; emphasis in original). By the time of her death, Lowther had long since broken from the doctrinaire Marxism Roy Lowther championed toward what he dismissively called an "intellectual type of poetry" (qtd. in Wiesenthal 56). She was increasingly experimenting with collage (as previously discussed), new lyricism, and a unique, nascent postmodern text of witness. Roy, a domineering misogynist, found it intolerable and humiliating.

Considering her familial and political situation within the far-Left Marxist communities of Vancouver, Lowther was particularly attuned to the shift away from revolutionary discourse across Vancouver's avant-garde. More specifically, Wiesen-thal highlights Lowther's turn away from the influence of Pablo Neruda, her beloved poet hero, the one she called "the world's greatest poet" ("Regard" 161) and "the dark jewel of history" ("Last Letter to Pablo" 223). Her rejection was a resistance to the "poet as visionary-patriot-sage: a vocation emphatically, exclusively, and immemori-ally male" (Wiesenthal 278). Neruda, it is worth remembering, positioned his own poetic persona as an extension of Walt Whitman's legacy – the pre-modern poet championed by Robert Duncan and Charles Olson in the Vancouver Poetry Confer-ence as the initiator of the literary tradition in which they wrote (leaving space for Wordsworth, too). Whitman, furthermore, was an imperialist poet who envisioned a universal culture (from America) overflowing all national borders, harmonizing the planet in a cosmic synergy predicated on American democracy. In contrast, Lowther was a materialist poet who, like Potrebenko, was increasingly conscious of the replication of oppressive politics, including gendered oppression, within the revolutionary community. In 1971, she published the poem "Woman," which, as in the pregnancy narratives of the same period (indeed, of the same year) discussed in chapter 6, recognizes the shattering of universal culture through female experience: "Remembering lonely sky I became a slave // to the whimpering womb, / that hollow mouth that never says Enough / until too late" (n. pag.).

Her poetry, while never the propagandistic doggerel or jaunty populism of her husband, was always politically attuned. Over the course of the early 1970s, how-ever, it registered the rattling of the political confidence of the far Left by various political currents underway in Canada and beyond. One important example for Vancouver leftists was the 1972 election of the New Democratic Party (NDP; for-merly the Co-operative Commonwealth Federation), a first in British Columbia for a party with openly socialist roots. Their tenure was decidedly a mixed success, however, as they introduced sweeping new reforms to labour relations, but simul-taneously cut funding to universities and arts organizations. Furthermore, in 1972, the Canada Council changed its funding policies and separated literature from the other arts. Categorization and specialization, those bugaboos that bissett had long railed against, were being reasserted as foundational principles for arts funding. The Intermedia Society was a quick victim of the change, dissolving itself that same year rather than face a more gradual and painful dissolution by attrition. It was an ending, writes Nancy Shaw, "that was perhaps a utopian gesture, in that it signi-fied a refusal on the part of the collective to give in to institutional constraints or, worse, become an institution itself" (96). The local interdisciplinary praxis resur-faced with the appearance of the artist-run Western Front centre, which sought to champion radical experimentation within institutional constraints and even, to a certain extent, to become an institution itself. The professionalism they embraced, however, meant an end to the radical imagination of Vancouver arts extending throughout the polis.

4 Neruda, Chile, and Further Disenchantments

The provincial NDP lost the next election in 1975 when the far-Right Social Credit party, under the leadership of W.A.C. Bennett's son William Bennett, a Christian conservative, regained power (and held it until 1991). International politics during the period also witnessed a quick swing from triumph to trough. Following the election of Salvador Allende in 1970, the first Marxist president elected in Latin America, Neruda won the Nobel Prize for Literature in 1971 (in spite of his past public praise for Stalin).[7] On 11 September 1973, however, the Chilean military staged a coup d'état that overthrew the democratically elected government and, with the tacit support of the United States, established a brutal dictatorship under Augusto Pinochet. Neruda died just twelve days after the coup as he prepared to escape Chile for Mexico – officially, he died of cachexia caused by cancer, though others insist he was assassinated.

The literary community was aghast and distraught. Writers like Tom Wayman, Dorothy Livesay, Gerry Gilbert, bill bissett, and Pat Lowther all wrote politically charged elegies for Neruda and for Chilean democracy more generally. Wayman's "the chilean elegies" are published in *Waiting for Wayman* and *Money and Rain* (and reprinted in *For Neruda, for Chile: An International Anthology*). bissett published a poem protesting the murder of Allende and calling for revolt: "change will cum nd thrs mor / uv us poor peopul than them nd / we ar lerning how" ("Chile" 40). Gilbert included a dense collage of headlines relating to the coup and Canada's role in the situation in *Moby Jane*. His text is reminiscent of Audrey Thomas's unravelling conclusion to *Mrs. Blood*, where the collage of public language documents the unravelling of the contemporary (revolutionary) subject. A key measure of agency and possibility disappeared from the literary subject in the march of the Chilean junta over democracy, backed by America and swiftly, perhaps cynically, recognized as a legitimate government by Pierre Trudeau's Canada.

Lowther, for her part, had been writing about Neruda since at least 1972, when she completed a suite of four "Letters to Pablo Neruda." These poems begin to mythologize the poet as a source of "holy water" ("Letter to Pablo 4" 220), a poignant admixture of religious figures (Jesus, Buddha) and epic hero (Odysseus). She added "Regard to Neruda" and "Last Letter to Pablo" to the set of response poems after his death. It is her startling long poem, though, "Chacabuco, The Pit," a 223-line documentary dirge on the brutal treatment of leftist political prisoners taken during the coup, that offers the clearest and sharpest sense of disenchantment: "let

---

7 Such controversy circulated even in Canadian literary circles, where, for instance, George Bowering described Neruda as a "Stalinist assassin" (*Words, Words, Words* 150).

musicians stop building / towers of sound, / let commerce fall / in convulsions: / we have deserved this" (196). The eight-part poem is structured as a grim prayer, with epigraphs taken from Psalm 137, Corinthians 15:52, and an ancient Mayan prayer, that speaks to the onset of despair, of a faith tested to the point of weeping. Psalm 137 also carries a poignant intertext with Elizabeth Smart's *By Grand Central Station I Sat Down and Wept*, where the same image is used to lament the violence of modern life.

For Potrebenko, meanwhile, Chile, and all it had come to symbolize politically, was quickly folded in with all of the other atrocities she had protested and marched against: "If I wasn't walking on picket lines, / I could walk across Canada [...] Several marches about Chile / would have taken me to the turnoff to Ashcroft, / finally limp-ing into Cache Creek / on an International Women's Day march" ("Days and Nights on the Picket Line" 6). It is a compelling and ultimately sad mapping of the terrain that she could have seen, the experiences she could have had had she not been fight-ing for a revolutionized country. A later poem from 1983 includes the confession that "[i]t is sometimes easier now / without the hatred, / without the chanters / except that the number of unemployed grows each year" ("Canadian Agriculture: 1946–1983" 49–50). Hope, here, is buried in a nostalgic reflection on what might have been, in the glimmer faintly gleaming from a barricade of lost causes: announc-ing the arrival of the post-avant, then, after the moment of futurist idealism.

Conclusion – "we stopped at nothing": Finding Nothing in the Avant-Garde Archive

The theme lies in the layers
made and unmade by the nudging lurching
spiraling down from nothing [...]

But still on the highest shelf of ever
washed by the curve of timeless returnings
lies the unreached unreachable nothing
whose winds wash down to the human shores
and slip shoving

into each thought nudging my footsteps now
as I turn to my brief night's ledge
Earle Birney, "November Walk Near
False Creek" (44, 51)

As a gesture toward a conclusion, this chapter leaves the time period in question, leaves the act of mapping out the various avant-garde networks in their unfolding, and assumes its place in the present, looking backward. I have offered throughout this book a series of microhistories of particular nodes of avant-garde collectives in the city and sought to illuminate those groups from the logic of their own formation, drawing attention, meanwhile, to the overarching movement toward increased possibilities for expression, for saying something, including against the strategic erasure of particular voices. In his closing remarks at the Approaching the Poetry Series conference in April 2013, Darren Wershler cautioned attendees against the pitfalls of reifying the ostensible subjects of their research by giving themselves too freely to the service of their stories ("Closing Remarks" n. pag.). The conference was focused on the readers and the poets of the Sir George Williams University (hereafter SGWU) reading series that ran from 1966 to 1975. His message addresses the problem of another generation of scholars paying homage (yet again) to a previous generation of Canadian poets that has not reproduced the means of their own production; that has not provided to the next generation(s) the conditions of material or intellectual or institutional support that they themselves received from the previous generation.[1] Wershler's plea is not just a generational gripe but also a more significant invitation to meditate on the function of the nature and utility of (digital) archival work in the present and to think about how we do the work of remembering the literary past. We change texts radically by translating them into new media, including into history, but the act of doing so does not necessitate our being in control or at least conscious of the changes we impose. In this chapter, then, I seek to register the shift out of the period in question and highlight how the idea of its failure has shaped our understanding of avant-garde work in the 1960s. This conclusion, then, offers a final thematic reading of the idea of failure, silence, and nothingness in the Vancouver avant-gardes 1959–75 as a reflection of the problem that haunts contemporary literary scholarship and microhistories and how such work alters the subjects it purports to represent.

Reflecting on the various approaches to the diverse materials archived in the spokenweb.ca digital repository, the home of the SGWU reading series archive, Wershler invokes various means by which contemporary scholars might approach the material without privileging the subject and by instead increasing engagement with the contemporary moment and its various technologies. The methodology Wershler maps out was once argued by Marshall McLuhan to be somewhat unnecessary, as the content of any medium becomes another medium that has been displaced.[2] The combination of this familiar McLuhanism with Wershler's instruction suggests a latent crisis in contemporary writing and its attendant scholarship: poetry, and the poetry reading series in general, once a means of discovering and advancing new ideas, has been displaced by other cultural modes of enquiry and representation and now serves the more limited role of content within those other especially digital media. While poetry plays a marginal role in the digital environment (even taking into account the rise of social media poetic forms, such as that developed by Rupi Kaur), this process of technological supplication and cultural displacement already occurred with early film, radio, and newspapers.

It strikes me that a model for wrestling with this paradoxical kind of simultaneous engagement with, resistance to, or doubt of the archives already exists in the work of the period in question. By circuitous way of conclusion to this discussion of avant-garde literary production in Vancouver between 1959 and 1975, I would like to return to *Tish* issue #21 discussed in chapter 1, published three years prior to the SGWU reading series in Montreal, as an instructive example in a broader discussion of the

---

1 See "Tish and Koot" by Christian Bök in *Open Letter* 12.8 (2006), and Jason Wiens's "Canonicity and Teachable Texts" response in *Open Letter* 14.3 (2010).
2 McLuhan writes, "The 'content' of any medium is always another medium [...] [but] the 'message' of any medium or technology is the change of scale or pace or pattern it introduces into human affairs" (*Understanding Media* 23–24).

problem of recording, remembering, and archiving. Such a discussion highlights the need for a historical consciousness as well as a technohistorical consciousness of the media involved in historicizing. What is especially striking about the avant-garde in Canada, and in Vancouver in the 1960s and early 1970s, is that they had already confronted and internalized the failure of expression, the boundary of unrepresentability, and the limitations of data, long anticipating the centrality of these issues in the digital archivization of their work. *Tish* 21, as previously discussed, followed shortly after the three-week-long Vancouver Poetry Conference. Having just witnessed the germinal event, and having recently gained editorial control of a definitive local small press magazine, the recently appointed *Tish* editors, David Dawson, Peter Auxier, David Cull, Dan McLeod, Daphne Marlatt, and Gladys Maria Hindmarch, had to make a series of editorial choices about how they would represent the conference. To contextualize the singularity of their decisions, it is worth juxtaposing their work with the much more prominent model of representing the conference via the audio recordings of the event. Former *Tish* editor Fred Wah recorded much of the conference on a 4-track, one-microphone Wollensack recorder. The recordings are consequently mostly monological, focused almost exclusively on the featured speaker of each event, even though attendees regularly comment on the uniquely dialogical nature of their experience in the course. As a result of the technical set-up, questions and comments from the audience and even other panelists are mostly indecipherable, effectively erased from the permanent record. In 2002, the Slought Foundation in Philadelphia built a web portal to house Wah's incredible collection of recorded lectures and readings. The website follows a similar monological orientation as Wah's recording by organizing the database around the names of the primary speakers (the "notable New American poets" described by the website) with no mention of the audience participants, the location, or other details or events surrounding the lectures, discussions, and readings. While the recordings and their internet portal are enormously useful, these resources exclusively privilege the perspective of the singular poet.

Participants at the conference, however, tend to speak of the Vancouver event as having been more collaborative, networked, and heteroglossic than either the recordings or the website suggests. When Robert McTavish asked about the conference's importance, for instance, interviewees Bowering, Copithorne, Marlatt, Butling, Wah, and others all discussed its importance *for themselves* as writers and subjects of the late modernist moment. Furthermore, each of the student participants were required to produce a journal of their experience, as Ginsberg explained, "our journals should be free-floating forms of anything of interest" (Hindmarch, "The Vancouver Conference Poetry Journals" 198). *Tish* 21, which commemorates the Vancouver conference, appropriately responds to this multivalenced experience by not just capturing the voices of great authors speaking, but also realizing: "the only possible form: a type of collage" (Dawson, Editorial 1). Most useful for the *Tish*

Figure C.1 Pauline
Butling, in the Tallman
home on W 37th Street,
in 1963. Photo by
Karen Tallman. Used
with permission.

editors at that time were their impressions and the inspiration they took from the
event. Collage registers an essential multidirectional multiplicity of consciousnesses
simultaneously overlapping and mutually informing. To ask why the *Tish* editors did
not use New American poetics to represent the event is to confront a gap between
the content and the methodology of its archivization. The past was already inaccessible, even as it was being enshrined and archived.

Thinking about the difference between polyvocalic and monological modes of
representation of literary reading series adds a note of doubt about the inevitability or naturalness of either type. This doubt, in turn, provides a key to recognizing
a mark of resistance embedded in the SGWU reading series in the readings and
performances by the poets themselves. After all, the Vancouver poetry scene, and its
aesthetic debates, dominated the SGWU reading series to the point that it is impossible to gloss over the terms and insinuations of those debates when attempting to
address the series historically, geographically, socially, or aesthetically. The series
was organized and hosted by a committee of SGWU English department professors,
including George Bowering and Roy Kiyooka. In private correspondence from the
period, Bowering confessed to having had no connection to the local Montreal literary scene; consequently, he was back in Vancouver by 1971. Kiyooka, also in correspondence, confessed a similar longing to return to Vancouver, and had moved back

Figure C.2 Roy Kiyooka laughs in 1963. Photo by Karen Tallman. Used with permission.

to the city by 1973. The space, place, and debates of Vancouver accordingly domi-nated the planning and organization of the series until at least 1972. It reached the point that Bowering was disciplined by the Department of English, the series' spon-sor, for, among other things, orchestrating their resources to fund his "West Coast poetry friends" (A. Bowering, Letter to Gladys Hindmarch n. pag.). In total, twenty-one of the sixty-six readers featured between 1966 and 1975 (which included three years of readings after the departures of Bowering and Kiyooka) were biographically connected to Vancouver. With regard to SGWU-VPC performance overlaps, four of seven of the featured poets in the VPC also performed at the SGWU reading series.[3] Reflecting the predominance of Vancouver's aesthetic interests in the SGWU read-ing series, another four poets that performed in the series were associated with the

---

3 These numbers are based on the recordings available via the spokenweb.ca recordings of the series. They are, without question, incomplete but also the most authoritative record to date. The very first reading on the website, for insight, begins by describing the night as the "second reading in our fall series." Those connected to Vancouver include, in order of appearance in the series, Phyllis Webb, Roy Kiyooka, Daryl Hines, George Bowering, Robert Creeley, bpNichol, Lionel Kearns, Earle Birney, bill bissett, Gladys Hindmarch, Robin Blaser, Stan Persky, Al Purdy, Daphne Marlatt, David Bromige, Frank Davey, Robert Hogg, Dorothy Livesay, Maxine Gadd, Andreas Schroeder, and George Bowering. Those associated with the Black Mountain school of poets include Margaret Avison, Irving Layton, Diane Wakoski, Joel Oppenheimer, Michael McClure, Robert Creeley, and Robert Duncan.

Black Mountain College school of poets. In other words, half of all readers in the series can be traced back to those deformative three weeks in Vancouver, 1963.

If their cultural inheritance instructed them to value first and foremost the human self, the individual in its broadest understanding, as the conduit for meaningful experience (in a spiritual, political, and historical sense), the mid-decade poets became increasingly attuned to the philosophical, spiritual, and aesthetic potential of the emptied self, and how forms of subjectivity govern us unconsciously. Instead of privileging agency, collage privileges the meaningful revelations of contingency, chance, and selflessness. In the words of Brion Gysin, Canada's first committed collagist author:

> Take your own words or the words said to be "the very own words" of anyone else living or dead. You'll soon see that words don't belong to anyone. Words have a vitality of their own and you or anybody else can make them gush into action [...] Since when do words belong to anybody. "Your very own words," indeed! And who are you?
>
> (*Back in No Time* 132)

Poignantly, one of the first notes in *Tish* 21 is a summary of a lecture by Robert Creeley that outlines the poet's entirely opposite sense of self: "Bob – consciousness, a form that is local, in the person, never exceeds the person" (Dawson, Editorial 3). In many respects, this paraphrase highlights a tension of representation between the monological recordings, which never exceed one person, versus the polyvocal collage of voices of the event itself and into which Creeley speaks. Hindmarch, in her journal of the events, bristled at the physical, unidirectional heirarchy of the VPC classroom: "The situation itself – seventy people, faces pulled in from the front, many of whom know each other from times past, is strange" ("The Vancouver Conference" 198). By the end of the session, she reports a "just this-it's-finally happening [...] feeling to it all" where the students were present, fully present and not lesser participants in the unfolding cutting edge of culture (199). The editorial collective of *Tish* 21 thus creatively represented the stimulating event involving New American poetics in Vancouver by creating a further or ancillary event: the deployment of a new aesthetic technology – the cut-up – which transformed the New American poets and their poetics into the content for a new kind of medium.

So what, then, did the effaced Canadian poets take from the named Americans? The poets in Vancouver, whether from the extended *Tish* group or from the emerging group of Canadian collagist consciousness-raising downtowners, were stimulated into believing that poetry had a role to play for themselves and against the brutal hand of history, as it were. Daphne Marlatt has said, "What was so liberating about that conference was that it was always encouraged: pay attention to where you are, here, now, where you are, here, now" (Marlatt, *The Line Has Shattered* n. pag.). What is particularly illuminating about the *Tish* response to the event, however, is the ease with which the authors incorporated the energy of the event into new aesthetic entanglements. Another account of the workshop in the same editorial expresses the ambivalence of the general animating spirit: "it is very hard to give any specifics. One gets, rather, a 'feel' of the contemporary movement and what its directions will be, and its immediate aims – i.e. an 'atmosphere'" (Dawson, Editorial 10). It was a starting point, not a historical end. Oddly, Burroughs (and silently Gysin) were held up as exemplars for the direction of future writing: "The best way to find out what <u>words</u> are saying, is to cut them up, rearrange them as Burroughs did" (Dawson, Editorial 8). Burroughs is an odd reference precisely because none of the poets participating in the VPC, and none of the previous generation of *Tish* editors, had explored cut-up textuality. His work was discussed, having been brought up by Allen Ginsberg (Bergé, *Vancouver* 9), who was at best an ambivalent champion of the method. Outside of the conference, and in private letters, Ginsberg actively wrestled with or argued against Burroughs for using the technique. In a dream sequence in his *Indian Journals*, he describes the cut-up unfavourably:

> Bill is in room with clippings of Time Magazine & Gysin – he has new method which infuriated the Critics or Bourgeois or someone or me or the *Artistes* are angry again & he's sitting there happily snarling sneers of glee in his suite in mid room – I don't understand it all no more & feel left out & I go to Austria feeling depressed.
>
> (n. pag.; emphasis in original)

In *Tish* 21, the editorial collage makes no mention of Gysin, the Canadian with Vancouver connections from whom Burroughs had learned and developed the technique (Burroughs, "The Cut-Up" 31–33). However, it does echo Gysin's personal philosophy almost precisely when it declares, "The poem is beyond our control. / When we enter the psyche that is in the language we are not entering our personal psyche but rather breaking through it" (Dawson, Editorial 6). Language and poetry become markers and evidence of our (i.e., human subjects, all) alienation, and language's elemental complicity in that alienation, and are not traces of our projection into, or our creation of, the world.

bpNichol, who performed at SGWU in 1968, attempted to come to terms with and articulate the significance of the aesthetic division he witnessed within the Canadian avant-garde literary community. In an unpublished essay written shortly before his Montreal reading, he wrote:

> the avant-garde in Canadian poetry has taken off in two seemingly different directions [...] the one has attempted to make the visual notation of language tie in with the sound of their poems as they write them – Victor Coleman, Dave Cull, George Bowering, Bob Hogg, Fred Wah, Frank Davey, William Hawking, & others. the other has taken the visual notation and extended it till it has become totally visual. ("Last Wall" n. pag.)

Nichol was trying to generalize the difference between the New American writing and the more collagic and visual experiments documented in chapters 1–4 – especially as found in Vancouver's little zines *Blewointment, Circular Causation,* and *radiofreerainforest,* as well as his own Toronto-based *grOnk* magazine and Ganglia Press. It is instructive that Nichol considered the essay to have failed, for whatever reason, and abandoned it. In hindsight, his analysis lacked a sufficiently McLuhan-esque attention to the implications of the different sensory orientations of these two groups. For McLuhan, attention to the singular voice and the sound of the voice projected over a landscape concocted a romantic heroism and a mythological environment. Accordingly, in Warren Tallman's estimation:

> For Olson speech is the Protean thing, the god itself, in a form of words. When on the last evening of the festival he read the conclusion of his Maximus poems, the locale was neither Gloucester nor Vancouver but his voice, his voice reading, which was its own first-last-everlasting place, like life. ("Poets in Vancouver" n. pag.)

In contrast, the collagists and concrete poets were much more suspicious of language and grammar and voice, as articulated in bill bissett's only book of literary theory (notably commissioned by Nichol in 1971):[4] "theyre trying to create yr mind for ya watch it" (*RUSH* 50). The wariness that language is somehow complicit with broader ideological systems elucidates the endeavour to break or destroy language as an attempt to escape its limitations: ignoring its semantic implication, and its spoken tactility, for its visual materiality was one attempt to escape its conceptual boundedness. Gysin's own imperative command to "[r]ub out the word," about as far from Tallman's celebration of the mythological power of language as is conceivable, connected more intimately to Nichol's own literary ambitions and, in McCaffery's terms, bissett's "anti-inscriptional strategies" ("Bill Bissett" 102). Thus, Nichol, in his private journals of 1968, the year of his SGWU reading, similarly wrote: "the space between words is greater than the nothingness of their visible signs" ("Notes on the New" n. pag.). Instead of remaking the world, or projecting oneself into the world through language, this kind of poet seeks out the world behind the arbitrary semiotic system of language and renders it material rather than total, visual rather than vocal. Poignantly, in an interview with George Bowering in 1971, Nichol mused on making a video of his visual works by "cutting them all up" à la Brion Gysin (Bowering, "Cutting" 21). Bowering used the phrase for the title of the interview.

---

4 See Gregory Betts and Derek Beaulieu, Afterword to *RUSH: what fuckan theory; a study uv language* (Toronto: BookThug, 2012), 113–22.

Figure C.3 bpNichol journal entry, 1968. Source: Simon Fraser Collections and Rare Books, bpNichol Fonds, November 1966, "Poems," 12a.9.2. Used with permission of the Estate of bpNichol.

Given its noticeably West Coast orientation, it is fair to characterize the SGWU reading series as the first re-presentation of the Vancouver literary community – or what Bowering called the "Vancouver Renaissance" in his introduction to Lionel Kearns in 1968 – in its full context (i.e., including many of its determining influences) outside of that locale, just as the VPC had been for the New American writers. Though it would be years, indeed decades, before authors and critics began to narrativize the dissolution of the unified 1960s avant-garde, this re-presentation reveals further evidence of the bifurcation of dominant aesthetics in the Vancouver avant-garde community. This divide introduces a significant problem in the archivization of the series, for how does one represent or archive doubt, division, and conflict? It is difficult enough to represent textual communities fairly, but the encoding of friendly fractures that reveal creative openings risks overdetermining those debates. Ignoring them, however, as Frank Davey attempts to do in his recent book on the subject *When Tish Happens*, obscures one of the most productive and essential creative fissures in Canadian literature outside of the ever-repeated nationalist-*contra*-universalist contest.[5] That is, the poetry of a generation of writers defined by a particular locale (Vancouver) at a particular moment (early 1960s) and unified by tight social bonds is marked by a sharp, internal philosophical difference about the role of the poet's language. What is particularly striking is the fact that one tendency of these writers was to *celebrate* this irreconcilability and the failure to arrive at a singular aesthetic as an essential characteristic of their aesthetic philosophy. What I am attempting to show here is that a significant portion of the Vancouver avant-garde poets embraced and explored doubt, absence, and incoherence – what I call the narrative or epiphany of *finding nothing* – directly in their writing.

Two writers who performed in the SGWU reading series, Phyllis Webb and Gerry Gilbert, demonstrate the value in attending to the representation of doubt in their aesthetics: finding nothing in their writing (or performance) implies an acceptance of uncertainty, incoherence, and contingency (i.e., lack of control) as inevitable and essential, clues to a greater cosmology. It is in the uncertain terms of such a cosmology, I contend, that we can discover the first resistance to the reification of 1960s poets and their poetry from within their own poetry and performances. The period has been increasingly narrativized in memoirs, critical studies, films, and various *Festschrifts*, making Vancouver 1959–75 a subject of literary history, subject to the same mythological pull of all historical narratives. Despite this fact, keys to resisting such a distortion are already embedded in the works themselves.

Gilbert, an important figure in the downtown literary scene in Vancouver, and a pioneer in collage and intermedial experimentation, used this doubt and his discovery of nothing as recurrent themes in his writing throughout the 1960s and early 1970s. In 1971, for instance, shortly after Gilbert travelled to Montreal to read at SGWU, he published *And*, a short, limited edition book, put out by bissett's Blew Ointment Press, structured around the concept of cumulative abundance. (His

---

5 Davey also rejects out of hand any difference between the New American writing and the anti-writing by the likes of Gysin, bissett, and Nichol because of the former's use of composition by field and chance-based methods ("The Poetry Reading and Reading Series" n. pag.). Whether or not the New Americans were entirely different from an aesthetic they rejected is a subject for a different context. The strikingly different aesthetics I map out were felt by people in the literary community.

Figure C.4 Gerry Gilbert reading at the Western Front, 1975. Photographer unknown. Source: Private collection of the author.

reading in Montreal largely consisted of readings from this work in progress.) The book features a series of thirty-one minimalist poetic meditations, each between two and fifty-one lines, linked by the eponymous conjunction "AND" in all caps. While the list-poem structure implies abundance, a productive poetic foundry of images and linguistic play, the poems themselves contradict the structure inasmuch as they tend to present negations that undo the appearance of plenty.[6] In one section, for instance, Gilbert writes about Toronto's iconic, countercultural Rochdale College by highlighting the school's disastrous eviction process, highlighting the institutionalized rules for evacuating the student body, emptying itself ultimately. In another, he writes about Vancouver through a self-negating character called nobody: "nobody fucking vancouver / nobody is this fabulous character who lives / on empty mountain / in dusty canada" (n. pag.). Many of these segments were delivered in Montreal, including "AND / Buddha: somebody stole my head again / i sed / AND."

Phyllis Webb, in 1965, the year before her SGWU reading, published a short volume called *Naked Poems* with Vancouver's Periwinkle Press, designed by visual artist Takao Tanabe. The sparse text in *Naked Poems* is as much a meditation on space and the absence of text as it is on bodies and the problem of presence in erotic

---

6 There is also a veiled echo of the (disputably) first concrete poem, Eugene Gomringer's 1952 "avenidas," which is also structured around a cycled use of "and" ("y").

NAKED POEMS
PHYLLIS WEBB

PHYLLIS WEBB
NAKED POEMS

Figure C.5 The cover of Phyllis Webb's *Naked Poems* (1965). Source: Private collection of the author.

encounter: "MOVING / to establish distance / between our houses. / It seems / I welcome you in. / Your mouth blesses me / all over. / There is room" (n. pag.). The paradox of space in this poem highlights the importance of the geography and architecture in which encounter happens: room is the established distance between them, their separation, as much as it is Plato's *khôra* (from *Timaeus*) or Heidegger's clearing; room is the space in which encounter takes place, the precondition that enables the possibility of union and presence. Other texts add meditations on chronology and the difference of textual representation versus experience: "*While you were away / I held you like this / in my mind*" (author's italics). Such a literature begins with absence and the attendant overflow of emotional experience; hence the simile "like this" refers to abstract reflection off the page and out of the world. In both cases, the embodied "perfection with exactitude" that the poem praises of itself requires the lover's absence. Stephen Collis writes extensively of Webb's poetry as one of communion, multitude, and intertextual tribute, but there is a countervailing exploration of absence, negation, and creative destruction in her writing, especially in *Naked Poems*: "walking in dark / walking in dark the presence of all / the absences we have known."

Webb followed up *Naked Poems*, and her SGWU reading, with fifteen years of silence – a period between book publications that many critics use to characterize her writing and career.[7] It is an intriguing fact that critics were led to this conclusion by Webb herself in her next book of poetry, *Wilson's Bowl*, published in 1980 by Toronto's Coach House Press. *Wilson's Bowl* begins with an authorial preface on the theme of nothing: "My poems are born out of great struggles of silence. This book has been long in coming. Wayward, natural and unnatural silences, my desire for privacy, my critical hesitations, my critical wounds, my dissatisfactions with myself and the work have all contributed to a strange gestation" (9). The book addresses the idea of anarchy (itself a politic predicated on the absence of hierarchical governance), especially as articulated and embodied by the life of Russian anarchist Pyotr Kropotkin, but introduces her developing resistance to Marxian and Freudian social analysis. The first section of the book is comprised of poems called "Poems of Failure" that explore the theme of doubt about the ability of the author and her language to represent her subject and the world accurately: "I grasp what I can. The rest / is a great shadow" (13).

Unlike Dennis Lee's disempowering experience of silence triggered by the realization of colonial language as articulated in his 1972 essay "Cadence, Country, Silence: Writing in Colonial Space," wherein the sound of his silence is a measure of his weakness as an interpolated subject in a colony of multiple empires, Webb's experience of silence and even failure is decidedly productive. In an interview with Smaro Kamboureli, Webb explains that "[i]n that fertile silence I am hearing many things and taking in a great deal" (Kamboureli, "Seeking Shape" 25). The fundamental openness to otherness and to the heterogeneous palimpsest of experience reverberates with the spirit of collage and multiconsciousness. Akin to John Cage's iconic silent composition "4'33," which was first performed in 1952, Webb's refusal to speak or sound her voice allows the world to rush into her writing and resound with the presence of absence. Writing is not an attempt to make mythology, or to overcome silence, or to project oneself forcefully against the world, but is a collaboration with silence: "I am not a person who writes everyday. I write when the lid comes off the pressure-cooker and it all arrives in a great rush [...] So I don't think the silence is [...] unnatural" (qtd. in Sujir 35).

Frank Davey, in *From There to Here* and later in *Canadian Literary Power*, argues that Webb's texts are marked by melodrama and failure and that this failing (and looming silence) is a synecdoche for "the end of modernism" (*Canadian Literary Power* 210). Laura Cameron rejects Davey's analysis by noting the productive postmodernism in Webb's shift away from a modernist aesthetic of perfection, universalism, and well-wrought poems for a fragmented poetry that highlights process over

---

7 See, for instance, George Woodcock's "In the Beginning Was the Question: The Poems of Phyllis Webb" (1986), Liza Potvin's "Phyllis Webb: The Voice That Breaks" (1993), Susan Drodge's "The Feminist Romantic" (1996), and Cristina María Gámez-Fernández's "Knowing That Everything Is Wrong: Existentialism in the Poetry of Phyllis Webb" (2007).

final product (n. pag.). In other words, she wasn't struggling with the collapse of one modality, but had already emerged within the postmodern. Indeed, her writing from the 1960s accords well with Bowering's sense of what makes a postmodernist:

> they question authority without having the temerity to offer another, whether Anglicanism, Fascism, history or myth. They are so much disposed against authority that they distrust any signs of it in themselves. They permit the signifiers to slip. Irony cannot, therefore, get a grip. Authors are long gone. Writers disappear among the readers. The very notion of a canon is at best tentative. ("Vancouver" 117)

Cameron's research has also pinpointed the composition dates of the "Poems of Failure" more precisely, from 7–13 September 1967, making these the first extant poems written after both *Naked Poems* and her SGWU reading.

The interest Webb and Gilbert showed in themes and formalisms of absence and negation also points to lingering doubts they possessed regarding the power of their own language, and to their inherent resistance to the God-is-now-speaking aesthetic that Tallman praised in Olson. But because they were writing this theme of negation into their work, rather than having it manifest from their subconscious, it is important to avoid reading the theme through the Freudian-inspired erotics of thanatos that circulated in Vancouver and was common in the popular imagination in the period. The same goes for the Lacanian notion of lack that was then being developed in his 1960–61 *Le transfert* seminar.[8] Instead, I would prefer to enlist another two psychological theorists, Gregory Bateson and Jurgen Ruesch, and their work on vision-*contra*-ideological systems. Of particular value is their concept of negative entropy,[9] which articulates the projection of disorder as the precondition for establishing the semblance of order. Bateson's work in the 1950s argued that there is an intrinsic connection between the visual system and ideology, such that sight itself is linked to and conditioned by the values of the looker. McLuhan would later twist

---

8 Freud used the Greek words for love and death, "eros" and "thanatos," to map out his notions of two drives within each individual: eros for life, creativity, love, and even species preservation; thanatos for death, destruction, hatred, and annihilation. The two drives intertwine, however, as a result of their conflict within the individual. Lack for Lacan, meanwhile, is always connected with desire that fills in the absence of being.

9 Which is different from the negative entropy that appears more prominently in Schrödinger's theoretical physics. Bateson, working from Freud more than Schrödinger, notes that internal desire and the encoding of the external world are intertwined such that our perspective is shaped by psychological and ideological forces (Ruesch and Bateson, *Communication* 177). Negative entropy, in this sense, is the means by which we must negate the actuality of the world in order to maintain an inner sense of order: "Negative entropy, value, and information, are in fact alike in so far as the system to which these notions refer is the man plus environment, and in so far as, both in seeking information and in seeking values, the man is trying to establish an otherwise improbable congruence between ideas and events" (179).

this idea into his delightful aphorism "I'll see it when I believe it." The implication, however, is that both the environment and also space itself must be evacuated, even destroyed, before we can realize or see our visual projections. Seeing and presence happen against the world as it is, and both depend upon unseeing and absence, respectively: the concepts of clearing, space, and *chora* become palimpsests imposed upon already otherwritten perspectives. There is no void upon which something new can be cast. Bateson and Ruesch's analysis of physical perception helps make sense of the semiotic difference between discovery and encounter, where only in the latter is the value of alterity and dialogue recognized. Encounter presages a concern with the erasure and loss precipitated by the act of speaking. Indeed, Bateson and Ruesch's work directly addresses the question of what is seen and simultaneously concealed in the act of looking at and understanding the world.

Taken as metaphor, though more precisely as metonymy, negative entropy helps to account for the eviscerating vision of Vancouver's poets in their appraisal of the socio-political and aesthetic environment. Consequently, absence – as in the absence of ideal forms – is a recurring motif used to characterize the socio-political and cultural landscape prior to the arrival of new kinds of literary and artistic modernisms into the city. The arrival of modernism is frequently set at 1963, with the VPC, but a more plausible date is 1959, when, by coincidence, Robert Duncan and Marshall McLuhan both first lectured in the city, Tallman began his public advocacy of New American aesthetics among his students, and Kenneth Patchen began working with Al Neil in poetry-jazz experiments and collaborations. Privileging the arrival of particular modernisms into the city involved the displacement of existing aesthetics: every other form of literary production happening in the city was reduced, defaced, or entirely effaced through this projection of a new, dominant modernism. Indeed, I have framed this chapter with an epigraph from a poem by Earle Birney, one of those poets so displaced, to acknowledge a continuity of aesthetics between Vancouver's modernisms, which stands in contrast to the narrative of the breakaway or oppositional new. To put this into concrete terms, *Tish* did not publish – indeed, steadfastly refused to publish – any Vancouver or Canadian writer that preceded them. *Blewointment*, in sharp contradistinction, published many of them, including work by Birney, Dorothy Livesay, Webb, Milton Acorn, Nellie McClung, and many others. The difference confirms the respective positions of *Tish* and *Blewointment* on multiplicity and alterity, and their willingness to represent Canadian literary history, including circulating and competing modernisms. As Tallman famously and fatuously characterized Vancouver in a group conversation with *Tish* poets in 1985, there had been writers "working in isolation," but there had been "no coherent scene whatsoever" prior to his own arrival and prior to *Tish* (Niechoda and Hunter 85). After that opening remark to the group, Gerry Gilbert immediately objected to Tallman's negation of the rest of the city's arts production by reminding him of the downtown poets, who were already active at the time. *Tish*ers Gladys Hindmarch and Frank Davey added credence and other evidence to Gilbert's objection, but none of them in that conversation cast even a passive eye at the writers before their generation.[10] This familiar negating narrative by those who came of age in the 1960s was intended to highlight the importance of the arrival of an active, vibrant modernism (or modernisms) into the city, but, as Bateson's theories of negative entropy suggest, the narrative equally erased extant modernisms and other modes of literary production already being practised by the likes of Birney, Dorothy Livesay, Malcolm Lowry, and Emily Carr, as well as the avant-gardisms of Jack Shadbolt, Lawren Harris, Al Neil, and Anne Charlotte Dalton, let alone the backdrop of a cultural genocide against the Indigenous inhabitants of the land that was then still unfolding across Canada. Bowering openly, gleefully confessed: "the poems actually became not only the making of poems but the making of history for us, and a geography for us and a mythology for us, for which we were absolutely reviled by those people back east" (Bowering et al. n. pag.). Gilbert objected to this claim, too, by reminding Bowering that the downtown poets also reviled the characteristic *Tish* "pomposity" (Niechoda and Hunter 85). It is perhaps for this reason that Gilbert wrote in his 1964 "Poem on a Folded Postcard" the instruction: "Do not believe / Vancouver" (n. pag.).

Gilbert, for his part, was distinctly more aware of both a palimpsestuous relationship among practising writers to the literary historical inheritance of Vancouver and British Columbia and of the existence of competing aesthetics in the city's past and present. His *BC Monthly* magazine, a follow-up project to his delightfully, deliriously messy *radiofreerainforest*, took its name from a collapsed literary publication from the 1920s as tribute and homage to the history of writing in the province. The first issue of the magazine had a special feature on a similar-minded endeavour to rethink and repurpose British Columbia's cultural heritage. It focused on the Deluxe group, an anarchist band of guerrilla activists bent on purchasing, and then repurposing, Bralorne, an abandoned mining town in the BC interior – the kind of interior ghost town used to house displaced Japanese Canadians in the Second World

---

10 In a similar manner, though, both the *Tish* and the downtown poets used the trope of the discovery of absence, and the destruction of that absence, to articulate their own presence as individual and collective poets. Thus, the interest in the proprioceptive act, presence, and the discovery of locale, or what Tallman has called the story of "[h]ow people come to possess their own imaginations" (qtd. in Niechoda and Hunter 84), begins with the encounter with margins, empty fields, and unwritten, unimagined landscapes. The writing itself begins with the discovery of nothing, of a space for new writing. This interest in bringing "Vancouver into presence," as Tallman writes in a different context (*In the Midst* 26), was not just a neo-colonial *Tish* aesthetic, deputized by the proper American authorities, but one that can be found echoing across other Vancouver forums such as the *Georgia Strait Writing Supplement*, *Iron*, *Blackfish*, and *Talon* little literary magazines. That last Tallman quote, for instance, comes from the first issue of Gilbert's *British Columbia Monthly* in a review of a new book by Stan Persky published by the *Georgia Strait Writing Supplement*. It is worth noting that outside the *Tish* group, some of those responsible for bringing the New American poetics to Vancouver, such as Stan Persky, George Stanley, and obviously Robin Blaser, originated or had significant links to the San Francisco literary community or could count themselves as legitimate contributors to its renaissance.

ISSN 0382-5272

VOLUME III   NUMBER 1   OCTOBER 1976

*

letter from HP
TRY IT collage by GREGG SIMPSON
ROY KIYOOKA & DAPHNE MARLATT IN CONVERSATION
TOM BURROWS & ROY KIYOOKA IN CONVERSATION
ARTIST & TYONEK ALASKA JULY 4 1971 by CAROLE ITTER
WHERE WERE YOU MONDAY AFTERNOON? by GERRY GILBERT
CUT OFF AT THE BROKEN ARMS by PAUL DE BARROS
5 POEMS by BRAD ROBINSON
THE GAME & THE LAKE by DAVID PHILLIPS
SINBAD THE GOOD & THE UGLY by BLANDIE & DOGWOOD
RECENT MURDERS NEAR WINDY POINT & BRIDGE LAKE by BRETT ENEMARK
3 STORIES by ANN IRELAND
CONVERSATIONS WITH MY MIND by PETER HLOOKOFF
LITTLE SOUNDS ALL OF WHOM AGREE by RAVING PAVAN(E)
BIRTHMARK by MARYBETH KNECHTEL
GEEK by SARAH SHEARD
BAJA CALIFORNIA by CAROLYN BORSMAN
CHINA by MALCOLM LOWRY
A LETTER & 2 POEMS FROM PINANG MALAYSIA by DAPHNE MARLATT
ORIENTAL SAGES by PAUL DRESMAN
EGUCHI by KOMPARU ZENCHIKU/TRANSLATION by SONJA ARNTZEN
ISRAEL SELLS PLUTONIUM TO SOUTH AFRICA by BOB ROSE
AN INTERVIEW WITH BRUCE LACEY
THE PHANTOM WITH THE VELVET EARLOBES by FIELDING DAWSON
AN INTERVIEW WITH VIC D'OR
VIC D'OR AT PARACHUTE CENTER CALGARY by VICTORI-AWE
TO MATTHEW by ANTONY
EXORCISE by PENNY CHALMERS
POEM by DAVID UU
FORT ST. JOHN by ALASTAIR MACLENNAN
A MARRIAGE CEREMONY FOR KAREN TALLMAN & BRIAN DEBECK by ROBIN BLASER
THE CEREMONY photo by TAKI BLUESINGER
CANADA'S TOP POET/VIC D'OR photo by TAKI BLUESINGER
linocuts by HAND STAMP ONLY
*
Copyright © 1976 reserved for the authors artists & their estates
*
EDITED & PRODUCED AT THE NEW ERA SOCIAL CLUB by GERRY GILBERT & BOB ROSE

CANADAS NATIONAL MAGAZINE
BOX 48884 VANCOUVER V7X 1A8 CANADA

Figure C.6 Cover of the *BC Monthly* 2.2 (February 1974). Source: Private collection of the author. Used with permission.

War. The Deluxe group had grown out of the Intermedia Society artists' collective, where they had learned to repurpose wood scraps into ever increasingly elaborate projects. They experimented with houses made entirely out of driftwood in Burrard Inlet (which the city quickly demolished) and later hosted elaborate "Pleasure Faires" where thousands of people would gather and make mischief without electricity for a weekend or more.

With a core group of twelve people, Deluxe had, on special occasions, between five hundred and three thousand active volunteers on their projects, which themselves drew thousands of attendees. The Bralorne mining village project was by far their most ambitious event in its attempt to establish a permanent home for their "social form" (Ridgeway et al. n. pag.). With "hundreds" of people prepared to move into the village they tried to create, they spent three months working with the Gold Dust Twins Settlement Society on the plans until the federal government intervened and overruled the intended resettlement (Ridgeway and Clemons 10). The way the Deluxe group imagined the effect of the repurposed town site is instructive: it would, among other things, correct "the gnawing apprehension that something is missing in [Canadians'] daily lives" ("The Bralorne Papers" 8). They thought of their initiative (even after the Bralorne failure) in distinctly revolutionary terms, punning on their commitment to a return to a "natural vacuum of responsibility [...] Revolution is re-cycling old materials. Re-cycling revolution is Deluxe" (Ridgeway and Clemons 8). The collage mindset had evolved into repurposing geography (though no thoughts were spared for St'at'imc people of the Nxwísten First Nation, on whose unceded territory the abandoned mine sits).

While it is easy to dismiss the hippie naïveté of the Deluxe Bralorne project, it is worth noting that their idealistic vision of potentials for urban life was similar in spirit, if not in kind, to celebrated architectural avant-gardists such as France's Le Corbusier, whose "Plan Voisin" for Paris was supposed to overcome the "appalling nightmares" of modern civic space (Le Corbusier n. pag.). Plan Voisin involved bulldozing an enormous swath of Paris, not unlike Hausmann's remodelling of the city before him, and would have literally rewritten the city in a grand repurposing of urban space. Like the British Columbians, however, Le Corbusier's motivating ambition was predicated on a rejection of the automobile and a realignment of urban space with nature: "You are under the shade of trees, vast lawns spread all round you. The air is clear and pure; there is hardly any noise." Silence was imagined as an anti-modern luxury, something to uncover and recover from the harsh clang of modern life. The Bralorne project was a similarly highly ambitious utopian effort intended to address the emptiness, the alienating impact, of urban space. It stands as evidence of the new possibilities opened up by the experimental praxis of the downtown Vancouver literary community – an earnest attempt to break through the hollowness of the colonial culture they inhabited and to re-imagine their locus through repurposing its refuse. In Gilbert's words, it was a "Big Try" (Letter to Sam

Abrams n. pag.). Such utopian projects and projections depend upon the destruction
of the past, especially the recent past, including its presumed failures. Such projects
signal the presence of a desire that needs to be filled, and a consciousness of that
ideological emptiness. The Bralorne failure was a significant symbolic loss for the
avant-garde in Vancouver: in Ian Ridgeway's words, "[p]erhaps that was the point
where the heady enthusiasm of the 60s turned into the tough-minded experience of
the 70s" (Ridgeway and Clemons 10).

All the while the Deluxe group was attempting to re-imagine the possibilities of
space and community, and repurpose the wasted materials created by urban expansion, the downtown poets and some of their newfound allies at *Tish*[11] were discovering the enormous potential of the wasted space of the poetic page. This spatial
consciousness depends upon seeing value in things deemed valueless, seeing through
absence to the possibility of presence. It follows that a consciousness of the presence
of absence also haunts the concrete and visual work of the period produced in the
same downtown milieu. David UU's essay "Beyond Concrete Poetry," published in
the third issue of Gilbert's *BC Monthly*, articulates the ambitions of that movement
as evacuating the surface content of language and struggling to encounter "what is
behind language" (n. pag.). He quotes bissett's poem "Young Masters of Pinto" on
the double negation that enables presence and writing in the concrete mode: "here,
now / writing this poem, / not knowing death / we derive form / from [...] it is the
dead / we thrive on, / that lulls us, ourselves, / into ghost wrappers." Recovering a
vaguely defined, more likely intuited, lost unity begins for UU by recognizing the
absence at the heart of our contemporary language: "not only are letters meaning-
less but naturally so are words and sentences and paragraphs." The rush to fill the
whole (empty) page partakes in rediscovering the magical, alchemical potential of
art that has been lamentably lost and in seeking new reanimated alphabets, words,
sentences, and paragraphs that could overcome the present absence. If you will
excuse the obvious allegory, the alphabet was not unlike an abandoned gold mine
they were hoping to revive.

Negation, then, seen as a self-inventing creative destruction or the space of
redemptive opening, or re-cycling revolution, proliferates in the avant-garde imagination in Vancouver. It collects the loose discourse surrounding negative theology
from especially Zen Buddhism[12] and negative philosophy from Nietzsche, Dada,
post-structuralism, and eventually Deconstruction, and even incorporates select
notions from quantum physics to acknowledge the importance of nothing within

---

11 Ian Ridgeway tells a lovely anecdote of *Tish* editor Peter Auxier discovering thirty-six-foot-long slabs of
old-growth lumber in a demolished factory and working with Deluxe to salvage the wood before it was
turned into backfill and lost. They salvaged thirty thousand pieces of the "priceless" lumber (Ridgeway and
Clemons, "Deluxe Text" 13–14).
12 As Gerry Gilbert mused: "Yeah, Zen was there" (Bowering et al., "Vancouver" n. pag.).

the essence of everything. Thus, Gilbert writes almost triumphantly, "I find / noth-ing / in these poems" ("Babyland" n. pag.). In *Naked Poems*, Webb writes that she is sad because "all my desire goes / out to the impossibly / beautiful" (n. pag.) – a beauty that is changed by desire, destroyed by the act of claiming it; hence its impossibility. Webb's texts and Gilbert's texts are both haunted by the destruction, the loss, of the conditions that enabled them: the pure rawness of nothing, the potential field before presence, and the impossibility for desire to fulfil itself. In the words of Alexan-dre Kojève in his famous lecture on Hegel that helped to launch post-structuralism: "Born of Desire, action tends to satisfy it, and can only do so by the 'negation,' the destruction, or at least the transformation, of the desired object [...] Thus, all action is 'negating'" (Kojève 4). The poems by Webb and Gilbert presented in their Mon-treal readings, while enacting this negation,[13] are already meditations on the conse-quences of eviscerating this thing that they desire.

Gerry Gilbert, "Song for the French Revolution, May 1968"

(LIBERTE, FRATERNITE, ET SENILITE)

but words for beauty of revolt are uncommon
uncummin to my lips tongue held tween teeth:
blood of sunsets is extraneous to us
who are lost in the flag of dreams

(MANDALA, MANTRA, AND YANTRA)

thru which we move like pawns,
sometimes weeping, sometimes laughing,
sometimes weeping laughing i can tell yu
of the glaciers i've seen
in hearts of GOVERNORS as we melt

---

13 Furthermore, in Kojève's words: "Generally speaking, the I of Desire is an emptiness that receives a real positive content only by negating action that satisfies Desire in destroying, transforming, and 'assimilating' the desired non-I. And the positive content of the I, constituted by negation, is a function of the negated non-I." Desire itself "is but a revealed nothingness, an unreal emptiness. Desire, being the revelation of an emptiness, the presence of the absence of a reality, is something essentially different from the desired thing, something other than a thing, than a static and given real being that stays eternally identical to itself" (5). Self and subjectivity are generated through this difference.

in each other's furnace, climbing pinnacles
of pentacles in frenzy to be whole(d.
(n. pag.)

"trip: Kokanee – Banff, Summer '70"

"there is mysticism that is
revolutionary
/one of "hair raisng [*sic*] liberation"
not CONTROL
is is is more
   areas of consciousness
          central mind
        th warp at high velocity
      matter-parabola becoming
     measured by mind's constructs
& what are we to do.

    the CITY, Vancouver & environs
   where there is a 13,000 year
     record of human life

In Derrida's discussion of various resistances to analysis, he claims that categories of truth (especially as established by psychoanalysis, but also, by extension, literary analysis and archivization) can be disputed convincingly only through disavowal, which ruptures the possibility of a truth claim from within a discourse. It is a useful theory by which to consider the notion of discovering or uncovering an abyss of nothingness at the heart of the language of the poem that these poets are writing. Similarly, Gilbert proposes that when "the silence arrives at the fact," the presence of this absence enables "a single uninterrupted poem / by means of the most direct and shortest image" ("Metro" n. pag.). Webb's *Naked Poems*, with its erotic minimalism, presents a similar anti-Imagism that marks the creative act with or by its own withdrawal: "You took / with so much gentleness / my dark" (n. pag.). Taking darkness is different from asserting or projecting presence, for it achieves presence only through double negation. For both Gilbert and Webb, the poetry performs a similar double negation: a disavowal that performs the collapsing of the possibility of poetry through the language of poetry. In the SGWU readings, both of these writers read works that articulate just such a strategic disavowal – including, specifically, a disavowal of work, performance, and the community of those gathered to hear them.

Given this thematic, theoretical, and practical interest in nothing and its corresponding link to disavowal, what particular challenge does this insistent nothingness pose to scholars and archivists seeking to preserve and represent these events, these performances, and these naked – denuded – poems? The SpokenWeb project has already made some progress in addressing this problem by including transcriptions of the readings in which both authors insist upon the incompleteness of the poems presented, as well as the inevitability of frustrated desire in the aesthetic act. Gilbert makes the prophetic joke in the middle of his performance that "[w]e're reading Canadian History" – an aside that is significantly the only extemporaneous comment he makes during his entire eighty-eight-minute set that he splits with David McFadden. While stage banter affords the audience the impression of presence and spontaneity, Gilbert's joke in contrast serves to deny his presence in the moment by insisting upon its historical inscription, as if enacting an absence or drawing attention to the gap between himself and his own writing. It is worth pointing out that Gilbert and McFadden read their work as a spontaneous dialogue, oscillating voices after a stanza or two, creating new tensions and sparks in their individual works by the sudden multiplicity and juxtaposition. While it is unclear who suggested the strategy, or why they chose to present their work this way, the strategy opens up their work to new intersections and dislocutions by chance encounters. It attempts to perform the dissembling spirit of collage. A schism opens up between the books read and the singularity of the collaged performance: the reading is unique, though the texts are already history. Gilbert would repeat the dialogic technique on reading tours with Daphne Marlatt years later, demonstrating some satisfaction with the experiment, and a willingness to repurpose a good idea.

Webb, pursuing a different performance strategy, makes numerous contextual remarks but also explicitly reminds her audience of the incompleteness of her reading. She describes texts she won't read and announces the insufficiency of her own voice to read her poems:

> I don't think I have the voice to read both sides of this poem tonight, there are two poems, one called "Breaking" and one called "Making." They're about the creative process, which involves both those things, but "Making" is rather long and a little hard to read, so I'll read "Breaking" which is better probably as a poem.

The irony of this announcement is poignant: making is hard, and because it involves breaking, she reads only a poem she has made called "Breaking," with its theme of creative destruction, and thereby avoids redundancy. The poem "Breaking" launches its own exploration of absence, rupture, and the predication of language on an impossible-to-fulfil desire: "Give us the wholeness, for we are broken. / But who are we asking, and why do we ask?" By transcribing only her extemporaneous remarks and not the poems about absence, the SpokenWeb website archive privileges the reading event and Webb's denial of its authority and completeness. Desire is unfulfilled even for those at the origin of this venture: those in attendance at the original reading. It leads one to imagine a transcription of the Vancouver Poetry Conference featuring only the audience dialogue, or only the "square" interruptions that frustrate Hindmarch and Ginsberg ("The Vancouver" 199) and that disappear in the Wah recordings, or a *Blewointment* version in which author names are completely stripped from all participants. These are all options in rendering the data of a poetic inheritance visible to present and future generations. Doing a numbers count based on gender, race, or sexual orientation is another way of making the hidden but inherent properties of communities visible. Another poem, "Rilke," that Webb reads speaks in splintered time signatures: "this page is a shadowed hall in duino castle. echoes the echoes. I don't know why I'm here." Poignantly, Ginsberg opened his first lecture in the VPC by admitting a similar disavowal: "I don't know what I'm doing here" (qtd. in Hindmarch, "The Vancouver" 198). Self-deprecation also helps to establish presence.

Conceptualizing the digital archivization and historical narrativization of this Canadian 1960s avant-garde praxis and poetics requires thinking beyond the historical anachronism of the recordings. The problem of rendering the reading series (and the Vancouver scene, in general) across multiple technological shifts is substantial, in this case moving from page to spoken word to analogue recording device to digitized translation and to online platforms where the hiss of the original cassette suddenly seems oddly organic and authentic. The persistence of the readings, now recast in the digital archives, provokes both a historical consciousness as well as a technohistorical consciousness of the media involved in historicizing. This haunting absence-presence has led me to digital media theorist Alexander Galloway's useful question "Are some things unrepresentable?" which becomes an essential problem when the task is representing texts that celebrate their insufficiency, their doubt, and their discovery of nothing *textually* or even *orally* with a voice speaking against its own speaking. Galloway distinguishes between data, the things that have been given (81), and information: "The worldly things, having previously been given, have now been given form" (82). For Galloway, following Jacques Rancière, the question of unrepresentability stems from the transformation of data into the realm of the aesthetic as information because "representation always has a relationship with the mode of production, not simply the ideological conceits and tricks of state power that are its epiphenomena" (92). Hence, how and why something is represented changes data in a manner at least analogous to Bateson's negative entropy, where the destruction of the world is precipitated by the act of perception. For Bateson and early post-structuralists, the determining agent was ideology, but post-Heideggerian contemporary media archaeologists, especially Wolfgang Ernst with his notion of the *fundus*, argue that the machinery used to represent data creates the perception by which ideology is encoded: as Ernst writes, "our perceptions are dependent on the signal-processing capacities of our devices" (17). Galloway makes a useful link between ideology, technology, and the society of control that Foucault warned about in the use of technology to prevent access to radical ideas. At the very least, when we return to the literature of the 1960s and 1970s, this technoconsciousness changes the orienting question from "what was it?" to "what are we doing to it?" The great irony that this chapter has tried, inevitably in vain, to highlight is that both Webb and Gilbert disrupt the possibility of an "it," of raw data in their reading and in their poetry. The "it" we recuperate, to protect and disseminate, is already information but, more point-edly, is really an arrow pointing at nothing; pointing, in fact, at a desire within the looker that can never be satisfied; "it" is an impossible beauty. As Webb writes in her poem "In This Place" from *Wilson's Bowl*: "We quake. We draw curtains / against the word's blaze" (66). It is at this stage that Lacan might become useful in addressing this complicated post-semiotic desire and lack, but that is a different project for a different book (but consider Clint Burnham's *The Only Poetry That Matters*, on the Lacanian inflection of Vancouver's Kootenay School of Writing, a great starting point in just such an investigation).

Finding nothing in the poems of avant-garde Vancouver 1959–75, however, evokes a threat acknowledged by Bateson, Derrida, McLuhan, Galloway, and Ernst of technology's destructive function that changes perception as it uncovers new ways to in-form data. To address Wershler's concern with which I began this conclusion, in that process, yet poignantly against that process, the poetry of both Gilbert and Webb encodes a disavowal that undoes the possibility of both poets' own memorialization from within.

Taken as metonymy for this project as a whole, the question of how to tell the story revolves around the even more central problem of what the story is and how it might be told without recourse to the archetypes of literary form. In the move from projective optimism through to avant-garde intermediation, in the shift from colonial violence to creating forums for oppressed voices to be heard (setting up the generations of radical work that has followed), the period in question already contained an awareness of its incompleteness and its unsettledness. Every individual mentioned in this book had a different experience of and set of opinions on the period in question. To record everything that took place, poem by poem, reading by reading, book by book, what was said and what was done, is a massive task worthy of Benjamin's *Arcades Project* or perhaps a Borgesian to-scale mapping as in his story "On Exactitude in Science." It might not, however, be useful here and now for enabling scholarly and literary extensions of the period, which is ultimately the hope for this review of a previous avant-garde: the instigation of further events that will continue to re-imagine the inaccessible past. The only possible form is a series of impressions, mixed with facts, gossip, literature, art, and images: in the end, only a type of collage.

Gary Lee-Nova, *A Small Electrical Storm in Element County* (1973; verso).
Used with permission. Collection of the Morris and Helen Belkin Art Gallery.

Appendix A:
Warren Tallman Elegy

Date: Tue, 5 Jul 1994 08:31:59 EST
Sender: UB Poetics discussion group
From: Robert Creeley
Subject: Warren Tallman

We've had the sad advice from his family that Warren Tallman died yesterday (July 4) in Vancouver, British Columbia, thankfully at home and without difficulty. It's hard to imagine the present fact of Canadian poetry and its relation to our own sans the immense effort which Warren Tallman made in his years as a teacher at the University of British Columbia, and, even more, as the indefatigable reader and friend of all the defining poets of both countries. In 1962, for example, Warren's students at UBC included Daphne Marlatt, Fred Wah, George Bowering, Gladys Hindmarch, Lionel Kearns, and David Bromige, among many others. The landmark 1963 Vancouver Poetry Conference was almost entirely Warren's remarkable invention, bringing together for the first time a decisive company of then disregarded poets such as Denise Levertov, Charles Olson, Allen Ginsberg, Robert Duncan, Margaret Avison, Philip Whalen and myself, together with as yet unrecognized younger poets of that time, Michael Palmer, Clark Coolidge and many more. Be it said that Warren wrote the first decisive piece on Jack Kerouac's skills as a writer, "Kerouac's Sound," published in the Evergreen Review. Donald Allen and he subsequently edited together POETICS OF THE NEW AMERICAN POETRY, a crucial backup of Don's initial anthology which, seemingly, changed everything. Warren's two substantial collections of essays report and review the tenets of poetry which underlie the revolution he had so much to do with.

All that can finally be checked out. What will be sorely missed is the singular insight and invention Warren brought to his relations with poetry and poets. He was a great reader, a great, great heart. Defined by the American Great Depression, he believed absolutely that books mattered, that what people can think of and so imagine is true, that it can really happen. So it was that he brought Robert Duncan first to Vancouver, to talk with his students in a series of meetings, all managed by the money they could themselves modestly and communally provide. Jack Spicer's last articulate lectures were fact of the same circumstance. I was able to teach for a year at UBC at a time when virtually no other job was possible, just that Warren BELIEVED. I cannot overemphasize the significance of such a power. It's as if Warren brought not only the US and Canada together in such interests, but that he really brought western Canada's poetry into the international world it now helps to define and keep possible.

Well, this can be the beginning, I hope, of what can now continue as Warren's work: bringing it all home, keeping the beat, making that joyful sound. Warren loved the sense of "mother tongue" always. He really knew how to listen.

Here's to you, brother, forever.

Robert Creeley

Appendix B:
Concrete Poetry

Edwin Varney, "Concrete Poetry," 1968:

Concrete – actual, real, immediate to experience, not abstract or general, the thing itself; as poetry, the graphic union of word as symbol for meaning and the poem as object. The poet's craft consists in somehow suspending the flux of experience as it eddies around him. The jewel in the whirlpool then, the poem itself must be placed before the reader's eyes like an explosion. "how can the poet reach out and touch you physically as say the sculptor does by caressing you with the objects you caress?" asks bpNichol who, answering goes on to say that the poet "creates a poem/object for you to touch and is not a sculptor for he is still moved by the language and sculpts with words."

The poem as object, sculptural or graphic, is as old as writing, Oriental pictograms, as well as Egyptian and Babylonian hieorglyphics [*sic*], are, to our eyes, just that – pictures which speak as language does. These early languages make sense through the eye's understanding, English mainly through the ear. [...] Concrete respects the integrity of the poem as object. The original itself must be the source for all reproductions. Language is treated as design as well as the medium for ideas. Just as each poem is a separate hieroglyph, a whole new language is built out of the totality of a poet's work; each poem is the basis for a new alphabet.

But since concrete poetry depends upon immediate reaction, it excludes the whole realm of myth from poetry. Since it is not linear there can be no sense of progression, no plot or story, no structuring of time elapsed. Concrete consequently eliminates the high voice, the diction of moral purpose and piety which has characterized most great western poetry.

Appendix C:
Glossary of Intermedia and Transdisciplinary Groups

The Cellar Musicians and Artists Society (1955–65): This jazz co-operative emerged in response to the rise in interest in jazz in Vancouver, as well as against the restrictive liquor consumption laws in the city. Famed for attracting top-drawer jazz performers (Charles Mingus, Coleman Hawkins, Pepper Adams, Don Cherry, etc.) to the city, it was also the site of Kenneth Patchen and Al Neil's collaborations in combining jazz and poetry. The Cellar staged a series of productions of plays by Samuel Beckett.

The New Design Gallery/Arts Club (1958; name changed to the hieroglyphics Arts Club Theatre): Founded by Bob Orchard, Jane Rule, Helen Sonthoff, Abraham Rogatnick, and Alan Balkind to create a forum for public lectures, readings, and performances. Marshall McLuhan gave his first lecture in Vancouver at the club, and later Lawrence Ferlinghetti performed with his avant-garde orchestra.

The Festival of the Contemporary Arts (1961–71): Conceived as an annual event by B.C. Binning and Charles Lankester to highlight the activities and interests of the new UBC Fine Arts Department, the FoCA evolved into a marquee event for North American avant-garde artists and thinkers. Guided by the philosophy of Marshall McLuhan, each iteration explored cutting-edge and intermedia work, featuring artists like Michael McClure, Andy Warhol, Jasper Johns, Ed Ruscha, Jack Spicer, Robert Duncan, and many others. Tensions emerged on campus about whether the festival should serve of niche coterie of experimentalists or the wider campus audience.

The Sound Gallery/Motion Studio (1966): Anticipating the Intermedia Society, the Sound Gallery grew out of musician and painter Gregg Simpson's studio and developed a space for interdisciplinary, events-based programming. Helen Goodwin orchestrated a multimedia dance and poetry series. Prominent participants included Sam Perry, Gregg Simpson, Judith Copithorne, Al Neil, Gerry Gilbert, and Gary Lee-Nova.

The Mandan Ghetto Gallery (1967): A co-operative gallery on 4th Avenue, orchestrated by bill bissett, Gregg Simpson, and Ian Wallace. The gallery lasted just seven months but hosted some of the most important exhibitions during the period, including two Dada-inspired literary-collage shows, and *Brazilia 73*, the first international exhibition of concrete poetry in Canada.

The Intermedia Society (1967–72): Inspired by the theories of Marshall McLuhan, the Intermedia Society was formed to explore the sensorium of art across the disciplines. Members included Werner Aellen, Iain Baxter, Michael de Courcy, Kate Craig, Arthur Erickson, Gary Lee-Nova, Glenn Lewis, Eric Metcalfe, Michael Morris, David Orcutt, Al Razutis, Jack Shadbolt, Vincent Trasov, Ed Varney, Gerry Gilbert, et cetera. Intermedia ended when federal funding dried up.

Intermedia made one of the first contributions anywhere in the world – and certainly in Canada – to a particular kind of collaborative avant-garde. The element of collaboration was rooted in a strong, functional democracy that demanded a loose-limbed, flexible, less-structured, co-operative approach to artistic endeavour. (Alvin Balkind, "On Ferment and Golden Ages," in *Vancouver Forum: Old Powers, New Forces*, 1992)

The New Era Social Club (1969): A co-operative arts and literature collective established the premises that became the centre for various groups, including the Image Bank, Intermedia, and the Vancouver Poem Company.

Intermedia Press (1969–81): The official book publishing arm of the Intermedia Society made creative use of the society's Roneo four-colour mimeo printer. The press actually outlived Intermedia by almost a decade, during which time they published fifty-five books of poetry and more than fifty books of prose work. The press's publications were edited by Ed Varney and Henry Rappaport, as well as John MacDonald for a time. As Ed Varney said, "We thought of ourselves as publishers of the 'downtown' writers, the eclectic, avant-garde, marginalized, emerging writers and poets who, for the most part, weren't associated with the academics at Simon Fraser University, UBC, or the poets associated with Tish" ("Publishing" n. pag.).

The Vancouver Poetry Front (1969–71): A collaborative poetry performance group that explored and pushed the boundaries of the poetry reading. For instance, on 14 November 1969, to acknowledge his 212th birthday, the group held a continuous reading of the work of William Blake from noon until 9:30 p.m. at the UBC Fine Arts Gallery. Members of the group included Judith Copithorne, Ed Varney, Maxine Gadd, Henry Rappaport, and Gerry Gilbert.

The Intermedia Video Band (1970–72): Founded by Ed Varney, this was another creative extrapolation project of the Intermedia Society's interdisciplinary activism.

The Poem Company (1970–74): Founded by John MacDonald, Henry Rappaport, and Ed Varney, the Poem Company published a weekly eight-page magazine (distributed free) in editions of three hundred copies. The group published over fifty editions of their magazine, which they bound and distributed also for free.

It quickly became an important site and distribution centre for Vancouver-based mail art.

The Image Bank (1970–74): Founded by Vincent Trasov, Gary Lee-Nova, and Michael Morris in 1970. Modelled after Ray Johnson's New York Correspondence School, the Image Bank was a distribution nexus for the exchange of images between artists and an archive of works shared. Jacob: "The often witty, ironic or parodical responses that were sent by artists from around the world would constitute the basis of an 'image bank' – a repertoire of recycled readymade or elaborated imagery and raw material for further reworking" ("Golden Streams" n. pag.).

The name was taken from William Burroughs's novel *Nova Express* (1964). It led to AA Bronson of General Idea (Toronto) visiting and expanding collaborations in the city, and Robert Filliou coming to the city in 1973. Bronson's visit led to Morris being named "Miss General Idea"; Filliou's visit led to the Vancouver group participating in "Art's Birthday: The Decca-Dance" celebration in Los Angeles in 1974. Trasov ran for mayor of Vancouver in 1974 in the guise of his alter-ego Mr. Peanut, and was endorsed as a candidate by Burroughs.

The New York Corres-Sponge Dance School of Vancouver (1970): Launched by Glenn Lewis in 1970: "The School was not a formal entity with a listed membership. People attended, took part if they felt like it" (Glenn Lewis n. pag.). In 1971, artist members began weekly swims at the Crystal Pool in Vancouver, often donning rubber shark fin bathing caps and swimming in synchronized formation. The Sponge Dance Swimmers included Lewis, Michael Morris, Vincent Trasov, Eric Metcalfe, and Kate Craig. Through the school, Lewis produced Sponge Step Alphabet, a series of silkscreen prints, in collaboration with Morris and Trasov. When the Vancouver Intermedia group visited New York City en masse in 1972, the NYCSDSoV organized and hosted a banquette at Gordon Matta-Clark's "Food" restaurant. It also contributed *The Great Wall of 1984* installation to the Image Bank's 1984 exhibition on utopias and dystopias.

Video Inn (1971): Michael Goldberg's Video Exchange Directory of people involved with porta-pack video.

The Isle of Avalon Society (1971–6): Founded by Gregg Simpson and David UU, and directed by UU, the Isle of Avalon Society was an intermedia group that combined theatre, poetry, music, and dance with occultic ritual and symbolisms. They orchestrated a kind of spiritual agitprop performance art they called "Ritual Theatre" that was designed to reinvigorate magic in the world. They took inspiration from André Breton's 1930 call for the complete "occultation" of Surrealism (Breton, "Second" 178).

Granville Grange Co-operative (1972): A co-operative interdisciplinary studio run by Glenn Toppings, Dallas Sellman, and D'arcy Henderson.

Babyland (1972): A sixteen-acre piece of property purchased by Mick Henry, Michael Morris, and Vincent Trasov (i.e., the Image Bank) and by Carole Itter at Roberts Creek, two hours from Vancouver by ferry. It was a meeting place for collaboration in a natural setting. Victor Coleman and Stan Bevington visited Babyland in its first year of operation.

Colour Bar Research (1972–4): Launched by Image Bank at Babyland, the Colour Bar Research project was, according to Scott Watson, "a multimedia modular environmental series of paintings, photographs, objects and films" ("Transmission Difficulties" 19). Orchestrated by Michael Morris, Vincent Trasov, Eric Metcalfe, and other visitors at Babyland, the project involved the creation of over one thousand wood blocks painted in colour spectrums. These bars were arranged and assembled, rearranged, and disassembled in various places in the natural environment, becoming through this constant permutation an "endless painting." See Wayne Baerwaldt's essay on the node in colour research (catalogue for the XXII Bienal Internacional de Sao Paulo, 1994).

The Vancouver Poetry Co-op (1973–5): The Vancouver Poetry Co-op had a core of ten poets and a total membership of about forty. It evolved from a weekly poets' group held at the Vancouver Public Library downtown in the winter of 1972–3 until the spring of 1974. Members included Mona Fertig, Cathy Ford, Gwen Hauser, Tim Lander, Nellie McClung, Ed Varney, and Eric Ivan Berg.

Luxe Radio Players (1974): Founded by Kate Craig and Glenn Lewis, the group collaborated on the writing and production of radio plays that were performed in front of live audiences and broadcast across North America. Other artists involved included Dana Atchley, Lowell Darling, and Willoughby Sharp.

The Western Front (1973–present): Named after the iconic battle lines in the First World War, the Western Front is an important artist-run centre in Vancouver, generally considered to be the successor to the Intermedia Society, which folded the year before it was founded. It was and remains much more of a professional operation, though still deeply invested in experimental and avant-garde production. The centre was founded by Martin Bartlett, Mo van Nostrand, Kate Craig, Henry Greenshow, Glenn Lewis, Eric Metcalfe, Michael Morris, and Vincent Trasov. Well connected with the Fluxus network, and visited by Robert Filliou, Dick Higgins, and Emmett Williams in its first years, the Western Front also maintained an active and important literary reading series. A number of books and many articles have been written about the remarkable centre, such as *Whispered Art History: Twenty Years at the Western Front* (1993), comprised of documents and essays tributing and analysing the first two decades of the forty-year-old institution.

Appendix D:
Letter to the Editor of the Georgia Straight

Letter to the Editor of the Georgia Straight
by Helen Potrebenko [spelled Potrehenko in issue; other misspellings as in original]
5.213 (1971) 26–29, pg 26

Editorial Staff of the Georgia Straight:

I never did like your paper much but was convinced that it served a particular community and was radical in its opposition to the status quo and representation of the counterculture. The trouble is that there ain't no such thing as a counterculture and the unemployed and disenchanted youth are simply a new subculture subservient to the dominant one. The higher levels of technology have made many of the youth obsolete since many workers are no longer necessary so a method must be found to keep them quiet or at least, under control, without disrupting the basic structures of capitalism. There are many ways of doing this and I'm beginning to think that if you were paid by the establishment to brainwash people, you wouldn't sound any different. I am not suggesting that you ARE paid, only that you've found a way which makes everybody happy of making a living.

As everyone is no doubt aware, one method of keeping youth under control is to give them drugs. If drugs are illegal then the users feel they are in some way disturbing the established order of things. In fact, they are not and drug using and selling is part of capitalism. The only objection is that you concentrate on soft drugs more than hard drugs but this can be remedied by making grass more difficult to get than speed or heroin. Further, in the end, grass and has can be legalized and everyone will go home happy feeling they have won a great victory.

Along with the supposed reprehensibility of drugs is this thing about sex. Everybody screws; it's not like the current waves of pornography-in-the-name-of-revolution was inventing some new solution to the old problems. Also, in the implication that repression is what causes all manner of personality problems, you were preceded by one of the daddies of capitalist ideologies, Freud. I am referring specifically to the article you printed some months ago abou the necessity for screwing kids by the age of 8. This kind of shit achieves several purposes. One is the Freudian

one of keeping people from looking beyond themselves for solutions to social problems. If they just learned to screw right from an early age, they wouldn't have these
hang-ups. The other purpose is to keep women down in order to preserve the hierarchical nature of society, among other worthy accomplishments. Promiscuous sex
and sexual objectification in a male chauvinist society leaves women (& children)
the losers, no matter how many Freudian or other justifications you propose.

Just recently through the vehicle of a prick named Rand Holmes, you have been
carrying on a tirade against education. It sounds like the sniveling of a bunch of
spoiled brats. Bourgeois kids pick up the necessary rudiments form their environment; if working-class kids didn't go to school they would never become literate, let
alone acquire any of the other technical skills required to survive in the society. As
for college education, it has always been the privilege of an elite. It is becoming less
so in Canada; they've loosened the gates that guarded the tower from the unwashed
rabble. Now what's happening is signifincat unemployment rates among holders of
college degrees. If anybody, or a lot more people than before, can get degrees, it's sure
the fuck obvious that degrees aren't worth anything. So what you're suggesting is that
we all leave again and leave the privileges to people who don't read your stupid rag:
Shaugnessy-British Properties children from whom the universities were built. The
rest of us dead-enders should stay where we are, at the dead-end.

The other service you perform quite nicely for the rulers is to romanticize poverty.
In an age when the capitalists don't need our services, we shouldn't bitch about being
hungry and not having a decent place to live. There's this pretty sotry in the Sun about
a little girl who goes with her parents into the bush and lives off the land. They carry
their own water and live in overcrowded houses (otherwise called communes) and read
by those romantically antique kerosene lamps. The story is called "A Child in a Prison
Camp" and is describing the concentration camps the Japanese were herded into during the Second World War. What did they have to complain about? Young people now
are doing voluntarily what the army had to force the Japanese to do. They wouldn't
even let them have schools at first, but then they were allowed to go as far as grade 8.

Although I am frequently shocked by your callousness and inhumanity, I was particularly incensed by the Rand Holmes comic of last Tuesday. Among other things,
he suggested sending cabs and food deliveries to teachers at unreasonable hours.
What, in the first place, is the extremes of psychologyical torture suggested supposed
to accomplish? Is the aim purely one of sadistic delight? Further, how are the delivery
people and cab-drivers supposed to feel about being used in this manner? It rarely
occurs to any elits that cabbies are also people and you don't differ in this respect.
How are cab-drivers supposed ot feel about driving around for nothing at 3 a.m.?
They don't mind that they don't quite make a decent living at the best of times? Well,
it probably serves them right. We work in the manner of all other suckers instead of
learning how to be rip-off artists like you sons-of-bitches.

Helen Potrebenko

Works Cited

5 B.C. Poets. Vancouver: The Poem Company/Intermedia, 1974.

Breathless Days 1959–1960: A Chronotropic Experiment. Published in conjunction with an exhibition of the same title, organized by and presented at the Morris and Helen Belkin Art Gallery, University of British Columbia, 16 April–2 June 2010.

"Intermedia Nights: A New Festival Concept Emerges." *Province*, 3 May 1968. http://www .michaeldecourcy.com/intermedia/ICF/ICF_05.htm.

"blewointment." *Encyclopedia of BC*. Accessed August 2016. https://knowbc.com/limited/Books /Encyclopedia-of-BC/B/blewointment.

"The Bralorne Papers: Autumn 1971." *BC Monthly* 1.1 (June/July 1972): 8.

"The Grateful Dead." *Mojo-Navigator News* 1.4 (30 August 1966). 1–6.

"Vancouver Gives Two Public Plazas Indigenous Names." *Vancouver Sun*, 18 June 2018.

Abel, Jordan. *The Place of Scraps*. Vancouver: Talonbooks, 2013.

Ackerely, Chris. "Explanatory Annotation." In *The Collected Poetry of Malcolm Lowry*, edited by Kathleen Scherf, 112, 239–356. Vancouver: University of British Columbia Press, 1992.

Adamowicz, Elza. *Surrealist Collage in Text and Image: Dissecting the Exquisite Corpse*. Cambridge: Cambridge University Press, 1998.

Ades, Dawn. "Exhibiting Surrealism." In *The Colour of My Dreams: The Surrealist Revolution in Art*, edited by Dawn Ades, 15–31. Vancouver: Douglas & McIntyre, 2011.

Agamben, Giorgio. *Homo Sacer: Sovereign Power and Bare Life*. Translated by Daniel Heller-Roazen. Stanford: Stanford University Press, 1998.

Apollinaire, Guillaume. "Les Fenêtres." In *The Self-Dismembered Man: Selected Later Poems of Guillaume Apollinaire*, translated by Donald Revell, 27–29. Middleton: Wesleyan University Press, 2004.

Aragon, Louis, Antonin Artaud, André Breton, Max Ernst, Robert Desnos, et al. "The Revolution First and Always." In *Surrealism*, edited by Mary Ann Caws, 201–2. Translated by Michael Richardson and Krzysztof Fijalkowski. London: Phaidon, 2004.

Aristotle. "On the Soul." In *The Complete Works of Aristotle*, translated by I. Bywater, 641–92. Rev. Oxford translation. Princeton: Princeton University Press, 1991.

– "The Poetics." In *The Complete Works of Aristotle*, translated by I. Bywater, 2316–41. Rev. Oxford translation. Princeton: Princeton University Press, 1991.

Armstrong, Jeannette. "Land Speaking." *Speaking for the Generations: Native Writers on Writing*, edited by Simon J. Ortiz, 175–94. Tucson: University of Arizona Press, 1998.

Arnold, Grant. "Ian Wallace: An Annotated Chronology." In *Ian Wallace: At the Intersection of Painting and Photography*, edited by Duncan McCorquodale, 317–33. Vancouver: Black Dog, 2012.

Arp, Hans. "Concrete Art." 1944. In *Manifesto: A Century of Isms*, edited by Mary Ann Caws, 24–25. Lincoln: University of Nebraska Press, 2000.

Assembly of First Nations. *Dismantling the Doctrine of Discovery*. Assembly of First Nations, January 2018. https://www.afn.ca/wp-content/uploads/2018/02/18-01-22-Dismantling-the-Doctrine-of-Discovery-EN.pdf.

Artaud, Antonin. "Lettre à volante." *La Révolution surréaliste* 8 (December 1926): 16.

Atwood, Margaret. "The Messianic Stance: West Coast Seen." In *Second Words: Selected Critical Prose 1960–1982*, 79–82. Toronto: House of Anansi Press, 1982.

Augaitis, Daina, ed. *Ian Wallace: At the Intersection of Painting and Photography*. Vancouver: Vancouver Art Gallery, 2012.

– "Ian Wallace: Framing a Practice." In *Ian Wallace: At the Intersection of Painting and Photography*, edited by Daina Augaitis, 16–31. Vancouver: Vancouver Art Gallery, 2012.

Auxier, Peter and Dan McLeod. "Calling the Guide." *Tish* 28 (1965): 12.

Avison, Margaret. "Geometaphysics." *Poetry: A Magazine of Verse* 70.6 (September 1947): 318–19.

– *I Am Here and Not Not-There: An Autobiography*. Erin: The Porcupine's Quill, 2009.

– Letter to Aaron Vidaver. 2 August 1999. http://filller.blogspot.ca/2007/08/letter-from-margaret-avison-990802.html.

– *Sliverick*. Edited by John W. Curry. Ottawa: CURVD H & Z, 2008.

Badiou, Alan. "The Idea of Communism." In *The Idea of Communism*, edited by Costas Douzinas and Slavoj Žižek, 1–14. New York: Verso, 2010.

Baerwaldt, Wayne. *Morris/Trasov Archive: Colour Research: XXII Bienal Internacional de Sao Paulo*. Winnipeg: Plug-In Editions, 1994.

Bakhtin, Mikhail. Rabelais and His World. Trans. H. Iswolsky. Bloomington: Indiana UP, 1984

Balkind, Alvin. "On Ferment and Golden Ages." In *Vancouver Forum 1: Old Power, New Forces*, edited by Max Wyman, 64. Vancouver: Douglas & Mcintyre, 1992.

Balkind, Alvin, Helen Goodwin, Iain Baxter, David Orcutt, Cortland Hultberg, Abraham Rogatnick, Takao Tanabe, Alvin Balkind, Sam Perry, Roy Kiyooka, and Helen Sonthoff. "The Medium Is the Message," press release, Festival of the Contemporary Arts, 1965. Collection of the Morris and Helen Belkin Art Gallery Archives, Belkin Art Gallery Fond, 13.4–5.12.

Banner, Stuart. *Possessing the Pacific: Land, Settlers, and Indigenous People from Australia to Alaska*. Cambridge, MA: Harvard University Press, 2007.

Barkaskas, Patricia Miranda. "*The Indian Voice* – Centring Women in the Gendered Politics of Indigenous Nationalism in BC, 1969–1984." MA thesis, University of British Columbia, 2009.

Barnard, Suzanne, and Bruce Fink, eds. *Reading Seminar XX: Lacan's Major Work on Love, Knowledge, and Feminine Sexuality*. New York: State University of New York Press, 2002.

Barnholden, Michael. *Reading the Riot Act: A Brief History of Riots in Vancouver*. Vancouver: Anvil, 2005.

Bartels, Kathleen S. Foreword to *The Colour of My Dreams: The Surrealist Revolution in Art*, edited by Dawn Ades, 12–13. Vancouver: Douglas & McIntyre, 2011.

Barthes, Roland. "The Death of the Author." In *Image Music Text*, translated by Stephen Heath, 142–48. New York: Noonday, 1977.

– *S/Z*. New York: Hill and Wang, 1974.

Barwin, Gary. "Squaring the Vowels: On the Visual Poetry of Judith Copithorne." *Jacket2*, 23 October 2013. http://jacket2.org/commentary/squaring-vowels.

Bataille, Georges. *Inner Experience*. 1954. Translated by Leslie Boldt. Albany: State University of New York Press, 1998.

Bate, David. *Photography and Surrealism: Sexuality, Colonialism and Social Dissent*. London: I.B. Tauris, 2004.

Bayard, Caroline. *The New Poetics in Canada and Quebec: From Concretism to Post-modernism.* Toronto: University of Toronto Press, 1989.

Bayard, Caroline, and Jack David. "George Bowering." In *Outposts/Avant-Postes*, 77–106. Erin: Press Porcépic, 1978.

Béalu, Marcel. "The Water Spider." Translated by Michael Bullock. *Prism* 15.2–3 (Summer 1976): 11–32.

Bellefleur-Attas, Mireille. *Léon Bellefleur and Surrealism in Canadian Painting (1940–1980): The Transmigration of an Ideology.* PhD thesis, University of London, Birbeck College, 2006.

Belton, Robert J. "Speaking with Forked Tongues: 'Male' Discourse in 'Female' Surrealism?" *Dada/Surrealism* 18 (1990): 50–62.

Benjamin, Walter. "Theses on Historical Materialism." Translated by Edmund Jephcott. In *Selected Writings*, vol. 4, *1938–1940*, 245–55. Harvard University Press, 2003.

Bergé, Carol. "Reading the Poem." *Tish* 22 (December 1963): 6.

– *The Vancouver Report.* New York: Fuck You Press, 1964.

Bernstein, Charles. *Attack of the Difficult Poems: Essays and Inventions.* Chicago: University of Chicago Press, 2011.

Betts, Gregory. *Avant-Garde Canadian Literature: The Early Manifestations.* Toronto: University of Toronto Press, 2012.

– "Severed from Roots: Settling Culture in Sheila Watson's Novels." MA thesis, University of Victoria, 2000.

Betts, Gregory, and derek beaulieu. Afterword to *RUSH: what fuckan theory; a study uv language*, by bill bissett, 113–22. Toronto: BookThug, 2012.

Betts, Gregory, and Ray Ellenwood. "Canada's Forgotten Surrealists: Joys and Sorrows of the AGO's Surrealist Summer." *Artfocus* 74 (December 2002): 6–8.

Bidini, Dave. "The Myths of Vancouver's Superiority Do the City a Disservice." *National Post*, 25 June 2011.

Birney, Earle. *The Damnation of Vancouver.* 1957. Toronto: McClelland & Stewart, 1977.

– "November Walk Near False Creek." In *The Collected Poems of Earle Birney*, vol. 2, 43–51. Toronto: McClelland & Stewart, 1975.

– "Poets and Painters: Rivals or Partners." *Canadian Art* 14.4 (Summer 1957): 148–50.

– *Spreading Time: Remarks on Canadian Writing and Canadian Writers, 1904–1949.* Montreal: Vehicule, 1989.

– "Vancouver Lights." In *The Collected Poems of Earle Birney*, vol. 1, 71–72. Toronto: McClelland & Stewart, 1975.

bissett, bill. "About in Search of Innocence: film by Len Forrest, director; Jack Long, camera; addressed to them both." 1963. In *RUSH: what fuckan theory; a study uv language*, edited by Gregory Betts and derek beaulieu, 103–5. Toronto: BookThug, 2012.

– "A Warm Place to Shit." In *Drifting into War.* Vancouver: Talonbooks, 1971.

– "Awake in th Red Desert." In *Awake in th Red Desert.* Vancouver: Talonbooks, 1968.

– "bare bones biography what els shudint i remember." In *Nobody Owns th Earth*, 93. Toronto: House of Anansi Press, 1971.

– "bend ovr so we can see whats in yr asshole." In *Sailor.* Vancouver: Talonbooks, 1978.

– "Canada." In *Selected Poems: Beyond Even Faithful Legends*, 137. Vancouver: Talonbooks, 1980.

– "Chile." *Capilano Review* 4 (Fall/Winter 1973): 40.

– *Drifting into War.* Vancouver: Talonbooks, 1971.

– "Evolution of Letters Chart." In *The Cosmic Chef Glee & Perloo Memorial Society Under the Direction of Captain Poetry Presents ... An Evening of Concrete.* Ottawa: Oberon Press, 1970.

– Introduction to *The Last Blewointment Anthology*, 7–9. Toronto: Nightwood Editions, 1985.

- Letter to Diane di Prima. 1971. York University, Clara Thomas Archives, Bill Bissett Fonds, F0266.
- Letter to Margaret Atwood. 1974. York University, Clara Thomas Archives, Bill Bissett Fonds, F0266.
- Letter to Shirley Gibson. 14 November 1974. York University, Clara Thomas Archives, Bill Bissett Fonds, F0266.
- *Pass th food release th spirit book*. Vancouver: Talonbooks, 1973.
- "a pome." In *Selected Poems: Beyond Even Faithful Legends*, 116. Vancouver: Talonbooks, 1980.
- "a pome in praise of all the quebec bombers." *Pass th food release th spirit book*. Vancouver: Talonbooks, 1973.
- *RUSH: what fuckan theory; a study uv language*. Vancouver: Blew Ointment Press, 1972; repr. Toronto: BookThug, 2012.
- *Stardust*. Vancouver: Blew Ointment Press, 1975.
- "a study uv language what can yew study." 1971. Reprinted in *RUSH: what fuckan theory; a study uv language*, edited by Gregory Betts and derek beaulieu, 85–102. Toronto: BookThug, 2012.
- Untitled. *Blewointment* 3.1 (November 1965).
- Untitled. In *Awake in th Red Desert*, 23. Vancouver: Talonbooks and See/Hear Productions, 1968.
- "we are haunted ..." *Blewointment* 1.2 (December 1963).
- "We Paint the Mirror in Wicker and Odalesque." *Blewointment* 1.2 (December 1963).
- "what im doing in these pomes." In draft of *We Sleep Inside Each Other All*, number 8 of 10 special editions, York University, Clara Thomas Archives, Bill Bissett Fonds, F0266.
- "whilst waiting for peter lore ... " *Blewointment* 1.2 (December 1963).
Blanchot, Maurice. *Lautrémont and Sade*. Translated by Stuart Kendall and Michelle Kendall. Stanford: Stanford University Press, 2004.
Blanton, Charles Daniel. *Epic Negation: The Dialectical Poetics of Late Modernism*. Oxford: Oxford University Press, 2015.
Blaser, Robin. "Departure (envoi-commiato." In *The Holy Forest: The Collected Poems of Robin Blaser*, 239. Rev. and expanded ed. Berkeley: University of California Press, 2008.
- "The Sky-stone." In *The Holy Forest: The Collected Poems of Robin Blaser*, 193–4. Rev. and expanded ed. Berkeley: University of California Press, 2008.
- "The Stadium of the Mirror." In *Image-Nations 1–12 & The Stadium of the Mirror*, 53–64. London: Ferry Press, 1974.
Blewointment [also Blewointment Press; blew ointment]. Edited by bill bissett. 17 issues, 1963–77.
Bly, Robert. "Time at Harvard." Interview by Francis Quinn. *Paris Review* 154 (Spring 2000). https://www.theparisreview.org/interviews/729/the-art-of-poetry-no-79-robert-bly.
Bök, Christian. "Tish and Koot." *Open Letter* 12.8 (Spring 2006): 97–104.
Borrows, John. "The Durability of *Terra Nullius*: Tsilhqot'in Nation v British Columbia." *University of British Columbia Law Review* 48.3 (2015): 701–42.
Boughn, Michael. "Canadian Poetry." In *Encyclopedia of American Poetry: The Twentieth Century*, edited by Eric L. Haralson, 122–25. New York: Routledge, 2001.
Bourassa, André G. *Surrealism and Québec Literature: History of a Cultural Revolution*. 1977. Translated by Mark Czarnecki. Toronto: University of Toronto Press, 1984.
Bowering, Angela. Letter to Gladys Hindmarch. 20 January 1969. Simon Fraser Special Collections, Gladys Hindmarch Fonds, MsC 34 Box 1.
Bowering, George. "Alphabiography." *Essays on Canadian Writing* 51 (1993): 296–320.
- "Cutting Them All Up." Interview with bpNichol. *Alphabet* 18/19 (1971): 18–21.

- Editorial. In *Tish No. 1–19*, edited by Frank Davey, 17. Vancouver: Talonbooks, 1975.
- "It's There You Can't Deny It." *Capilano Review* 1.1 (Spring 1972): 28.
- "Kerouac's Brother." *Tish* 22 (December 1963): 5.
- "The Most Remarkable Thing about Tish." *Tish* 20 (August 1963): 2.
- Review of Blaser and Levertov. *Tish* 30 (June 1965): 6–7.
- "Songs & Wisdom: An Interview with Audrey Thomas." *Open Letter* 4.3 (Spring 1979): 7–31.
- "Tuesday Night." In *Tish No. 1–19*, edited by Frank Davey, 136. Vancouver: Talonbooks, 1975.
- "Vancouver as Postmodern Poetry." *Colby Quarterly* 29.2 (June 1993). 102–18.
- *Words, Words, Words: Essays and Memoirs*. Vancouver: New Star Books, 2012.
Bowering, George, Lionel Kearns, and Gerry Gilbert. "Vancouver Poetry in the 60s." *BC Monthly* 3.3 (December 1976).
Bowker, Gordon. *Apparently Incongruous Parts: The Worlds of Malcolm Lowry*. Metuchen, NJ: Scarecrow Press, 1990.
- *Pursued by Furies: A Life of Dylan Thomas*. London: FaberFinds, 2009.
Brandon, Ruth. *Surreal Lives: The Surrealists, 1917–1945*. New York: Grove Press, 199.
Brandt, Di. *Questions i asked my mother*. Winnipeg: Turnstone Press, 1987.
Bray, Joe, Alison Gibbons, and Brian McHale. Introduction to *The Routledge Companion to Experimental Literature*, edited by Joe Bray, Alison Gibbons, and Brian McHale, 118. New York: Routledge, 2012.
Bringhurst, Robert. *Ocean Paper Stone: The Catalogue of an exhibition of printed objects which chronicle more than a century of literary publishing in British Columbia*. Vancouver: William Hoffer, 1984.
Breton, André. "A Letter to Seers." 1925. In *Manifestoes of Surrealism*, translated by Richard Seaver and Helen R. Lane, 195–204. Ann Arbor: University of Michigan Press, 1972.
- "Les Mots sans rides." *Littérature* 7 (December 1922): 12–14.
- "Manifesto of Surrealism." 1924. In *Manifestoes of Surrealism*, translated by Richard Seaver and Helen R. Lane, 1–48. Ann Arbor: University of Michigan Press, 1972.
- *Nadja*. 1928. Translated by Richard Howard. New York: Grove Press, 1960.
- "Reply to a Survey." 1924. In *Lost Steps*, translated by Mark Polizzotti, 83–84. Lincoln: University of Nebraska Press, 1996.
- "Second Manifesto of Surrealism." 1930. In *Manifestoes of Surrealism*, translated by Richard Seaver and Helen R. Lane, 117–194. Ann Arbor: University of Michigan Press, 1972.
- "Taking Stock of Surrealism." 1952. *Vie des Arts* 20.80 (Autumn 1975): 16–88.
Breton, André, Paul Éluard, Benjamin Péret, Georges Sadoul, Pierre Unik, André Thirion, René Crevel, Louis Aragon, René Char, Maxime Alexandre, Yves Tanguy, and Georges Malkine. "Boycott the Colonial Exposition." *Le Surréalisme au service de la revolution* (3–4 (December 1931). Reprinted in *Tracts surréalistes et declarations collectives 1922–39*, 194–5. Paris: Le Terrain Vague, 1980.
Brooker, Bertram. "When We Awake!" In *Yearbook of the Arts in Canada*, edited by Bertram Brooker, 1–17. Toronto: Macmillan, 1928–29.
Brown, Jim. Email correspondence with author. 13 January 2013.
Browne, Colin. "Scavengers of Paradise." In *The Colour of My Dreams: The Surrealist Revolution in Art*, edited by Dawn Ades, 245–62. Vancouver: Douglas & McIntyre, 2011.
Bullock, Michael. "An Interview with Michael Bullock." *British Columbia Library Quarterly* 36–38 (1972): 5–19.
- *Randolph Cranstone and the Glass Thimble*. London: Marion Boyars, 1977.
- "Surrealism's Janus Head." *Vancouver Surrealist Newsletter* 1 (1981): 1–4.

Burns, Wayne. "Voices in Limbo." *Canadian Literature* 24 (1965): 77–79.

Bürger, Peter. "Avant-Garde and Neo-Avant-Garde: An Attempt to Answer Certain Critics of Theory of the Avant-Garde." *New Literary History* 41 (2010): 695–715.

– *Theory of the Avant-Garde*. 1974. Translated by Michael Shaw. In *Theory and History of Literature*, vol. 4, edited by Wlad Godzich and Jochen Schulte-Sasse. Minneapolis: University of Minneapolis Press, 1984.

Burke, Kenneth. *Surrealism: A Dissenting Opinion*. New York: New Directions, 1940.

Burke, Peter. "Overture: The New History, Its Past, and Its Future." In *New Perspectives on Historical Writing*, 1–23. University Park: Pennsylvania State University Press, 1991.

Burnham, Clint. *The Only Poetry That Matters: Reading the Kootenay School of Writing*. Vancouver: Arsenal Pulp Press, 2011.

Burroughs, William S. *APO-33*. New York: Fuck You Press, 1965.

– *APO-33*. San Francisco: Beach Books, 1968.

– "The Cut-Up Method of Brion Gysin." *Yugen* 8 (1962): 31–33. http://www.ubu.com/papers /burroughs_gysin.html.

Butler, Judith. *Bodies That Matter: On the Discursive Limits of "Sex."* New York: Routledge, 1993.

Butling, Pauline, and Susan Rudy. *Writing in Our Time: Canada's Radical Poetries in English (1957–2003)*. Waterloo: Wilfrid Laurier University Press, 2005.

Cain, Stephen. "André Breton in Canada." In "Surrealism in Canada," edited by Gregory Betts and Beatriz Hausner. Special issue, *Open Letter* 15.3 (Summer 2013): 37–59.

Cameron, Laura. "Phyllis Webb's 'Struggles of Silence' and the Making of *Wilson's Bowl*." Paper presented at Congress of the Humanities, Victoria, British Columbia, University of Victoria, 3 June 2013.

Campbell, Lara, Dominique Clément, and Gregory S. Kealey. *Debating Dissent: Canada and the Sixties*. Toronto: University of Toronto Press, 2012.

Campos, Augusto de, Décio Pignatari, and Haroldo de Campos. "plano-piloto para poesia concreta." *Noigandres* 4 (1958). Reprinted as "plano-piloto para poesia concreta / pilot plan for concrete poetry," translated by the authors, in *Concrete Poetry: A World View*, edited by Mary Ellen Solt, 70–72. Bloomington: Indiana University Press, 1968.

Capperdoni, Alessandra. "Feminist Poetics as Avant-Garde Poetics." *Open Letter* 14.3 (Summer 2010): 33–51.

Carlson, Tim. "bill bissett." *bill bissett: Essays on His Works*. Toronto: Guernica, 2002. 13–49.

Carr, Emily. *Dear Nan: Letters of Emily Carr, Nan Cheney and Humphrey Toms*. Edited by Doreen Walker. Vancouver: University of British Columbia, 1990.

– "Hundreds of Thousands: The Journals of an Artist." In *The Complete Writings of Emily Carr*, 653–893. Toronto: University of Washington Press, 1993.

– *Opposite Contraries: The Unknown Journals of Emily Carr and Other Writing*. Edited by Susan Crean. Toronto: Douglas & McIntyre, 2003.

Carstairs, Catherine. "Food, Fear, and the Environment in the Long Sixties." In *Debating Dissent: Canada and the Sixties*, 29–45. Toronto: University of Toronto Press, 2012.

Cartwright, Miriam. "Michael Bullock The First Fifty Years and Family." ABC BookWorld. Accessed August 2016. https://abcbookworld.com/writer/bullock-michael/.

Cawsey, Fred. "Stress Must Be on Literature as Art." *Ubyssey* 49.33 (January 1968): 1.

Chevalier, Tracy. *Contemporary Poets*. Chicago: St. James Press, 1991.

Chidholm, Louey, and Amy Steedman. *A Staircase of Stories*. London: Thomas Nelson, 1920.

Choucha, Nadia. *Surrealism & the Occult: Shamanism, Magic, Alchemy, and the Birth of an Artistic Movement*. Rochester: Destiny Books, 1992.

Clinton, Martina. *Something in*. grOnk series 5, no. 4. Toronto: Ganglia Press, 1971.

– *Yonder Glow*. Vancouver: Blew Ointment Press, 1971.

Cohen, Leonard. *The Favourite Game & Beautiful Losers*. Toronto: McClelland & Stewart, 2009.

Coleman, Bob. *Improvisations*. Kingston: Derwydon Press, 1977.

Coleman, Elizabeth. "War with LSD." *Blewointment* 9.1 (July 1967).

Collins, Bradford R. "Les peintres hermétique de la côte ouest du Canada/Canadian West Coast Hermetics." *Vie des arts* 20.80 (Autumn 1975): 38–41, 92–93.

Collis, Stephen. "Of the Dissolved: On George Bowering's Serials and Procedures." In *Taking Measures: George Bowering Selected Serial Poems*, edited by Stephen Collis, 1–16. Vancouver: Talonbooks, 2019.

– "The Call to Be Disobedient: On Michael Nardone." In "Avant Canada: On the Canadian Avant-Garde," edited by Gregory Betts and Katie L. Price. Special issue, *Jacket2* (2016).

Copithorne, Judith. *Arrangements*. Vancouver: Intermedia Press, 1973.

– "A Personal and Informal Introduction and Checklist Regarding Some Larger Poetry Enterprises in Vancouver Primarily in the Earlier Part of the 1960s." *University of the Fraser Valley Research Review* 3.1 (Winter 2010): 54–63.

– "Famine." *Blewointment* 1.2 (December 1963).

– "How do you ever know? / You never do." In *Returning*, 18–19. Vancouver: Press One, 1972.

– *Miss Tree's Pillow Book*. Vancouver: Intermedia Returning Press, 1971.

– "This was drawn last year ..." *Blewointment* 2.4 (September 1964).

– Untitled. *Circular Causation* 2 (1969): 2.

Coulthard, Glen. *Red Skin, White Masks: Rejecting the Colonial Politics of Recognition*. Minneapolis, MN: University of Minnesota Press, 2014.

– "The Colonialism of the Present." Interview by Andrew Bard Epstein. *Jacobin*, January 2015. https://www.jacobinmag.com/2015/01/indigenous-left-glen-coulthard-interview/.

Coupey, Pierre. "An Allegory of Love." In *Poets Market*. Vancouver: Talonbooks, 1968.

– Email interview with author. 10 July 2012.

– Interview with author. 8 December 2019.

– Letter to Henri Chopin. 24 March 1966. Simon Fraser Rare Books and Special Collections, xx 205-03-4-0-1.

Craig, Blanche. *Collage: Assembling Contemporary Art*. London: Black Dog, 2008.

Cram, Carol M. "The West Coast Surrealists." *Vie des Arts* 30.120 (1985): 36–91.

Creeley, Robert. *Collected Prose*. Champaign: Dalkey Archive, 2001.

Culley, Peter. "Because I Am Always Talking: Reading Vancouver into the Western Front." In *Whispered Art History: Twenty Years at the Western Front*, edited by Keith Wallace, 189–97. Vancouver: Arsenal Pulp Press, 1993.

Davey, Frank. *aka bpNichol: A Preliminary Biography*. Toronto: ECW Press, 2012.

– "Dear Fred, David, George, others:." *Open Letter* 2 (March 1966): 3.

– *Earle Birney*. Studies in Canadian Literature. Toronto: Copp Clark, 1971.

– Editorial. In *Tish No. 1–19*, edited by Frank Davey, 13. Vancouver: Talonbooks, 1975.

– Editional. *Tish* 20 (August 1963): 10.

– Introduction. In *Tish No. 1–19*, edited by Frank Davey, 7–11. Vancouver: Talonbooks, 1975.

– *Canadian Literary Power*. Edmonton: NeWest Press, 1994.

– "Of the North Shore." In *Tish No. 1–19*, edited by Frank Davey, 139. Vancouver: Talonbooks, 1975.

– "One Man's Look at 'Projective Verse.'" In *Tish No. 1–19*, edited by Frank Davey, 101–3. Vancouver: Talonbooks, 1975.

- "Surviving the Paraphrase." In *Surviving the Paraphrase*, 1–12. Winnipeg: Turnstone Press, 1983.
- "The Poetry Reading and Reading Series, Revisted by Amodern." London Open Mic Poetry Archive. Accessed August 2016. https://www.londonpoetryopenmic.com/frank-davey-blog /the-poetry-reading-and-reading-series-revisted-by-amodern.
- "The Present Scene." *Delta* 18 (June 1962): 1.
-, ed. *Tish No. 1–19*. Vancouver: Talonbooks, 1975.
- "Two Retrospects." In *Tish No. 1–19*, edited by Frank Davey, 423–4. Vancouver: Talonbooks, 1975.
- *When Tish Happens: The Unlikely Story of Canada's "Most Influential Literary Magazine."* Toronto: ECW Press, 2011.
Davis, Stephen. *Old Gods Almost Dead: The 40-Year Odyssey of the Rolling Stones*. New York: Broadway Books, 2001.
Dawn, Leslie. *National Visions, National Blindness: Canadian Art and Identities in the 1920s*. Vancouver: University of British Columbia Press, 2006.
Dawson, David. Editorial. *Tish* 21 (September 1963): 1.
De Beauvoir, Simone. *The Second Sex*. 1949. Translated by H.M. Parshley. New York: Vintage Books, 1989.
De Courcy, Michael. "The Intermedia Catalogue." 2009. http://intermedia.vancouverartinthesixties .com/introduction/default.
Dean, John, and Ralph Steadman. "Rituals of the Herd." *Rolling Stone*, 7 October 1976, 38.
Degentesh, Katie. "Legitimate and Illegitimate Poems." *Boston Review*, 6 December 2012. http:// www.bostonreview.net/forum/poetry-brink/legitimate-and-illegitimate-poems.
Deleuze, Gilles and Félix Guattari. *What is Philosophy?* New York: Verson, 1994.
Derrida, Jacques. *Specters of Marx: The State of the Debt, the Work of Mourning, and the New International*. Translated by Peggy Kamuf. New York: Routledge, 1994.
Dikeakos, Christos. "Serial photo-collages." *The Capilano Review*. 4 (Fall/Winter 1973): 59–63.
Di Prima, Diane. Letter to Bill Bissett. October 1970. York University, York University, Clara Thomas Archives, Bill Bissett Fonds, F0266.
- "Revolutionary Letters #9." *Blewointment* 5.2 (August 1968).
Djwa, Sandra. *Professing English: A Life of Roy Daniels*. Toronto: University of Toronto Press, 2002.
Douglas, Stan. "Interview: Ian Wallace on Cinema." In *Ian Wallace: At the Intersection of Painting and Photography*, edited by Duncan McCorquodale, 109–13. Vancouver: Black Dog, 2012.
Douglas, Vasiliki. *Introduction to Aboriginal Health and Health Care in Canada: Bridging Health and Healing*. Mannheim: Springer, 2013.
Douzinas, Costas, and Slavoj Žižek. Introduction to *The Idea of Communism*, edited by Costas Douzinas and Slavoj Žižek, vii–xi. New York: Verso, 2010.
Doyle, Laura. "Geomodernism, Postcoloniality, and Women's Writing." In *The Cambridge Companion to Modernist Women Writers*, edited by Maran Linett, 129–45. Cambridge: Cambridge University Press, 2010.
- "Liberty, Race, and Larsen in Atlantic Modernity: A New World Genealogy." *Geomodernisms: Race, Modernism, Modernity*, edited by Laura Doyle and Laura Winkiel, 51–76. Bloomington: Indiana University Press, 2005.
Doyle, Laura, and Laura Winkiel. "Introduction: The Global Horizons of Modernism." In *Geomodernisms: Race, Modernism, Modernity*, edited by Laura Doyle and Laura Winkiel, 1–14. Bloomington: Indiana University Press, 2005.
Drodge, Susan. "The Feminist Romantic: The Revisionary Rhetoric of Double Negative, Naked Poems, and Gyno-text." PhD thesis, Memorial University of Newfoundland, 1996.

Drucker, Johanna. "Visual Poetics: An International View." In "99 Poets/1999: An International Poetics Symposium," edited by Charles Bernstein. Special issue, *boundary 2* 26.1 (Spring 1999): 100–104.

Drumbolis, Nick. *Myth as Math: Calendrical Significance in the Mosaic Census of the Sons of Israel*. Toronto: Letters Bookshop, 2007.

Duncan, Robert. *The H.D. Book*. Berkeley: University of California Press, 2011.

– "Ideas of the Meaning of Form." *Kulchur* 1:4 (1961): 60–75.

– *Fictive Certainties*. 1955. New York: New Directions, 1985.

– "For the Novices of Vancouver." In *Tish No. 1–19*, edited by Frank Davey, 253–7. Vancouver: Talonbooks, 1975.

– "Electric Iron." *Robert Duncan: The Collected Early Poems and Plays*. Berkeley: University of California Press, 2012. 177.

– "Man's Fulfillment in Order and Strife." *Caterpillar* 8/9 (October 1969): 229–49.

Eagleton, Terry. *After Theory*. London: Perseus Books, 2003.

– *Wittgenstein: The Terry Eagleton Script, the Derek Jarman Film*. London: British Film Institute, 1993.

Editorial. *Tish* 21 (September 1963).

Eliade, Mircea. *Occultism, Witchcraft, and Cultural Fashions: Essays in Comparative Religion*. Chicago: U Chicago P, 1976.

Ellenwood, Ray. *Egregore: A History of the Montréal Automatist Movement*. Toronto: Exile Editions, 1992.

Ellingham, Lewis, and Kevin Killian. *Poet Be Like God: Jack Spicer and the San Francisco Renaissance*. Hanover: Wesleyan University Press, 1998.

Ernst, Max. *Beyond Painting and Other Writings by the Artist and His Friends*. Edited by Robert Motherwell. New York: Wittenborn, Schultz, 1948.

Ernst, Wolfgang. *Digital Memory and the Archive*. Minneapolis: University of Minnesota Press, 2012.

Faas, Ekbert. "An Interview with Robert Duncan." *boundary 2* 8.2 (Winter 1980): 1–19.

Faas, Ekbert, and Maria Trombacco. *Robert Creeley: A Biography*. Kingston: McGill-Queen's University Press, 2001.

Faas, Ekbert, and Sabrina Reed, eds. *Irving Layton & Robert Creeley: The Complete Correspondence, 1953–1978*. Montreal: McGill-Queen's University Press, 1990.

Farebrother, Rachel. *The Collage Aesthetic in the Harlem Renaissance*. Farnham: Ashgate, 2009.

Farrell, Lance. *Ten Pomes*. Vancouver: Blew Ointment Press, 1971.

Farrell-Ward, Lorna. "Tradition/Transition: The Keys to Change." In *Vancouver: Art and Artists 1931–1983*, 14–33. Vancouver: Vancouver Art Gallery, 1983.

Fawcett, Brian. "Frank Davey's Tish." *Dooneyscafe*, 8 June 2011. https://dooneyscafe.com/frank-daveys-tish/.

Finch, Elizabeth. "Collage." In *The Exquisite Corpse: Chance and Collaboration in Surrealism's Parlor Game*, edited by Kanta Kochhar-Lindgren, Davis Schneiderman, and Tom Denlinger, 116–26. Lincoln: University of Nebraska Press, 2009.

Finlay, Ian Hamilton, and Stephen Scobie. "The Insider." In *Concrete Poetry: An Exhibition in Four Parts*. Vancouver: Fine Arts Gallery, University of British Columbia, 1969. Exhibition catalogue.

Filreis, Al. *Counter-revolution of the Word: The Conservative Attack on Modern Poetry, 1945–1960*. Chapel Hill: University of North Carolina Press, 2007.

Fitzgerald, F. Scott. *The Great Gatsby*. 1925. Cambridge: Cambridge University Press, 1991.

Fitzpatrick, Anne. *Late Modernism: Odysseys in Art*. Mankato, MN: Creative Education, 2006.

Flint, F.S. "The History of Imagism." *Egoist* 2:5 (1 May 1915): 70–71.

Fleming, John. "Jack Shadbolt: A Study of a Canadian Painter." MA thesis, University of Victoria, 1979.

Foisy, Gilles. "Notes on the Process." In *Canadian West Coast Hermetics: The Metaphysical Landscape*. Vancouver: Fine Arts Gallery, University of British Columbia, 1973.

Fong, Deanna and Karis Shearer. Introduction. In *Wanting Everything: Gladys Hindmarch, The Collected Works*, xiii–xxxvi. Vancouver: Talonbooks, 2020.

Freeman, Barbara Claire. "A Union Forever Deferred: Sexual Politics after Lacan." *Qui Parle* 4.2 (Spring 1991). 119–31.

Friedman, Susan. "Periodizing Modernism: Postcolonial Modernities and the Space/Time Borders of Modernist Studies." *Modernism/Modernity* 13.3 (2006): 425–43.

– *Planetary Modernisms: Provocations on Modernity across Time*. New York: Columbia University Press, 2015.

– "Planetarity: Musing Modernist Studies." *Modernism/modernity* 17.3 (September 2010): 471–99.

Frye, Northrop. Afterword to *Hetty Dorval*, by Ethel Wilson, 113–16. New Canadian Library. Toronto: McClelland & Stewart, 1990.

Gadd, Maxine. "the happy vision gone." In *Lost Language: Selected Poems of Maxine Gadd*, edited by Daphne Marlatt and Ingrid Klassen, 76–77. Toronto: Coach House Press, 1982.

Galloway, Alexander. *The Interface Effect*. Cambridge: Polity Press, 2012.

Gámez-Fernández, Cristina. "'Knowing That Everything Is Wrong': Existentialism in the Poetry of Phyllis Webb." *Canadaria: Revista Canaria de Estudios Canadienses* 1 (2007): 40–54.

Gauvreau, Claude. "The Oval Mayonaisse and the Back of the Medieval Chair." In *Entrails*, translated by Ray Ellenwood, 137. Toronto: Exile Editions, 1991.

Geiger, John. *Nothing Is True – Everything Is Permitted: The Life of Brion Gysin*. New York: The Disinformation Company, 2005.

Genter, Robert. *Late Modernism, Art, Culture, and Politics in Cold War America*. Philadephia: University of Pennsylvania Press, 2010.

Gilbert, Gerry. *And*. Vancouver: Blew Ointment Press, 1971.

– "Babyland Blues." In *Money*. Vancouver: York Street Commune, 1971.

– "Friday the 13th." In *Journal to the East*. Vancouver: Blew Ointment Press, 1974.

– Letter to Sam Abrams. 6 August 1972. Simon Fraser University Special Collections and Rare Books, Gerry Gilbert Fonds, MsC 14.1.1.

– "Metro." In *Journal to the East*. Vancouver: Blew Ointment Press, 1974.

– "Poem on a Folded Postcard." In *White Lunch*. Vancouver: Periwinkle Press, 1964.

– "Song for the French Revolution, May 1968." In *Money*. In *Georgia Straight Writing Supplement*, Vancouver Series 2 (1971).

– "Thought for Penny." In *Journal to the East*. Vancouver: Blew Ointment Press, 1974.

Ginsberg, Allen. *Indian Journals*. New York: Grove Press, 1996.

Ginsberg, Allen, and Yves Le Pellec. "A Collage of Voices: An Interview with Allen Ginsberg." *Revue francaise d'etudes americaines* 39 (February 1989): 91–111.

Golding, Alan. "'The New American Poetry' Revisited, Again." *Contemporary Literature* 39.2 (Summer 1998): 180–211.

Goldsmith, Kenneth. *Uncreative Writing: Managing Language in the Digital Age*. New York: Columbia University Press, 2011.

Grace, Sherrill. "Midsummer Madness and the Day of the Dead: Joyce, Lowry, and Expressionism." In *Joyce/Lowry: Critical Perspectives*, edited by Patrick A. McCarthy, 9–20. Lexington: University Press of Kentucky, 1997.

Green, Paul. "Remembering Michael Bullock." ABC BookWorld. Accessed August 2016. http://www.abcbookworld.com/view_author.php?id=378.

Greenhill, Ralph. "Early Photography in Canada." *Canadian Art* 22.3 (May/June 1965): 56.

Griffin, Kevin. "An Era Ended at the VAG When Tony Emery Resigned." Art from the Archives Series. *Vancouver Sun*, 25 March 2015. https://vancouversun.com/news/staff-blogs/art-from-the-archive-an-era-ended-at-the-vag-when-tony-emery-resigned/.

– "In Vancouver: Robert Rauschenberg, aka Bob." *Vancouver Sun*, 6 April 2012. https://vancouversun.com/news/staff-blogs/in-vancouver-robert-rauschenberg-aka-bob/.

Grindon, Gavin. "Surrealism, Dada, and the Refusal of Work: Autonomy, Activism, and Social Participation in the Radical Avant-Garde." *Oxford Art Journal* 34.1 (2011): 79–96.

Gysin, Brion. "About the Cut-ups." 1964. In *Back in No Time: The Brion Gysin Reader*, edited by Jason Weiss, 125–31. Middletown: Wesleyan University Press, 2001.

– *Back in No Time: The Brion Gysin Reader*. Edited by Jason Weiss. Middleton: Wesleyan University Press, 2001.

– "An Encomium for Allen Ginsberg." 1984. In *Back in No Time: The Brion Gysin Reader*, edited by Jason Weiss, 287–8. Middleton: Wesleyan University Press, 2001.

– "Cut Me Up." In *Minutes to Go*, by Sinclair Beiles, William S. Burroughs, Gregory Corso, and Brion Gysin, 42–46. Paris: Two Cities Editions, 1960.

Haggerty, Joan. *Daughters of the Moon*. New York: Bobbs-Merrill, 1971.

Halpin, Marjorie. *Jack Shadbolt and the Coastal Indian Image*. Vancouver: University of British Columbia Press, 1986.

Harris, David W. *See* UU, David.

Harris, Oliver. "Cutting Up the Corpse." In *The Exquisite Corpse: Chance and Collaboration in Surrealism's Parlor Game*, edited by Kanta Kochhar-Lindgren, Davis Schneiderman, and Tom Denlinger, 82–103. Lincoln: University of Nebraska Press, 2009.

Harris, Lawren. *A Disquisition on Abstract Painting*. New York: Rous & Mann Press, 1954.

Harrison, Julia, and Regna Darnell. *Historicizing Canadian Anthropology*. Vancouver: University of British Columbia Press, 2006.

Hardt, Michael, and Antonio Negri. *Empire*. Cambridge: Harvard University Press, 2000.

– *Multitude: War and Democracy in the Age of Empire*. New York: Penguin, 2004.

Harvie, David. *Eiffel: The Genius Who Reinvented Himself*. Gloucestershire: Sutton, 2006.

Hauser, Gwen. "Power to the People." In *Pomegranate: A Selected Anthology of Vancouver Poetry*, edited by Nellie McClung, 38–39. Vancouver: Intermedia Society, 1975.

– "What Did the Underground Ever Do For Women." In "What Isn't Tantrik." Special issue, *Blewointment* (December 1973): 4.

Hemingway, Ernest. *The Sun Also Rises*. 1926. New York: Scribner's, 1954.

Henripin, Jacques, John P. Humphrey, Lola M. Lange, Jeanne Lapointe, Elsie Gregory MacGill, and Doris Ogilvie. *Report of the Royal Commission on the Status of Women in Canada*. Ottawa: Information Canada, 1967–70. https://epe.lac-bac.gc.ca/100/200/301/pco-bcp/commissions-ef/bird1970-eng/bird1970-eng.htm.

Herzmann, G., and T. Curran. "Experts' Memory: An ERP Study of Perceptual Expertise Effects on Encoding and Recognition." *Memory & Cognition* 39.3 (2011): 412–32.

Heyman, George, and Scott Lawrance. "Circular Causation." *Circular Causation* 1 (Spring 1969).

Heyman, Jorg (also George). "Ghost Dance." In "Th Combined Blew Ointment Picture Book nd th News," edited by bill bissett. Special issue, *Blewointment* (December 1972).

Hilder, Jamie. "Concrete Poetry and Conceptual Art: A Misunderstanding." *Contemporary Literature* 54.3 (Fall 2013): 578–614.

- "Concrete Poetry: From the Procedural to the Performative." In *Letters: Michael Morris and Concrete Poetry*, edited by Scott Watson and Jana Tyner, 111–24. London: Black Dog, 2015.

Hindmarch, Gladys Maria. Email interview with the author. 25 January 2013.

- *A Birth Account.* Vancouver: New Star Books, 1976.

- Interview with the author. 11 December 2019.

- "Review of Blew Ointment One." *Tish* 22 (December 1963): 12–13.

- "The Vancouver Poetry Conference Journals." 1963. *Wanting Everything: Gladys Hindmarch, The Collected Works*, edited by Deanna Fong and Karis Shearer, 195–205. Vancouver: Talonbooks, 2020.

Honeyman, Scott, and Bill Bachop. "Police Battle Mob at Stones' Concert as Firebombs, Rocks, Bottles Hurled." *Vancouver Sun*, 5 June 1972, 1.

Hong, Cathy Park. "Delusions of Whiteness in the Avant-Garde." *Lana Turner*, 7. https://arcade .stanford.edu/content/delusions-whiteness-avant-garde.

Truth and Reconciliation Commission of Canada. *Honouring the Truth, Reconciling for the Future: Summary of the Final Report of the Truth and Reconciliation Commission of Canada.* Winnipeg: Truth and Reconciliation Commission of Canada, 2015. http://www.trc.ca/assets /pdf/Honouring_the_Truth_Reconciling_for_the_Future_July_23_2015.pdf.

Hopkins, Budd. "Modernism and the Collage Aesthetic." *New England Review* 18.2 (Spring 1997): 5–12.

Howard, Victor, and Julia Skikavich. "Unemployment Relief Camps." *Canadian Encyclopedia*, 17 March 2015. https://www.thecanadianencyclopedia.ca/en/article/unemployment-relief-camps.

Hunt, Ron. "Icteric and Poetry Must Be Made by All/Transform the World: A Note on a Lost and Suppressed Avant-Garde and Exhibition." https://translatingpracticesblog.blogspot .com/2010/09/icteric-can-be-seen-as-avant-garde.html.

Hurley, Grant. "The Lyric West: Reading the Vancouver Poetry Society, 1916–1974." MA thesis, University of British Columbia, 2012.

Irvine, Dean. *Editing Modernity: Women and Little-Magazine Cultures in Canada 1916–1956.* Toronto: University of Toronto Press, 2008.

- "Immigrants, Exiles, and Expatriates." In *The Oxford Handbook of Modernisms*, edited by Peter Brooker, Andrzej Gąsiorek, Deborah Longworth, and Andrew Thacker, 873–95. Oxford: Oxford University Press, 2010.

Itter, Carole. *Location Shack.* 1982. Selections reprinted in *Into the Night Life: Canadian Writers and Artists at Work*, 31–35. Toronto: Nightwood Editions, 1986.

Jacob, Luis. *Golden Streams: Artists' Collaboration and Exchange in the 1970s.* Mississauga, ON: Blackwood Gallery, University of Toronto at Mississauga, 2002.

Jameson, Fredric. *Postmodernism, or, the Cultural Logic of Late Capitalism.* Durham: Duke University Press, 1991.

Janssen, Renske. "Then and Now and Art and Politics: An Interview with Ian Wallace." In *Ian Wallace: A Literature of Images*, edited by Vanessa Joan Müller, Beatrix Ruf, and Nicolaus Schafhausen, 138–69. Zürich: Sternberg Press, 2008.

Jarry, Alfred. *Ubu roi: Drama in 5 Acts.* 1896. Norfolk: New Directions, 1961.

Jonaitis, Aldona. *Art of the Northwest Coast.* Seattle: University of Washington Press, 2006.

Jukelevics, Nicette. "A Bibliography of Canadian Concrete, Visual and Sound Poetry 1965–1972." MA thesis, Sir George William University, 1974.

Kamboureli, Smaro. Preface to *Trans.Can.Lit: Resituating the Study of Canadian Literature*, edited by Smaro Kamboureli and Roy Miki, vii–xv. Waterloo: Wilfred Laurier University Press, 2007.

– "Seeking Shape, Seeking Meaning: An Interview with Phyllis Webb." *West Coast Line* 25.3 (1991): 25.

Kargbo, Marian. "Musqueam Indian Reserve: A Case Study for Community Development Purposes." MA thesis, University of British Columbia, 1965.

Kiyooka, Roy. *The Fontainebleau Dream Machine*. Toronto: Coach House Press, 1977.

– Letter to Judy Copithorne. 4 October 1971. In *Transcanada Letters*, 167. Edmonton: NeWest Press, 2005.

– Letter to Sheila Watson. 19 February 1971. In *Transcanada Letters*, 110. Edmonton: NeWest Press, 2005.

– "miscellaneous 4/66." In *transcanada letters*. Vancouver: Talonbooks, 1975.

Klobucar, Andrew. "Line Breaks: West Coast Line, Past and Present." *Books in Canada* 28.7 (October 1999): 14.

Kojève, Alexandre. Introduction to *The Reading of Hegel: Lectures on the Phenomenology of Spirit*. 1947. Repr. Ithaca: Cornell University Press, 1980.

Kraus, Rosalind. *The Originality of the Avant-Garde and Other Modernist Myths*. Cambridge: MIT Press, 1985.

Kristeva, Julia. "L'engendrement de la formule." *Tel Quel* 37 (1969).

Kröller, Eva-Marie. "Roy Kiyooka's *The Fontainebleau Dream Machine*: A Reading." *Canadian Literature* 113–14 (Summer 1987): 47–61.

Kruz, Jerry. *The Afterthought: West Coast Rock Posters and Recollections from the '60s*. Vancouver: Rocky Mountain Books, 2014.

Kuskis, Alex. "Collaborative Collage Painting: Marshall McLuhan & Mansaram." *McLuhan Galaxy* (blog), 6 August 2012. https://mcluhangalaxy.wordpress.com/2012/08/06/collaborative-collage-painting-marshall-mcluhan-mansaram/.

Lachance, Bertrand. "frosting." *Blewointment* (March 1972): 58–59.

Lachs, John. Review of *lost angel mining company*, by bill bissett. *Alphabet* 18–19 (1971): 50–53.

Lane, Patrick. "(Auto)Biographical Notez." In "Spanish Fleye – 'wun,'" edited by David UU. Special issue, *Tamarack Review* (1966).

Laroque, Yves. "Cours général de surréalisme au Canada anglais." Doctoral thesis, Paris, Université de Paris 1 (Panthéon-Sorbonne), 1996.

– "Grace Pailthorpe et Reuben Mednikoff à Vancouver. La transmission du surréalisme au Canada Anglais, 1942–1946." *RACAR: Canadian Art Review* 32.1–2 (2007): 35–44.

Larisey, Peter. *Light for a Cold Land: Lawren Harris's Life and Work*. Toronto: Dundurn Press, 1993.

Latour, Bruno. *We Have Never Been Modern*. 1991. Translated by Catherine Porter. Cambridge: Harvard University Press, 1993.

Lawrance, Scott. "blood sutra." In "Th Combined Blew Ointment Picture Book nd th News," edited by bill bissett. Special issue, *Blewointment* (December 1972).

Le Corbusier. "Plan Voisin, Paris, France, 1925." Fondation Le Corbusier. Accessed May 2011. http://www.fondationlecorbusier.fr/corbuweb/morpheus.aspx?sysId=13&IrisObjectId=6159&sysLanguage=en-en&itemPos=2&itemSort=en-en_sort_string1%20&itemCount=2&sysParentName=Home&sysParentId=65.

Leclerc, Denise. *The Crisis of Abstraction in Canada: The 1950s*. Ottawa: National Gallery of Canada, 1992.

Lederman, Marsha. "In Vancouver, Surrealism in a Native Mask." *Globe and Mail*, 3 June 2011. http://www.theglobeandmail.com/arts/in-vancouver-surrealism-in-a-native-mask/article582058/.

Lee, Sueyeun Juliette. "Shock and Blah: Offensive Postures in 'Conceptual' Poetry and the Traumatic Stuplime." *Volta* 41 (May 2014). http://www.thevolta.org/ewc41-sjlee-p1.html.

Le Fur, Yves. "Magical Notebooks." In *The Colour of My Dreams: The Surrealist Revolution in Art*, edited by Dawn Ades, 237–42. Vancouver: Douglas & McIntyre, 2011.

Lesh, Phil. "1965." Onstage interview with Jay Blakesberg. YouTube video, 2 January 2015.

Lewis, Glenn. *Bewilderness – The Origins of Paradise*. Exhibition catalogue. Vancouver: Vancouver Art Gallery, 1978

Lewis, Pericles. *The Cambridge Introduction to Modernism*. Cambridge: Cambridge University Press, 2007.

Lewis, Wyndham. *The Enemy: A Review of Art and and Literature*, vol. 1. London: Arthur Press, 1927.

Levertov, Denise. Letter to the Editor. In *Tish No. 1–19*, edited by Frank Davey, 223–24. Vancouver: Talonbooks, 1975.

Lowndes, Joan. "The Spirit of the Sixties by a Witness." In *Vancouver: Art and Artists 1931–1983*, 142–51. Vancouver: Vancouver Art Gallery, 1983.

Lowther, Pat. "Chacabuco, The Pit." In *Collected Works of Pat Lowther*, edited by Christine Wiesenthal, 191–98. Edmonton: NeWest Press, 2010.

– "Last Letter to Pablo." In *Collected Works of Pat Lowther*, edited by Christine Wiesenthal, 161. Edmonton: NeWest Press, 2010.

– "Regard to Pablo Neruda." In *Collected Works of Pat Lowther*, edited by Christine Wiesenthal, 161. Edmonton: NeWest Press, 2010.

– "Scatter Poem." *Ganglia* 3 (1966).

– "Woman." *Blackfish* 2 (Fall 1971).

– "Infinite Mirror Trip: Multi-Media Experience of the Universe." 1974. In *Collected Works of Pat Lowther*, edited by Christine Wiesenthal, 104–10. Edmonton: NeWest Press, 2010.

Luckyj, Natalie. *Other Realities: The Legacy of Surrealism in Canadian Art*. Kingston: Agnes Etherinton Art Centre, 1978.

Ludwar, Terry. Introduction to "Letters to Robin Blaser, 1955–1958," by Jack Spicer. *Line* 9 (Spring 1987): 26–28.

Mallarmé, Stéphane. "A Throw of the Dice." Translated by E.H. Blackmore. In *Collected Poems and Other Verse*, edited by Elizabeth McCombie, 161–81. Oxford: Oxford University Press, 2006.

Mancini, Donato. "The Young Hate Us {1}: Can Poetry be Matter." In *The Vispo Anthology: Visual Poetry 1998–2008*, edited by Nico Vassilakis and Crag Hill, 63–68. Seattle, WA: Fantagraphics, 2012.

Maracle, Lee. *Bobbi Lee, Indian Rebel*. 1975. Toronto: Women's Press, 1990.

Mariani, Philomena. *Global Conceptualism: Points of Origin 1950s–1980s*. New York: Queens Museum of Art, 1999.

Marlatt, Daphne. *Ana Historic*. 1988. Toronto: House of Anansi Press, 2004.

– "Correspondences: Selected Letters." *Line* 13 (1989): 5–31.

– "Given This Body: An Interview with Daphne Marlatt." With George Bowering. *Open Letter* 4.3 (1979): 32–88.

– Interview with the author. 12 December 2019.

– Interview. *The Line Has Shattered*, dir. Robert McTavish. Vancouver: Non-Inferno Media, 2013. DVD.

– "Long Ongoing Line." *Periodics* 3 (Fall 1978). Reprinted in *Geist*, http://www.geist.com/findings/long-ongoing-line/.

– "Musing with Mothertongue." In *Gynocritics: Feminist Approaches to Canadian and Quebec Women's Writing*, edited by Barbara Godard, 223–26. Toronto: ECW Press, 1987.

– "On Care." *Tish* 30 (June 1965): 2.

– *Rings*. Vancouver: *Georgia Straight Writing Supplement*, 1971.

– *What Matters*. Toronto: Coach House Press, 1980.

Marx, Karl, and Friedrich Engels. *The Communist Manifesto*. 1848 in German, 1850 in English, translated by Samuel Moore. London: Penguin Books, 2002.

Mathews, Mike. Letter to the Editor. In *Tish No. 1–19*, edited by Frank Davey, 72. Vancouver: Talonbooks, 1975.

Mathews, Timothy. "Reading Translation in Apollinaire." In *One Poem in Search of a Translator: Re-writing "Les Fenêtres" by Apollinaire*, edited by Eugenia Loffredo and Manuella Perteghella, 29–52. Bern: Peter Lang, 2009.

Mayne, Seymour. *Manimals*. Vancouver: Very Stone House, 1969.

– *Mutetations*. Vancouver: Very Stone House, 1969.

McCaffery, Steve. "Bill Bissett: A Writing outside Writing." In *North of Intention: Critical Writings 1973–1986*, 93–106. New York: Roof Books, 2000.

– *Carnival: The First Panel, 1967–70*. Toronto: Coach House Books, 1970.

– *Carnival: The Second Panel, 1970–75*. Toronto: Coach House Books, 1975.

– Introduction to *Rational Geomancy: The Kids of the Book Machine: The Collected Research Reports of the Toronto Research Group, 1973–1982*, edited by Steve McCaffery, 9–22. Vancouver: Talonbooks, 1992.

– "The Martyrology as Paragram." *Open Letter* 6.5–6 (1986): 191–206.

– *North of Intention: Critical Writings 1973–1986*. New York: Roof Books, 2000.

McCarthy, Patrick A. Introduction to *Joyce/Lowry: Critical Perspectives*, edited by Patrick A. McCarthy, 1–8. Lexington: University Press of Kentucky, 1997.

McLeod, Dan. "Goodbye." *Tish* 22 (December 1963): 1–2.

McLeod, Neil. *Indigenous Poetics in Canada*. Waterloo: Wilfred Laurier University Press, 2014.

McGann, Jerome. *Radiant Textuality: Literature after the World Wide Web*. New York: Palgrave, 2001.

McLuhan, Andrew. "The Etymology of Marshall McLuhan's 'The Medium Is the Message.'" *Medium.com*, 6 January 2020. https://medium.com/@andrewmcluhan/the-etymology-of -marshall-mcluhans-the-medium-is-the-message-1e3ce266f67b.

McLuhan, Marshall. *Culture Is Our Business*. New York: Ballantine Books, 1972.

– "Electronic Revolution: Revolutionary Effects of New Media." 1959. In *Understanding Me: Lectures and Interviews*, edited by Stephanie McLuhan and David Stains, 1–11. Toronto: McClelland & Stewart, 2003.

– *The Gutenberg Galaxy: The Making of Typographic Man*. Toronto: University of Toronto Press, 1962.

– *Mechanical Bride: Folklore of Industrial Man*. Boston: Beacon Press, 1968.

– "Notes on Burroughs." In *Media Research: Technology, Art and Communication*, edited by Michel A. Moos, 86–91. Amsterdam: OPA Amsterdam B.V., 1997.

– "Playboy Interview." 1969. In *Essential McLuhan*, edited by Eric McLuhan and Frank Zingrone, 233–69. Toronto: House of Anansi Press, 1995.

– *Understanding Media: The Extensions of Man*. New York: Signet Books, 1964.

McRandle, Paul. "Julius Carlebach, Antiques and Art Objects, 943 Third Avenue." *Surrealist NYC*, 31 January 2013. http://tmblr.co/Zh-yKtd4XHaP.

McRobbie, Kenneth. *Eyes without a Face*. Toronto: Gallery Editions, Isaacs Gallery, 1960.

McTavish, Robert, dir. *The Line Has Shattered*. Vancouver: Non-Inferno Media, 2013. DVD.

McWhirter, George. "Poem for Michael Bullock." *Trek* 22 (Fall 2008): 48.

Meijer-Kline, Karen. *Secret Wisdom of the West Coast Esoteric and Occult Practice in British Columbia*. Exhibit guide. Rare Books and Special Collections, University of British Columbia, 1–31 August 2012.

Michelson, Peter. "A Materialist Critique of Robert Duncan's Grand Collage." *boundary 2* 8.2 (Winter 1980): 21–43.

Miller, Henry. "The Tropic of Cancer." In *Burning City: Poems of Metropolitan Modernity*, edited by Tim Conley and Jed Rasula, 171. Notre Dame: Action Books, 2012.

Miller, Tyrus. *Late Modernism: Politics, Fiction, and the Arts between the Wars.* Berkeley: University of California Press, 1999.

Milne, Heather. Interview with Daphne Marlatt. In *Prismatic Publics: Innovative Canadian Women's Poetry and Poetics*, edited by Heather Milne and Kate Eichhorn, 242–51. Toronto: Coach House Books, 2009.

Molesworth, Helen. *Leap Before You Look: Black Mountain College 1933–1957.* New Haven: Yale University Press, 2015.

Morris, Michael, ed. *Concrete Poetry.* Vancouver: Morris and Helen Belkin Art Gallery, 1969. Exhibition catalogue.

Morton, Murray. "Its Manifesto." In *Limbo: A Paraliterary Journal of Survivalism*, edited by Murray Morton, i–v. Vancouver: Neo-Surrealist Press, 1964.

Mota, Miguel, and Paul Tiessen. *The Cinema of Malcolm Lowry: A Scholarly Edition of Lowry's "Tender Is the Night."* Vancouver: University of British Columbia Press, 1990.

Mufti, Aamir R. "Global Comparitism." *Critical Inquiry* 31 (Winter 2005): 487.

Murray, Heather. "Literary History as Microhistory." In *Home-work: Postcolonialism, Pedagogy, and Canadian Literature*, edited by Cynthia Sugars, 405–22. Ottawa: University of Ottawa Press, 2004.

Murray, Joan. *Canadian Collage.* Oshawa: Robert McLaughlin Gallery, 1997.

– *Confessions of a Curator: Adventures in Canadian Art.* Toronto: Dundurn Press, 1996.

Nasgaard, Roald. *Abstract Painting in Canada.* Vancouver: Douglas & McIntyre, 2008.

Niechoda, Irene, and Tim Hunter. "A Tishstory." In *Beyond TISH: New Writing, Interviews, Critical Essays*, edited by Douglas Barbour, 83–98. Edmonton: NeWest, 1991.

Neil, Al. "Guess Work." In "Splendor Solis." Special section, *Georgia Straight Writing Supplement* (June 1970): 12.

– "Sam." In *Vancouver: Art and Artists 1931–1983*, 152. Vancouver: Vancouver Art Gallery, 1983.

Neufert, Andreas. "Ten Rolls of 8mm Film Documenting Wolfgang Paalen's Journey through British Columbia in Summer 1939." In *The Colour of My Dreams: The Surrealist Revolution in Art*, edited by Dawn Ades, 229–35. Vancouver: Douglas & McIntyre, 2011.

Nichol, bp. "from bp to David fr *Spanish Fleye*." 1966. In *Meanwhile: The Critical Writings of bpNichol*, edited by Roy Miki, 23. Vancouver: Talonbooks, 2002.

– Interview with Gladys Hindmarch, Daphne Marlatt, Pierre Coupey, Dwight Gardiner, and Brian Fisher. *Capilano Review* 8/9 (Fall 1975/Spring 1976): 313–46.

– Interview with Nicette Jukelevics. 26 June 1974. In "A Bibliography of Canadian Concrete, Visual and Sound Poetry 1965–1972," 127–34. MA thesis, Sir George William University, 1974.

– Introduction to *Ganglia Press Index, 1964–1983.* Toronto: Ganglia Press, 1983.

– "Introduction to *The Arches: Selected Poems of Frank Davey*." 1980. In *Meanwhile: The Critical Writings of bpNichol*, edited by Roy Miki, 245–62. Vancouver: Talonbooks, 2002.

– "Last Wall and Test a Minute." Simon Fraser University Special Collections and Rare Books, bpNichol Fonds, Notebook 1968, MsC 1223, November 1966.

– *Late October grOnk Mailout.* Toronto: Ganglia Press, 1970.

– "Not What the Siren Sang But What the Frag Meant." In *Konfessions of an Elizabethan Fan Dancer*, 25. 1967. Toronto: Coach House Books, 2004.

– "Notes on the New Writing." Simon Fraser University Special Collections and Rare Books, bpNichol Fonds, Notebook 1968, MsC 12.
– "The Typography of Bill Bissett." In draft of *We Sleep Inside Each Other All*, number 8 of 10 special editions. York University, York University, Clara Thomas Archives, Bill Bissett Fonds, F0266.
Niechoda, Irene, and Tim Hunter. "A Tishstory." In *Beyond TISH: New Writing, Interviews, Critical Essays*, edited by Douglas Barbour, 83–98. Edmonton: NeWest Press, 1991.
O'Brian, John, Naomi Sawada, and Scott Watson. Introduction to *All Amazed: For Roy Kiyooka*, 5–10. Vancouver: Emily Carr Institute of Art and Design, 2002.
O'Connelly, Barbara. "There Were Dreams." *grOnk* 2.4 (1967).
Obrist, Hans-Ulrich. "The Hang of It: Hans Ulrich Obrist Talks with Pontus Hulten." *Artforum International* 36.8 (April 1997): 74–79, 113–14.
Olson, Charles. *Collected Prose*. Edited by Donald Allen and Benjamin Friedlander. Berkeley: University of California Press, 1997.
– "Human Universe." In *Selected Writings of Charles Olson*, edited by Robert Creeley, 53–68. New York: New Directions, 1966.
– "I, Maximus of Gloucester, to You." In *The Maximum Poems*, edited by George F. Butterick, 5–8. Berkeley: University of California Press, 1983.
– Letter to Robert Creeley. 1 December 1951. In *Charles Olson & Robert Creeley: The Complete Correspondence*, vol. 8, edited by George F. Butterick, 213–14. Santa Rosa: Black Sparrow Press, 1987.
– "Mayan Letters." In *Selected Writings of Charles Olson*, edited by Robert Creeley, 69–132. New York: New Directions, 1966.
– "Projective Verse." 1950. In *Selected Writings of Charles Olson*, edited by Robert Creeley, 15–30. New York: New Directions, 1966.
– *The Special View of History*. Berkeley: Oyez, 1970.
Pacey, Desmond. *Ethel Wilson*. New York: Twayne, 1967.
Patchen, Kenneth. *Hallelujah Anyway*. New York: New Directions, 1967.
Peacock, Molly. *The Paper Garden: Mrs. Delaney [Begins Her Life's Work] at 72*. Toronto: McClelland & Stewart, 2010.
Percival, Walter. *Leading Canadian Poets*. Toronto: Ryerson Press, 1948.
Perry, Sam. "Maximus of Gloucester from Dogtown: Charles Olson Personal Locus." In *Tish No. 1–19*, edited by Frank Davey, 204–10. Vancouver: Talonbooks, 1975.
– "Osseous Roots." *Tish* 28 (1965): 9–10.
Persky, Stan. "Bibliographic Soap Opera." *Tish* D (February 1969).
Peters, Carl. *Textual Vishyuns: Image and Text in the Work of bill bissett*. Vancouver: Talonbooks, 2011.
Philip, J.B. "Charles Olson Reconsidered." *Journal of American Studies* 5.3 (1971): 293–305.
Plato. "The Republic." 400 BCE. In *Plato: Six Great Dialogues*, edited and translated by Benjamin Jowett, 186–460. Mineola, NY: Dover, 2007.
Pollock, Della. "Performing Writing." In *The Ends of Performance*, edited by Peggy Phelan and Jill Lane, 73–103. New York: New York University Press, 1998.
– *Telling Bodies Performing Birth: Everyday Narratives of Childbirth*. New York: Columbia University Press, 1999.
Polyck-O'Neill, Julia. "Rematerializing the Immaterial: A Comparative Study of Vancouver's Conceptual Visual Arts and Writing." PhD Dissertation, Brock University, 2021.
Pope, Alexander. "Epistle to a Lady: Of the Characters of Women." 1743. In *Eighteenth Century Verse*, edited by Roger Lonsdale, 248–54. New York: Oxford University Press, 1989.

Potrebenko, Helen. "Canadian Agriculture: 1946–1983." In *Walking Slow*, 49–50. Vancouver: Lazara, 1985.

– "Days and Nights on the Picket Line." In *Walking Slow*, 6. Vancouver: Lazara, 1985.

– "The New Society." In *Walking Slow*, 3. Vancouver: Lazara, 1985.

– *Taxi!* Vancouver: New Star Books, 1975.

– *Walking Slow*. Vancouver: Lazara, 1985.

Potsmurth, Zarmsby. "on Collage being All." *Blewointment* 1.2 (December 1963).

Potvin, Liza. "Phyllis Webb: The Voice That Breaks." *Canadian Poetry: Studies, Documents, Reviews* 32 (Summer 1993). http://canadianpoetry.org/volumes/vol32/potvin.html.

Pound, Ezra. *ABC of Reading*. New York: New Directions, 1960.

– *Guide to Kulchur*. 1952. New York: New Directions, 1970.

– "How to Read." In *Literary Essays of Ezra Pound*, edited by T.S. Eliot, 15–40. Norfolk: New Directions, 1954.

– *Make It New*. London: Faber & Faber, 1934.

– "The Serious Artist." *Literary Essays of Ezra Pound*, edited by T.S. Eliot, 41–57. Norfolk: New Directions, 1954.

– "The Twelve Dialogues of Fontenelle." In *Pavannes and Divisions*, 45–58. New York: Alfred Knopf, 1918.

Querengesser, Neil. "Journeyworks." *Canadian Literature* 150 (Autumn 1996): 180–82.

Rancière, Jacques. "Separated, We Are Together." Translated by Nicolas Vieillescazes. In *Ian Wallace: A Literature of Images*, edited by Vanessa Joan Müller, Beatrix Ruf, and Nicolaus Schafhausen, 100–107. Zürich: Sternberg Press, 2008.

Read, Herbert. Introduction to *International Surrealist Exhibition Catalogue*, 12–13. London: New Burlington Galleries, 1936.

Reid, Jamie. Letter to the Editors. *Tish* 29 (1965): 2.

– "one man civilization: a review of bill bissett over time." Talonbooks. Accessed August 2016. https://talonbooks.com/meta-talon/one-man-civilization-a-review-of-bill-bissett-over-time.

– "The Pome Wuz a Store end Is th Storee: th Erlee Daze uv Blewointment." In *bill bissett: Essays on His Works*, edited by Linda Rogers, 15–23. Toronto: Guernica Editions, 2002.

– "Reading." Vancouver: Western Front, 1975. Video, 57:26. https://vimeo.com/139729985.

Remy, Michel. *Surrealism in Britain*. Aldershot: Ashgate, 1999.

Rhodes, Shane. "X: Poems & Anti-Poems (an interview)." *Toronto Quarterly*, 17 September 2013. http://thetorontoquarterly.blogspot.ca/2013/09/shane-rhodes-x-poems-anti-poems.html.

Rhodes, Michael. Untitled. In *Concrete Poetry: An Exhibition in Four Parts*. Vancouver: Fine Arts Gallery, University of British Columbia, 1969. Exhibition catalogue.

Ribemont-Dessaignes, Georges, Jacques Prévert, and Raymond Queneau. *Un Cadavre*. Paris: Publisher not identified, 1930.

Ribkoff, Fred. "Daphne Marlatt's 'Rings': An Extension of the Proprioceptive." *Essays on Canadian Writing* 50 (Fall 1993): 231–46. Accessed via EBSCOhost.

Ricou, L.R. "No Writing Here at All: Review Notes on Writing Native." In *Native Writers and Canadian Writing*, edited by William H. New, 294–306. Vancouver: University of British Columbia Press, 1990.

Ridgeway, Ian, and Dan Clemons. "Deluxe Text." Simon Fraser Special Collections and Rare Books, Gerry Gilbert Fonds, MsC 14.1, Folder 1.2.

Roediger, David. R. *Colored White: Transcending the Racial Past*. Berkeley: University of California Press, 2002.

Rogers, Janet Marie. "MOQW/MOQW?ESPEYE?WIXT." In *Resisting Canada: An Anthology of Poetry*, edited by Nyla Matuk, 130–33. Montreal: Signal Editions, 2019.

Rosemont, Penelope, ed. *Surrealist Women: An International Anthology*. London: Athlone Press, 1998.

Rosenthal, Edna. *Aristotle and Modernism: Aesthetic Affinities of T.S. Eliot, Wallace Stevens, and Virginia Woolf*. Brighton, UK: Sussex Academic Press, 2008.

Roy, Marina. "Corporeal Returns: Feminism and Phenomenology in Vancouver Video and Performance, 1968–1983." *Canadian Art* 18.2 (Summer 2001): 58–65.

Ruesch, Jurgen, and Gregory Bateson. *Communication: The Social Matrix of Psychiatry*. 1951. London: Transaction, 2006.

Ruscheinsky, Lynn. "Travelling in the United States of Male Supremacy." In *the fascist branding pomes #2*, by Gwen Hauser, 4. Vancouver: Blew Ointment Press, 1974.

Saint-Martin, Lori. "Mourning Absence, Fighting Absence: From Literary Manspreading toward Cultural Parity." CWILA, 16 June 2017.

Salloum, Sheryl. "John Vanderpant and the Culture Life of Vancouver, 1920–1939." *BC Studies* 97 (Spring 1993): 38–51.

– *Malcolm Lowry: Vancouver Days*. Toronto: Harbour, 1987.

Samaltanos, Katia. *Apollinaire: Catalyst for Primitivism, Picabia, and Duchamp*. Ann Arbor: UMI Research Press, 1984.

Sarah, Robyn. "About Margaret Avison." In *The Essential Margaret Avison*, 60–62. Erin: Porcupine's Quill, 2010.

Savage, Jon. "Real English Tea Made Here." *Frieze* 114 (April 2008).

Scobie, Stephen. *bpNichol: What History Teaches*. Vancouver: Talonbooks, 1984.

Seligmann, Kurt. "A Conversation with a Tsimshian." *Minotaure* 12–13 (1939): 66–69. Reprinted in *The Colour of My Dreams: The Surrealist Revolution in Art*, edited by Dawn Ades, 221–2. Vancouver: Douglas & McIntyre, 2011.

Shadbolt, Doris. "Our Relation to Primitive Art." *Canadian Art* 5.1 (October & November 1947): 14–16.

Shadbolt, Jack. "A Personal Recollection." In *Vancouver: Art and Artists 1931–1983*, 34–41. Vancouver: Vancouver Art Gallery, 1983.

Shaw, B. "The Promised Land." In "Th Combined Blew Ointment Picture Book nd th News," edited by bill bissett. Special issue, *Blewointment* (December 1972).

Shaw, Nancy. "Expanded Consciousness and Company Types: Collaboration since Intermedia and the N.E. Thing Co." In *Vancouver Anthology*, edited by Stan Douglas, 91–110. Vancouver: Talonbooks, 2011.

Shepheard, David. "Saussure's Vedic Anagrams." *Modern Language Review* 77.3 (July 1982): 513–23.

Siegal, Ethan. "What Is the Physics of Nothing?" *Forbes*, 22 September 2016. https://www.forbes.com/sites/startswithabang/2016/09/22/what-is-the-physics-of-nothing/#3061023275f8.

Simmins, Richard. Review of *The Collage Show*. *Province*, 26 March 1971.

Simpson, Gregg. "Canadian West Coast Hermetics: The Metaphysical Landscape." *Lodgistiks* 1.2 (1971).

– "Hermetic Series 1970–1975." greggsimpson.com. Accessed August 2016. http://www.greggsimpson.com/Hermetic.html.

– *Luminous Desires: Collected Writings*. Kingston: Derwydon Press, 1977.

– "The Quest." In "Splendor Solis." Special section, *Georgia Straight Writing Supplement* (June 1970): 3–10.

– "The Triumph of the Surreal." *Georgia Straight*, 1970. http://www.greggsimpson.com/Chrono_Triumph.html.

– "The Vancouver School of Collage." 3 April 1971. http://www.greggsimpson.com/Vancouver_School_of_Collage.html

– "The West Coast Surrealist Group: A Chronology 1965–2014." http://www.greggsimpson.com /westcoastsurrealists.html.

Spahr, Juliana, and Stephanie Young. "Numbers Trouble." *Chicago Review* 53.2 (Autumn 2007): 88–111.

Spatola, Adriano. *Towards Total Poetry*. Los Angeles: Otis Books/Seismicity Editions, 2008.

Solt, Mary Ellen. *Concrete Poetry: A World View*. 1968. Bloomington: Indiana University Press, 1970.

Sova, Dawn B. *Edgar Allan Poe: A Literary Reference to His Life and Work*. New York: Infobase, 2007.

Stanley, George. *Vancouver: A Poem*. Vancouver: New Star Books, 2008.

Stein, Gertrude. *Everybody's Autobiography*. New York: Random House, 1937.

– "Portraits and Repetition." In *Lectures in America*, 166–69. New York: Random House, 1935.

Stevens, Wallace. "Notes Toward a Supreme Fiction." 1942. In *Collected Poems of Wallace Stevens*, 380–408. New York: Knopf, 1993.

– "An Ordinary Evening in New Haven." In *Poems*, 949. New York: Vintage Books, 1959.

Sujir, Leila. "Addressing a Presence: An Interview with Phyllis Webb." *Prairie Fire* 9.1 (Spring 1988): 35.

Surrealism in Canadian Painting. Exhibition Catalogue. London: London Public Library and Art Museum, 1964.

Swedenborg, Emanuel. *The Delights of Wisdom Concerning Conjugal Love after which follow Pleasures of Insanity Concerning Scortatory Love*. New York: John Allen, 1849.

Tallman, Warren. "A Brief Reintroduction to Tish." In *Beyond TISH: New Writing, Interviews, Critical Essays*, edited by Douglas Barbour, 115–19. Edmonton: NeWest Press, 1991.

– *Godawful Streets of Man*. Toronto: Coach House Books, 1977.

– *In the Midst: Writings 1962–1992*. Vancouver: Talonbooks, 1992.

– Letter to Robert Creeley. 30 May 1962. Reprinted in *Minutes of the Charles Olson Society* 30 (April 1999): 7–9.

– "Poets in Vancouver: Margaret Avison, Robert Creeley, Robert Duncan, Allen Ginsberg, Denise Levertov, Charles Olson and Philip Whalen, from July 24 through August 16." Simon Fraser University Special Collections and Rare Books, Warren Tallman Fonds, MsC 26 Box 13. Also available online at http://vidaver.wordpress.com/tag/charles-olson/.

– "Wonder Merchants: Modernist Poetry in Vancouver during the 1960's." 1974. *Open Letter* 3.6 (1976–77): 175–207.

Theall, Donald. *The Medium Is the Rear View Mirror: Understanding McLuhan*. Montreal: McGill-Queen's University Press, 1971.

– *The Virtual Marshall McLuhan*. Montreal: McGill-Queen's University Press, 2001.

Taylor, Felicity. *The Grey Guide to Artist-Run Publishing & Circulation / Le Petit Gris: guide de l'édition en art et de la distribution autogérée*. Montreal: Artist-Run Centres and Collectives Conference, 2017.

Thomas, Audrey. "Aquarius." In *Lovers & Escorts*, 17. Ottawa: Oberon, 1977.

– *Mrs. Blood: A novel*. Vancouver: Talonbooks, 1970.

Thomas, Dylan. *The Love Letters of Dylan Thomas*. Naperville: Sourcebooks, 2001.

Tiessen, Paul. "From Literary Modernism to the Tantramar Marshes: Anticipating McLuhan in British and Canadian Media Theory and Practice." *Canadian Journal of Communication* 18.4 (1993): 451–67.

– Introduction to *The 1940 Under the Volcano: A Critical Edition*, edited by Paul Tiessen, xix–lxxiiii. Ottawa: University of Ottawa Press, 2015.

– Introduction to *The Letters of Malcolm Lowry and Gerald Noxon: 1940–1952*, edited by Paul Tiessen, 1–21. Vancouver: University of British Columbia Press, 1988.

Tish No. 1–19. Edited by Frank Davey. Vancouver: Talonbooks, 1975.

Tomaszewska, Lara. "Borderlines of Poetry and Art: Vancouver, American Modernism, and the Formation of the West Coast Avant-Garde, 1961–69." Dissertation, University of British Columbia, 2011.

Turner, Michael. "Expanded Literary Practices." *Vancouver Art in the Sixties.* Accessed August 2016. http://expandedliterarypractices.vancouverartinthesixties.com/.

– "Visual Poems, Imaginary Museums." In *Letters: Michael Morris and Concrete Poetry,* edited by Scott Watson and Jana Tyner, 125–46. London: Black Dog, 2015.

UU, David (David W. Harris). "Advent of Heliocentrum." *Lodgistiks* 4 (1976).

– "Before the Golden Dawn." *Lodgistiks* 4 (1976).

– "Beyond Concrete Poetry." *British Columbia Monthly* 1.3 (December 1972).

– "Composition (after pellan)." *Blewointment* 5.1 (January 1967).

– *Diary of a Metempsychotic.* Kingston: Derwyddon Press, 1976.

– *Gideon Music.* Vancouver: Blew Ointment Press, 1967.

– *High C: Selected Sound and Visual Poems 1965–1983.* Toronto: Underwhich Editions, 1990.

– "Homage to Andre Breton." *Lodgistiks* (January 1975).

– Letter from David Harris (later UU) to bill bissett. 17 August 1966 (Letter 88). York University, Clara Thomas Archives, Bill Bissett Fonds, F0266.

– Letter from David Harris (later UU) to bill bissett. 18 August 1966 (Letter 88). York University, Clara Thomas Archives, Bill Bissett Fonds, F0266.

– Letter from David Harris (later UU) to bill bissett. 30 June 1971 (Letter 116). York University, Clara Thomas Archives, Bill Bissett Fonds, F0266.

– "Magic and the Goddess." In "Splendor Solis." Special section, *Georgia Straight Writing Supplement* (June 1970): 11.

– "The Magicians Manifesto." In "Isle of Avalon." Special issue, *grOnk* 7.1 (September 1970).

– "Maquette Pour Une Fontaine (after louis archambault)." *Blewointment* 5.1 (January 1967).

– "Note for Aurea Mediocritas." *Blewointment* 5.1 (January 1967).

– Untitled. Artist's statement. *Canadian West Coast Hermetics: The Metaphysical Landscape.* Vancouver: Fine Arts Gallery, University of British Columbia, 1973.

– "The ODinity." *Canadian West Coast Hermetics: The Metaphysical Landscape.* Vancouver: Fine Arts Gallery, University of British Columbia, 1973.

– "page 177." In *Before the Golden Dawn.* Toronto: Weed/flower Press, 1971.

– "Sleep Descending." *Lodgistiks* 4 (1976).

– "Une Famile (after archambault)." *Blewointment* 5.1 (January 1967).

van Doesburg, Theo. "Basis of Concrete Painting." In *Manifesto: A Century of Isms,* edited by Mary Ann Caws, 520. Lincoln: University of Nebraska Press, 2000.

van Doesburg, Theo, Piet Mondrian, and Antony Kok. "De Stijl 1919–1920." In *Concrete Poetry: A World View,* edited by Mary Ellen Solt, 11. Bloomington: Indiana University Press, 1970.

Varney, Ed. "Concrete Poetry." In *Concrete Poetry,* edited by Michael Morris. Vancouver: Morris and Helen Belkin Art Gallery, 1969. Exhibition catalogue.

– "Concrete Poetry." In *The Poem Company.* Edited by Ed Varney. Vancouver: Intermedia Press and the Poem Company, 1972.

– "Lori-ann Latremouille and Surrealism." *An Open Book: A Catalogue of Artworks from the Surrey Art Gallery's Permanent Collection,* 2004. http://www.surrey.ca/culture-recreation/1541 .aspx.

– "On Lions Gate Bridge." In *Human Nature,* 5. Vancouver: Intermedia Press, 1974.

– "Publishing / Origins of Intermedia Press, Inc." 2011. ABC BookWorld. Accessed August 2016. https://abcbookworld.com/essay/essay-15716/

– "Remembering Michael Bullock." ABC BookWorld. Accessed August 2016. http://www
    .abcbookworld.com/view_author.php?id=378.
– Untitled. Artist's statement. *Canadian West Coast Hermetics: The Metaphysical Landscape*.
    Vancouver: Fine Arts Gallery, University of British Columbia, 1973.
Vicari, Justin. *Mad Muses and the Early Surrealists*. Jefferson: McFarland & Company, 2012.
von Meier, Kurt. "Michael Morris' Book." Originally in *ArtsCanada Magazine* (August 1969).
    Reprinted on KurtvonMeier.com. Accessed August 2016. https://www.kurtvonmeier.com
    /michael-morris-book.
Vowel, Chelsea. *Indigenous Writes: A Guide to First Nations, Métis, and Inuit Issues in Canada*.
    Winnipeg: Portage & Main Press, 2016.
Wakefield, Pauline. "Salvaging Sound at Last Sight: Marius Barbeau and the Anthropological
    'Rescue' of Nass River Indians." *ESC* 30.3 (September 2004): 57–88.
Walbohm, Samara. "Representations of the Native Condition in Watson's *The Double Hook* and
    Deep Hollow Creek." In *Adjacencies: Minority Writing in Canada*, edited by Lianne Moyes,
    Licia Cantonm and Dominic Beneventi, 80–102. Toronto: Guernica, 2004.
Waldman, Diane. *Collage, Assemblage, and the Found Object*. New York: Harry N. Abrams, 1992.
Wall, Jeff. *Landscape Manual*. Vancouver: UBC Fine Arts Gallery, 1969.
– "Meaningness." *Free Media Bulletin* 1 (1969).
Wallace, Ian. "A Literature of Images." *Free Media Bulletin* 1 (1969).
– Email correspondence with the author. 18 December 2019.
– "Literature – Transparent and Opaque." In *Concrete Poetry: An Exhibition in Four Parts*.
    Vancouver: Fine Arts Gallery, University of British Columbia, 1969. Exhibition catalogue.
– "Photography and the Monochrome: An Apologia, an Exegesis, an Interrogation." In *Cameres
    Indiscretes*. Barcelona, Spain: Centre d'art santa Monica, 1992.
Wallace, Keith. "A Particular History: Artist-Run Centres in Vancouver." In *Vancouver Anthology:
    A Project of the Or Gallery*, edited by Stan Douglas, 29–52. Vancouver: Talonbooks, 2011.
Walsh, Nigel, and Andrew Wilson, eds. *Sluice Gates of the Mind: The Collaborative Work of Dr.
    Grace W. Pailthorpe and Reuben Mednikoff*. Leeds: City Art Gallery, 1998.
Warlick, M.E. *Max Ernst and Alchemy: A Magician in Search of Myth*. Austin: University of Texas
    Press, 2001.
Warner, Simon. *Text and Drugs and Rock 'n' Roll: The Beats and Rock Culture*. London: Bloomsbury,
    2013.
Watson, Dave. "Vancouver Easter Be-In." *Georgia Straight*, 8 May 1997. http://burnerboys
    .pbworks.com/w/page/11207088/Easter%20Be-In.
Watson, Scott. "Art and Photography." In *Art and Photography*. Vancouver: Vancouver Art
    Gallery, 1984.
– "Mirrors: Michael Morris's Letter Paintings and Drawings, and the Problem of Nothing." In
    Letters: Michael Morris and Concrete Poetry, edited by Scott Watson and Jana Tyner, 55–86.
    London: Black Dog, 2015.
– "Transmission Difficulties: Vancouver Paintings in the 1960s." *Vancouver Art in the Sixties*.
    http://transmissiondifficulties.vancouverartinthesixties.com/. Accessed August 2016.
Webb, Phyllis. *Naked Poems*. Vancouver: Periwinkle Press, 1965.
– *Wilson's Bowl*. Toronto: Coach House Books, 1980.
Weins, Jason. "Canonicity and Teachable Texts: A Response to Christian Bök's 'TISH and
    KOOT.'" *Open Letter* 14.3 (Summer 2010): 162–69.
– "'I may be trying to tell what I renounce': George Bowering's Post-*Tish* Poetics." *Open Letter*
    11.1 (Spring 2001): 83–93.

Wershler, Darren. Closing remarks at Approaching the Poetry Series, Concordia University, Montreal, 6 April 2013.

Whitaker, Reg, Gregory Kealey, and Andrew Parnaby. *Secret Service: Political Policing in Canada from the Fenians to Fortress America*. Toronto: University of Toronto Press, 2012.

Whitelaw, Anne. "Placing Aboriginal Art at the National Gallery of Canada." *Canadian Journal of Communication* 31.1 (2006). http://www.cjc-online.ca/index.php/journal/article/view/1775/1897.

Wiesenthal, Christine. *The Half-Lives of Pat Lowther*. Toronto: University of Toronto Press, 2005.

Willmott, Glenn. *Unreal Country: Modernity in the Canadian Novel in English*. Montreal: McGill-Queen's University Press, 2002.

Wilson, Andrew. "The Unconscious Is Always Right." In *Sluice Gates of the Mind: The Collaborative Work of Dr. Grace W. Pailthorpe and Reuben Mednikoff*, edited by Nigel Walsh and Andrew Wilson, 11–38. Leeds: City Art Gallery, 1998.

Wilson, Edward O. *Half-Life: Our Planet's Fight for Life*. New York: W.W. Norton, 2016.

Wilson, Norman. "Intermedia Nights – Movements of the Mind – in Which People Were Catalysts." *Province*, 27 May 1968. http://www.michaeldecourcy.com/intermedia/ICF/ICF_18.htm.

Wilson, Richard Albert. *The Miraculous Birth of Language*. 1937. London: J.M. Dent, 1949.

Witt, Andrew. "Nostalgia's Weathered Change." Review of Stan Douglas's *Vancouver Anthology*. *Mainlander*, 15 July 2011. http://themainlander.com/2011/07/15/review-nostalgias-weathered-charge/.

Wood, Denis, with John Fels and John Krygier. *Rethinking the Power of Maps*. New York: Guilford Press, 2010.

Woodcock, George. Editorial. *Canadian Literature* 1.1 (1959): 3–4.

– "In the Beginning Was the Question: The Poems of Phyllis Webb." *Queen's Quarterly* 93.3 (1986): 527–45.

– Interview with Malcolm Muggeridge. *CBC Monday Evening*, 8 July 1974. CBC Digital Archives. http://www.cbc.ca/archives/categories/arts-entertainment/media/marshall-mcluhan-the-man-and-his-message/the-destroyer-of-civilization.html.

– "Elegy for Fur-Covered Motor Horns: Note on Surrealism in England." *Limbo* 1.1 (February 1964): 49–52.

Woolf, Virginia. "Professions for Women." 1942. In *The Broadview Anthology of British Literature*, 1850–53, edited by Joseph Black, Leonard Conolly, Kate Flint, Isobel Grundy, Roy Liuzza, Jerome McGann, Anne Prescott, Barry Qualls, and Claire Waters. Toronto: Broadview Press, 2015.

– *Orlando: A Biography*. 1928. New York: Harcourt, 2006.

Wunderli, Peter. "Saussure's Anagrams." In *The Cambridge Companion to Saussure*, edited by Carol Sanders, 174–85. Cambridge: Cambridge University Press, 2004.

Zajonc, R.B. "Attitudinal Effects of Mere Exposure." *Journal of Personality and Social Psychology* 9.2 (1968): 1–27.

Zebrowitz, L.A., and Y. Zhang. "Neural Evidence for Reduced Apprehensiveness of Familiarized Stimuli in a Mere Exposure Paradigm." *Social Neuroscience* 7.4 (2012): 347–58.

Žižek, Slavoj. "Courtly Love, or, Woman as Thing." In *The Norton Anthology of Theory and Criticism*, 2nd ed., edited by Vincent B. Leitch, 2407–27. New York: W.W. Norton, 2010.

– *In Defence of Lost Causes*. London: Verso, 2009.

Zukofsky, Louis, ed. "Preface – 'Recencies' in Poetry." In *An "Objectivists" Anthology*, 24–25. Dijon: To Publishers, 1932.

Index

Bush, Jack, 158
Butler, Judith, 282
Butling, Pauline, 115, 273, 305–6
Butz, Earl, 106

Cage, John, 39, 315
Cain, Stephen, 227–8
Callaghan, Morley, 24
Cameron, Laura, 315–16
Campbell, Joseph, 152
Campbell, Lara, 1
Canada Council for the Arts, 66, 68, 106, 140,
  173, 220, 300
Canadian Broadcasting Corporation (CBC),
  55, 236–7
Canadian Fiction Magazine, The (magazine),
  43
Canadian Literature (magazine), 56, 243
Canadian Poetry Magazine (magazine), 27,
  29, 32
Canadian Vorticists, 15, 16n
Canadian West Coast Art: Native and
  Modern (exhibition), 234–5, 238
Canadian West Coast Hermetics: The
  Metaphyiscal Landscape (exhibition), 219,
  254, 258–60
Candelaria, Frederick, 43, 175
Capilano Review, The (magazine), 16n, 44,
  59–61, 163, 182, 187, 220
Carlson, Chuck, 43
Carlson, Tim, 106, 121
Carr, Emily, 35, 174, 232–5, 238, 318
Carr, Wayne, 160
Carroll, Lewis, 187
Carter, Jim, 176
Cartwright, Miriam, 247
Cawsey, Fred, 242
Cellar Musicians and Artist Society, The, 40,
  55, 248, 333
Centre (magazine), 99
Cézanne, Paul, 152
Chagall, Marc, 86
Char, René, 233
Cherry, Don, 333
Chevalier, Tracy, 245n17
Chidholm, Louey, 204
Chilkat First Nation, 232n

Chisholm, Sweeney, 243
Chopin, Henri, 74, 184
Choucha, Nadia, 223, 225
Choy, Wayson, 6
Christensen, Paul, 90n8
Christopher, Ken, 160
Chrystos, 42
Circular Causation (magazine), 43, 59, 126,
  146, 174, 220, 310; Issue 2, 180
City Lights (magazine), 32, 74, 197–8
City Lights Books, 74–5
CIV/n (magazine), 80
Claus, Carlfriedrich, 197
Clément, Dominique, 1
Clements, Marie, 58
Clemons, Dan, 320
Clinton, Martina, 52, 125, 135, 149, 160, 176,
  181, 183, 194–5, 201, 203
Coach House Press, 315
Cobblestone Press, 42
Cochrane, Maureen, 146, 148
Cohen, Leonard, 174, 254
Cold War, 1, 26, 290–2
Coleman, Bob, 221n2, 264–5
Coleman, Elizabeth, 139
Coleman, Victor, 61, 227, 309, 336
collage: about, 14, 94–7, 129, 135–78, 215,
  276, 299, 301, 305–6, 308, 312, 315, 324;
  Blewointment, 121, 126, 147; in *Tish*,
  90–2, 99, 103, 123; representation, 152;
  Surrealism, 247, 258, 262; visual poetry,
  105–6, 137, 150, 159–60, 167, 169, 172–4,
  176, 185, 186, 193, 310; visuality, 103, 163,
  228–9. *See also* cut-ups
Collage, The, 168
Collage Show, The (exhibition), 159–61, 163
Coleridge, Samuel Taylor, 287
Collins, Aileen, 80
Collins, Bradford, 245, 258
Collins, Eleanor, 55
Collins, Jess, 97
Collis, Stephen, 44–5, 101, 228, 314
colonialism, 3–10, 16–17, 25, 29, 33–4, 46–7,
  49–50, 99–100, 126, 182, 204, 209–10, 212,
  266, 300, 315, 318, 326; vs. Surrealism,
  215–16, 230, 233, 240, 254. *See also*
  post-colonialism